Social Psychology in Transition

Contributors

Frances E. Aboud *McGill University, Montreal, Canada*

Erika Apfelbaum *Laboratoire de Psychologie Sociale, Université de Paris VII, Paris, France*

John W. Berry *Queen's University, Kingston, Ontario, Canada*

André C. deCarufel *University of North Carolina at Chapel Hill, North Carolina*

Richard deCharms *Washington University, St. Louis, Missouri*

Morton Deutsch *Teachers College, Columbia University, New York, New York*

Kenneth J. Gergen *Swarthmore College, Swarthmore, Pennsylvania*

Ram Harré *Oxford University, Oxford, England*

Gustav Jahoda *University of Strathclyde, Glasgow, Scotland*

Charles A. Kiesler *University of Kansas, Lawrence, Kansas*

Ian Lubek *University of Guelph, Gueph, Ontario, Canada*

Joseph Lucke *University of Kansas, Lawrence, Kansas*

Gregory B. Markus *University of Michigan, Ann Arbor, Michigan*

William J. McGuire *Yale University, New Haven, Connecticut*

Alan Moffitt *Carleton University, Ottawa, Ontario, Canada*

John T. Partington *Carleton University, Ottawa, Ontario, Canada*

Ragnar Rommetveit *University of Oslo, Oslo, Norway*

Peter Schönbach *Ruhr-Universität, Bochum, Germany*

Paul F. Secord *Queens College, City University of New York, New York*

Dennis J. Shea *Washington University, St. Louis, Missouri*

Caryll Steffens *Carleton University, Ottawa, Ontario, Canada*

Lloyd H. Strickland *Carleton University, Ottawa, Ontario, Canada*

Wolfgang Stroebe *Universität Marburg, Marburg, Germany*

Paul G. Swingle *University of Ottawa, Ottawa, Ontario, Canada*

Henri Tajfel *University of Bristol, Bristol, England*

Warren Thorngate *University of Alberta, Edmonton, Alberta, Canada*

Harry C. Triandis *University of Illinois, Champaign-Urbana, Illinois*

Robert B. Zajonc *University of Michigan, Ann Arbor, Michigan*

Social Psychology in Transition

Edited by

Lloyd H. Strickland

Carleton University
Ottawa, Canada

Frances E. Aboud

McGill University
Montreal, Canada

and

Kenneth J. Gergen

Swarthmore College
Swarthmore, Pennsylvania

PLENUM PRESS · NEW YORK AND LONDON

Library of Congress Cataloging in Publication Data

Main entry under title:

Social psychology in transition.

    Based on a conference held at Carleton University, July 1974.
    Includes bibliographies and index.
    1. Social psychology–Congresses. 2. Social psychology–Research–Congresses. I. Strickland, Lloyd. II. Aboud, Frances. III. Gergen, Kenneth J. [DNLM: 1. Psychology, Social Congresses. HM251 S679 1974]
HM251.S675   301.1   76-22439
ISBN 0-306-30918-1

©1976 Plenum Press, New York
A Division of Plenum Publishing Corporation
227 West 17th Street, New York, N.Y. 10011

Printed in United States of America

ACKNOWLEDGMENTS

Two sets of acknowledgments must accompany this book. With respect to the conference, "Priorities and Paradigms for Social Psychology," appreciation must go to the various agencies that enabled the codirectors, Lloyd Strickland and Henri Tajfel, to organize the meeting in the first instance. Generous financial support came from several sources: The Human Factors Panel of the North Atlantic Treaty Organization, the Canada Council, and Carleton University. Dean R.A. Wendt of Carleton provided initial impetus and constant support through preparations for the conference, as an official of the University, as a colleague, and as a friend. Deserving special acknowledgment is Helen Durie, from Carleton, administrative assistant to the codirectors, who typed, organized, paid bills, made reservations, answered all questions, and became the single participant who was truly indispensable. If no other person deserves singular mention, the many social psychologists who attended have earned a collective "Thanks." They created a climate for one another that seems to have brought out the best of both formal and informal contributors. We trust that the products of the conference printed herein will reflect the credit they deserve.

For help in the preparation of this collection, we gratefully acknowledge Dean Wendt's support through Carleton University's Arts Research and Publication Fund. Again, the editors must tender collective appreciation to a portion of the participants, the contributors to the volume. They rewrote conference papers and critiques, prepared new manuscripts in response to our requests, and displayed their continued commitment to the solution of problems of "priorities and paradigms" long after the last conference session.

This book is dedicated to those individuals whose names and institutional affiliations (in 1974) appear on page 347. They were the participants in the conference, "Priorities and Paradigms in Social Psychology," whose attendance made that symposium, and this volume, possible.

Lloyd H. Strickland

Carleton University

CONTENTS

vii

SECTION I

INTRODUCTION

PRIORITIES AND PARADIGMS

The Conference and the Book

LLOYD H. STRICKLAND

Occurrence of the conference, *Research Paradigms and Priorities in Social Psychology*, held at Carleton University in July 1974, was perhaps inevitable—it appears now to be a symposium whose time had come. A number of different agents and agencies were implicated in the event, but if it had been held elsewhere, under different auspices, it doubtless would have had a similar focus and many of the same participants. Through a variety of minor accidents, supplemented by several major efforts, it grew from a fantasy first shared in Anne Tajfel's kitchen to a reality held in a relatively new university in the national capital of Canada. As will be seen, this was an appropriate locale for a number of reasons.

If the conference was indeed a kind of reaction, what factors initiated the sequence of planning, invitation, and participation that produced it? They were a set of pressures, proclamations, and papers, all of which helped define what can now be construed as social psychology's "crisis" in 1973 and 1974, as evident in Europe as in North America. The field seemed to be under attack from many sides, and there were multiple symptoms of an underlying malaise. Some of these symptoms were informal and emotional, others more formal and scholarly. There was the constant input from dismayed students and from other groups in society on both sides of the Atlantic; many of these people refused to buy, and almost all of them chose to question, the "knowledge" claimed by

LLOYD H. STRICKLAND · Carleton University, Ottawa, Ontario, Canada.

social psychologists and the values and practices that lay behind it. There was a host of articles disputing the long-term usefulness of procedures that had been taken as part of the social psychologist's stock-in-trade, like laboratory experimentation, deception, reliance on analysis of variance, and so on. There were cogent essays like Smith's (1972) review of the series *Advances in Experimental Social Psychology*; this paper questioned severely some of the theoretical– empirical bases of then current social psychology. There were major efforts, like the volume edited by Israel and Tajfel (1972), which, although primarily reflecting assessments of social psychology's status from various European points of view, at least starkly demonstrated a different set of "priorities and paradigms" from those which North Americans had come to take for granted. There was the contemporaneous volume by Harré and Secord (1972), whose radically different premise was a "conception of man as an actor . . . it is not the person himself who is the subject of analysis, but the character he plays. If man is indeed a self-directing agent . . . it makes imminent sense for the behavioral scientist to treat him as such" (p. 313). This view was, of course, discrepant from an implicitly accepted notion of man as an emitter of responses, an organism to be manipulated and then monitored in the way general experimental psychologists are supposed to perform these operations, and whose social nature and social context might be interesting, but coincidental. Social psychology's situation was well described by Leonard Berkowitz, who was quoted by Smith (1972) in the aforementioned review:

> . . . it seems to me . . . that social psychology is now in a "crisis stage," in the sense that Kuhn used this term in his book *The Structure of Scientific Revolutions*. We seem to be somewhat at a loss for important problems to investigate and models to employ on our research and theory. It is certainly time to take stock and see where we are and where we should go. (p. 86)

The geographical setting of the conference itself provided good reason for its design. A contrast of the "priorities and paradigms" of European social psychologists with those of Americans promised to be especially fruitful for an audience wherein young Canadian social psychologists were heavily represented. There has seemed to be pressure for a somewhat different "style" of social psychology to emerge in Canada (e.g., Berry, 1974). This pressure stems in part from the unique cultural and geographical environments of the Canadian social psychologist and the people he chooses to study. These, when combined with the often vast distances between both subcultures and psychology departments, help define the young and varied character of most Canadian graduate programs. Such factors have served to slow contact among junior social psychologists within Canada, and between them and the often conflicting but usually stimulating research values and practices in other parts of the world. The conference was in part an attempt to obviate these impediments.

The general organization of the conference reflected all of these considerations. A number of participants were invited by the codirectors, Lloyd Strickland and Henri Tajfel, either as authors or as discussants of a major paper. Many of them were among the most prominent social psychologists in Europe, Britain, and North America; however, some were relatively unknown graduate students or recent Ph.D.'s, either in (or from) Canadian graduate programs or studying outside Canada. Authors were invited to discuss the "paradigms and priorities" issue with special reference to their areas of interest, and they were matched with discussants appropriate for these areas. With a core program quickly established and announced, applications from the general community of social psychologists were invited and rapidly received. Several additional major papers were submitted, more discussants were enlisted, and the conference quickly grew to its maximum enrollment of 60 participants. This number was set by available funds, space at Carleton's meeting facilities, and the prejudices of the co-directors, who had attended far too many of those larger meetings which so quickly break up into small groups while communication among members of the larger collection of colleagues ceases.

The conference proved to be a significant one for the participants. There were never less than 90% of the registrants present at a scheduled session, and the proportion of participants actually involved in discussion was higher than anyone seemed able to recall. This led not only to searching evaluations of individual papers, but also to some of the most honest, articulate, and publicly open discussions of central and sensitive issues ever recorded and published. Near the close of the conference, a general meeting was held regarding publication of the proceedings. A five-member conference editorial board (Aboud, Gergen, Jahoda, Strickland, and Tajfel) was elected. Aboud, Gergen, and Strickland were named editors, and at a subsequent meeting, Strickland was designated "senior editor." Without exception it was decided that (a) some of the original conference papers might be omitted from an eventuating book, and (b) post-conference papers might be invited, submitted, and possibly included. Both of these possibilities have become realities, as the description of the following sections will indicate.

Organization of the Book

We have attempted to organize the contents of this book in a way that would not do violence to the thrust of any given paper. This was relatively easy, because the papers tended to address themselves primarily either to theoretical problems or to proposals for (or illustrations of) new research strategies. We have avoided the temptation of forcing the appearance of coherence on the contributions as a collection. The critiques of social psychology have been heterogeneous, and it was felt in the present instance that the field would be best served by embodying herein varied points of view and proposals for future "priorities and paradigms" articulated at and as a result of the conference.

In Section II are reprinted three of the most frequently cited passages from recent literature dealing with the present scientific status and alternative research futures in social psychology. The article by Gergen (1973) has been discussed and debated orally as frequently as any journal paper in the recollection of this editor, and the controversy it stimulated has also been carried on in print (Gergen, 1974; Manis, 1975; Schlenker, 1974). Many of us who have helped turn out the hundreds of (largely) unread studies that annually fill our journals have, of course, harbored secret suspicions that we were not really "scientists" in the same way that physiological psychologists down the hall were. (Incidentally, not all physiological psychologists feel they are cornering *the* scientific truths—see Webster, 1973). So Gergen's assertions that social psychological processes are the psychological counterparts of cultural norms and that theories of social behavior are simply reflections of contemporary history doubtless confirmed a lot of worries not frequently bruited about; they also implied the necessity for alternative research strategies for those of us who continue to believe that we have been concerned with very important questions, and that there must be a pony there someplace.

McGuire's paper shares several misgivings with Gergen's, but seems still to harbor the conviction that, if we have indeed focused on a trivial version of "reality" with too-simple (-minded?) models and an overconcern with hypothesis testing instead of more creative hypothesis generation, there are nevertheless regularities among social phenomena that we may yet observe if we but train ourselves and our students to do so. "Relevant" laboratory experiments and field experiments have failed as replacements for pointless validation of inconsequential, linearly-derived, and laboratory-tested hypotheses; McGuire's call for employment of notions like bidirectional causality, of time series analyses, of multivariate designs, of archival data, etc., provides a number of tactical suggestions for coping with the revised conception of what the social psychologist can "know."

The chapter, "Experiments in Social Psychology" from Harré and Secord (1972), is one of the most thorough indictments of the laboratory experiment, the device that has been the most frequently employed research tool of the social psychologist. There are, of course, many criticisms of this research style in the literature by now, so that a catalog of even the better experiments on experiments would itself lead to a bibliography of several pages. What distinguishes the Harré—Secord analysis is its *argument* that the laboratory experiment has been an inappropriate tool for the subject matter we had assumed we were studying—man's social behavior. If man is construed as an acting, information-seeking, and information-generating agent, instead of a behaving, information-processing machine, then use of a technique appropriate for the latter is logically inappropriate for the former. It can lead only to scrutiny of atypical behaviors in improbable and transient situations, while the goal of our efforts, the explanation of social behavior, will continue to elude us.

These three papers—Gergen's, which argues for sobering acknowledgment of the temporal limits of what we can know; McGuire's proclamation of the inadequacy of our past paradigm and, as well, of our recent attempts to break out of it; and the Harré and Secord analysis of the laboratory experiment's inadequacies for social psychology—all help define the context within which the idea of the Carleton Conference was developed.

Section III is comprised of four papers in the tradition of those just discussed, papers which examine the appropriateness of assumptions of our approach to scientific work, as well as their implications. The first, by Apfelbaum and Lubek, was prepared specifically for the conference. They discern three limitations of social psychological work on conflict: (1) the definition of the subject matter, "conflict," which seems restricted to a cold-war model involving two roughly equal antagonists, and which is focused on resolutions in terms of the "legitimate" strategies allowed by the investigator; (2) the passive acceptance by social psychologists of this definition, which is itself a product of the sources of support for the research; and (3) the adoption of a "game-theoretic" model in the analysis of conflict. Thus, we have concealment of certain kinds of conflicts and of certain classes of conflicting parties. Apfelbaum and Lubek's indictment of social psychologists who, they assume, should have known better receives a strong second by Paul Swingle and a powerful rebuttal from Morton Deutsch. Both these critiques were included in this book, as they provide two anchors for the "space" in which criticisms like Apfelbaum and Lubek's may be located for assessment. The three discussions serve as a valuable package of opinion for anyone interested in the social psychology of conflict.

It was stated earlier that the editorial committee had been empowered to elicit postconference papers from participants, papers which might be expansions of some of the discussion sparked by the formal presentations. The next three contributions are of this type. Rommetveit's essay on "emancipatory social psychology" was invited after several conference discussions closed with participants requesting him to elaborate on his assertion that the aim of social psychologists should be to give man more choices, not to demonstrate how few he actually has. His premise is that our basic question should be a Kantian "What is man?" He decries the fact that our field has gained its "legitimate" status through *lack* of concern with this question, and he offers prescriptions based on as unlikely a combination of sources as hermeneutic–dialectic philosophy (e.g., Apel, 1968) on the one hand, and psychophysiology (e.g., Hebb, 1974) on the other, as to how to expand man's self-control and rational choice. Research like that of Michotte and Piaget is seen as increasing man's range of choices, and hence the richness of his life, as results are fed back to him. It is striking to consider that the factor that Gergen sees to be frustrating social psychology (i.e., that the feedback from psychologist to society will alter the character of the causal relations of concern) is instead for Rommetveit an advantage to be pursued.

In the third chapter of Section III, Warren Thorngate supplies a different view of the limitations of social psychology, in another paper invited as a result of the author's significant contribution to the conference proceedings. He elaborates on the implication of "postulates of impotence" in a detailed conjecture that social psychology's subject matter may simply be too complex; we can never know very much, especially acting as the scientists we have tried to be. This, of course, is a different kind of criticism from the others considered here, with a stronger tone of finality.

However, Thorngate administers, with the discussion of limits to understanding, the prescription of a dose of pride. If we must remain essentially ignorant and our research techniques inadequate to the task, we are nevertheless sophisticated in comparison to self-proclaimed social philosophers—we should be proud of our efforts and, indeed, publicize their merit. We are again called upon to take advantage of the main impediment to a scientific social psychology (i.e., enlightenment effects) as discussed by Gergen and exploit it as urged by Rommetveit.

Section III ends with a paper by Kiesler and Lucke, an early version of which was presented at the meetings of the Society of Experimental Social Psychology in 1974, following the Carleton Conference. This invited revision seconds the note of optimism in Thorngate's paper and urges social psychologists to be more theoretically adventurous, not less. The authors suggest that one of our major problems is not that we lack a single "scientific" theoretical paradigm to show for our effort, but rather that we do not have enough of them. The suggestion is not that we cannot reach the scientific goals we have set for ourselves; rather, we have taken too narrow a view of what may be legitimately constitute "science," and it is this narrowness which has so limited social psychology's progress. To the suggestion that we should terminate our empirical research, shown to be so replete with problems, they reply that the unacceptable alternative is a sacrifice of our critical efforts and a substitution for them of dogmatic proclamation.

Section IV is in part a response to the questions about priorities and paradigms raised in Sections II and III. The paper by Zajonc (a revision of which has been published elsewhere) is one that departs drastically from previous treatments of individual differences by social psychologists. His development of the "confluence model," wherein the developing person is construed as part of his own intellectual environment, his employment of archival data, and his use of basic mathematical modeling techniques are eloquent illustrations of some of the methodological alternatives suggested by McGuire. The critique by a social psychologist, Stroebe, focuses on potential pitfalls of such an approach, as well as on the model's and method's potential advantage; the critique of a developmental psychologist, Moffit, clearly demonstrates that the kind of misgivings voiced by Apfelbaum and Lubek in Section III will not disappear with the substitution of new paradigms for the old. Moffit shares with Rommetveit and Thorngate a concern for the social psychologist's responsibility to the public that supports him. Thus, the unit that consists of a new model, its endorsement, and its castigation illustrates dramatically some of the problems which must be faced by social psychologists as they gather the courage and competence to move outside their restricted research spheres. One may conjecture that the reasons their theoretical work has been so seldom criticized is that (a) there has been comparatively little of it, as Kiesler suggests, and (b) it has been in traditionally "safe" areas, quite probably ignored by those not already committed to it.

What Zajonc endeavors in the area of intellectual development, Rommetveit attempts for psycholinguistics, or, more properly, for the area of interpersonal communication. He argues that a traditional, "pre-Newtonian" psycholinguistics, which focuses on linguistic competence and the analysis of utterances *in vacuo*, is doomed to modest achievements. Rather, he develops conception of *inter-subjectivity* in which communication is seen primarily as a social event. He proposes an analysis of the drafting of *metacontracts*, which must exist between parties for a meaningful communicative exchange to occur, along with examination of these contracts' premises (complementarity of the interactors' intentions, their ability to "take the role of the other," etc.). Peter Schonbach discusses the perilous fragility of the metacontracts that interactors design and is not optimistic about the theoretical and empirical fruitfulness of Rommetveit's analysis. Frances Aboud endorses Rommetveit's explanation of how words convey meaning in a social contract but notes, like Schonbach, that words may be only secondary to the real meaning of a communication, and thus that Rommetveit's analysis will need elaboration.

The Triandis–Berry–Jahoda contribution presents another proposal for a "new paradigm" along with evalutions of it. Triandis' point of departure is the argument, derived from Gergen's, that the transitory nature of social psychological findings will keep the field from achieving scientific status; he argues that this is due not to the nature of the subject matter itself, but to our choice of variables and strategies. The former are often trivial, selected because of easy manipulation and measurement, not for importance; the latter are chosen to detect small differences, not large generalities. The cross-cultural approach is proposed as an alternative, particularly one in which our data are those reflecting how people in different cultures think about social behaviors. It is presented as a first concrete proposal, complete with some supporting data, for the new methodology seen as essential by Harré and Secord (1972).

Although Triandis' work is applauded by Jahoda, his optimism that the analysis of subjective cultures will be the "kind of rescue boat for those of us adrift at sea" is not. Jahoda argues that it is unlikely that we would achieve any "laws" of cross-cultural generality, since social psychologists now lack any kind of adequate theoretical framework for cross-cultural data. Berry sees cultural analysis more positively, suggesting that a good place to start is with *behavioral mapping* within the ecological framework. A worry is that social psychologists are generally poorly trained and theoretically unacculturated, with respect to working in societies other than their own. Nevertheless, Triandis' approach is seen as a promising alternative to the paradigms that have characterized social psychology in the past.

In the fourth chapter of Section IV, deCharms and Shea propose that personal causation is a primary human experience, while the notion of physical causation is but a derivative thereof. This is a novel conception, because it seems, in the brief history of social psychology's concern with attribution processes, to have been assumed that just the *reverse* were true. This was quite possibly so because of our research paradigm's stress on "objectivity," which would lead us to avoid anything that smacked of anthropomorphism. They develop an extension of this argument that employs a distinction between imposed and intrinsic relevance of the person's behavior, one leading to a differentiation between intentional *actions* and imposed *behaviors*. The implications for research and for society of this revised conception of causal attribution are discussed in several contexts, but primarily with respect to the authors' attempts to train school teachers and their pupils to transform certain of their imposed (by the system) behaviors into intentional actions—to become less like pawns and more like origins. Strong exception to the assumptions implicit in this revised causal paradigm, as well as for the research it has generated, is taken by both critics. Partington's reservation reflects a concern that the possible *negative* consequences of a belief in personal control are ignored by deCharms and Shea, as are the positive implications of less primitive, "interdependent modes" of causality. Similar reservations are expressed by Steffens, who questions the consequences of using a "simplistic" framework to conceptualize acute social problems. Of concern also to her is the risk of theoretical violence that will be done by premature substitution of a paradigm based on the study of intuitive understanding rather than on the study of behavior.

The final chapter in this section, by Henri Tajfel, is presented here almost as a "case study" which employs an analytic method and a source of data quite different from that presented by other authors here but whose need was anticipated by Gergen. It may be seen as a response to one of the perceived weaknesses of the field, which was voiced several times during the conference: the need for more cross-disciplinary research and analysis. It was pointed out in discussions that the paradigm problems facing social psychologists were partly a function of researchers' narrowness; that reworking our present rules for asking questions within the confines of our discipline, without comparing frameworks to those of others in the social sciences, could scarcely aid attempts to break out of old paradigms and into new ones. Tajfel's paper considers conceptualizations by an eminent economist, Hirschman, on "exit" and "voice" options that individuals may exercise to control their interaction with business organizations or other social institutions. He then compares these conceptualizations with those of "social mobility" and "social change," developed in his own more recent writings, which have argued that social psychologists must attend more to intergroup phenomena and less to the sort of general psychology that examines social behavior in a cultural vacuum. In the method and analysis of this paper, one may observe the possibilities that exist for both social psychology's subject matter and its theoretical base. Indeed, if social psychologists are going to have anything of consequence to say about social processes "out there," it is absolutely crucial that we compare our own theoretical formulations to those of other social scientists who are *always* concerned with the "out there," lest we end up talking to ourselves.

Section V reflects another product of the conference that the editors were "instructed" to consider in assembling the contents of this book, that is, viewpoints representative of the many graduate students in attendance. Three vehicles are employed to this end: (1) an edited version of one student-oriented discussion session, during which participants considered the impact of the discipline's power structure on its paradigms and priorities; (2) an analysis of both the discussion and of the editorial efforts that followed it by the person who initiated the event, Ian Lubek; and (3) a view of future research strategies by a young Ph.D. candidate dedicated to their development and use, Andre deCarufel. These three statements foretell the diversity in social psychology which is likely to replace whatever vestiges of uniformity that remain after its current agonizing self-appraisal.

References

Apel, K. O. Scientifik, Hermeneutik, Ideologie Kritik: Entwer einer Wissenschafts lehre in erkenntnisanthropologischer Sicht. *Man and the World*, 1968, 1, 37–63.

Berry, J. W. Canadian psychology: Some social and applied emphases. *The Canadian Psychologist*, 1974, 15, 132–139.

Gergen, K. J. Social psychology as history. *Journal of Personality and Social Psychology*, 1973, 26, 309–320.

Gergen, K. J. Social psychology, science and history: A rejoinder. Unpublished manuscript, Swarthmore College, 1974.

Harré, R., and Secord, P. *The explanation of social behaviour*. Oxford: Blackwell, 1972.

Hebb, D. O. What psychology is about. *American Psychologist*, 1974, 29, 74–88.

Israel, J., and Tajfel, H. *The context of social psychology: A critical assessment*. London: Academic Press, 1972.

McGuire, W. J. The yin and yang of progress in social psychology: Seven koans. *Journal of Personality and Social Psychology*, 1973, 26, 446–456.

Manis, M. Comments on Gergen's "Social psychology as history," *Personality and Social Psychology Bulletin*, 1975, 1, 450–455.

Schlenker, B. R. Social psychology and science. *Journal of Personality and Social Psychology*, 1974, 29, 1–15.

Smith, M. B. Is experimental social psychology advancing? *Journal of Experimental Social Psychology*, 1972, 8, 89–96.

Webster, W. Assumptions, conceptualizations, and the search for the function of the brain. *Physiological Psychology*, 1973, 1, 346–350.

Zajonc, R. Birth order and intellectual development. *Psychological Review*, 1975, 82, 74–88.

THE CRITICAL CONTEXT OF THE CONFERENCE

SOCIAL PSYCHOLOGY AS HISTORY

KENNETH J. GERGEN

An analysis of theory and research in social psychology reveals that while methods of research are scientific in character, theories of social behavior are primarily reflections of contemporary history. The dissemination of psychological knowledge modifies the patterns of behavior upon which the knowledge is based. It does so because of the prescriptive bias of psychological theorizing, the liberating effects of knowledge, and the resistance based on common values of freedom and individuality. In addition, theoretical premises are based primarily on acquired dispositions. As the culture changes, such dispositions are altered, and the premises are often invalidated. Several modifications in the scope and methods of social psychology are derived from this analysis.

The field of psychology is typically defined as the science of human behavior, and social psychology as that branch of the science dealing with human interaction. A paramount aim of science is held to be the establishment of general laws through systematic observation. For the social psychologist, such general laws are developed in order to describe and explain social interaction. This traditional view of scientific law is repeated in one form or another in almost all fundamental treatments of the field. In his discussion of explanation

KENNETH J. GERGEN · Swarthmore College, Swarthmore, Pennsylvania. I am much indebted to the following persons for their thoughtful appraisal of various phases of this analysis: Shel Feldman, Mary Gergen, Kenneth Hammond, Louise Kidder, George Levinger, Paul Rosenblatt, Ralph Rosnow, M. Brewster Smith, Siegfried Streufert, Lloyd Strickland, Karl Weick, and Lawrence Wrightsman.

Reprinted by permission from *Journal of Personality and Social Psychology*, 1973, **26**, 309–320.

in the behavioral sciences, DiRenzo (1966) pointed out that a "complete explanation" in the behavioral sciences "is one that has assumed the invariable status of law" (p. 11). Krech, Crutchfield, and Ballachey (1962) stated that "whether we are interested in social psychology as a basic science or as an applied science, a set of scientific principles is essential" (p. 3). Jones and Gerard (1967) echoed this view in their statement, "Science seeks to understand the factors responsible for stable relationships between events" (p. 42). As Mills (1969) put it, "social psychologists want to discover causal relationships so that they can establish basic principles that will explain the phenomena of social psychology" (p. 412).

This view of social psychology is, of course, a direct descendent from eighteenth century thought. At that time the physical sciences had produced marked increments in knowledge, and one could view with great optimism the possibility of applying the scientific method to human behavior (Carr, 1963). If general principles of human behavior could be established, it might be possible to reduce social conflict, to do away with problems of mental illness, and to create social conditions of maximal benefit to members of society. As others later hoped, it might even be possible to transform such principles into mathematical form, to develop "a mathematics of human behavior as precise as the mathematics of machines" (Russell, 1956, p. 142).

The marked success of the natural sciences in establishing general principles can importantly be attributed to the general stability of events in the world of nature. The velocity of falling bodies or the compounding of chemical elements, for example, are highly stable events across time. They are events that can be recreated in any laboratory, 50 years ago, today, or 100 years from now. Because they are so stable, broad generalizations can be established with a high degree of confidence, explanations can be empirically tested, and mathematical transformations can be fruitfully developed. If events were unstable, if the velocity of falling bodies or the compounding of chemicals were in continuous flux, the development of the natural sciences would be drastically impeded. General laws would fail to emerge, and the recording of natural events would lend itself primarily to historical analysis. If natural events were capricious, natural science would largely be replaced by natural history.

It is the purpose of this paper to argue that social psychology is primarily an historical inquiry. Unlike the natural sciences, it deals with facts that are largely nonrepeatable and which fluctuate markedly over time. Principles of human interaction cannot readily be developed over time because the facts on which they are based do not generally remain stable. Knowledge cannot accumulate in the usual scientific sense because such knowledge does not generally transcend its historical boundaries. In the following discussion two central lines of argument will be developed in support of this thesis, the first centering on the impact of the science on social behavior and the second on historical change. After examining these arguments, we can focus on alterations in the scope and aims of the field suggested by this analysis.

Impact of Science on Social Interaction

As Back (1963) has shown, social science can fruitfully be viewed as a protracted communications system. In the execution of research, the scientist receives messages transmitted by the subject. In raw form, such messages generate only "noise" for the scientist. Scientific theories serve as decoding devices which convert noise to usable information. Although Back has used this model in a number of provocative ways, his analysis is terminated at the point of decoding. This model must be extended beyond the process of gathering and decoding messages. The scientist's task is also that of communicator. If his theories prove to by useful decoding devices, they are communicated to the populace in order that they might also benefit from their utility. Science and society constitute a feedback loop.

This type of feedback from scientist to society has become increasingly widespread during the past decade. Channels of communication have developed at a rapid rate. On the level of higher education, over eight million students are annually confronted by course offerings in the field of psychology, and within recent years, such offerings have become unexcelled in popularity. The liberal education of today entails familiarity with central ideas in psychology. The mass media have also come to realize the vast public interest in psychology. The news media carefully monitor professional meetings as well as journals of the profession. Magazine publishers have found it profitable to feature the views of psychologists on contemporary behavior patterns, and specialty magazines devoted almost exclusively to psychology now boast readerships totaling over 600,000. When we add to these trends the broad expansion of the soft-cover book market, the increasing governmental demand for knowledge justifying the public underwriting of psychological research, the proliferation of encounter techniques, the establishment of business enterprises huckstering psychology through games and posters, and the increasing reliance placed by major institutions (including business, government, military, and social) on the knowledge of in-house behavioral scientists, one begins to sense the profound degree to which the psychologist is linked in mutual communication with the surrounding culture.

Most psychologists harbor the desire that psychological knowledge will have an impact on the society. Most of us are gratified when such knowledge can be utilized in beneficial ways. Indeed, for many social psychologists, commitment to the field importantly depends on the belief in the social utility of psychological knowledge. However, it is not generally assumed that such utilization will alter the character of causal relations in social interaction. We do expect knowledge of function forms to be utilized in altering behavior, but we do not expect the utilization to affect the subsequent character of the function forms themselves. Our expectations in this case may be quite unfounded. Not only may the application of our principles alter the data on which they are based, but the very development of the principles may invalidate them. Three lines of argument are pertinent, the first stemming from the evaluative bias of psychological research, the second from the liberating effects of knowledge, and the third from prevalent values in the culture.

Prescriptive Bias of Psychological Theory

As scientists of human interaction, we are engaged in a peculiar duality. On the one hand, we value dispassionate comportment in scientific matters. We are well aware of the biasing effects of strong value commitments. On the other hand, as socialized human beings, we harbor numerous values about the nature of social relations. It is the rare social psychologist whose values do not influence the subject of his research, his methods of observation, or the terms of description. In generating knowledge about social interaction, we also communicate our personal values. The recipient of knowledge is thus provided with dual messages: Messages that dispassionately *describe* what appears to be, and those which subtly *prescribe* what is desirable.

This argument is most clearly evident in research on personal dispositions. Most of us would feel insulted if characterized as low in self-esteem, high in approval seeking, cognitively undifferentiated, authoritarian, anal compulsive, field dependent, or close-minded. In part, our reactions reflect our acculturation; one need not be a psychologist to resent such labels. But in part, such reactions are created by the concepts utilized in describing and explaining phenomena. For example, in the preface of *The Authoritarian Personality* (Adorno, Frenkel-Brunswik, Levinson, & Sanford, 1950), readers are informed that "In contrast to the bigot of the older style, [the authoritarian] seems to combine the ideas and skills of a highly industrialized society with irrational or anti-rational beliefs" (p. 3). In discussing the Machiavellian personality, Christie and Geis (1970) noted

> Initially our image of the high Mach was a negative one, associated with shadowy and unsavory manipulations. However ... we found ourselves having a perverse admiration for the high Machs' ability to outdo others in experimental situations. (p. 339)

In their prescriptive capacity such communications become agents of social change. On an elementary level, the student of psychology might well wish to exclude from public observation behaviors labeled by respected scholars as authoritarian, Machiavellian, and so on. The communication of knowledge may thus create homogeneity with respect to behavioral indicators of underlying dispositions. On a more complex level, knowledge of personality correlates may induce behavior to insubstantiate the correlates. Not so strangely, much individual difference research places the professional psychologist in a highly positive light. Thus, the more similar the subject is to the professional in terms of education, socioeconomic background, religion, race, sex, and personal values, the more advantageous his position on psychological tests. Increased education, for example, favors cognitive differentiation (Witkin, Dyk, Faterson, Goodenough, & Karp, 1962), low scores in authoritarianism (Christie & Jahoda, 1954), open-mindedness (Rokeach, 1960), etc. Armed with this information, those persons unflattered by the research might overcompensate in order to dispel the injurious stereotype. For example, women who learn they are more persuasible than men (cf. Janis & Field, 1959) may retaliate, and over time the correlation is invalidated or reversed.

While evaluative biases are easily identified in personality research, they are by no means limited to this area. Most general models of social interaction also contain implicit value judgments. For example, treatises on conformity often treat the conformer as a second-class citizen, a social sheep who foregoes personal conviction to agree with the erroneous opinions of others. Thus, models of social conformity sensitize one to factors that might lead him into socially deplorable actions. In effect, knowledge insulates against the future efficacy of these same factors. Research on attitude change often carries with it these same overtones. Knowing about attitude change flatters one into believing that he has the power to change others; by implication, others are relegated to the status of manipulanda. Thus, theories of attitude change may sensitize one into guarding against factors that could potentially influence him. In the same way, theories of aggression typically condemn the aggressor, models of interpersonal bargaining are disparaging of exploitation, and models of moral development demean those at less than the optimal stage (Kohlberg, 1970). Cognitive dissonance theory (Brehm & Cohen, 1966; Festinger, 1957) might appear to be value free, but most studies in this area have painted the dissonance reducer in most unflattering terms. "How witless" we say, "that people should cheat, make lower scores on tests, change their opinions of others, or eat undesirable foods just to maintain consistency."

The critical note underlying these remarks is not inadvertent. It does seem unfortunate that a profession dedicated to the objective and nonpartisan development of knowledge should use this position to propagandize the unwitting recipients of this knowledge. The concepts of the field are seldom value free, and most could be replaced with other concepts carrying far different valuational baggage. Brown (1965) has pointed to the interesting fact that the classic authoritarian personality, so roundly scourged in our own literature, was quite similar to the "J-type personality" (Jaensch, 1938), viewed by the Germans in a highly positive light. That which our literature termed rigidity was viewed as stability in theirs; flexibility and individualism in our literature were seen as flaccidity and eccentricity. Such labeling biases pervade our literature. For example, high self-esteem could be termed egotism; need for social approval could be translated as need for social integration; cognitive differentiation as hair-splitting; creativity as deviance; and internal control as egocentricity. Similarly, if our values were otherwise, social conformity could be viewed as prosolidarity behavior; attitude change as cognitive adaptation; and the risky shift as the courageous conversion.

Yet, while the propagandizing effects of psychological terminology must be lamented, it is also important to trace their sources. In part the evaluative loading of theoretical terms seems quite intentional. The act of publishing implies the desire to be heard. However, value-free terms have low-interest value for the potential reader, and value-free research rapidly becomes obscure. If obedience were relabeled alpha behavior and not rendered deplorable through associations with Adolph Eichman, public concern would undoubtedly be meager. In addition to capturing the interest of the public and the profession, value-loaded concepts also provide an expressive outlet for the psychologist. I have talked with countless graduate students drawn into psychology out of deep humanistic concern. Within many lies a frustrated poet, philosopher, or humanitarian who finds the scientific method at once a means to expressive ends and an encumbrance to free expression. Resented is the apparent fact that the ticket to open expression through the professional media is a near lifetime in the laboratory. Many wish to share their values directly, unfettered by constant demands for systematic evidence. For them, value-laden concepts compensate for the conservatism usually imparted by these demands. The more established psychologist may indulge himself more directly. Normally, however, we are not inclined to view our personal biases as propagandistic so much as reflecting "basic truths."

While the communication of values through knowledge is to some degree intentional, it is not entirely so. Value commitments are almost inevitable by-products of social existence, and as participants in society we can scarcely dissociate ourselves from these values in pursuing professional ends. In addition, if we rely on the language of the culture for scientific communication, it is difficult to find terms regarding social interaction that are without prescriptive value. We might reduce the implicit prescriptions embedded in our communications if we adopted a wholly technical language. However, even technical language becomes evaluative whenever the science is used as a lever for social change. Perhaps our best option is to maintain as much sensitivity as possible to our biases and to communicate them as openly as possible. Value commitments may be unavoidable, but we can avoid masquerading them as objective reflections of truth.

Knowledge and Behavioral Liberation

It is common research practice in psychology to avoid communicating one's theoretical premises to the subject either before or during the research. Rosenthal's (1966) research indicated that even the most subtle cues of experimenter expectation may alter the behavior of the subject. Naive subjects are thus required by common standards of rigor. The implications of this simple methodological safeguard are of considerable significance. If subjects possess preliminary knowledge as to theoretical premises, we can no longer adequately test our hypotheses. In the same way, if the society is psychologically informed, theories about which it is informed become difficult to test in an uncontaminated way. Herein lies a fundamental difference between the natural and the social sciences. In the former, the scientist cannot typically communicate his knowledge to the subjects of his study such that their behavioral dispositions are modified. In the social sciences such communication can have a vital impact on behavior.

A single example may suffice here. It appears that over a wide variety of conditions, decision-making groups come to make riskier decisions through group discussion (cf. Dion, Baron, & Miller, 1970; Wallach, Kogan, & Bem, 1964). Investigators in this area are quite careful that experimental subjects are not privy to their thinking on this matter. If knowledgeable, subjects might insulate themselves from the effects of group discussion or respond appropriately in order to gain the experimenter's favor. However, should the risky shift become common knowledge, naive subjects would become unobtainable. Members of the culture might consistently compensate for risky tendencies produced by group discussion until such behavior became normative.

As a general surmise, sophistication as to psychological principles liberates one from their behavioral implications. Established principles of behavior become inputs into one's decision making. As Winch (1958) has pointed out, "Since understanding something involves understanding its contradiction, someone who, with understanding, performs X must be capable of envisioning the possibility of doing not X" (p. 89). Psychological principles also sensitize one to influences acting on him and draw attention to certain aspects of the environment and himself. In doing so, one's patterns of behavior may be strongly influenced. As May (1971) has stated more passionately, "Each of us inherits from society a burden of tendencies which shapes us willy-nilly; but our capacity to be conscious of this fact saves us from being strictly determined" (p. 100). In this way, knowledge about nonverbal signals of stress or relief (Eckman, 1965) enables us to avoid giving off these signals whenever it is useful to do so; knowing that persons in trouble are less likely to be helped when there are large numbers of bystanders (Latané & Darley, 1970), may increase one's desire to offer his services under such conditions; knowing that motivational arousal can influence one's interpretation of events (cf. Jones & Gerard, 1967) may engender caution when arousal is high. In each instance, knowledge increases alternatives to action, and previous patterns of behavior are modified or dissolved.

Escape to Freedom

The historical invalidation of psychological theory can be further traced to commonly observed sentiments within western culture. Of major importance is the general distress people seem to feel at the diminution of their response alternatives. As Fromm (1941) saw it, normal development includes the acquisition of strong motives toward autonomy. Weinstein and Platt (1969) discussed much the same sentiment in terms of "man's wish to be free," and linked this disposition to the developing social structure. Brehm (1966) used this same disposition as the cornerstone of his theory of psychological reactance. The prevalence of this learned value has important implications for the long-term validity of social psychological theory.

Valid theories about social behavior constitute significanct implements of social control. To the extent that an individual's behavior is predictable, he places himself in a position of vulnerability. Others can alter environmental conditions or their behavior toward him to obtain maximal rewards at minimal costs to themselves. In the same way that a military strategist lays himself open to defeat when his actions become predictable, an organizational official can be taken advantage of by his inferiors and wives manipulated by errant husbands when their behavior patterns are reliable. Knowledge thus becomes power in the hands of others. It follows that psychological principles pose a potential threat to all those for whom they are germane. Investments in freedom may thus potentiate behavior designed to invalidate the theory. We are satisfied with principles of attitude change until we find them being used in information campaigns dedicated to changing our behavior. At this point, we may feel resentful and react recalcitrantly. The more potent the theory is in predicting behavior, the broader its public dissemination and the more prevalent and resounding the reaction. Thus, strong theories may be subject to more rapid invalidation than weak ones.

The common value of personal freedom is not the only pervasive sentiment affecting the mortality of social psychological theory. In western culture there seems to be heavy value placed on uniqueness or individuality. The broad popularity of both Erikson (1968) and Allport (1965) can be traced in part to their strong support of this value, and recent laboratory research (Fromkin, 1970, 1972) has demonstrated the strength of this value in altering social behavior. Psychological theory, in its nomothetic structure, is insensitive to unique occurrences. Individuals are treated as exemplars of larger classes. A common reaction is that psychological theory is dehumanizing, and as Maslow (1968) has noted, patients harbor a strong resentment at being rubricated or labeled with conventional clinical terms. Similarly, blacks, women, activists, suburbanites, educators, and the elderly have all reacted bitterly to explanations of their behavior. Thus, we may strive to invalidate theories that ensnare us in their impersonal way.

Psychology of Enlightenment Effects

Thus far we have discussed three ways in which social psychology alters the behavior it seeks to study. Before moving to a second set of arguments for the historical dependency of psychological theory, we must deal with an important means of combatting the effects thus far described. To preserve the transhistorical validity of psychological principles, the science could be removed from the public domain and scientific understanding reserved for a selected elite. This elite would, of course, be co-opted by the state, as no government could risk the existence of a private establishment developing tools of public control. For most of us, such a prospect is repugnant, and our inclination instead is to seek a scientific solution to the problem of historical dependency. Such an answer is suggested by much that has been said. If people who are psychologically enlightened react to general principles by contradicting them, conforming to them, ignoring them, and so on, then it should be possible to establish the conditions under which these various reactions will occur. Based on notions of psychological reactance (Brehm, 1966), self-fulfilling prophecies (Merton, 1948), and expectancy effects (Gergen & Taylor, 1969), we might construct a general theory of reactions to theory. A psychology of enlightenment effects should enable us to predict and control the effects of knowledge.

Although a psychology of enlightenment effects seems a promising adjunct to general theories, its utility is seriously limited. Such a psychology can itself be invested with value, increase our behavioral alternatives, and may be resented because of its threats to feelings of autonomy. Thus, a theory that predicts reactions to theory is also susceptible to violation or vindication. A frequent occurrence in parent–child relations illustrates the point. Parents are accustomed to using direct rewards in order to influence the behavior of their children. Over time, children become aware of the adult's premise that the reward will achieve the desired results and become obstinate. The adult may then react with a naive psychology of enlightenment effects and express disinterest in the child's carrying out the activity, again with the intent of achieving the desired ends. The child may respond appropriately but often enough will blurt out some variation of, "you are just saying you don't care because you really want me to do it." In Loevinger's (1959) terms, ". . . a shift in parentmanship is countered by a shift in childmanship" (p. 149). In the popular idiom, this is termed reverse psychology and is often resented. Of course, one could counter with research on reactions to the psychology of enlightenment effects, but it is quickly seen that this exchange of actions and reactions could be extended indefinitely. A pscyhology of enlightenment effects is subject to the same historical limitations as other theories of social psychology.

Psychological Theory and Cultural Change

The argument against transhistorical laws in social psychology does not solely rest on a consideration of the impact of science on society. A second major line of thought deserves consideration. If we scan the most prominent lines of research during the last decade, we soon realize that the observed regularities, and thus the major theoretical principles, are firmly wedded to historical circumstances. The historical dependency of psychological principles is most notable in areas of focal concern to the public. Social psychologists have been much concerned, for example, with isolating predictors of political activism during the past decade (cf. Mankoff & Flacks, 1971; Soloman & Fishman, 1964). However, as one scans this literature over time, numerous inconsistencies are found. Variables that successfully predicted political activism during the early stages of the Vietnam war are dissimilar to those which successfully predicted activism during later periods. The conclusion seems clear that the factors motivating activism changed over time. Thus, any theory of political activism built from early findings would be invalidated by later findings. Future research on political activism will undoubtedly find still other predictors more useful.

Such alterations in functional relationship are not in principle limited to areas of immediate public concern. For example, Festinger's (1957) theory of social comparison and the extensive line of deductive research (cf. Latané, 1966) are based on the dual assumption that (a) people desire to evaluate themselves accurately, and (b) in order to do so they compare themselves with others. There is scant reason to suspect that such dispositions are genetically determined, and we can easily imagine persons, and indeed societies, for which these assumptions would not hold. Many of our social commentators are critical of the common tendency to search out others' opinions in defining self and they attempt to change society through their criticism. In effect, the entire line of research appears to depend on a set of learned propensities, propensities that could be altered by time and circumstance.

In the same way, cognitive dissonance theory depends on the assumption that people cannot tolerate contradictory cognitions. The basis of such intolerance does not seem genetically given. There are certainly individuals who feel quite otherwise about such contradictions. Early existentialist writers, for example, celebrated the inconsistent act. Again, we must conclude that the theory is predictive because of the state of learned dispositions existing at the time. Likewise, Schachter's (1959) work on affiliation is subject to the arguments made in the case of social comparison theory. Milgram's (1965) obedience phenomenon is certainly dependent on contemporary attitudes toward authority. In attitude change research, communicator credibility is a potent factor because we have learned to rely on authorities in our culture, and the communicated message becomes dissociated from its source over time (Kelman & Hovland, 1953) because it does not prove useful to us *at present* to retain the association. In conformity research, people conform more to friends than nonfriends (Back, 1951) partly because they have learned that friends punish deviance in contemporary society. Research on causal attribution (cf. Jones, Davis, & Gergen, 1961; Kelley, 1971) depends on the culturally dependent tendency to perceive man as the source of his actions. This tendency can be modified (Hallowell, 1958) and some (Skinner, 1971) have indeed argued that it should be.

Perhaps the primary guarantee that social psychology will never disappear via reduction to physiology is that physiology cannot account for the variations in human behavior over time. People may prefer bright shades of clothing today and grim shades tomorrow; they may value autonomy during this era and dependency during the next. To be sure, varying responses to the environment rely on variations in physiological function. However, physiology can never specify the nature of the stimulus inputs or the response context to which the individual is exposed. It can never account for the continuously shifting patterns of what is considered the good or desirable in society, and thus a range of primary motivational sources for the individual. However, while social psychology is thus insulated from physiological reductionism, its theories are not insulated from historical change.

It is possible to infer from this latter set of arguments a commitment to at least one theory of transhistorical validity. It has been argued that the stability in interaction patterns upon which most of our theories rest is dependent on learned dispositions of limited duration. This implicitly suggests the possibility of a social learning theory transcending historical circumstance. However, such a conclusion is unwarranted. Let us consider, for example, an elementary theory of reinforcement. Few would doubt that most people are responsive to the reward and punishment contingencies in their environment, and it is difficult to envision a time in which this would not be true. Such premises thus seem transhistorically valid, and a primary task of the psychologist might be that of isolating the precise function forms relating patterns of reward and punishment to behavior.

This conclusion suffers on two important counts. Many critics of reinforcement theory have charged that the definition of reward (and punishment) is circular. Reward is typically defined as that which increases the frequency of responding; response increment is defined as that which follows reward. Thus, the theory seems limited to post hoc interpretation. Only when behavior change has occurred can one specify the reinforcer. The most significant rejoinder to this criticism lies in the fact that once rewards and punishments have been inductively established, they gain predictive value. Thus, isolating social approval as a positive reinforcer for human behavior was initially dependent on post hoc observation. However, once established as a reinforcer, social approval proved a successful means of modifying behavior on a predictive basis (cf. Barron, Heckenmueller, & Schultz, 1971; Gewirtz & Baer, 1958).

However, it is also apparent that reinforcers do not remain stable across time. For example, Reisman (1952) has cogently argued that social approval has far more reward value in contemporary society than it did a century ago. And while national pride might have been a potent reinforcer of late adolescent behavior in the 1940s, for contemporary youth such an appeal would probably be aversive. In effect, the essential circularity in reinforcement theory may at any time be reinstigated. As reinforcement value changes, so does the predictive validity of the basic assumption.

Reinforcement theory faces additional historical limitations when we consider its more precise specification. Similar to most other theories of human interaction, the theory is subject to ideological investment. The notion that behavior is wholly governed by external contingency is seen by many as vulgarly demeaning. Knowledge of the theory also enables one to avoid being ensnared by its predictions. As behavior modification therapists are aware, people who are conversant with its theoretical premises can subvert its intended effects with facility. Finally, because the theory has proved so effective in altering the behavior of lower organisms, it becomes particularly threatening to one's investment in autonomy. In fact, most of us would resent another's attempt to shape our behavior through reinforcement techniques and would bend ourselves to confounding the offender's expectations. In sum, the elaboration of reinforcement theory is no less vulnerable to enlightenment effects than other theories of human interaction.

Implications for an Historical Science of Social Behavior

In light of the present arguments, the continued attempt to build general laws of social behavior seems misdirected, and the associated belief that knowledge of social interaction can be accumulated in a manner similar to the natural sciences appears unjustified. In essence, the study of social psychology is primarily an historical undertaking. We are essentially engaged in a systematic account of contemporary affairs. We utilize scientific methodology, but the results are not scientific principles in the traditional sense. In the future, historians may look back to such accounts to achieve a better understanding of life in the present era. However, the psychologists of the future are likely to find little of value in contemporary knowledge. These arguments are not purely academic and are not limited to a simple redefinition of the science. Implied here are significant alterations in the activity of the field. Five such alterations deserve attention.

Toward an Integration of the Pure and Applied

A pervasive prejudice against applied research exists among academic psychologists, a prejudice that is evident in the pure research focus of prestige journals and in the dependency of promotion and tenure on contributions to pure as opposed to applied research. In part, this prejudice is based on the assumption that applied research is of transient value. While it is limited to solving immediate problems, pure research is viewed as contributing to basic and enduring knowledge. From the present standpoint, such grounds for prejudice are not merited. The knowledge that pure research bends itself to establish is also transient; generalizations in the pure research area do not generally endure. To the extent that generalizations from pure research have greater transhistorical validity, they may be reflecting processes of peripheral interest or importance to the functioning of society.

Social psychologists are trained in using tools of conceptual analysis and scientific methodology in explaining human interaction. However, given the sterility of perfecting general principles across time, these tools would seem more productively used in solving problems of immediate importance to the society. This is not to imply that such research must be parochial in scope. One major shortcoming of much applied research is that the terms used to describe and explain are often relatively concrete and specific to the case at hand. While the concrete behavioral acts studied by academic psychologists are often more trivial, the explanatory language is highly general and thus more broadly heuristic. Thus, the present arguments suggest an intensive focus on contemporary social issues, based on the application of scientific methods and conceptual tools of broad generality.

From Prediction to Sensitization

The central aim of psychology is traditionally viewed as the prediction and control of behavior. From the present standpoint, this aim is misleading and provides little justification for research. Principles of human behavior may have limited predictive value across time, and their very acknowledgment can render them impotent as tools of social control. However, prediction and control need not serve as the cornerstones of the field. Psychological theory can play an exceedingly important role as a sensitizing device. It can enlighten one as to the range of factors potentially influencing behavior under various conditions. Research may also provide some estimate of the importance of these factors at a given time. Whether it be in the domain of public policy or personal relationships, social psychology can sharpen one's sensitivity to subtle influences and pinpoint assumptions about behavior that have not proved useful in the past.

When counsel is sought from the social psychologist regarding likely behavior in any concrete situation, the typical reaction is apology. It must be explained that the field is not sufficiently well developed at present so that reliable predictions can be made. From the present standpoint, such apologies are inappropriate. The field can seldom yield principles from which reliable predictions can be made. Behavior patterns are under constant modification. However, what the field can and should provide is research informing the inquirer of a number of possible occurrences, thus expanding his sensitivities and readying him' for more rapid accommodation to environmental change. It can provide conceptual and methodological tools with which more discerning judgments can be made.

Developing Indicators of Psychosocial Dispositions

Social psychologists evidence a continuous concern with basic psychological processes, that is, processes influencing a wide and varied range of social behavior. Modeling the experimental psychologist's concern with basic processes of color vision, language acquisition, memory, and the like, social psychologists have focused on such processes as cognitive dissonance, aspiration level, and causal attribution. However, there is a profound difference between the processes typically studied in the general experimental and social domains. In the former instance, the processes are often locked into the organism biologically; they are not subject to enlightenment effects and are not dependent on cultural circumstance. In contrast, most of the processes falling in the social domain are dependent on acquired dispositions subject to gross modification over time.

In this light, it is a mistake to consider the processes in social psychology as basic in the natural science sense. Rather, they may largely be considered the psychological counterpart of cultural norms. In the same way a sociologist is concerned with measuring party preferences or patterns of mobility over time, the social psychologist might attend to the changing patterns of psychological dispositions and their relationship to social behavior. If dissonance reduction is an important process, then we should be in a position to measure the prevalence and strength of such a disposition within the society over time and the preferred modes of dissonance reduction existing at any given time. If esteem enhancement appears to influence social interaction, then broad studies of the culture should reveal the extent of the disposition, its strength in various subcultures, and the forms of social behavior with which it is most likely associated at any given time. Although laboratory experiments are well suited to the isolation of particular dispositions, they are poor indicators of the range and significance of the processes in contemporary social life. Much needed are methodologies tapping the prevalence, strength, and form of psychosocial dispositions over time. In effect, a technology of psychologically sensitive social indicators (Bauer, 1969) is required.

Research on Behavioral Stability

Social phenomena may vary considerably in the extent to which they are subject to historical change. Certain phenomena may be closely tied to physiological givens. Schachter's (1970) research on emotional states appears to have a strong physiological basis, as does Hess's (1965) work on affect and pupillary constriction. Although learned dispositions can overcome the strength of some physiological tendencies, such tendencies should tend to reassert themselves over time. Still other physiological propensities may be irreversible. There may also be acquired dispositions that are sufficiently powerful that neither enlightenment nor historical change is likely to have a major impact. People will generally avoid physically painful stimuli, regardless of their sophistication or the current norms. We must think, then, in terms of a *continuum of historical durability*, with phenomena highly susceptible to historical influence at one extreme and the more stable processes at the other.

In this light, much needed are research methods enabling us to discern the relative durability of social phenomena. Cross-cultural methods could be employed in this capacity. Although cross-cultural replication is frought with difficulty, similarity in a given function form across widely divergent cultures would strongly attest to its durability across time. Content analytic techniques might also be employed in examining accounts of earlier historical periods. Until now, such accounts have provided little except quotations indicating that some great thinker presaged a pet hypothesis. We have yet to tap the vast quantities of information regarding interaction patterns in earlier periods. Although enhanced sophistication about behavior patterns across space and time would furnish valuable insights regarding durability, difficult problems present themselves. Some behavior patterns may remain stable until closely scrutinized; others may simply become dysfunctional over time. Man's reliance on a concept of deity has a long history and is found in numerous cultures; however, many are skeptical about the future of this reliance. Assessments of durability would thus have to account for potential as well as actual stability in phenomena.

While research into more durable dispositions is highly valuable, we should not therefore conclude that it is either more useful or desirable than studying passing behavior patterns. The major share of the variance in social behavior is undoubtedly due to historically dependent dispositions, and the challenge of capturing such processes "in flight" and during auspicious periods of history is immense.

Toward an Integrated Social History

It has been maintained that social psychological research is primarily the systematic study of contemporary history. As such, it seems myopic to maintain disciplinary detachment from (a) the traditional study of history and (b) other historically bound sciences (including sociology, political science, and economics). The particular research strategies and sensitivities of the historian could enhance the understanding of social psychology, both past and present. Particularly useful would be the historian's sensitivity to causal sequences across time. Most social psychological research focuses on minute segments of ongoing processes. We have concentrated very little on the function of these segments within their historical context. We have little theory dealing with the interrelation of events over extended periods of time. By the same token, historians could benefit from the more rigorous methodologies employed by the social psychologist as well as his particular sensitivity to psychological variables. However, the study of history, both past and present, should be undertaken in the broadest possible framework. Political, economic, and institutional factors are all necessary inputs to understanding in an integrated way. A concentration on psychology alone provides a distorted understanding of our present condition.

References

Adorno, T. W., Frenkel-Brunswik, E., Levinson, D. J., and Sanford, R. N. *The authoritarian personality.* New York: Harper, 1950.

Allport, G. W. *Pattern and growth in personality.* New York: Holt, Rinehart & Winston, 1965.

Back, K. W. Influence through social communication. *Journal of Abnormal and Social Psychology*, 1951, 46, 9–23.

Back, K. W. The proper scope of social psychology. *Social Forces*, 1963, 41, 368–376.

Barron, R., Heckenmueller, J., and Schultz, S. Differences in conditionability as a function of race of subject and prior availability of a social reinforcer. *Journal of Personality*, 1971, 39, 94–111.

Bauer, R. (ed.) *Social indicators.* Cambridge, Mass.: M.I.T. Press, 1969.

Brehm, J. W. *A theory of psychological reactance.* New York: Academic Press, 1966.

Brehm, J. W., and Cohen, A. R. *Explorations in cognitive dissonance.* New York: Wiley, 1966.

Brown, R. *Social psychology.* Glencoe, Ill.: Free Press, 1965.

Carr, E. H. *What is history?* New York: Knopf, 1963.

Christie, R., and Jahoda, M. (eds.) *Studies in the scope and method of "The authoritarian personality."* Glencoe, Ill.: Free Press, 1954.

Crowne, D. P., and Marlowe, D. *The approval motive: Studies in evaluative dependence.* New York: Wiley, 1964.

Dion, K. L., Baron, R. S., and Miller, N. Why do groups make riskier decisions than individuals? In L. Berkowitz (ed.), *Advances in experimental social psychology*, Vol. 5. New York: Academic Press, 1970.

DiRenzo, G. (ed.) *Concepts, theory and explanation in the behavioral sciences.* New York: Random House, 1966.

Eckman, P. Communication through non-verbal behavior: A source of information about an interpersonal relationship. In S. S. Tomkins and C. Izard (eds.), *Affect, cognition and personality.* New York: Springer, 1965.

Erickson, E. Identity and identity diffusion. In C. Gordon and K. J. Gergen (eds.), *The self in social interaction*, Vol. 1. New York: Wiley, 1968.

Festinger, L. *A theory of cognitive dissonance.* Evanston, Ill.: Row, Peterson, 1957.

Fromkin, H. L. Effects of experimentally aroused feelings of undistinctiveness upon valuation of scarce and novel experiences. *Journal of Personality and Social Psychology*, 1970, 16, 521–529.

Fromkin, H. L. Feelings of interpersonal undistinctiveness: An unpleasant affective state. *Journal of Experimental Research in Personality*, 1972, 6, 178–185.

Fromm, E. *Escape from freedom.* New York: Rinehart, 1941.

Gergen, K. J., and Taylor, M. G. Social expectancy and self-presentation in a status hierarchy. *Journal of Experimental and Social Psychology*, 1969, 5, 79–92.

Gewirtz, J. L., and Baer, D. M. Deprivation and satiation of social reinforcers as drive conditions. *Journal of Abnormal and Social Psychology*, 1958, 57, 165–172.

Hallowell, A. I. Ojibwa metaphysics of being and the perception of persons. In R. Tagiuri & L. Petrullo (eds.), *Person, perception and interpersonal behavior*. Stanford: Stanford University Press, 1958.

Hess, E. H. Attitude and pupil size. *Scientific American*, 1965, 212, 46–54.

Jaensch, E. R. *Der Geqentypus*. Leipzig: Barth, 1938.

Janis, I. L., and Field, P. B. Sex differences and personality factors related to persuasibility. In I. Janis and C. Hovland (eds.), *Personality and persuasibility*. New Haven: Yale University Press, 1959.

Jones, E. E., Davis, K. E., and Gergen, K. J. Role playing variations and their informational value for person perception. *Journal of Abnormal and Social Psychology*, 1961, 63, 302–310.

Jones, E. E., and Gerard, H. B. *Foundations of social psychology*. New York: Wiley, 1967.

Kelley, H. H. *Causal schemata and the attribution process*. Morristown, N.J.: General Learning Press, 1971.

Kelman, H., and Hovland, C. "Reinstatement" of the communicator in delayed measurement of opinion change. *Journal of Abnormal and Social Psychology*, 1953, 48, 327–335.

Kohlberg, L. Stages of moral development as a basis for moral education. In C. Beck and E. Sullivan (eds.), *Moral education*. Toronto: University of Toronto Press, 1970.

Krech, D., Crutchfield, R. S., & Ballachey, E. L. *Individual in society*. New York: McGraw-Hill, 1962.

Latané, B. Studies in social comparison—Introduction and overview. *Journal of Experimental Social Psychology*, 1966, 2(Suppl. 1).

Latané, B., and Darley, J. *Unresponsive bystander: Why doesn't he help?* New York: Appleton-Century-Crofts, 1970.

Loevinger, J. Patterns of parenthood as theories of learning. *Journal of Abnormal and Social Psychology*, 1959, 59, 148–150.

Mankoff, M., and Flacks, R. The changing social base of the American student movement. *Journal of the American Academy of Political and Social Science*, 1971, 395, 54–67.

Maslow, A. H. *Toward a psychology of being*. New York: Van Nostrand-Reinhold, 1968.

May, R. Letters to the Editor. *New York Times Magazine*, April 18, 1971, p. 100.

Merton, R. K. The self-fulfilling prophecy. *Antioch Review*, 1948, 8, 193–210.

Milgram, S. Some conditions of obedience and disobedience to authority. In I. D. Steiner and M. Fishbein (eds.), *Current studies in social psychology*. New York: Holt, Rinehart & Winston, 1965.

Mills, J. *Experimental social psychology*. New York: Macmillan, 1969.

Reisman, D. *The lonely crowd*. New Haven: Yale University Press, 1952.

Rokeach, M. *The open and closed mind*. New York: Basic Books, 1960.

Rosenthal, R. *Experimenter effects in behavioral research*. New York: Appleton-Century-Crofts, 1966.

Russell, B. *Our knowledge of the external world*. New York: Menton Books, 1956.

Schachter, S. *The psychology of affiliation*. Stanford: Stanford University Press, 1959.

Schachter, S. The interaction of cognitive and physiological determinants of emotional states. In L. Berkowitz (ed.), *Advances in experimental social psychology*, Vol. 1. New York: Academic Press, 1970.

Skinner, B. F. *Beyond freedom and dignity*. New York: Knopf, 1971.

Soloman, F., and Fishman, T. R. Youth and peace: A psycho-social study of student peace demonstrators in Washington, D.C. *Journal of Social Issues*, 1964, **20**, 54–73.

Wallach, M. A., Kogan, N., and Bem, D. J. Diffusion of responsibility and level of risk taking in groups. *Journal of Abnormal and Social Psychology*, 1964, **68**, 263–274.

Weinstein, F., and Platt, G. M. *The wish to be free.* Berkeley: University of California Press, 1969.

Winch, P. *The idea of a social science and its relation to philosophy.* New York: Humanities Press, 1958.

Witkin, H. A., Dyk, R. B., Faterson, H. F., Goodenough, D. R., and Karp, S. A. *Psychological differentiation.* New York: Wiley, 1962.

THE YIN AND YANG OF PROGRESS
IN SOCIAL PSYCHOLOGY
Seven Koan

WILLIAM J. McGUIRE

We describe the current dissatisfactions with the paradigm that has recently guided experimental social psychology—testing of theory-derived hypotheses by means of laboratory manipulational experiments. The emerging variant of doing field experiments does not meet the criticisms. It is argued that an adequate new paradigm will be a more radical departure involving, on the creative side, deriving hypotheses from a systems theory of social and cognitive structures that takes into account multiple and bidirectional causality among social variables. On the critical side, its hypotheses testing will be done in multivariate correlational designs with naturally fluctuating variables. Some steps toward this new paradigm are described in the form of seven koan.

The Paradigm Recently Guiding Experimental Social Psychology

When the 19th Congress met three years ago in London, and certainly a half-dozen years back at the Moscow Congress, social psychology appeared to be

WILLIAM J. McGUIRE · Yale University, New Haven, Connecticut. This paper is based on an address given at the Nineteenth Congress of the International Union of Scientific Psychology at Tokyo in August 1972.

Reprinted by permission from *Journal of Personality and Social Psychology*, 1973, **26**, 446–456.

in a golden age. It was a prestigious and productive area in which droves of bright young people, a sufficiency of middle-aged colonels, and a few grand old men were pursuing their research with a confidence and energy that is found in those who know where they are going. Any moments of doubt we experienced involved anxiety as to whether we were doing our thing well, rather than uncertainty as to whether it needed to be done at all.

The image of these golden boys (and a few, but all too few, golden girls) of social psychology, glowing with confidence and chutzpah only six years back at the Moscow Congress, blissfully unaware of the strident attacks which were soon to strike confusion into the field, brings to mind a beautiful haiku of Buson that goes

> Tsurigane-ni
> Tomarite nemuru
> Kochō kana

which I hasten to translate as follows:

> On a temple bell
> Settled, asleep,
> A butterfly.

We social psychology researchers know all too well that the peaceful temple bell on which we were then displaying ourselves has now rudely rung. During the past half-dozen years, the vibrations which could be vaguely sensed at the time of the Moscow meeting have gathered force. Now the temple bell has tolled and tolled again, rudely disturbing the stream of experimental social psychological research and shaking the confidence of many of us who work in the area.

The first half of this paper is devoted to describing the three successive waves of this current history. First, I shall describe the experimental social psychology paradigm that has recently guided our prolific research. Second, I shall discuss why this recent paradigm is being attacked and what, superficially at least, appears to be emerging in its place. Third, I shall say why I feel the seemingly emerging new paradigm is as inadequate as the one we would replace. Then, in the second half of this paper I shall offer, in the form of seven koan, my prescriptions for a new paradigm, more radically different from the recent one, but more in tune with the times and the march of history than is the variant that is supposedly emerging.

The Old Paradigm

What was the experimental social psychology paradigm which until recently had been unquestioningly accepted by the great majority of us but which now is being so vigorously attacked? Like any adequate paradigm it had two aspects, a creative and a critical component (McGuire, 1969, pp. 22–25). By the creative aspect, I mean the part of our scientific thinking that involves hypothesis generation, and by the critical aspect, I mean the hypothesis-testing part of our work.

The creative aspect of the recent paradigm inclined us to derive our hypotheses from current theoretical formulations. Typically, these theoretical formulations were borrowed from other areas of psychology (such as the study of psychopathology or of learning and memory), though without the level of refinement and quantification which those theories had reached in their fields of origin.

The critical, hypothesis-testing aspect of the recent paradigm called for manipulational experiments carried out in the laboratory. The experimental social psychologist attempted to simulate in the laboratory the gist of the situation to which he hoped to generalize, and he measured the dependent variable after deliberately manipulating the independent variable while trying to hold constant all other factors likely to affect the social behavior under study. In brief, the recent paradigm called for selecting our hypotheses for their relevance to broad theoretical formulations and testing them by laboratory manipulational experiments. McGuire (1965) presented an emphatic assertion of this recent paradigm in its heyday.

Assaults on the Old Paradigm

During the past several years both the creative and the critical aspects of this experimental social psychology paradigm have come under increasing attack. The creative aspect of formulating hypotheses for their relevance to theory has been denounced as a mandarin activity out of phase with the needs of our time. It has been argued that hypotheses should be formulated for their relevance to social problems rather than for their relevance to theoretical issues. Such urgings come from people inside and outside social psychology, reflecting both the increasing social concern of researchers themselves and the demands of an articulate public for greater payoff from expensive scientific research. While many of us still insist with Lewin that "There is nothing so practical as a good theory," the extent to which the pendulum has swung from the theoretically relevant toward the socially relevant pole is shown in the recent upsurge of publications on socially important topics of ad hoc interest, such as bystander intervention, the use of local space, the mass media and violence, the determinants of love, responses to victimization, and nonverbal communication.

At least as strong and successful an assault has been launched on the critical aspect of the recent paradigm, namely, the notion that hypotheses should be tested by manipulational laboratory experiments. It has been urged that laboratory experiments are full of artifacts (such as experimenter bias, demand character, and evaluation apprehension) which make their results very hard to interpret. Ethical questions also have been raised against the laboratory social experiments on the grounds that they expose the participants to an unacceptable amount of deception, coercion, and stress.

In place of the laboratory manipulational experiment, there has been a definite trend toward experiments conducted in field settings and toward correlational analysis of data from naturalistic situations. A variety of recent methodological advances (which we shall list under Koan 5) has made alternative hypothesis-testing procedures more attractive.

The attacks on the old paradigm of theory-derived hypotheses tested in laboratory manipulational experiments have certainly shaken confidence in that approach. At the same time, there is some suggestion of an emerging new paradigm which has as its creative aspect the derivation of new hypotheses for their ad hoc interest and social relevance. And in its critical aspect, this new paradigm involves testing these hypotheses by field experiments and, where necessary, by the correlational analysis of naturalistic data. McGuire (1967, 1969) described in more detail the worries about the recent paradigm and the nature of the purportedly emerging one. Higbee and Wells (1972) and Fried, Gumpper, and Allen (1973) suggested that reports by McGuire, by Sears and Abeles (1969), etc., of the demise of the recent paradigm may be exaggerated, but perhaps they have underestimated the time that must intervene before a change of vogue by the leaders shows up in mass analysis of the methods used in published research.

More Basic Questions Regarding Both the Recent and Emerging Paradigms

My own position on the relative merits of the recent paradigm and this supposedly emerging new paradigm is a complex and developing one which I have detailed in print (McGuire, 1965, 1967, 1969) so the reader will be spared here a recital of my Byzantine opinions on this issue. Instead, I am raising the more fundamental issue of whether or not both the recent and the seemingly emerging paradigms which I have just described fail to come to grips with the deeper questions which lie behind our present unease. It seems to me that any truly new paradigm that ultimately arises from the present unrest is going to be more radically different from the recent one than is the supposedly emerging paradigm I have just depicted. It will represent a more fundamental departure on both the creative and the critical sides.

Inadequacies on the Creative Side

The switch from theory relevance to social relevance as the criterion in the creative, hypothesis-generating aspect of our work seems to me to constitute only a superficial cosmetic change that masks rather than corrects the basic problem. Socially relevant hypotheses, no less than theoretically relevant hypotheses, tend to be based on a simple linear process model, a sequential chain of cause and effect which is inadequate to simulate the true complexities of the individual's cognitive system or of the social system which we are typically trying to describe. Such simple *a*-affects-*b* hypotheses fail to catch the complexities of parallel processing, bidirectional causality, and reverberating feedback that characterize both cognitive and social organizations. The simple sequential model had its uses, but these have been largely exploited in past progress, and we must now deal with the complexities of systems in order to continue the progress on a new level.

The real inadequacy of the theory-derived hypotheses of the recent paradigm is not, as those now advocating socially relevant hypotheses insist, that it focused on the wrong variables (those that were theory rather than problem relevant). Rather, the basic shortcoming of the theory-relevant and the socially relevant hypotheses alike is that they fail to come to grips with the complexities with which the variables are organized in the individual and social systems.

Inadequacies of the Critical Aspect of the Recent Paradigm

The critical, hypothesis-testing aspect of the purportedly emerging paradigm also has the defect of being but a minor variant of the recent experimental social psychology paradigm rather than the fundamental departure which is called for. Let me first describe some of the deep epistemological uneasiness some of us have been expressing about the manipulational laboratory experiment that was the hypothesis-testing procedure of the recent paradigm. The crux of this objection is that we social psychologists have tended to use the manipulational laboratory experiment not to test our hypotheses but to demonstrate their obvious truth. We tend to start off with a hypothesis that is so clearly true (given the implicit and explicit assumptions) and which we have no intention of rejecting however the experiment comes out. Such a stance is quite appropriate, since the hypothesis by its meaningfulness and plausibility to reasonable people is tautologically true in the assumed context. As Blake said, "Everything possible to be believ'd is an image of truth."

The area of interpersonal attraction will serve to illustrate my point. The researcher might start off with a *really* obvious proposition from bubba-psychology, such as "The more someone perceives another person as having attitudes similar to his own, the more he tends to like that other person." Or a somewhat more flashy researcher, a little hungrier for novelty, might hypothesize the opposite. That is, he could look for certain circumstances in which the generally true, obvious hypothesis would obviously be reversed. He might hypothesize exceptional circumstances where attitudinal similarity would be anxiety arousing and a source of hostility; for example, if one loves one's wife, then one might actually dislike some other man to the extent that one perceives that other as also loving one's wife. Or another exceptional reversal might be that some people may think so poorly of themselves that they think less well of another person to the extent that the other person is like themselves. If the negative relationship is not found, we are likely to conclude that the person did not have a sufficiently low self-image, not that the hypothesis is wrong. Both the original obvious hypothesis and the obvious reversed hypothesis are reasonable and valid in the sense that if all our premises obtained, then our conclusion would pretty much have to follow.

Experiments on such hypotheses naturally turn out to be more like demonstrations than tests. If the experiment does not come out "right," then the researcher does not say that the hypothesis is wrong but rather that something was wrong with the experiment, and he corrects and revises it, perhaps by using more appropriate subjects, by strengthening the independent variable manipulation, by blocking off extraneous response possibilities, by setting up a more appropriate context, etc. Sometimes he may have such continuous bad luck that he finally gives up the demonstration because the phenomenon proves to be so elusive as to be beyond his ability to demonstrate. The more persistent of us typically manage at last to get control of the experimental situation so that we can reliably demonstrate the hypothesized relationship. But note that what the experiment tests is not whether the hypothesis is true but rather whether the experimenter is a sufficiently ingenious stage manager to produce in the laboratory conditions which demonstrate that an obviously true hypothesis is correct. In our graduate programs in social psychology, we try to train people who are good enough stage managers so that they can create in the laboratory simulations of realities in which the obvious correctness of our hypothesis can be demonstrated.

It is this kind of epistemological worry about manipulational laboratory experiments that a half-dozen years back caused a number of observers (e.g., McGuire, 1967) to urge social psychology to search for interrelations among naturally varying factors in the world outside the laboratory. Out of these urgings has come the critical aspect of the apparently emerging paradigm which I have described above, calling for research in the field rather than in the laboratory.

Inadequacies of the Critical Aspects of the Purportedly Emerging New Field Experiment Paradigm

Recently, I have come to recognize that this flight from the laboratory manipulational experiment to the field study, which I myself helped to instigate, is a tactical evasion which fails to meet the basic problem. We would grant that in the field we put the question to nature in a world we never made, where the context factors cannot be so confounded by our stage management proclivities as they were in the laboratory. But in this natural world research, the basic problem remains that we are not really testing our hypotheses. Rather, just as in the laboratory experiment we were testing our stage-managing abilities, in the field study we are testing our ability as "finders," if I may use a term from real estate and merchandising. When our field test of the hypothesis does not come out correctly, we are probably going to assume not that the hypothesis is wrong but that we unwisely chose an inappropriate natural setting in which to test it, and so we shall try again to test it in some other setting in which the conditions are more relevant to the hypothesis. Increasing our own and our graduate students' critical skill will involve making us not better hypothesis testers or better stage managers but rather better finders of situations in which our hypotheses can be demonstrated as tautologically true. Though I shall not pursue the point here, other objections to the laboratory experiment, including ethical and methodological considerations, that have been used (McGuire, 1969) to argue for more field research, could similarly be turned against experiments conducted in the natural environment.

What I am arguing here is that changing from a theory-relevant to a socially relevant criterion for variable selection does not constitute a real answer to the basic problem with the creative aspect of our recent social psychology paradigm. And again, the switch from laboratory to field manipulation does not meet the basic objection to the critical aspect of the old paradigm. Neither the recent paradigm nor the supposedly emerging one really supplies the answer to our present needs. The discontent is a quite healthy one, and we should indeed be dissatisfied with the recent paradigm of testing theory-derived hypotheses by means of laboratory manipulational experiments. But our healthy discontent should carry us to a more fundamentally new outlook than is provided by this supposedly emerging variant paradigm of testing socially relevant hypotheses by experiments in natural settings.

Sources of the New Social Psychology

The Ultimate Shape of the New Paradigm

What I have written in the previous section suggests my general vision of what the more radically different new paradigm for social psychology will look like. On the creative side, it will involve theoretical models of the cognitive and social systems in their true multivariate complexity, involving a great deal of parallel processing, bidirectional relationships, and feedback circuits. Since such complex theoretical formulations will be far more in accord with actual individual and social reality than our present a-affects-b linear models, it follows that theory-derived hypotheses will be similar to hypotheses selected for their relevance to social issues. Correspondingly, the critical aspect of this new paradigm involves hypothesis testing by multivariate time series designs that recognize the obsolescence of our current simplistic *a*-affects-*b* sequential designs with their distinctions between dependent and independent variables.

But I feel somewhat uncomfortable here in trying to describe in detail what the next, radically different paradigm will look like. It will be hammered out by theoretically and empirically skilled researchers in a hundred eyeball-to-eyeball confrontations of thought with data, all the while obscured by a thousand mediocre and irrelevant studies, which will constitute the background noise in which the true signal will be detected only gradually. Trying to predict precisely what new paradigm will emerge is almost as foolish as trying to control it.

But there is a subsidiary task with which I feel more comfortable and to which I shall devote the rest of this paper. I have come to feel that some specific tactical changes should be made in our creative and critical work in social psychology so as to enhance the momentum and the ultimate sweep of this wave of the future, whatever form it may take. I shall here recommend a few of these needed innovations and correctives, presenting them as koans and commentaries thereon, to mask my own uncertainties.

Koan 1: The Sound of One Hand Clapping . . . and the Wrong Hand

One drastic change that is called for in our teaching of research methodology is that we should emphasize the creative, hypothesis-formation stage relative to the critical, hypothesis-testing stage of research. It is my guess that at least 90% of the time in our current courses on methodology is devoted to presenting ways of testing hypotheses and that little time is spent on the prior and more important process of how one creates these hypotheses in the first place. Both the creation and testing of hypotheses are important parts of the scientific method, but the creative phase is the more important of the two. If our hypotheses are trivial, it is hardly worth amassing a great methodological arsenal to test them; to paraphrase Maslow, what is not worth doing, is not worth doing well. Surely, we all recognize that the creation of hypotheses is an essential part of the scientific process. The neglect of the creative phase in our methodology courses probably comes neither from a failure to recognize its importance nor a belief that it is trivially simple. Rather, the neglect is probably due to the suspicion that so complex a creative process as hypothesis formation is something that cannot be taught.

I admit that creative hypothesis formation cannot be reduced to teachable rules, and that there are individual differences among us in ultimate capacity for creative hypothesis generation. Still, it seems to me that we have to give increased time in our own thinking and teaching about methodology to the hypothesis-generating phase of research, even at the expense of reducing the time spent discussing hypothesis testing. In my own methodology courses, I make a point of stressing the importance of the hypothesis-generating phase of our work by describing and illustrating at least a dozen or so different approaches to hypothesis formation which have been used in psychological research, some of which I can briefly descirbe here, including case study, paradoxical incident, analogy, hypothetico—deductive method, functional analysis, rules of thumb, conflicting results, accounting for exceptions, and straightening out complex relationships.

For example, there is the intensive case study, such as Piaget's of his children's cognitive development or Freud's mulling over and over of the Dora or the Wolf Man cases or his own dreams or memory difficulties. Often the case is hardly an exceptional one—for example, Dora strikes me as a rather mild and uninteresting case of hysteria—so that it almost seems as if any case studied intensively might serve as a Rorschach card to provoke interesting hypotheses. Perhaps an even surer method of arriving at an interesting hypothesis is to try to account for a paradoxical incident. For example, in a study of rumors circulating in Bihar, India after a devastating earthquake, Prasad found that the rumors tended to predict further catastrophes. It seemed paradoxical that the victims of the disaster did not seek some gratification in fantasy, when reality was so harsh, by generating rumors that would be gratifying rather than further disturbing. I believe that attempting to explain this paradox played a more than trivial role in Festinger's formulation of dissonance theory and Schachter's development of a cognitive theory of emotion.

A third creative method for generating hypotheses is the use of analogy, as in my own work on deriving hypotheses about techniques for inducing resistance to persuasion, where I formulated hypotheses by analogy with the biological process of inoculating the person in advance with a weakened form of the threatening material, an idea suggested in earlier work by Janis and Lumsdaine. A fourth creative procedure is the hypothetico—deductive method, where one puts together a number of commonsensical principles and derives from their conjunction some interesting predictions, as in the Hull and Hovland mathematico—deductive theory of rote learning, or the work by Simon and his colleagues on logical reasoning. The possibility of computer simulation has made this hypothesis-generating procedure increasingly possible and popular.

A fifth way of deriving hypotheses might be called the functional or adaptive approach, as when Hull generated the principles on which we would have to operate if we were to be able to learn from experience to repeat successful actions, and yet eventually be able to learn an alternative shorter path to a goal even though we have already mastered a longer path which does successfully lead us to that goal. A sixth approach involves analyzing the practitioner's rule of thumb. Here when one observes that practitioners or craftsmen generally follow some procedural rule of thumb, we assume that it probably works, and one tries to think of theoretical implications of its effectiveness. One does not have to be a Maoist to admit that the basic researcher can learn something by talking to a practitioner. For example, one's programmed simulation of chess playing is improved by accepting the good player's heuristic of keeping control of the center of the board. Or one's attitude change theorization can be helped by noting the politician's and advertiser's rule that when dealing with public opinion, it is better to ignore your opposition than to refute it. These examples also serve to remind us that the practitioner's rule of thumb is as suggestive by its failures as by its successes.

A seventh technique for provoking new hypotheses is trying to account for conflicting results. For example, in learning and attitude change situations, there are opposite laws of primacy and of recency, each of which sometimes seems valid; or in information integration, sometimes an additive or sometimes an averaging model seems more appropriate. The work by Anderson trying to reconcile these seeming conflicts shows how provocative a technique this can be in generating new theories. An eighth creative method is accounting for exceptions to general findings, as when Hovland tried to account for delayed action effect in opinion change. That is, while usually the persuasive effect of communications dissipates with time, Hovland found that occasionally the impact actually intensifies over time, which provoked him to formulate a variety of interesting hypotheses about delayed action effects. A ninth creative technique for hypothesis formation involves reducing observed complex relationships to simpler component relationships. For example, the somewhat untidy line that illustrates the functional relationship between visual acuity and light intensity can be reduced to a prettier set of rectilinear functions by hypothesizing separate rod and cone processes, a logarithmic transformation, a Blondel–Rey-type threshold phenomenon to account for deviations at very low intensities, etc.

But our purpose here is not to design a methodology course, so it would be inappropriate to prolong this list. Let me say once again, to summarize our first koan, that we have listened too long to the sound of one hand clapping, and the less interesting hand at that, in confining our methodology discussion almost exclusively to hypothesis testing. It is now time to clap more loudly using the other hand as well by stressing the importance of hypothesis generation as part of psychological methodology.

Koan 2: In This Nettle Chaos, We Discern This Pattern, Truth

I stress here the basic point that our cognitive systems and social systems are complex and that the currently conventional simple linear process models have outlived their heuristic usefulness as descriptions of these complex systems. In our actual cognitive and social systems, effects are the outcome of multiple causes which are often in complex interactions; moreover, it is the rule rather than the exception that the effects act back on the causal variables. Hence, students of cognitive and social processes must be encouraged to think big, or rather to think complexly, with conceptual models that involve parallel processing, nets of causally interrelated factors, feedback loops, bidirectional causation, etc.

If we and our students are to begin thinking in terms of these more complex models, then explicit encouragement is necessary since the published literature on social and cognitive processes is dominated by the simple linear models, and our students must be warned against imprinting on them. But our encouragement, while necessary, will not be sufficient to provoke our students into the more complex theorizing. We shall all shy away from the mental strain of keeping in mind so many variables, so completely interrelated. Moreover, such complex theories allow so many degrees of freedom as to threaten the dictum that in order to be scientifically interesting, a theory must be testable, that is, disprovable. These complex theories, with their free-floating parameters, seem to be adjustable to any outcome.

Hence, we have to give our students skill and confidence and be role models to encourage them to use complex formulations. To this end we have to give greater play to techniques like computer simulation, parameter estimation, multivariate time series designs, and path analysis (as discussed further in Koan 5) in our graduate training programs.

Koan 3: Observe. But Observe People Not Data

In our father's house there are many rooms. In the total structure of the intelligentsia, there is a place for the philosopher of mind and the social philosopher, as well as for the scientific psychologist. But the scientific psychologist can offer something beside and beyond these armchair thinkers in that we not only generate delusional systems, but we go further and test our delusional systems against objective data as well as for their subjective plausibility. Between the philosopher of mind and the scientific psychologist there is the difference of putting the question to nature. Even when our theory seems plausible and so ingenious that it deserves to be true, we are conditioned to follow the Cromwellian dictum (better than did the Lord Protector himself) to consider in the bowels of Christ that we may be wrong.

But I feel that in our determination to maintain this difference we have gone too far. In our holy determination to confront reality and put our theory to the test of nature, we have plunged through reality, like Alice through the mirror, into a never-never land in which we contemplate not life but data. All too often the scientific psychologist is observing not mind or behavior but summed data and computer printout. He is thus a selfincarcerated prisoner in a platonic cave, where he has placed himself with his back to the outside world, watching its shadows on the walls. There may be a time to watch shadows but not to the exclusion of the real thing.

Perhaps Piaget should be held up as a role model here, as an inspiring example of how a creative mind can be guided in theorizing by direct confrontation with empirical reality. Piaget's close observation of how the developing human mind grapples with carefully devised problems was much more conducive to his interesting theorizing than would have been either the armchair philosopher's test of subjective plausibility or the scientific entrepreneur's massive project in which assistants bring him computer printouts, inches thick.

The young student typically enters graduate study wanting to do just what we are proposing, that is, to engage in a direct confrontation with reality. All too often, it is our graduate programs which distract him with shadows. Either by falling into the hands of the humanists he is diverted into subjectivism and twice-removed scholarly studies of what other subjectivists have said; or, if he falls under the influence of scientific psychologists, he becomes preoccupied with twice-removed sanitized data in the form of computer printout. I am urging that we restructure our graduate programs somewhat to keep the novice's eye on the real rather than distracting and obscuring his view behind a wall of data.

Koan 4: To See the Future in the Present, Find the Present in the Past

One idea whose time has come in social psychology is the accumulation of social data archives. Leaders of both the social science and the political establishments have recognized that we need a quality-of-life index (based perhaps on trace data, social records, self-reports obtained through survey research, etc.). Such social archives will also include data on factors which might affect subjective happiness, and analyses will be done to tease out the complex interrelations among these important variables. The need for such archives is adequately recognized; the interest and advocacy may even have outrun the talent, energy, and funds needed to assemble them.

In this growing interest in social data archives, one essential feature has been neglected, namely, the importance of obtaining time series data on the variables. While it will be useful to have contemporaneous data on a wide variety of social, economic, and psychological variables, the full exploitation of these data becomes possible only when we have recorded them at several successive points in time. Likewise, while a nationwide survey of subjective feelings and attitudes is quite useful for its demographic breakdowns at one point in time, the value of such a social survey becomes magnified many times when we have it repeated at successive points in history. It is only when we have the time series provided by a reconstructed or preplanned longitudinal study that we can apply the powerful methodology of time series analyses which allow us to reduce the complexity of the data and identify causality.

Hence, my fourth koan emphasizes the usefulness of collecting and using social data archives but adds that we should collect data on these variables not only at a single contemporaneous point in time, but also that we should set up a time series by reconstructing measures of the variables from the recent and distant past and prospectively by repeated surveys into the future.

Koan 5: The New Methodology Where Correlation Can Indicate Causation

If we agree that the simple linear sequence model has outlived its usefulness for guiding our theorizing about cognitive and social systems, then we must also grant that the laboratory manipulational experiment should not be the standard method for testing psychological hypotheses. But most graduate programs and most of the published studies (Higbee & Wells, 1972) focus disproportionately on descriptive and inferential statistics appropriate mainly to the linear models from the recent paradigm. The methods taught and used are characterized by obsolescent procedures, such as rigorous distinction between dependent and independent variables, two-variable or few-variable designs, an assumption of continuous variables, the setting of equal numbers and equal intervals, etc.

It seems to me that we should revise the methodology curriculum of our graduate programs and our research practice so as to make us better able to cope with the dirty data of the real world, where the intervals cannot be preset equally, where the subjects cannot be assigned randomly and in the same number, and where continuous measures and normal distributions typically cannot be obtained. In previous writings in recent years, I have called attention to advances in these directions which I mention here (McGuire, 1967, 1969), and Campbell (1969) has been in the forefront in devising, assembling, and using such procedures.

Our graduate programs should call the student's attention to new sources of social data, such as archives conveniently storing information from public opinion surveys, and to nonreactive measures of the unobtrusive trace type discussed by Webb and his colleagues.

Our students should also be acquainted with the newer analytic methods that make more possible the reduction of the complex natural field to a manageable number of underlying variables whose interrelations can be determined. To this end, we and our students must have the opportunity to master new techniques for scaling qualitative data, new methods of multivariate analysis, such as those devised by Shepard and others, and the use of time series causal analyses like the cross-lag panel design. More training is also needed in computer simulation and techniques of parameter estimation.

Mastery of these techniques will not be easy. Because we older researchers have already mastered difficult techniques which have served us well, we naturally look upon this retooling task with something less than enthusiasm. We have worked hard and endured much; how much more can be asked of us? But however we answer that question regarding our obligation to master these techniques ourselves, we owe it to our students to make the newer techniques available to those who wish it, rather than requiring all students to preoccupy themselves with the old techniques which have served us so well in reaching the point from which our students must now proceed.

Koan 6: The Riches of Poverty

The industrial countries, where the great bulk of psychological research is conducted, have in the past couple of years suffered economic growing pains, which, if they have not quite reduced the amount of funds available for scientific research, at least have reduced the rate at which these funds have been growing. In the United States, at least, the last couple of years have been ones of worry about leveling scientific budgets. It is my feeling that the worry exceeds the actuality. In the United States' situation, psychology has in fact suffered very little as compared with our sister sciences. As an irrepressible optimist I am of the opinion that not only will this privileged position of psychology continue but also that the budgetary retrenchment in the other fields of science is only a temporary one and that, in the long run, the social investment in scientific research will resume a healthy, if not exuberant, rate of growth. I recognize that this optimism on my part will do little to cheer scientists whose own research programs have been hard hit by the financial cuts. To my prediction that in the long run social investment in science will grow again after this temporary recession, they might point out (like Keynes) that in the long run we shall all be dead.

I persist in my Dr. Pangloss optimism that things are going to turn out well and even engage in gallows humor by saying that what psychological research has needed is a good depression. I do feel that during the recent period of affluence when we in the United States could obtain government funds for psychological research simply by asking, we did develop some fat, some bad habits, and some distorted priorities which should now be corrected. While we could have made these corrections without enforced poverty, at least we can make a virtue of necessity by using this time of budgetary retrenchment to cut out some of the waste and distraction so that we shall emerge from this period of retrenchment stronger than we entered it.

The days of easy research money sometimes induced frenzies of expensive and exhausting activity. We hired many people to help us, often having to dip into less creative populations, and to keep them employed the easiest thing to do was to have them continue doing pretty much what we had already done, resulting in a stereotyping of research and a repetitious output. It tended to result in the collection of more data of the same type and subjecting it to the same kinds of analyses as in the past. It also motivated us to churn out one little study after another, to the neglect of the more solitary and reflective intellectual activity of integrating all the isolated findings into more meaningful big pictures.

Affluence has also produced the complex research project which has removed us from reality into the realm of data as I discussed in Koan 3. The affluent senior researcher often carried out his work through graduate assistants and research associates, who, in turn, often have the actual observations done by parapsychological technicians or hourly help, and the data they collect go to cardpunchers who feed them into computers, whose output goes back to the research associate, who might call the more meaningful outcome to the attention of the senior researcher, who is too busy meeting the payrolls to control the form of the printout or look diligently through it when it arrives. A cutback in research funds might in some cases divert these assistants into more productive and satisfying work while freeing the creative senior researcher from wasting his efforts on meeting the payroll rather than observing the phenomena.

I am urging here, then, that if the budgetary cutbacks continue instead of running ever faster on the Big Science treadmill, we make the best of the bad bargain by changing our research organization, our mode of working, and our priorities. I would suggest that rather than fighting for a bigger slice of the diminishing financial pie, we redirect our efforts somewhat. We should rediscover the gratification of personally observing the phenomena ourselves and experiencing the relief of not having to administer our research empire. Also, I think we should spend a greater portion of our time trying to interpret and integrate the empirical relationships that have been turned up by the recent deluge of studies, rather than simply adding new, undigested relationships to the existing pile.

Koan 7: The Opposite of a Great Truth Is Also True

What I have been prescribing above is not a simple, coherent list. A number of my urgings would pull the field in opposite directions. For example, Koan 1 urges that our methodology courses place more emphasis on the creative hypothesis-forming aspect of research even at the cost of less attention to the critical, hypothesis-testing aspect, but then in Koan 5 I urged that we, or at least our students, master a whole new pattern of hypothesis-testing procedures. Again, Koan 3 urges that we observe concrete phenomena rather than abstract data, but Koan 4 favors assembling social data archives that would reduce concrete historical events to abstract numbers. My prescriptions admittedly ride off in opposite directions, but let us remember that "consistency is the hobgoblin of little minds."

That my attempt to discuss ways in which our current psychological research enterprise could be improved has led me in opposite directions does not terribly disconcert me. I remember that Bohr has written, "There are trivial truths and great truths. The opposite of a trivial truth is plainly false. The opposite of a great truth is also true." The same paradox has appealed to thinkers of East and West alike since Sikh sacred writings advise that if any two passages in that scripture contradict one another, then both are true. The urging at the same time of seemingly opposed courses is not necessarily false. It should be recognized that I have been giving minidirectives which are only a few parts of the total system which our psychological research and research training should involve. Indeed, I have specified only a few components of such a total research program. Any adequate synthesis of a total program must be expected to contain theses and antitheses.

I have asserted that social psychology is currently passing through a period of more than usual uneasiness, an uneasiness which is felt even more by researchers inside the field than by outside observers. I have tried to analyze and describe the sources of this uneasiness as it is felt at various levels of depth. I have also described a few of the undercurrents which I believe will, or at any rate should, be part of the wave of the future which will eventuate in a new paradigm which will lead us to further successes, after it replaces the recent paradigm, which has served us well but shows signs of obsolescence.

A time of troubles like the present one is a worrisome period in which to work, but it is also an exciting period. It is a time of contention when everything is questioned, when it sometimes seems that "the best lack all conviction, while the worst are full of passionate intensity." It may seem that this is the day of the assassin, but remember that "it is he devours death, mocks mutability, has heart to make an end, keeps nature new." These are the times when the "rough beast, its hour come round at last, slouches toward Bethlehem to be born." Ours is a dangerous period, when the stakes have been raised, when nothing seems certain but everything seems possible.

I began this talk by describing the proud and placid social psychology of a half-dozen years back, just before the bell tolled, as suggesting Buson's beautiful sleeping butterfly. I close by drawing upon his disciple, the angry young man Shiki, for a related but dynamically different image of the new social psychology which is struggling to be born. Shiki wrote a variant on Buson's haiku as follows:

> Tsurigane-ni
> Tomarite hikaru
> Hotaru kana.

Or,

> On a temple bell
> Waiting, glittering,
> A firefly.

References

Campbell, D. T. Reforms as experiments. *American Psychologist*, 1969, **24**, 409–429.

Fried, S. B., Gumpper, D. C., and Allen, J. C. Ten years of social psychology: Is there a growing commitment to field research? *American Psychologist*, 1973, **28**, 155–156.

Higbee, K. L., and Wells, M. G. Some research trends in social psychology during the 1960s. *American Psychologist*, 1972, **27**, 963–966.

McGuire, W. J. Learning theory and social psychology. In O. Klineberg and R. Christie (eds.), *Perspectives in social Psychology*. New York: Holt, Rinehart & Winston, 1965.

McGuire, W. J. Some impending reorientations in social psychology. *Journal of Experimental Social Psychology*, 1967, **3**, 124–139.

McGuire, W. J. Theory-oriented research in natural settings: The best of both worlds for social psychology. In M. Sherif and C. Sherif (eds.), *Interdisciplinary relationships in the social sciences*. Chicago: Aldine, 1969.

Sears, D. O., and Abeles, R. P. Attitudes and opinions. *Annual Review of Psychology*, 1969, **20**, 253–288.

EXPERIMENTATION IN PSYCHOLOGY

R. HARRÉ AND P. F. SECORD

Loss of Verisimilitude due to Manipulative Restrictions

1. The experimental set-up destroys the possibility of the study of the very features that are essential to social behavior in its natural setting.

2. This can be illustrated from another field, from the revolutionary studies in perception by J. J. Gibson (1966);

    a. The traditional perception experiment required

        (i) a physically restrained person,

        (ii) that his attention be directed wholly to simple sensations, out of which, it was assumed, perceptions are built.

    b. Gibson showed that

        (i) simple sensations have little to do with how the world is actually perceived, and that

        (ii) perception is actually achieved by the apprehension of invariants in the environment through a process of active exploration.

3. Analogous restrictions appear in social psychological studies of personality judgment where the "stimulus" person is presented in terms of absurdly

---

R. HARRÉ · Oxford University, Oxford, England. P. F. SECORD · Queens College, CUNY, New York. Reprinted with permission from Harré, R., and Secord, P. *The explanation of social behavior.* Oxford: Blackwell, 1972.

limited information, such as bodily silhouette, or a few attitude statements purported to be his, and where the perceiver is severely restricted in the form of judgment he may make.

4. Common to all types of overly restrictive experiments is the conception of people as information-*processing* machines, rather than information-*seeking* and information-*generating* agents. Thus information is deliberately restricted, and *inter*action prevented. But in judging personality in life situations, as in perception of the world of things, social exploration to discover or invent bases underlying the judgments is required.

Loss of Verisimilitude due to Conceptual Naiveté

1. Empirical concepts: Psychological reactance experiments are vitiated as possible bases for generalizing to real social life by failure to appreciate the immense complexity of the concepts involved, particularly in these experiments, the concept of free action.

2. Theoretical concepts: Dissonance studies also suffer from confusion and lack of clarity on the theoretical side.

a. The central theoretical concept, "dissonance," oscillates in meaning between a feeling and a logical relation.

b. It seems that careful examination of the procedures used shows that in some cases the laboratory situation itself contains social factors of sufficient strength to produce the results of apparent "forced compliance."

Critique of the Analogy between Human Characteristics and the Variables and Parameters of Physical Science

1. Random assignment of people to treatments in effect relegates important person parameters to the category of the unknown, guaranteeing that the experimental results, even when positive, will be incomplete, and sometimes trivial or banal.

2. There are two senses of the world "variable" with different logics.

a. That used when people are manipulated to experience differing amounts of some characteristic or state, e.g., anxiety;

b. That used when each person in a class has an attribute at a different level, but different people have the attribute in differing amounts, strengths or levels, e.g., intelligence.

Note. It is in sense (a) that the concept is used in physics, and upon which the logic of the classical experimental method rests, while it is in sense (b) that a good many crucial human characteristics are variables, though there are some which are variables in sense (a).

The relative importance of b-type characteristics compared with the relative unimportance of a-type characteristics in generating readiness to social behavior guarantees that much experimental work issues only in banalities.

c. The reduction of person parameters to zero can vitiate a whole field of experiment. For example, learning studies which eliminate idiosyncratic methods of learning effectively eliminate *all* methods of learning which occur outside the learning laboratory.

The Psychological Laboratory as a Special Kind of Society

1. Consequential difficulties:
   a. Participants in experiments try to fulfill the experimenter's hypotheses, however cleverly he tries to conceal them.
   b. It has been established that experimenters subtly suggest to participants how to behave (and by calling them "subjects" delude themselves into thinking that they are not taking part in the experiment as intelligent agents).
2. Attempted solutions:
   a. Attempts to eliminate these difficulties by eliminating experimenters or replacing them by machines must fail, since people react differently to machines and to people.
   b. The stimulus conditions cannot be neatly correlated with the behavioral results, but must be extended to include the participant and the experimenter and their views of what is going on, as integral and idiosyncratic elements in each "experiment."

The Psychological Experiment as an Interaction between Strangers

1. The general form of such interaction:
   a. Names are not known.
   b. Interactions fall into two classes.
   (i) Nonverbal interactions, which may be quite elaborate.
   (ii) Verbal interactions.
2. Verbal interactions:
   a. These often take the form of rituals.
   (i) This is possible when there are clear role definitions.
   (ii) This is necessary for the protection of honor and the concealment of self.
   b. Nonritualistic interactions open up time perspectives through monitored disclosures of biographies and plans, and often take place within a game framework.
3. Interactions between strangers do not usually lead to permanent social relations. This permits

    a. deliberate falsification of biographies in self-presentation,

    b. inadvertent falsifications of biographies, which are not worth correcting.

    4. The formal character of much stranger interaction is probably the most important point for the critique of the experiment, in that in this mode of interaction selves are protected, or overexposed. It is easy to see how this can affect the results of "forced compliance" experiments, for instance.

Earlier we asserted that adopting a mechanical model of man, a Humean and externalistic view of cause, and logical positivism as a method had a profound influence on the way in which experimentation is carried out. The present chapter provides some documentation for this assertion. The most general effect of these conceptions is to introduce constraints that distort the phenomena being studied and that block out considerations that play a vital part in a naturalistic situation.

The Limitation of Information and the Inhibition of Natural Forms of Response

Experimental constraints take many forms, so many, indeed, that the concept has an open texture and can scarcely be defined. However, the following points are obvious and crucial. The amount of information provided the person may be severely restricted. The physical structure of the experiment may make certain responses impossible. The psychological structure of the experiment may inhibit certain responses and encourage others. In fact, the very capacities to behave in various ways may be created or abrogated by the laboratory situation.

The brilliant work of Gibson (1966) on perception provides an excellent illustration of how certain experimental constraints operated for almost a hundred years to blind us to the true character of perception and its relation to sensation. This has occurred in apparently objective psychophysical experiments, because the person has been restricted to the role of a passive observer. Normally his head is held in a fixed position by apparatus, and he is asked to focus upon a fixed point in the visual field. Psychophysical investigations focus upon such simple stimulus variables as intensity, area or volume, and frequency. These can be neatly varied and correlated with sensory experiences as long as the person is assigned a passive role.

This research emphasis has led psychologists to conceive of perception as a complex process of interpretation in which simple sensations provide the basic information for the perceptual process. But Gibson has shown clearly that the kinds of sensations that a person experiences in psychophysical experiments have little to do with how he perceives the world outside the laboratory. When in his experiments, Gibson placed his subjects in an active exploratory role, he found that the crucial explanation of how we perceive lies in apprehending the invariances in our environment through *active exploration*. This activity, which has always been eliminated from psychophysical experiments by rigorous controls, allows the person to respond to higher order variables in the environment that provide the true basis for the kinds of perceptual experience that occur outside the laboratory. If Gibson's view is correct, then no amount of experimentation in the framework of psychophysics would enable us to explain everyday perceptual phenomena.

According to Gibson, the useful dimensions of perception are those that specify the environment and the observer's relation to the environment. Perhaps this is clearest in his studies of the sense of touch. What he shows is the variable and chaotic nature of sensation in contrast to the clarity and simple order in the environment. For example, when pressing a rigid object with a finger there is an increase and then a decrease of sensation, actually a flow of changing intensities. But the perception is of a constant rigidity of the surface. Furthermore, a person can discriminate correctly between two protuberant surfaces, one rigid and the other yielding, when he presses them, but not when they are pressed on the passive skin.

Or, when one lifts an object, the judgment of its weight is easier than when it is allowed simply to press downward against the supported resting hand. In active lifting, a whole set of additional inputs is involved, stemming from the receptors of the joints of the fingers, wrist, and arm. Instead of presenting itself as a kaleidoscope of sensory information, this complex input from a dozen body joints is apprehended by the person as simply the weight or mass of the object. The person is responding to higher order, sequential properties of the environment as he interacts with it. He responds to the mass of the object with only the vaguest (if any) awareness of the complex set of sensations that theoretically occur.

The unhappy consequences of unconsidered psychophysical constraints for our knowledge of perception are not an isolated example. We have an analogous but largely unrecognized problem in many other areas of experimental research and even in the last place where it might be expected—social psychology! Because we social psychologists were also trained in a relatively narrow, behavioristic tradition, many of the experiments we conduct have meaning only in a kind of never-never land of behavior that is forever inapplicable to behavior outside the laboratory, except in the most limited sense. In part this is true because of the manner in which the experimenter structures the behavior of the person serving as a subject through the assumption that behavior is a complex of simple behaviors. If we abandon the basic theoretical assumptions of behaviorist psychology, this prescription of the form of experiments is no longer tenable. This is why we must pay strict attention to the meaning of laboratory experiments and their relevance to ordinary behavior. We must discover the strategy for making empirical studies and for designing experiments that permit the person to behave as he would outside the laboratory under similar conditions. For many areas of social behavior we may even need to abandon the laboratory for the actual world.

In the typical psychophysical experiment, the person plays the part of an information-processing machine. The judgmental aspect of his behavior is emphasized, and those other aspects of the perceptual process that operate in nonlaboratory situations, such as exploration, are excluded. Such defects are not limited to psychophysical experiments. At the 1967 convention of the Western Psychological Association, a study was presented on judging personality from body-type silhouettes. The human figure was presented in silhouette form ranging from very fat through athletic to very lean, and the people serving in the study were asked to arrange the figures on various personality traits such as lazy, religious, and so on. Naturally the judges were able to carry out this task with considerable agreement. The fat types were lazy; athletic types were energetic. The thin ones were the most religious. The outcome of the experiment was predicted quite successfully by the experimenter, because he, too, was able to examine how he might process the same restricted information.

In this experiment and in many others, the information provided (body silhouettes only) is so limited that there is virtually only one way that the person can process it—a way that fits the hypothesis. Such experiments tell us little that we did not know in advance of the experiment. Such trivial experiments can be made more meaningful by providing more complex information so that the person has a choice of several alternative means of processing it. The treatment of a person as an information-processing machine does not necessarily condemn our experiment as trivial. This will depend upon the degree to which the simplifying procedure falsifies the actual process. The role of silhouettes in forming ideas about another person has to be considered in relation to the real situation in a social context to answer this question.

The misuse of the information-processing model applies to many other studies in psychology. As one more illustrative case, we refer to a program of published research on the relation between liking for a person and the amount of similarity between the liker and the person he is judging (Byrne, Griffit, and Stefanik, 1967).

The dominant experimental paradigm that runs through most of this research on interpersonal attraction and similarity is as follows: the person is asked to read a set of attitude items representing the responses of a hypothetical stranger, and to make a judgment about probable liking of him and probable enjoyment of working with him, as well as a variety of other attributes. For different hypothetical stimulus persons, the proportion of attitude statements congruent with the individual's own attitudes is varied. Byrne and his colleagues find that the larger the proportion of similar attitudes depicted as belonging to the hypothetical stranger, the greater the interpersonal attraction of the individual toward him, as deduced by them from the answers to another question-naire.

In this paradigm, the judge is given extremely limited information, sup-posedly about another person, and asked to make quantitative ratings of his potential attraction to that person. He cannot act as would one person toward another outside the laboratory, for two main reasons. First, he is deprived of the rich input we normally receive concerning another person—the only information he has is a set of attitude statements and he is not, in fact, in contact with another person at all. Second, he cannot react with warmth and friendliness as he would in a face-to-face situation, but is limited to choosing a point on a quantitative scale of attraction from which, of course, no rewarding or discour-aging feedback can be expected. Moreover, the context of judgment is one in which the experimenter specifically tells the person that the purpose of the experiment is to see how accurate he can be in making such judgments.

Placed in a situation like this, most people, but by no means all, indicate greater attraction toward the more similar stranger. Using mean ratings, a roughly linear relation is found. However, some individuals do not process the information in this way. Apparently some show that there is little relation for them between similarity and attraction, and others show a reverse relation.

What is glaringly wrong here is the contrast between the laboratory situation, in which the action of the participants is confined to a series of dispassionate judgments based upon written descriptions, and the face-to-face situation where a person reacts to another person with warmth and friendliness and a feeling of spontaneous liking which may be encouraged or inhibited by the meaning the other person's responses have for him. The dissimilarity between the life situa-tion and the laboratory situation is so marked that the laboratory experiment really tells us *nothing* about the genesis of liking and friendship among real people.

Disparity between the Concepts Appropriate to Natural Situations and Those Defining the Laboratory Situation

A further aspect of the problem of generalizing from laboratory experiments to real life may be taken from the series of experiments on *psychological reactance* by Brehm (1966). "Psychological reactance" is the name given to an effect that occurs when a person or a situation imposes some restrictions upon another individual's choices. The individual experiences an increased motivation to carry out the behavior that is forbidden. Parents will immediately recognize this phenomenon. The mere banning of some activities is often sufficient to ensure that a child will engage in them.

The problem that we find with this line of research is the failure to make any careful analysis of the concept of psychological reactance, in particular as it is to be applied in naturally occurring situations. Instead, like any well-trained experimenter who has digested or absorbed in some way the themes of logical positivism, Humean causation, and a mechanistic model of man, Brehm *begins* by setting up a series of experiments. Participants are told that they are free to do certain things, and this freedom is later restrained or threatened. Increased motivation to carry out the restricted actions is tested for. Because the experiments involve explicit operations, the confirmation of the hypothesis is considered to validate the concept of psychological reactance, and the operations to clarify its meaning. But what has actually happened is that "reactance" has been studied only in the very restricted form tacitly defined by the "experiments." *That* throws virtually no light on reactance outside the laboratory, that is, bloody minded behavior as it is known to parents, or the more general psychological phenomenon which is the theme of the proverb that the other man's grass is always greener, etc.

A key problem in getting to grips with the variety of real life "reactance" situations is the specification and application of the concept of free behavior. This is done in a prescribed way in the experiment, and the concept defined by fiat, but outside the laboratory, it is not at all clear what it means for behavior to be free, for behavior to be restricted, and whether these concepts form an exclusive disjunction. Austin's analysis of the concept of voluntary action shows that the conceptual complexity in this area is very great (Austin, 1966). What kind of behavior is a person ordinarily free to engage in? Is he bound by social convention? Is he bound by his own standards? What structural constraints exist outside the laboratory? If other agents constrain his behavior in any way, which of these create reactance and which do not? Brehm's experiments, like so many others, modeled after logical positivistic tenets, do not answer any of these questions.

As we noted earlier, the popular dissonance theory experiments suffer from some of the same limitations*. Like Brehm, dissonance theorists are attempting to introduce cognitive elements into the explanation of behavior. But because of the constraints exerted by the tacit mechanistic paradigm, this move toward mentalism is handled gingerly indeed.

All of the proponents of dissonance theory try manfully to stay at the operational level. Scarcely a single study by any of the major dissonance experimenters appears in which they attempt to measure or ascertain the presence of dissonance in an experiential or phenomenological sense, that is, as something a person might *feel*! They set up situations that should create dissonance, they deduce what changes would occur if dissonance were present, and they ascertain whether these changes do in fact occur. More than 200

*See Harré, R., and Secord P. *The explanation of social behavior,* Chapter One, Oxford: Blackwell, 1972.

studies of this kind have been carried out—an enormous investment of time and energy.

But the fruits of such work are more meager than they need be, because the paradigm is mechanical and operational. In spite of the recent publication of the 900-page book *Consistency theory* (Abelson *et al.*, 1968), much of which is devoted to so-called theoretical discussion of dissonance theory, no single writer or combination of writers has given sufficient specification to the theory, even on such an elementary matter as whether dissonance is a feeling or a logical relation, so that we can move from the idea of dissonance between two cognitive elements (a logical notion) to an experimental situation or a nonlaboratory situation where we can say with any surety that dissonance (an emotion or feeling) will be aroused, and that it will have certain effects. Indeed we have no clear criteria for telling when a state of dissonance exists.

This state of affairs obtains because psychologists, by and large, still believe that the way to clarify concepts is to invent experimental operations and to do experiments. They overlook the fact that such procedures, if they are to be used at all, have still to be linked up with social situations outside the laboratory, situations that are described by the subtle and enormously refined terms and concepts of ordinary language. In the present state of dissonance theory, to do an actual experiment, one has to take a giant conceptual leap from the formal idea of two elements in a dissonant relation to some concrete situation which is employed in the experiment. There is little theory to guide us.

These theoretical problems have gradually come to light through the experimental work and subsequent analysis conducted by experimenters in this field. An outstanding example is the now classical, early experiment on dissonance theory conducted by Festinger and Carlsmith (1959). Participants in the experiment were induced to tell the next participant (actually an accomplice of the experimenter) that the dull, boring task they had just completed was interesting, exciting, fun, and enjoyable. Those engaging in this attitude-discrepant behavior for a small payment had fewer cognitions consonant with their behavior than those receiving a large reward, and thus were expected to reduce this dissonance by changing their attitude toward the task in the direction of the behavior. Thus, we have a situation where the smaller the incentive to engage in attitude-discrepant behavior, the greater the attitude change in the direction of one's behavior. Some subsequent experiments produced comparable results. Other investigators (Elms and Jarris, 1965), however, found just the opposite, obtaining an amount of attitude change directly proportional to the payments received.

This impasse led both to further experimental work and to more theoretical analysis of the meanings of these various experimental situations. For example, Carlsmith, Collins, and Helmreich (1966) point out that in the original Festinger and Carlsmith experiment, the participant was asked to make a *public* statement which conflicted with his private belief, and furthermore, that the person to whom he made this statement was unaware that this conflicted with the private belief. But in one experiment obtaining opposite results, the participant was asked to write an essay in favor of a position he did not agree with. He was assured that it would be anonymous, and that only the experimenter (who knew that it did not express a private belief) would read it. They argue that the latter task may create no dissonance—the participant is cooperating for good reasons, clear to himself and the experimenter. Role play participants engaged in a face-to-face deception; essay writers carried out an intellectual task involving no deception. An analysis by Rosenberg (1965) emphasizes the possibility that experimental situations such as the original Festinger and Carlsmith study induce anxious concern in the participant that his performance is being evaluated, and that the more he is paid, the greater his suspicion and concern, thus, the less his attitude change. Participants may assign any of a variety of meanings to these experimental situations, meanings that would presumably produce different amounts of dissonance and lead to different relations between the incentives offered and the amount of attitude change. This suggests not only that laboratory investigators must take into account the participant's interpretation of the experimental situation, but also that they must specifically work with theory that provides a place for the meanings that participants attach to experimental situations.

Variables, Parameters, and Causal Mechanisms

In the most common form of experimental design, the independent variable is established by setting up levels of treatment, with people being assigned at random to the several levels. The object is to compare the several experimental groups with respect to the dependent variable, which is some form of behavior of the people in the various groups. We are not concerned here with the problems arising in this procedure, which have been competently treated elsewhere (Campbell and Stanley, 1963). Instead, our objective is to point out certain logical and strategic limitations of this widely accepted method of doing psychological science.

In experiments conducted in the natural sciences, another class of operations other than the correlation of independent and dependent variables plays a vital part. These are operations involving parameters. These are factors that are held constant, factors that are *measured and specified*. For example, an experiment plotting the relation between the pressure and the volume of a gas might be conducted with temperature and every other possible relevant variable held constant. In this way the identity of all samples of gas is ensured, and so the inverse correlation of pressure and volume can be treated as a phenomenon produced by the same causal mechanism, in every case. While this sometimes has an analogue in psychological experiments, in the latter there are certain important parameters which remain unknown. These are the parameters associated with the characteristics of a person. People are assigned at random to the various treatments. In this way it is thought that these unknown parameters are of no consequence, because they will have random effects on the dependent variable, from one treatment to another, random effects whose limits are known through the application of statistical theory. In this way, it is assumed, the same explanation of the behavior can be assumed.

But there are circumstances under which this method of eliminating individual differences creates a serious problem, limiting the conclusions which might be drawn from an experiment. Most experiments produce only relatively small mean differences from one treatment level to another. Thus, while the general mean differences in the dependent variable relate in a systematic way to the treatments, only a minor proportion of the persons in each treatment group are clearly different on the dependent variable from those in another treatment group. The crucial limitation inherent in this state of affairs is that, since the person parameters are not identified, measured, or specified, those people in the treatment groups responsible for the positive outcome of the findings cannot be identified, other than nominally. This means that the experimental results yield a conclusion which is of value only in an actuarial sense, not a causal one. Having done an experiment on, say, the efficacy of two different drugs, and having obtained positive results, one might then say that one drug will work better than another in the sense that if it is given to a large number of patients, more will be helped than would be in the case for the other drug. But the experiment yields no information enabling the prediction of which persons will be helped by the drug, and who will not, and what the mechanism of action of the drug within the biochemistry of a person will be. That is, statistical methods do not enable one to isolate genuinely causal relations.

The basic problem here is one of interaction between the levels of treatment and the unknown person parameters. Since the design makes no provision for assessing this interaction, the relation between the independent variable and dependent variable must be thought of as correlational rather than causal. For a causal statement to be made, we need to have some knowledge of the manner in which the experimental treatment leads the person to produce the behavior observed. One of the minimal requirements for this knowledge is specification of the interaction between the independent variable and the relevant person parameters, i.e., we must have *some* idea of the causal mechanism at work, or, in the case of the social behavior of people, of the meanings they perceive, of the plans they conceive, and of the reasons they have for their actions.

It might be argued that the carrying out of numerous experiments using different independent variables in relation to the same dependent variable would gradually yield results that could be added up to give us a comprehensive view of the causal factors producing a particular effect. But if all of the experiments have the structure described above, this does not follow. For each experiment contains unknown person parameters which are apt to interact with the independent variable to produce different effects. Since these parameters are unknown, we continue to have only correlational and not causal information. Moreover, the assumption that the various independent variables would themselves be additive is gratuitous: the possibility of interaction among them must be assumed.

Another attempt to rebut this logic might lie in the argument that the independent variable of one experiment is the parameter of the next experiment. Now, this might certainly be true in some cases. But here we must recognize a fundamental difference between two uses of the term *variable*. The first and proper use of independent variable is found where persons can be manipulated so as to display varying amounts of an attribute, as where they are made to feel more confident or less confident through exposing them to a series of success or failure experiences. The other use of the term variable cannot appropriately be regarded as an independent variable; this pertains to those attributes which the individual possesses in some relatively fixed amount, such as intelligence, but which differ from person to person. It is these variables that constitute person parameters, and they are not dealt with in experiments.

One consequence of doing experimental work in which the person parameters are allowed to remain unknown would seem to be that the generalizations that are produced are apt to be banal—certainly of little use for understanding the behavior of individuals. Those experiments that are replicable are the ones that will get published and that will receive the most attention. But the model guarantees that these findings will be banal or trivial, because the conditions have to be extremely general to hold across the idiosyncracy of persons. We end up not being able to say anything much about the conditions of social behavior or about the behavior of particular people in particular sets of conditions because most specific social behavior depends on idiosyncratic features of people, such as their aims, beliefs, and current emotional states. It is true that human beings have a certain degree of commonality in their physiological makeup, and even certain commonalities in their social experience. But only a small number of very specialized kinds of experiments can capitalize on this to yield useful generalizations. And when social behavior is the object of study, the widely varying life experiences to which individuals have been exposed is simply too great to ignore. The theoretical solution to this problem would seem to be to develop a typology of individuals, so that experiments can admit individual variance as a part of the design.

This notion of person parameters allows us to obtain a somewhat clearer view of the effects of experimental constraints, discussed in the first part of this chapter. The effect of many types of experimental constraints is to *reduce the person parameters toward zero*. We previously illustrated this in connection with psychophysical experiments. Another example comes from the learning of nonsense syllables. Speaking of learning nonsense syllables through the use of associations, Woodworth and Schlosberg (1954) make the following statement:

> Such aids in memorizing are naturally regarded with much favour by O, but E would like to be rid of them. They make the learning task less uniform and introduce variability and unreliability into the quantitative results. Besides, E wants to study the formation of new associations, not O's clever utilization of old ones. (p. 708)

Miller, Galanter, and Pribram (1960) point out that by arranging the experiment so as to eliminate these individual differences, the experimenter is changing the very character of the phenomenon he wishes to study—forcing it into a form that he finds more convenient, and thereby discovering nothing of how persons left to their own devices would learn a list of nonsense syllables. The apparent desirability of controlling person parameters is only an illusion; the most usual consequence is that the experimental relation studied has no counterpart outside the laboratory. In the social world, the phenomena studied in the laboratory interact with numerous parameters, so that functional relationships are radically altered.

The Experiment as a Social Event

There is a subset of person parameters which deserves special comment because it has no counterpart in natural science. This set pertains to the participant's notions of what the experiment is about, and what his relation is to the experimenter. An interaction between any two people is guided by certain rules or expectations, and the laboratory situation is no exception to this principle. In any particular experiment, we have a radical alteration of the social structure and the rules of action that would prevail outside of the laboratory, and we have the invocation of some kind of social structure that characterizes the laboratory.

Surely the actions of participants in experiments are in part a function of this laboratory structure. To the extent that this is radically different from the social structure outside the laboratory in which similar behavioral phenomena occur, we are unlikely to discover anything that can be transferred to life situations. And surely we need to know how participants in an experiment construct and construe the social world of the laboratory, if we are to understand their behavior and if we are to tie it up with the world outside the laboratory.

Some of the recent work on the social psychology of the experiment by Orne and Gustafson (1965) and Rosenthal *et al.* (1966) is relevant here. Orne, for example, has shown that many experiments have what he calls *demand characteristics.* Acting as an agent, the participant perceives through various slight clues what behavior is appropriate to the experimenter's hypothesis. And if he is motivated to cooperate, he helps the experimenter to get the right results.

Rosenthal has attempted to demonstrate what he calls *experimenter bias*, by which he means that the experimenter, unbeknown to himself, subtly suggests to the participants that they should behave in a certain way.

But Rosenthal's solution to this problem is curious, and betrays an inappropriate model of human action. His solution is to eliminate the experimenter entirely, if possible, using tape recorders, blind experimenter mechanical contraptions, and so on, to eliminate the human element from the investigative side. He fails to see that the participants, being human, are still going to construct certain meanings to provide themselves with a framework for interpreting the experiment, and that this construction of meaning is going to relate to the way in which they behave, and to the kind of personality they present.

We are reminded here of an experiment in which participants played a game with two kinds of opponents. One half of the participants were told they were playing the game with a computer, and the other half that they were playing the game with a person stationed in the next room. In both groups the moves made by the opponents were exactly the same. Yet the participants in the two groups used very different strategies and modes of play, depending on whether they thought they were playing with a person or with a computer. So a totally computerized experiment would itself provide a kind of experimenter bias that would prevent generalization to human interaction situations outside the laboratory. What leads psychologists into thinking that such an experimental situation would be desirable is clearly an unthinking assumption of the mechanistic model of man and Humean notions of causation.

A schematic model more adequate than the prevailing one might take the following form:

$$\text{If } C_1, C_2, C_3, \ldots, C_n, \text{ then } B \text{ by virtue of } P \times E$$

In this model, C stands for conditions, including both physical and social ones, B stands for the ensuing behavior, P stands for a set of person parameters, and E stands for a set of experimenter parameters. This model takes into account the nature of the person and his current state of mind and body, as well as the actions of the experimenter. Also included in the person parameters are the participant's views of the laboratory experiment. We cannot afford to continue thinking of the participant as an empty organism or a mechanical robot. We are going to have to investigate the phenomenology of people in experiments, and we cannot any longer think of the experimenter as a nonperson. We are going to have to put the person back into experimental psychology.

While the logic of the experiment calls for a schematic model of the kind sketched above, its practical application is not an easy task. Specification of person parameters and person–experimenter interactions will require considerable conceptual and empirical work. We are not suggesting, for example, that conventional measures of personality would be fruitful for this model. On the contrary, as we shall see in more detail later, the dispositional or trait concept of personality fails to take account of the situational nature of human action. It may be necessary to develop a kind of typology of people in connection with each set of phenomena subjected to study. The central problem is to discover those person parameters that interact with a given set of phenomena. Obviously many person parameters will be irrelevant to particular phenomena and can safely be ignored, but others will have a vital significance.

Finally we would draw attention to the fact that the traditional psychological experiment, considered as a social interaction, is one of the kinds of interaction between strangers, and could be studied as an episode of that kind. It might well show certain important analogies with other situations in which strangers interact socially.

Let us begin by considering the general form of interactions between strangers. Typically they do not know each other's names. An *a priori* analysis of "when strangers meet" yields the following possibilities of structure: The primary distinction will be between those interactions in which nothing is said, and those in which, to a greater or less extent, the medium of exchange is words. Nonverbal interactions may be very elaborate. One of the authors was entertained during a night-flight across the Atlantic by the interaction between a young man and a girl across the aisle. Convention decreed that while it was yet night no verbal interchange could take place, as being a good deal too intimate, yet by whistling complicated tunes and tapping with his fingers, the young man contrived to indicate his interest in music, while by studied indifference the girl was able to indicate her interest in the young man. When dawn broke they were at last released from the shackles of propriety and began to talk vehemently. We are happy to report that they left the plane together planning to share a taxi up to London.

A good many verbal interactions between strangers are constrained by highly developed rituals, as in many customer–salesman interactions, such as the rituals governing calls at service stations, purchases in a shop, paying conductors on buses, and the like. In the cases just mentioned there is a clear role definition for each participant and that determines which ritual is performed. By adhering to the role definitions other aspects of the self are protected. Even when there are no clear role definitions, interaction between strangers occurs under powerful conventions giving it a highly ritualistic character. Most, if not all cultures, have definite rituals by which this situation is handled. They have important features in common. These involve devices for the protection of honor, such as the elaborate methods embodied in Polynesian ritual for finding out a stranger's name without asking him, and they have their informal counterparts in the West. They also involve devices for the regulation of the rate and degree of self-disclosure, and a general preparedness to go through a face-work ritual if one party oversteps the mark, revealing, say, an embarrassing difference in social class. There is good reason to suppose that these devices come into operation

automatically in psychological experiments, in that these have the social character of interactions between strangers calling for the following through of the
appropriate ritual. Far from penentrating into the reality of social interactions
psychological experiments which are deliberately restricted so as to be in fact
interactions between strangers are practically guaranteed to lead to self-
protecting rituals, which ensure only graduated and tentative self-disclosure.

This reasoning is supported by a series of experiments reported by Jourard
and Kormann (1968), in which the experimenter varied the extent to which he
disclosed information about himself, and obtained quite different results for
differing amounts of disclosure.

Any further interaction between strangers involves the opening up of time
perspectives. The adjacent passengers may exchange biographies, thus opening
perspectives into the past, or they may exchange plans, opening the future.
Introducing new dimensions of interaction in this way can radically alter the
nature of the interaction. It needs very little observation to notice that competitive, game elements make their appearance very early on in the developing
situation, and biographies may be disclosed in a manner only intelligible from a
game perspective. The authors have noticed this feature of psychological experiments when informally discussing their participation in experiments with people
who have been "subjects."

A final, and indeed vital point concerns time perspectives. Interactions
between strangers do not usually lead to permanent social relations. This fact has
two important effects upon such interactions as those aboard planes. The first is
that the authenticity of exchanged biographies is a matter of little importance.
This has two different effects upon self-presentation. A biography may be
deliberately falsified so as to present a more favorable picture, with the fairly
certain knowledge that it will not be called into question, then or later. Much
more common is the falsification that occurs through some early disclosure
being misunderstood, and the subsequent effort to correct that misunderstand-
ing being too bothersome to undertake. The fact the interactants will probably
not meet again permits a degree of self-disclosure not generally risked by those
who must allow for further social interaction with the people involved. Quite
extraordinary degrees of intimacy are possible in these situations since they do
not have to be paid for later, as it were. It is worth considering that both these
features may be present in social psychological experiments. Whatever time
perspectives are opened up in the course of the experiment may lack authenticity, and there may be degrees of self-disclosure unthinkable in apparently
corresponding situations in real life.

From the point of view of the critique of the standard sort of experiment
the formal character of interactions between strangers may be the most important feature of the experiment. In formal interactions the selves of the interactants are protected from each other, so if the scientist conceals himself behind
a formal treatment of his "subjects" they too will be protected by a complemen-

tary formal response. Consider, for example, the "forced compliance" experiment, where P is asked to play a role that commits him to acting in accordance with opinions, which are not his own. If his response is to take a formal stand, it may well be that he is less committed to the attitude-discrepant behavior than he would be if he behaves in a less formal way, following the lead of a less formal complementary interactant E. In the former case the dissonance aroused would be much less. This analysis of the character of interaction between strangers is consistent with an analysis by Friedman (1967) of the behavior of people serving in experiments who are unacquainted with one another. His study suggests that the results of much experimental work produces only a psychology of interaction between strangers.

References

Abelson, R. P., *et al.* (eds.). *Theories of cognitive consistency.* Chicago: Rand McNally, 1968.

Austin, J. L. *Philosophical papers.* London: Oxford, 1966, Chap. 6.

Brehm, J. W. *A theory of psychological reactance.* New York: Academic Press, 1966.

Byrne, D., Griffit, W., and Stefaniak, D. Attraction and similarity of personality characteristics, *Journal of Personality and Social Psychology*, 5, 1967, 82–90.

Campbell, D. T., and Stanley, M. C. *Experimental and quasi-experimental designs for research.* Chicago: Rand McNally, 1963.

Carlsmith, K. M., Collins, B. E., and Helmreich, R. L. Studies in forced compliance, *Journal of Personality and Social Psychology*, 4, 1966, 1–13.

Elms, A. C., and Jarris, I. L. Counter-norm attitudes induced by consonant versus dissonant conditions of role-playing. *Journal of Experimental Research and Personality*, 1, 1965, 50–60.

Festinger, L., and Carlsmith, J. M. Cognitive consequences of forced compliance. *Journal of Abnormal Social Psychology*, 58, 1959, 203–210.

Friedman, N. *The social nature of psychological research.* New York: Basic Books, 1967.

Gibson, J. J. *The senses considered as perceptual systems.* London: Allen & Unwin, 1966.

Jourard, S. M., and Kormann, L. A. Getting to know the experimenter, *Journal of Humanistic Psychology*, 8, 1968, 155–159.

Miller, G. A., Galanter, E. A., and Pribram, K. H. *Plans and the structure of behavior.* New York: Holt-Dryden, 1960.

Orne, M. T., and Gustafson, L. A. Effects of perceived role and role success on the detection of deception. *Journal of Applied Psychology*, 49, 1965, 412–417.

Rosenberg, M. J. When dissonance fails. *Journal of Personal and Social Psychology*, 1, 1965, 28–42.

Rosenthal, R., *et al.* Data desirability, experimenter expectancy, and the results of psychological research. *Journal of Personal and Social Psychology*, 3, 1966, 20–7.

Woodworth, R. S., and Schlosberg, H. *Experimental psychology.* London: Methuen, 1954.

SECTION III

PRIORITIES AND PROBLEMS

RESOLUTION VERSUS REVOLUTION?
The Theory of Conflicts in Question

ERIKA APFELBAUM AND IAN LUBEK

Prologue: The Drinking Water in Chicago

Scientists often engage in interdisciplinary research on important problems facing society. In the 1950s, social psychologists worked on the problem of conflict; in the 1970s, other scientists tackled "environmental pollution." Although the present chapter covers only the area of conflict research, this prologue will digress briefly to examine a fictional pollution problem—the analogy, if any, to the discussion of conflicts that follow must be left for the reader to draw.

In 1968, at the time of the Democratic National Convention, it was believed by some Chicago city officials that a group of Yippies planned to sabotage the city's drinking water by adding to it quantities of LSD. The alleged plot never materialized, and people were not able to "turn on" with tap-water that week. Not since the debate on fluoridation had the media focused so much attention on the mechanics of a water supply system. Since then problems about the supply of water (and various additives thereto), although perhaps not the most common topic of conversation at cocktail parties, have increasingly concerned

ERIKA APFELBAUM · Laboratoire de Psychologie sociale, Université de Paris VII, 18 rue de la Sorbonne, Paris 5, France. IAN LUBEK · University of Guelph, Guelph, Ontario, Canada (visiting the Laboratoire de Psychologie sociale, 1975–6, under a joint grant from Canada Council and le Ministère des Affaires étrangères). Erika Apfelbaum has developed the basic arguments of this chapter in two previous papers (Apfelbaum, 1974a,b); the concept of domination–recognition conflicts is further developed in the present chapter. Ian Lubek has made substantive contributions, and aided in the reorganization, documentation, and translation of this and earlier formulations. K. Gergen has helpfully commented on the previous version (Apfelbaum, 1974b): his thoughtful contributions are hereby gratefully acknowledged.

scientists. Let us build on this base of common sense information a hypothetical pollution problem that may yet face Chicago someday.

A group of leading scientists are contacted by city officials and told that the city's drinking water is gradually becoming polluted—this is a serious social problem, so funds from government, philanthropic foundations, and corporations are granted the scientists to find a way to prevent or resolve the pollution. Several different laboratories, each borrowing theory and technology from chemistry, begin seeking the cure to the city's water pollution problem. One group says boiling the water is best; another says filtering; a third group says chemicals should be added to purify the water, etc. Each group makes great technical progress, isolates interesting variables, develops a friendly rivalry, publishes papers, and becomes a group of experts on water purification, even founding a *Journal of Pollution Resolution.*

As with all scientific groups, there are critics. Some claim that water purification is an engineering orientation to the problem, that pollution should first be approached from a broader, theoretical framework that encompasses the whole scope of pollution processes. Some claim that by borrowing so heavily from chemistry, the questions to be asked in the research programs are severely limited in range to those that can be answered in test tubes. Some claim that there is a bias from the beginning tied to the origin of the research: that the scientists were given the problem of cleaning up the water by the very same groups (the city and local industries) who have always dumped waste into the lake. In accepting the problem as defined for them, scientists are led to ignore the questions of the sources of pollution and of who might profit from concentrating only on the short-term water purification solution, instead of a long-range analysis of the etiology and functions of pollution. Questions such as these, if followed through in Ralph Nader fashion, are liable to disturb the status quo; and anyway, since they are extraneous to the problem immediately at hand, the scientists simply bypass them and continue to develop techniques of water purification.

Some citizens picket against industry, but these are labeled marginal elements of society and their claims are ignored. A great number of fish die, a few people die from eating the fish, and some fishermen lose their jobs, but meanwhile the scientists accelerate the refinement of their techniques to combat the ever-rising pollution. On the eve of the evacuation of the city of Chicago (due to toxic levels of air pollution), the water purification plants are still managing to keep the pollution index for the drinking water of the City Council and wealthy water subscribers at an "acceptable" level. As for the scientists, until the moment that they board the buses, they still maintain the myth that pollution is just a transitory event that can be resolved through science.

I. Overview

When research priorities and paradigms are discussed, the area of conflicts may serve as the perfect example of how we can now raise in social psychology a certain number of questions both about this one area of current interest and about many others. More than twenty years of research have accumulated, and in the three-year period 1971–1973, over one hundred *experimental* studies claiming to deal with conflict were listed in *Psychological Abstracts* under the headings "conflict," "bargaining," and "negotiation." In three journals of perhaps special interest to social psychology, the *Journal of Personality and Social Psychology*, the *Journal of Experimental Social Psychology*, and the *Journal of Conflict Resolution*, between 1970 and 1973 there appeared about 80 articles on these topics.

The area fits closely Moscovici's notion of the genesis of social psychology: "the initial idea that has stimulated the beginnings of our discipline was the desire to understand the conditions necessary to the functioning of society"[1] ... (Moscovici, 1970, p. 56). The apparent link between research on conflicts and real-world social issues (especially those posed by the American social milieu, where the pioneering research was done) can perhaps be traced to Lewin who

> had devoted much of his scientific work to furthering the understanding of the practical day-by-day problems of modern society. His book, *Resolving Social Conflicts* (1948) presents many of his sociopsychological analyses which deal with such important social problems as the effects of prejudice, methods of facing oppression, conflict in industry, conflict in marriage, morale in time of war, and methods of changing prejudiced groups. (Deutsch, 1968, p. 465)

As conflict research blossomed within social psychology, the preoccupations of the late 1950s superimposed upon the research a specific paradigm as well as a particular Weltanschauung quite appropriate to that particular sociotemporal context. However, during the past 20 years, changes have occurred both in society's *focus* on conflicts, and in the actual *kinds of conflicts* that occur in the real world. The Cold War has been replaced by "détente." The big power race to stockpile the largest nuclear arsenal has been replaced by competition for sales of conventional weapons (i.e., planes and missiles), and the concept of "total war" no longer grabs the headlines; instead, our attention is focused on smaller, localized conflicts, e.g., urban guerrilla, ghetto, terrorist, and liberation struggles.

It therefore seems appropriate at this time in history to evaluate the findings of this research area and to question how creative and/or meaningful it still is. Our aim is not merely to review the literature as a balance sheet of empirical findings, but to ask how well the original *paradigm* on which conflict research is based has kept abreast of the actual real-world *occurrences* of conflict. The posing of this question implies that the initial paradigm is inadequate because it is time-locked, an argument we shall advocate throughout this paper. Even if we were to accept the viewpoints of researchers such as Rapoport (1970), Deutsch

---

[1] Our translation.

(1969, p. 1076), or Schelling (1963),[2] who assume that the original paradigm provides a model general enough to deal with all levels of conflict (interpersonal, intergroup, and international), we still might question the adequacy of this assumed model to account for all presently existing forms of conflicts. Using the area of conflicts as the focus of discussion, the more general question of the sensitivity of social psychology research to the Zeitgeist is raised.

In this paper, we shall first briefly paint the scenario for the development of research on conflicts and attempt to show how the Zeitgeist of the 1950s became deeply embedded in the initial research paradigm. Consequently, 20 years later, when we survey briefly some aspects of the literature of the 1970s, it still can be seen how the initial choice of paradigm and its subsequent inadequate expansion have confined the research to a narrow, particular context. Considering the total *scope* of possible conflicts, it will be pointed out that a whole range of conflict phenomena have been *excluded* from scrutiny. The continued use of the initial format for the study of conflicts has also prevented us from dealing with the question of the changing *functions* of conflicts in our society. A broader conceptualization is needed to handle the expressions and functions of "domination–recognition conflicts." Finally, we shall argue that certain status quo values and mechanisms have maintained the theory of conflicts in an inadequate state of development: change is necessary.

II. Bargaining Conflicts: The Paradigm of the 1950s

Before attempting to focus attention on the existing findings of researchers on conflicts, let us first consider the underlying ideology, values, and beliefs that have affected the initial formulation of the model. These have as well contributed to the perpetuation of this model and to the exclusion from modern research of a whole range of phenomena. Thus, it is necessary to examine the literature not just for the research *results* (i.e., the answers to the research questions posed since the 1950s by social psychologists), but we must also become sensitive to the kinds of *questions omitted* up to now, and the kinds of questions *still to be asked,* before we can claim to provide a complete analysis of conflicts (with emphasis on its plural nature).

A. The Cold War Concept of Conflict and the Game-Theoretical Model

Although interest in conflicts predated the 1950s the earlier work was not as systematic as the coherent, growing body of literature that followed and gave shape to the area. Two interlinked elements, the socio–historical–political climate and the development of a new model in the social sciences, simultaneously influenced both the conception and the definition of conflicts at that time (and, we shall contend, their aftereffects are still prevalent today).

---

[2] In the preface of his book, Schelling notes the "enlightening similarities between . . . deterring Russians and deterring one's own children" (p. v).

The first element, that of the social milieu, was dominated by the very real problem confronting American society: the Cold War. Thus Deutsch, for example, reflects on how his early work in social psychology in the late 1940s was "shadowed by the atomic cloud," and how thereafter "I turned my social concern about the possibilities of nuclear war into a theoretically oriented investigation of cooperation and competition" (1969, p. 1076). A rereading of the editorial from the first issue of the *Journal of Conflict Resolution*[3] reinforces the estimate of the magnitude of impact that the "total war fear" and the Cold War Zeitgeist had on the theoretical approach taken toward conflicts by the social sciences. "By far the most important practical problem facing the human race today is that of international relations—more specifically, the prevention of global war" (1957, p. 1). Although this same editorial asserts that the study of conflict will enlarge knowledge in all areas (e.g., personality, home, industry), "These, however, we regard as less urgent than the problem of war" (p. 2). Similarly, Fleming (1966, pp. 136–7), Trefousse (1966, pp. xi–xxi), Rapoport (1971, Chapter 7), and Frank (1970, Chapter 8), all comment on the pervasiveness of the Cold War in everyday life from 1945 to the late 1960s. To cite one more example, Schelling (1963, Chapter 1), in a paper presented early in 1959 to a conference on "International Relations in the Mid-Twentieth Century," refers to war and international affairs as the primary reasons for studying the strategy of conflict. We will return shortly to the implications and consequences that this Cold War preoccupation has had for the conduct of research. The specter of two equally armed superpowers, each with a similar mistrust of the other's motivations and a strong desire to win, loomed as the paramount model of conflict in the 1950s.[4]

The second element to affect conflict research greatly was the adoption by social psychology of the game-theoretical model, which contributed to limit the kind of conflict with which research is presently concerned. The notion of conflict that arises from a dependence on this model fits cosily with the Cold War perspective. The appeal of game theory to social psychologists interested in conflicts was not just an historical accident. Game theory was simultaneously emerging in other areas of social science as a model for dealing with rational conflict behaviors. One can see how certain features of game theory would appear attractive to social psychology, still struggling at the time to define its autonomy: (a) its appearance as a tight, strong formalization seemed to provide the adequate paradigm and situation for an experimental laboratory approach (especially the prisoner's dilemma game); (b) its orientation toward winning (i.e., developing a rational strategy in a conflict of interests situation) complemented the prevalent preoccupation of social psychologists and society; and (c) it also carried with it, implicitly, a ready-made conception of conflict, which would

---

[3] This journal evolved out of the *Bulletin of the Research Exchange for the Prevention of War*, founded in 1952, primarily by social psychologists (Sargent and Williamson, 1966).
[4] Cf. Bronfenbrenner's mirror image hypothesis (1961).

spare social psychologists the necessity of building from scratch an independent conflict theory.

With the Cold War in mind as the prototypical conflict, and the game theory paradigm now available for researchers, the spotlight was shone on *conflicts of interests*, i.e., on the achievement of a satisfactory *division of resources* among *identical protagonists.*

A direct implication is that conflict becomes conceptualized as "a kind of contest, in which the participants are trying to win" (Schelling, 1963, p. 3). In such contests, even if there is a certain degree of competition to win at the expense of the other, nonetheless both sides must *share* a *common* definition of what is at stake. In the Cold War, both parties compete to gain spheres of influence and/or a partitioning of the world's resources; but this competition could not be possible unless they both similarly value the ultimate goal of global supremacy, and share, as well, similar perceptions of each other, what Bronfenbrenner (1961) has described as the mirror image hypothesis. Game theory, as well, implies that both partners are similarly geared toward the same goal: an immediate (and short-term oriented) beneficial outcome based on *internally consistent and stable values* and whose sole difference lies in *momentary diverging interests.* Thus, in dealing with conflicts of interests, one presumes a mutual agreement on the most important values: "There is a common interest in reaching outcomes that are not enormously destructive of values of both sides" (Schelling, 1963, p. 5). The basic shared values between the partners constitutes the crux of our notion of similarity.

Concentrating on conflicts of interests has oriented research toward exclusive concern for conflicts between fundamentally similar and homogeneous protagonists. By contending that the Cold War conception of conflict is still prevalent, we mean that current research still accepts the premise that there is always a *basic consensus among the parties about which goals and values are* meaningful, i.e., there is a fundamental conformity of outlook and agreement about the underlying basis for their rival interests. But the generality and goodness of fit of such assumptions are called into question when we consider a variety of other conflicts, such as those which oppose powerless and dominant groups, as we shall shortly argue.

By accepting the assumption of similarity between the opponents, the Cold War/Game Theory model carries with it an even deeper set of assumptions about the very nature of man. The assumptions that both partners share the same set of values, pursue the same ultimate goals, agree to the predefined rules of the game, and use the same preestablished means to achieve these goals, make them both exemplars of a "universal" man, whose prime motive is based on the gain-maximizing principle. Thus, the dominant paradigm in research on conflicts depicts a system that evaluates anyone along universalistic and unidimensional indices. When this paradigm—which implies the similarity and universality of opponents—is then inappropriately superimposed on struggles involving powerless versus dominant parties, the result is that any "differentness," or individuality (i.e., heterogeneity of ends, values, and/or goals), is denied to the separate opponents. Thus this research, to borrow terms from the study of colonial politics, adopts an imperialistic point of view and an "integration" attitude toward the powerless that assumes "the right to live given to another at the very condition that he becomes what we are . . . which means ignoring or killing him first"[5] (Jaulin, 1970, p. 11).

The adoption of game theory models has had another major consequence for the study of conflicts. Game theory provides a conception of conflict as "a phenomenon *sui generis* regardless of its origin and content" (Rapoport, 1970, p. 1). As a consequence, it deals mainly with the final stage of the confrontation for which the theory seeks solutions. This has had two main effects on both the theory of conflicts and the range of research problems which have been given priority.

First, it narrows down the definition of conflict: it limits the phenomenon to a *state*—a specific moment rather than an on-going process. Thus conflict becomes *a state of diverging interests* (represented by the payoff matrix) *for two interdependent and clearly defined opponents.* The definition is broad enough that indeed all conflicts can *at one point or another in time,* be represented by such a paradigm. This has strengthened the assumption that the game paradigm provides a general enough model to deal with conflicts, be they interpersonal, inter-group or inter-nation, irregardless of differences in situational context and/or historical development. Such a view neglects consideration of how the unique features of each conflict—and each level of conflict—can affect its *processes*, which modify in turn, not only the outcomes, but the actual choice of ends, means, and above all, the nature of the interdependence itself.

An even more implicit consequence of game theory's aim to seek rational optimal solutions to a conflict (as described by the utility matrix), is the premise that conflicts are terminated if—and as soon as—the appropriate solution is found. This, in turn, has preoccupied researchers with studies of negotiation and *bargaining*—particularly appropriate given both the concern with the Cold War and, as we shall now argue, with the *resolution* of such a conflict.

B. Orthopedy: The Cure Approach

The Zeitgeist of the 1950s, together with the success of psychologists during World War II in solving pressing real-world problems, transferred to psychologists a practical concern for the *prevention* and *resolution* of conflicts, what we shall call a "cure approach."[6] Retrospectively reporting on his theorizing and research (ca. 1950), Deutsch (1969) also indicates his concern about the relevance of a

---

[5] Our translation.

[6] See, for example, the *Journal of Social Issues* (Russell, 1961), which devotes a whole issue to "Psychology and Policy in Nuclear Age."

theory of cooperation and competition "to the prevention of a nuclear holocaust" (p. 1076). He also suggests that his "later work [which has been described under such labels as "interpersonal conflict," "bargaining," "conflict resolution"] is directly related to the question of preventing destructive conflicts" (p. 1077). Similarly, as pointed out earlier, the editors who founded the *Journal of Conflict Resolution*[7] had emphasized "the prevention of Global War" as the "most important practical problem facing the human race today" (1957, p. 1), and argued further for greater application of the new research methods in the social sciences to the real-world problems of prevention of war.

This provided impetus for social scientists to stretch existing concepts and research approaches (e.g., interpersonal perception and group dynamics) in order to provide relevant answers to the problem facing society, namely, *how to resolve a conflictual confrontation between two protagonists with diverging interests.* Thus given the already mentioned Cold War conception and the heavy reliance on game theory, the added search for a "cure" for conflict spurred on social psychologists to engage in research to provide *answers to questions* that they had neither formulated in their own (discipline's) terms nor recast in a specific social psychological formulation of conflicts.

To the problem of how to resolve (or prevent) conflicts, a variety of solutions was proposed, depending on the orientations and implicit beliefs of the researchers. Some answered in terms of social perceptions and improvement of human relations, others concentrated on the conditions for improvement of human abilities to behave cooperatively; they sought the best strategies to reach agreements and maximize profits. In any case, despite surface differences, what everyone really investigated was how best to solve a specific conflict, that originating from the Cold War conception. The debate that pitted Deutsch and Krauss (1960) against Kelley (1965) about whether communication was better for settling conflict than a proper use of threat illustrates some of the "different" solutions that were investigated. While each strategy may provide valid answers to the specific problems posed, we would argue that the Cold War Game Theory and Cure approaches have seriously restricted the range of questions askable in the first place: hence, any answers provided to these questions will apply only to a narrow range of the total possible scope of conflicts.

Another severe limitation for the cure approach is its blindness to the *causal sources* of *current* conflicts. In seeking the means to reduce and alleviate conflict, one ignores the reasons for its essential existence and how those reasons, in turn, affect its development. This lack of concern for the causes is aided and abetted by the game-theoretical model, which focuses attention on the final confrontation, as we have already seen. According to Schelling, "the study of the strategy of conflict [which falls within the theory of games] takes the view that most conflict situations are essentially bargaining situations" (1963, p. 5). Thus, the emphasis has been more on the orthopedic aspects of conflicts than

---

[7] The choice of this name is itself symptomatic.

on the etiological or semiological ones. A direct consequence is the exclusion *a priori*, from scientific investigation, of the question of the extent to which conflicts can be paths towards social change. Similarly ignored is the more general analysis of their processes, their various functions, and their very place in the dynamics of society. Both the game theory and cure approaches give priority to the study of negotiation and bargaining—they focus attention on the outcomes, not on the causal development of conflicts.

Probing more deeply within the implicit assumptions of the cure approach, one discovers a basic underlying idea that conflict is a temporary, perhaps almost accidental, phenomenon that creates a pathological state of imbalance in the society. Conflicts, then, have to disappear—or be cured—in order to restore a sane and stable society. Thus, contained within the orthopedic approach is a utopian image of a social world exempt from conflicts. Under these assumptions, the social psychology of conflicts has created and maintained the illusion that conflicts are just *incidents de parcours*—hazards of the road.

C. The Marriage of Convenience: Is the Honeymoon Over?

Sometimes science makes strange bedfellows. Research on conflicts seems to be the product of a marriage of convenience between a limiting definition of the problem and the utilization of the Cold War/Game model. The wedding takes place in the 1950's, in a fallout shelter, symbolic of the Cold War atmosphere. The groom confines himself to a study of *conflict resolution* as is done by those pioneering North American social psychologists who work to solve problems of their specific social milieu. The bride limits her conception of conflicts to that offered by game theory. This focuses mainly on the final confrontation between two *identical* (homogeneous) opponents with *limited* diverging interests—it reduces the large social phenomenon to a brief, static episode, implying that the historical and dynamic aspects are irrelevant to the conduct of conflicts and to the determination of their outcomes. This wedding has been largely responsible for producing the current generation of research on conflicts. The bride and groom have brought with them, as dowry, certain very definite and strong assumptions about the nature and the functions of conflicts. The important point is that this conception of conflict, reasonably accepted within the 1950s' Cold War Zeitgeist, has been left critically unchanged and unchallenged ever since. One principal consequence of continued maintenance of this definition has been to block the development of a larger, more encompassing theory of conflict and to exclude from scientific investigation certain other types of conflicts, their specific processes, and their functions within society. The reevaluation has now become inevitable, due to the appearance of new types of conflicts in our present-day society. But a reconsideration could have occurred earlier, since there have been many empirical realities since the 1950s that quite clearly do not fit the original definition; they should have raised questions of the original paradigm's appropriateness. To take just one example, Horowitz notes that, during 1962, President Kennedy's advisors mistakenly superimposed this concept onto the Cuban missile crisis, treating it as part of the traditional conflict between U.S. and U.S.S.R. superpowers. "It was not a simple two-person struggle, but one interpreted by Cuba—and much of the Third World—as a struggle between big powers acting arrogantly and a small power acting with principles to preserve its autonomy and sovereignty" (1970, p. 284). Thus, one can see the limitations of the 1950s' concept of conflict, which ignored the possibility of a substantively different form of conflict. In particular, the importance of the central role played by the "small power" Cuba should have been acknowledged and integrated in the analysis. Anomalies in normal science are often the trigger for a paradigm shift (cf. Kuhn, 1970).

In summary, much of the research of the past 20 years has been devoted to questions of providing solutions to particular conflicts: those conflicts which are structured (*formés*), expressed (*formulés*) and definable (*formulables*). Their goals are clearly specified and are equally accepted by the opposing parties. Each of them has a clearly defined identity and a *mutually* legitimated social role within the conflict. The prevalent view of life in the 1950s was dominated by the threat of a total war between superpowers. Their contest to divide up the resources available (for example, Europe and Southeast Asia) focused priority on problems involving the bargaining processes rather than on an examination of the conflict's total dynamics. Such an emphasis on bargaining conflicts between similar parties concealed from researcher's attention other kinds of conflicts, especially those which confront opponents who are in a relationship of domination.

D. Pseudovariables in Research on Conflicts

Some may say that it is unwarranted to affirm that research has exclusively dealt with similar partners. They will argue that the question of conflict between different parties has already been studied in the literature, e.g., by manipulating the power variable. They will note that about 20% of the studies published (1970–1973) in the three social psychological journals mentioned earlier deal with the question of how the inequality of power affects the outcomes of negotiation. However, as one manipulates the independent variables in these experiments, "power disparity" or "asymmetry of the opponent's positions," what is really being varied is purely the structural features of the predefined game situation: that is, the "power disparity" is operationalized exclusively by unequal distribution of initial resources and means (cf. Apfelbaum, 1974a, pp. 133–150). These experiments further assume that both partners fully accept the rules of the game, and the imposed characterization of power and powerlessness. But as has been elsewhere argued, this power disparity is represented within the experimental situation as if it were complete, established, and legitimate. This

> excludes the possibility (or, at least, the perceived possibility) of challenging the
> legitimacy and of moving the conflict to terrains other than those defined by the

initial situation. Within the situation itself, no alternative is explicitly available to the subjects which could allow this challenge; the only way to do so is to refuse to participate in the experiment and this precisely has been ruled out by their volunteering for the experiment. (Apfelbaum, 1974a, p. 136)

Those who do *not* show up for the experiment are not even counted, and those who do not play by the rules or "do not understand the instructions" have their data discarded from analyses. Of course, subject loss is a regular hazard of experimentation, but in this particular case it has precise implications about the type of phenomena that are ruled out of scrutiny, such as rebelliousness, riots, or aggression. The game-theoretical model ignores all who leave the situation or violate the rules. Only "universal," rule-following subjects need apply!

To take a more specific example from the literature, several studies (e.g., Hornstein, 1965; Gahagan and Tedeschi, 1969; Deutsch and Krauss, 1960) all purport to show that, under certain conditions powerless individuals are cooperative. Since the initial experimental situation excludes a whole range of behavioral options, i.e., a real choice of actions, such results may reflect not a genuine behavior but simply the realization by the powerless people of their impotency in this system, which maintains the perception that social inequality is fixed and unchangeable (cf. Apfelbaum, 1974a). Differences in power are thus only the *apparent* features under investigation. One should say more accurately that these studies deal with differences in power between "universal," rule-following subjects, with the least powerful party having absolutely no contractual power, having no say about the terrains within which the conflict is defined, nor in the definition of his own goals or values, etc. Thus, independent variables are introduced and hypotheses are tested within contexts that are selected on the basis of the properties of a *model* rather than of the *real* phenomena: the "power" manipulated as the independent variable is a pseudovariable. The basic framework and general perspective remain unchanged. We have tried to spare the step of making a coherent and more widely encompassing theoretical analysis and, as a result, we have reduced phenomena such as exploitation, struggles of underprivileged and powerless groups, to a few structural variables (or pseudo-variables) within a time-locked model, without radically gaining new insights into the reality of certain conflicts. In our urge to face relevant problems, we have, in fact, operationalized them out of existence and reduced them to dimensions that exclude any possibility of a truly relevant and enlightening approach.

E. *Tacked-On Variables*

A quick perusal of the more than 80 studies on conflicts (1970–1973)[8] demonstrates that games are still "in," something Bernard had already pointed out in 1965. At present, they have become so well integrated in the discipline

[8] See *Journal of Conflict Resolution, Journal of Experimental Social Psychology,* and *Journal of Personality and Social Psychology.* Thanks to B. Personnaz for assistance.

that they are recognized as the legitimate tool to use for conflict research. Just as with Binet's often cited remark that intelligence is that which is measured by his test, conflict has become that which is created by the experimental game. A disservice is thus done to both intelligence and conflict. The popularity of games *per se* has led to a stream of research and to an exploration of variables; some of these are pseudovariables, such as power (in that the limitation of the Cold War/Game Theory/Cure model does not permit its genuine operationalization), while others may be considered as "tacked-on" variables, in that they are not even *apparently* theoretically linked to the bargaining model and/or conflict resolution. As an example, about 40% of the above-mentioned studies employ a personality variable. The rationale for such studies is unclear unless they express another implicit assumption that the causes of conflict and competition are to be sought in the personalities of the protagonists rather than in the immediate situational context or the broader conditions of the society.

Let us look at one of these seemingly irrelevant variables—sex—which appears as an independent variable in over 25% of the studies. One wonders just what the connection might be between studies involving this variable and the initial conflict resolution preoccupation. What is the relevance altogether of studies showing differences in behavior between men and women? If men turn out to be more cooperative than women, will there be suggestions that women then be excluded from the arena of international and national decision-making spheres (they already are!)? And if the contrary is found, will it be recommended that women take over the policy making of our respective countries? It is most probable that this research was not done for policy purposes. This type of data is not generated by a theory, nor oriented toward practical problems nor ultimately intended to affect social change. What then is the purpose of this research?

This proliferation of personality variables may be a response to Rapoport's suggestion to build up a behavioral theory of conflicts from experimental data based on the game paradigm (Rapoport, 1970, p. 40). If so, such a theory would be inadequate because of the inherent narrowness of the initial approach. Another possible explanation is the familiar apparatus syndrome: many of these studies seem comparable to those from a laboratory where an expensive machine has just been installed. One is guaranteed by the machine's presence that the next few years will see a certain number of studies dealing with parametric and hardware-oriented questions, largely irrelevant to the main theoretical concerns. At best, this serves the purpose of increasing one's list of publications. If one considers the scientific journals as one market—but there are others—conflicts and experimental games still can be easily sold after 20 years. This is quite an achievement! Perhaps, one should add to the previous list of limitations on the framing of research questions, the current motivations of researchers. Given the unrelatedness to theory of certain tacked-on variables, one must question whether these experiments search for a social psychological formulation, search for social reforms, search for significant social forces and factors, or merely search for a significant F! Steiner (1974) gives "run(ning) off one more variation of the Prisoner's Dilemma" as one example of easy projects for graduate students "that could be completed in a few months and be sanctioned by a journal editor" (p. 102).

III. Domination—Recognition Conflicts

The pervasiveness of the inheritance of the Cold War/Game Theory Model-/Cure approach has excluded from scientific investigation all the struggles that do not fit the characteristic model of a structured conflict between similar parties with legitimate roles. This blind eye is presently all the more noticeable as the Cold War in its initial form—and the type of conflict associated with its image—has presently faded and, other forms of conflicts have taken over the front pages of the newspapers.[9]

These newer[10] conflicts all express (a) struggles against the hold that a limited and dominating group with society maintains on political, cultural, and social choices and decisions, and (b) the legitimate desire of left-out categories of individuals to have a say in the decisions affecting their future. The reader can readily list examples of struggles, even more recent than those of women, Blacks, Palestinians, or Basques. In any case, such conflicts can spring up in the most diverse and unexpected sectors of social life and geographical location. They, however, all have as a common feature a confrontation between two *fundamentally heterogeneous* opponents, the inequality lying in the differential access to the decision-making concerning values and rules that control our social future. Therefore, we will refer to these latter forms of conflicts, for short, as *domination* conflicts, although what will be meant is more precisely "domination—recognition" conflicts, since hand in hand with the struggle against domination goes a battle for the redefinition of a social identity, as will be argued shortly.

Compared to the definable, expressed, and structured conflicts—the bargaining conflicts—on which research has focused up to now, we might characterize these new conflicts as undefinable, unexpressed, and unstructured. They do not initially aim toward clearly determined and fixed ends, except for a general objective of undoing an established situation of oppression. Nor is the powerless opponent in such conflicts definable by a clearly fixed and recognized social role. Rather, ends and opponents crystallize during the course of conflict as a

[9] This paper will not attempt to analyze the causes of such a shift of forms. The reader is referred to the work of sociologists such as Touraine (1974, 1975) for an analysis of this phenomenon.

[10] "New" is probably not entirely appropriate, since many of these conflicts existed previously in an endemic form, but become acute and manifest different expressions according to the specific historical—sociological context.

by-product of the dynamics of the struggle itself. There is, indeed, such a fundamental disparity between bargaining conflicts and domination struggles that a complete overhaul of the "old" general model of conflicts is inevitable. We must reconsider and redefine the characteristics of the opponents, the nature of the stakes, the modes of expression of conflicts, as well as their functions within society, with concern given to both a historical and dynamic framework.

A. Invisibles

The very nature of domination conflicts opposes, on the one hand, standard, formally and socially recognized groups, which accept and act according to the norms and values of the dominant society, and, on the other hand, any of those collectivities which have been denied at the outset a socially recognized role in the history of a given society. This latter group will be called "invisibles." [11] Invisibles have thus no legal, autonomous existence and as a direct consequence, no contractual power. The dominant group has set up various means to maintain categories of people, through tradition, authority, and media control, in a position of being oppressed—thus, invisible—as has been the case, for example, with Blacks in America as well as with women all over the world. [12] The dominant group does not recognize, or chooses to ignore, the very existence of the invisibles and, when expressed, their claims to be recognized as partners who participate fully in the decision regarding the fundamental options for society. Even a formally recognized entity, such as small power Cuba, can be, as we have seen earlier, ignored and rendered invisible.

But more generally, invisibles within a social system are given a one-dimensional identity by the dominants, who label them exclusively in terms of their biological, cultural, geographical, or historical genesis—hence, age, sex, "race," ethnic groups. [13] This categorization has often rendered them invisible even unto themselves, reinforcing their loss of identity, making them unable to recognize their potency as a group. Thus, they are generally, at the outset, only potential members and adherents to a particular struggle—what sociologists refer to as

[11] This is similar to what Fields (1974), in discussing the implications of the conflict in Northern Ireland, calls a "non-entity." Another term used is "minority," which is quite precise if we have in mind its etymological meaning of "having less" rather than its usual and confusing usage "less numerous." Because of this possible confusion, we prefer the term "invisible" by which we emphasize the inequality not in terms of "having less," but in its aspect of being ignored or unseen, and hence "having no say."

[12] Women, for example, have for centuries been quietly "integrated." They have ingeniously been maintained in their proper place, i.e., "barefoot, pregnant, and in the kitchen." Such a combination, aided by the soap powders and washing machines of modern society, is bound to produce invisibility and has concealed from *women themselves* their common views and how their claims may be legitimate.

[13] Such an ascribed unidimensional categorization is maintained by the dominants through mechanisms of stereotyping, legislation (segregation, Apartheid), and media control, hindering any further reorganization of a separate identity.

"quasi-groups." It is usually only a small number of invisibles who start to express their dissent, who no longer accept the rules imposed on them—the rules of the game!—and the place society assigned to them by these rules. Many so-called wildcat strikes, not formally recognized and organized by unions, have brought people together in a common struggle and helped them to discover and define the commonality of their problems *through the conflict itself.* It is the struggle and the conflict itself, as it progresses, that shapes the social reality of the invisible group and helps to define an identity for each of its members. The very existence of this group, as well as the definition of its aims, thus *emerge* during the struggle and *through* it. This, in turn, transforms the nature of the conflict itself. The killing of four students on the Kent State campus suddenly defined for students across America their role in the conflict: as Dick Gregory commented "on that day they woke up and found themselves the new Niggers of America" (Gregory, 1971). The temporarily united students produced further confrontations with increased numbers for a short time thereafter. One implication of the continuous possibility of the emergence of new invisibles is the social scientist's inability to establish, at any given moment, an exhaustive inventory of involved parties and their conflicts.

But more important, what has to be stressed is the very close link between *identity and conflict*; identity evolves in the process of the domination conflict. For it is only by refusing the identity imposed upon him by the social system and by developing a new identity for himself that an invisible can become a vital part of his society.

B. Stakes and Ends

The development of this new identity stems from a rise of consciousness of the inequity of the dominant value system and/or a conception of social reality priorities. Domination conflicts thus involve the questioning of the values which sustain the running of a society and the power that enforces its rules. Their general aim is to regain a certain control over the rules that orient the future directions of a given society, and to act on the domination relation which binds the opponents. More specific and limited goals often spring out of the actions of invisibles and are thus partially, if not entirely, created by the dynamics of the conflict itself, as a process similar to the rise of identity, discussed earlier.

However, by all means, domination conflicts are fundamentally different from bargaining conflicts both in their aims and, as will be argued below, in their expressions. Domination conflicts cannot be dealt with from the standpoint of simple negotiations within a fixed game for at least three reasons. First, their general aim is an attempt to *change power* rather than (as in bargaining conflicts) to force the power to yield and to negotiate a compromise. Second, invisibles cannot—and do not aim to—initiate dialogue with their dominating opponents as long as the latter set the rules of dialogue in their own terms and the location on their own grounds. Third, prior to negotiation is the need to assert *for others as well as for themselves,* their very existence, the right to have a say in the development of society and in the determination of the rules of the game.

C. Expressions and Functions

In this light we have to reexamine the actions undertaken by invisibles. The repeated denial of their very existence and claims may force them into various attention-drawing devices, e.g., highjackings, kidnappings, bike demonstrations against car pollution, hunger or wildcat strikes, and the so-called terrorist actions, which, for a group excluded from channels of decision making, serve as the only means still available to them for gaining recognition and visibility. Some invisible groups adamantly refuse both to play the game by the rules and to play it in the home ballpark of the dominant value groups; they drop out (Flower children) and develop their own ways (creating communes, free schools, free breakfast programs, etc.).

In our role as citizens, we can, according to our personal system of values, condemn or applaud the incidents at the Munich Olympics or the SLA kidnapping of Patricia Hearst. But as scientists, we can neither ignore these events nor disregard their political nature. Social science must go beyond society's categorization of these acts as "illegal," attempt to understand their meaning, and place them within a more adequate theory, e.g., view them as struggles in which *invisibles attempt to be heard.* These acts are expressions of such domination conflicts, revealing the powerlessness of their initiators to intervene legitimately within the system; they represent to a certain extent accusations made against the society itself.

In bargaining conflicts, the moves have *one* major purpose: namely, reaching within a predefined structure the optimal compromise solution (without fundamentally changing the opponents themselves). Moves within domination conflicts, however, have *multiple* functions. They are offensive *attacks,* directed toward the excluding group; but, at the same time, they communicate certain *demands,* e.g., the need for recognition of their existence, as the minimal starting point. Thus, so-called illegal acts are, in addition, an *alerting signal* that manifests the very existence of the invisibles to society. Simultaneously, for their own collectivity, these acts serve as rallying points for group self-identification. These expressions of action by the invisibles have a structuring function on the whole collectivity: they contribute directly to the process by which the invisibles specify their identity as a group, determine their autonomy, and define their niche in social life. As a consequence, these acts bring into the foreground possibilities of new identities, previously concealed by mechanisms of oppression, that serve as alternatives for those ready to break free from the excluding and paralyzing categorization (mainly biological) imposed by the dominant group.

IV. Oversights in the Theory of Conflicts—Some Implications for Social Psychology

If we reevaluate the existing studies in the light of the above-mentioned phenomena, it is clear that there is no place within the current approach to conflicts for an adequate consideration of domination struggles.

First, within the prevalent model, research that can most directly be considered as dealing with domination problems, such as the studies on power differences, deals merely with inequality of resources, never with inequality of rights to express dissent.

Second, we have earlier explained how, by defining *a priori* the legitimate means to resolve conflicts, one cannot account for—and recognize—attention-getting devices or original resistance activities, such as certain forms of aggression, highjacking, riots, hunger strikes, or dropping out. No experiment can reveal such events, which moreover show the inadequacy of dealing with domination conflicts as if they were problems of negotiation.

Third, as we have already pointed out, the current model conceives of the strictly linear development of conflicts; the partners, the goals, as well as the nature of the conflict itself being defined *a priori*, remain unchanged throughout the moves of the game. This model is, therefore, unable to account for the dynamics that are central to the understanding of domination struggle, of the rise of identity of the invisibles, and how they define and change themselves and their aims as the conflict progresses. Apfelbaum (1974a) has argued elsewhere that the way experiments are designed virtually excludes the "possibility of detecting any truly *interpersonal* and bilateral consequences of unequal power structures. The fact that accomplices were used to play the role of (the powerful opponent) shows implicitly, in several of these experiments, that (his) changes in attitude are of little interest. This meets the more general implicit assumption that the more powerful individual remains stable 'because the change he has caused should have optimal value for him and there is no reason for him to change' (Schopler, 1965, p. 205)." (p. 141).

Further, this research trend is implicitly geared to serve one side of the confronting protagonists, as one of the conclusions of Tedeschi, Lindskold, Horai, and Gahagan (1969) somewhat naively reveals: "thus, if a source has power and is maximizing his own gains, he should use his power exploitatively against a weak opponent" (p. 260).

The commitment to a model and consequently to a theoretical position has been a strong determinant of what is included in the situation, what is measured, and what is made salient. What falls outside the boundaries of the model is labeled irrelevant, or passed on to another area. Thus, questions of who wishes to reach agreements, on which bases they are discussed, and whose interests they best serve, are never raised. Therefore, the powerless (invisible) individual or group in the conflict finds all his *self-defined* claims, demands and goals ignored. Ignored, as well, is the fact that to become visible he often can only resort to "illegal" means of expression. Either overtly, by ignoring these questions, or covertly, by assuming without further investigation that all men are alike, strive for identical goals, and respond to the same set of values ("universal man"), social psychology reflects a certain value system which excludes, as illegitimate, certain claims and actions that are part of real-world conflicts, even though not always recognized as such by the dominant society. In applying to a certain category of conflicts an alien framework, instead of attempting to analyze those struggles from within, in the invisibles' own terms, social psychology contributes to perpetuating this value system and simultaneously validating the exclusion and nonrecognition of other possible conflicts. Thus, any potential revolutionary aim that is, or can be, inherent in such conflicts is taken out of scrutiny: research on conflicts is made somewhat aseptic.

Unless we are willing to expand our framework of analysis, then the claim of humanistic action-oriented social psychologists that their experiments to "foster the application of psychological knowledge to the welfare of men" (Deutsch, 1959, p. 1092), will, for the moment, remain a somewhat pious wish. We do not deny the good will and honesty of this claim, but we are saying that it cannot be really fulfilled as long as we attempt to apply results found only within the specific bargaining model. The dice are *a priori* loaded: at present we can only give solutions and strategies that benefit exclusively those members of a conflict who share with us the beliefs of universal man, i.e., those which we have included in our model.

Up to now, phenomena such as riots, prisoners' revolts, and more generally, various "acts of deviance" have been pigeon-holed into separate broad research areas, for example, violence, deviance, marginality; they have, therefore, remained imbued with certain domain assumptions, largely carried over from legal traditions (and definitions). In particular, they are viewed through a Manichean framework of what is good or bad for *society*. Such a dichotomy, which opposes, on the one hand, the social order (with conflict resolution returning a balance to the ordered world) and, on the other, the disorders, is too narrow.[14] It ignores the functions that these acts can serve for the *individuals who commit them* (for example, an identity recognition function); more gen-

---

[14] "Some conflicts [which] are fruitful and some [which] are not—some conflict processes [which] lead to resolution and integration, some [which] lead to disintegration and disaster . . . We prefer peace to war and the creative conflicts that move toward resolution to uncreative conflicts which lead to mental breakdown in the individual, disintegration in the family, disruption of the organization, factionalism in the political unit, and mass destruction of life and property on the international scale" (Editorial Board, 1957, p. 2). This distinction between creative versus uncreative—see also the distinction between constructive versus destructive conflicts (Deutsch, 1973, p. 17)—carries with it the same underlying Manichean connotation.

erally, it ignores the possibility that "illegal acts" are expressions of conflicts and have underlying political significance.[15]

One of the consequences of expanding the theory of conflicts to incorporate domination conflicts is that there is no longer a need for a fundamental and meaningful dissociation between conflict and marginality. Their intertwining can be vividly demonstrated in the writing of Jackson (1970), wherein he describes how the repression of marginality leads to its politicization and its transformation into a domination conflict reformulation.

> ... the last ten years have brought an increase in the percentage of blacks [in these prisons] for crimes that can *clearly* be traced to political–economic causes. There are still some blacks here who consider themselves criminals—but not many (p. 31)... Very few men imprisoned for economic crimes or even crimes of passion against the oppressor feel that they are really guilty. Most of today's black convicts have come to understand that they are the most abused victims of an unrighteous order ... now with the living conditions deteriorating, and with the sure knowledge that we are slated for destruction, we have been transformed into an implacable army for liberation. (p. 30)

Another implication from broadening the theory of conflicts is that we abandon the notion of an ideal sane society in which conflicts are temporary imbalances to be quickly resolved or in which conflicts with destructive consequences can be transformed into constructive ones.[16]

Conflicts should thus be looked at as indicators of a certain "state of society" and as an integral part of the dynamic processes by which society acts as the agent of its own transformation.

V. Status Quo versus Change?

What are the processes within social psychology that perpetuate the traditional definition of conflict? Within any scientific discipline, there will always be certain vested interests in the way things are currently done and in the avoidance of problems that might point toward drastically differentiating the needs for basic social changes. There are also vested interests in maintaining a particular conception of conflict which allows only partial aspects of the phenomenon to be revealed. The selective attention which characterizes this area of research

---

[15] Serving as a guest news editor on Radio Luxembourg (October 4, 1975) Jean-Paul Sartre offered the following commentary on the alleged murders of policemen and guardia civila by two members of the Basque Nationalist organization, ETA, and three members of Revolutionary Anti-Fascist Patriotic Front: "[In the present situation of Spain] the murder of a Spanish policeman is not an illegal act [*une faute*], it is a political event" (our translation).

[16] This refers to what Deutsch (1973) defines as the basic question of his book: "how to prevent conflict from being destructive. The point is *not* how to eliminate or prevent conflict, but rather how to make it productive" (p. 17).

reflects not only the past preoccupation of society, mentioned at the beginning of this presentation, but also society's current values; these values have been readily adopted by social psychology without much critical attempt at analysis, which might put them into perspective. Even if not explicitly recognized, certain precise political and ideological choices are present (e.g., ignoring invisible groups, seeking to resolve conflict). These orient the research into particular directions and serve the status quo society by legitimating its values and certain of its policies and decisions.

Kelman (1970) has argued at a more general level,

> that social research, in its conception and application, may be marked by a bias in favor of the status quo . . . The researchers and the research sponsors are in a position to define what is problematic—to decide what questions are to be asked to provide the framework within which answers will be organised. (p. 85)

He further suggests that the reason why social research is more likely to favor the status quo over social change is that "status quo assumptions tend to be built into the definition of the research questions and the frame of reference within which the research is carried out" (p. 85). With specific reference to conflicts, we would further argue that certain types of conflicts have been concealed from investigation: those which are inconvenient for the maintenance of a certain status quo. The initial conception of conflict has been used as the basic criterion of a categorization and thus determines what is relevant and irrelevant for research, as well as what will be the legitimate and illegitimate features of the conflicts. This categorization fixes the facts, events, and phenomena in a certain perspective and light. It is indeed difficult to understand the logic of certain real-world phenomena (such as disturbances or riots) within this particular and limited framework. Never having included in its research the idea that a riot may have something to do with the attention-seeking activities of an invisible group, the social psychology of conflicts by default has no scientific evidence that counters the common sense, mass media view that civil disturbances are signs that people demanding changes are intent to destroy a certain way of life rather than signs of the needs for change in society.

The original categorization excludes these aspects of conflicts and shoves them into other areas. Thus, progressively, we have scattered and segmented various moments of conflicts into a variety of independent areas of research (e.g., violence, aggression, victimology, social movements, collective behavior, and coalition formation). Although they belong to the same reality, they have become autonomous areas adopting differing theoretical models, languages, and methods; this makes their links almost impossible to grasp.

The exclusion of broad aspects of conflicts is legitimized by the already existing, and scientifically recognized, separate domains of investigation. And the prophecy becomes self-fulfilling: having divided up conflicts into smaller areas, social psychology need make no attempt to integrate the differing results;

in thus freeing itself from its own contradictions, it reconfirms the correctness of the original limited choices that have been made.

Not only do we have to reconcile the various aspects of conflicts within a consistent articulated theoretical framework, but we have to reformulate the problem of conflicts so as to encompass the various points of view which emanate from our society. We can no longer afford the luxury of an elitist, limited view that neglects the true concerns and preoccupations of those invisible groups who cannot themselves carry out the reformulation of their own problems, because they have no access to the corridors of power.

Some groups presently involved in conflicts and struggles for identity recognition (such as Blacks, youth, women) have made attempts to be heard, but to be heard *in their own terms*; these have encountered a systematic deafness by scientists, whereby these researchers have reduced to their own framework, using their own tools and models, how *they* perceive invisible groups to be living and expressing their struggles. In so doing, they deny invisibles the means and the time to elaborate their own tools and approach, so that their self-perception (in their own terms) can be added to a theory.

As Cedric X (Clark) notes in the editorial of one issue of the *Journal of Social Issues* (1973):

> It is an historical fact that whatever black thinkers have articulated as relevant, appropriate, and good has been used as the basis of the defining criteria for what most established systems define as irrelevant, inappropriate and poor. It is for this reason that we have today no established fields in psychology concerned with exploitation, racism, oppression, colonialism, paternalism, capitalism, imperialism, etc. In their stead, we have such specialized areas as deviance, criminality, population, aggression, behavioral control, etc. (p. 4)

Of course, one may contend that these discourses are partisan, and indeed they are. But they are no less objective (i.e., free from values of implicit assumptions) than the original formulation of research on conflicts, some of whose domain assumptions have already been described (see pp. 74–80). Kelman argues that

> We must re-examine our assumptions about scientific objectivity and its relationship to the value preferences of the individual social scientist and of his society. We must recognize that *social research—particularly on significant social issues—cannot be value-free nor is there any reason that it should be* ... We are only deluding ourselves when we claim to be value-free. What we must do instead is to rethink the criteria for scientific objectivity in our field, recognizing the inevitable involvement of social value in the research process. [Emphasis added (1970, pp. 81–82)]

The systematic refusal to hear certain claims and points of view is characteristic of social psychology's lack of sensitivity to the Zeitgeist and furthermore may foretell the discipline's destiny. We must abandon certain initial assumptions, in particular the postulate that we evolve in a stable social system.

One of the perspectives within which conflicts should and could be placed is that of dynamic social change; at present, the persistent neglect of social change, noted by Sherif (1970), clearly exists within this particular area of research. For the neighboring discipline of sociology, Coleman (1969) points out that

> the current neglect (of social change) leads one to suspect that the whole discipline . . . has evolved toward the study of social statics and become impotent in the face of change . . . Social change, social movements, conflicts, and collective behavior are the underpriviledged areas of social research. They are not only backward at present, they are not catching up. (Cited by Sherif, 1970, p. 144.)

VI. The Function of Questioning for Social Psychology

In the process of developing the arguments in this chapter, we were led to raise questions at several different levels of analysis: while these questions were targeted specifically toward research in, and the theory of, conflicts, they might also be more generally applied to other areas of social psychology. First, we questioned the limitations of the current, static theory, i.e., we questioned the appropriateness of certain socio–historical–political implicit assumptions for *current* real-world conflicts, especially domination–recognition struggles; we also questioned whether the current perspective on the *functions* of conflicts is still up to date. Second, we have only begun to question whether social psychology plays a *repressive* role, in that by continuing to apply an initial time-locked formulation, our attention may actually be detracted from *emerging* problems. This has repercussions for both the kind of theory constructed, and perhaps even the kind of policies implemented (cf. Horowitz, 1970; Wenner, 1973). Third, we have questioned the function of the present artificial *categorization*, the demarcation of boundaries around research territories, which supports a certain status quo in the structure of science, the structure of theory, and quite possibly the structure of society. Only when these kinds of questions have been analyzed in greater detail can one begin to envision a broader, more encompassing theory of conflicts: this chapter attempts to lay a partial groundwork for such an effort.

At the same time, however, there remains with the authors one further question, untreated in this paper, a certain nagging doubt; perhaps no theory can–nor should it be able to–account for real-life conflicts.[17] A reading of Fields' (1974) research on the conflict in Northern Ireland should be sufficient to create in most readers the strong sense that any "psychologizing" formulation

---

[17] "By analyzing these larger conflicts in terms of individual dynamics and interaction theories," we are "psychologizing . . . the too common application of theories and techniques of psychology to social and practical problems . . . psychologizing makes plausible an interpretation of events and societies as the microcosm of human behaviors in a vacuous context, lacking regard for political reality and social systems" (Fields, 1974, pp. 21–22).

is woefully inadequate to explain the day-to-day realities of that long-lived struggle.

Epilogue: Dedication

This paper is dedicated to the memory of Angel Otaegui, Juan Paredes Manot, Jose Humberto Baena Alonso, Ramon Garcia Sanz, and Jose Luis Sanchez Bravo Sollas, sentenced for the alleged murder of policemen and guardia civila under an antiterrorism law (decreed) and executed September 27, 1975, by Franco's firing squads.

References

Apfelbaum, E. On conflicts and bargaining, in L. Berkowitz (ed.), *Advances in experimental social psychology*, Volume 7, pp. 103–156. New York: Academic Press, 1974a.

Apfelbaum, E. Conflicts: Resolution or revolution? In quest of the implicit and the invisible. Unpublished manuscript, presented at the Conference on Research Priorities and Paradigms in Social Psychology, Ottawa, Canada, 1974b.

Bernard, J. Some current conceptualizations in the field of conflict. *American Journal of Sociology*, 1965, **70**, 442–454.

Bronfenbrenner, U. The mirror image in Soviet–American relations: A social psychologist's report. *Journal of Social Issues*, 1961, 17(3), 45–56.

Coleman, J. S. Methods of sociology, in R. Bierstedt (ed.), *Design for sociology: Scope, objectives, and methods*. Philadelphia: American Academy of Political and Social Science, 1969. [Cited in Sherif (1970).]

Deutsch, M. Field theory in social psychology, in G. Lindzey and E. Aronson (eds.), *The handbook of social psychology*, 2nd ed., Volume 1. Reading Mass.: Addison-Wesley, 1968, pp. 412–487.

Deutsch, M. Socially relevant science: Reflections on some studies of interpersonal conflict. *American Psychologist*, 1969, **24**, 1076–1092.

Deutsch, M. *The resolution of conflict: Constructive and destructive processes*. New Haven, Conn.: Yale Univ. Press, 1973.

Deutsch, M., and Krauss, R. M. The effect of threat upon interpersonal bargaining. *Journal of Abnormal and Social Psychology*, 1960, **61**, 181–189.

Editorial Board. An editorial. *Journal of Conflict Resolution*, 1957, **1**, 1–2.

Fields, R. M. *A society on the run: A psychology of Northern Ireland*. Hammondsworth, Middlesex, England: Penguin, 1974.

Fleming, D. F. The costs and consequences of the Cold War. *The Annals of the American Academy of Political and Social Science*, 1966, **366**, 121–138.

Frank, J. D. *Sanity and survival: Psychological aspects of war and peace*. New York: Vintage, 1967.

Gahagan, J. P., and Tedeschi, J. T. Shifts of power in a mixed-motive game. *Journal of Social Psychology*, 1969, **77**, 241–252.

Gregory, D. *Dick Gregory at Kent State*. New York: Poppy Records, 1971.

Hornstein, H. A. The effects of different magnitudes of threat upon interpersonal bargaining. *Journal of Experimental Social Psychology*, 1965, **1**, 282–293.

Horowitz, I. L. Deterrence games; From academic casebook to military codebook, in P. Swingle (ed.), *The structure of conflict*, pp. 277–296. New York: Academic Press, 1970.

Jackson, G. *Soledad brother: The prison letters of George Jackson.* New York: Bantam Books, 1970.

Jaulin, R. *La Paix blanche.* Paris: Editions du Seuil, 1970.

Kelley, H. H. Experimental studies of threat in interpersonal negotiations. *Journal of Conflict Resolution*, 1965, 9, 79–105.

Kelman, H. C. The relevance of social research to social issues: Promises and pitfalls. *The Sociological Review Monograph*, 1970, **16**, 77–99.

Kuhn, T. S. *The structure of scientific revolutions,* 2nd ed., Chicago: Univ. of Chicago Press, 1970.

Moscovici, S. Preface, in D. Jodelet, J. Viet, and P. Besnard (eds.), *La psychologie sociale: Une discipline en mouvement*, pp. 9–64. Paris: Mouton, 1970.

Rapoport, A. *Conflict resolution in the light of game theory and beyond,* in P. Swingle (ed.), *The structure of conflict*, pp. 1–44. New York: Academic Press, 1970.

Rapoport, A. *The big two: Soviet–American perceptions of foreign policy.* New York: Pegasus, 1971.

Russell, R. W. (ed.), Psychology and policy in a nuclear age. *Journal of Social Issues*, 1961, **17**(3).

Sargent, S. S., and Williamson, R. C. *Social psychology,* 3rd ed., New York: Ronald Press, 1966.

Schelling, T. C. *The strategy of conflict.* New York: Oxford Univ. Press, 1963.

Sherif, M. On the relevance of social psychology. *American Psychologist*, 1970, **25**, 144–156.

Steiner, I. Whatever happened to the group in social psychology? *Journal of Experimental Social Psychology*, 1974, **10**, 94–108.

Tedeschi, J. T., Lindskold, S., Horai, J., and Gahagan, J. P. Social power and the credibility of promises. *Journal of Personality and Social Psychology*, 1969, **13**, 253–261.

Trefousse, H. L. (ed.) *The Cold War: A book of documents.* New York: Capricorn Books, 1966.

Touraine, A. *Pour la sociologie.* Paris: Editions du Seuil, 1974.

Touraine, A. Les nouveaux conflits sociaux. *Sociologie du Travail*, 1975, **17**(1), 1–17.

Wenner, J. *The Rolling Stone interview: Dan Ellsberg.* San Francisco: Straight Arrow Publishers, 1973.

X (Clark), C. Introduction: Some reflexive comments on the role of editor. *Journal of Social Issues*, 1973, **29**(1), 1–9.

CRITIQUE
On Cursing the Darkness versus Lighting a Candle

MORTON DEUTSCH

Let me state my view of the paper, "Resolution versus revolution?" directly and bluntly: despite my sympathy with some of the aims of its authors, I think it represents a failure typical of some who like to think of themselves as "radical social psychologists." The failure is in offering no new ideas, no new insights, no new programs, and in resorting to exhortation for others to go out and find the promised land. In the guise of being a radical critique, there is an invocation of the holy term "revolution" and the sacred groups of "Blacks," "Youth," and "Women" in order to sanctify pronouncements about the social psychology of conflict. Despite its appeal to current ideological virtues, I believe there is very little that is truly radical about a paper which is content to present a caricature rather than an accurate portrait of the field it is assessing and which proposes nothing specific about how social psychologists could foster, through their scientific work, the values it favors.[1]

---

[1] The paper is particularly irritating to me because of its distorted presentation of my views. Without exception, all of the references to my work on conflict attribute views to me which do not accurately represent what is stated in the work to which they refer. Sometimes the distortion represents a selective presentation out of its context, other times it reflects a straw man of their own creation. For example, on p. 78 they state that I (along with Rapoport and Schelling) assume that the original paradigm (of the Cold War) provides a model general enough to deal with all levels of conflict. There is nothing in the reference or in *any* of my writing which indicates that I believe that the Cold War provides

---

MORTON DEUTSCH · Teachers College, Columbia University, New York. Preparation of this paper has been supported by the National Science Foundation grant SOC 74-02477.

The poverty of ideas is masked by the derogation of the work that has already been done and by the setting up of "straw men" of their own creations in order to demonstrate the appropriateness of their critical analysis. The fact is, however, that lacking any clear ideas, not having made a theoretical analysis, they are not in a position to assess what is relevant or what is not relevant to getting to the "promised land." There may be little or much of value in past work but without some detailed, systematic theoretical thinking on their part, how will they really know? In their paper, Apfelbaum and Lubek are concerned with "invisible groups." How would they know, for example, whether research on "trust and suspicion" (using the PD game) is relevant to "invisible groups" unless they did some thinking about the conditions affecting group formation? I have given considerable thought to the conditions of group formation (Deutsch, 1973) and believe that I can make the case for "trust" being one of the centrally relevant factors. As a result of not doing the necessary detailed thinking and possibly, also, as a result of too much concern with being ideologically fashionable, the radical social psychologist may be blind to the insights he or she might obtain from work that it is stylish for them to denigrate.

As I turn now to a more specific response to some of the points in their paper, I do not want to be in the position of defending all of the research that has been placed under the rubric of "the social psychology of conflict." Much of the work, as is true in many areas of the social and natural sciences, is mindless. We agree that too much work has involved grinding out studies employing a modish research paradigm (such as the PD game) without any significant ideas underlying these studies. However, I take exception to many of the other points they make. Let me go down the list one by one:

(1) Their first point appears to be that social psychologists have accepted the definition of conflict that society handed to them and the problems that society has given them to study, and in so doing they are functioning more like

---

a general model of conflict. In fact, the opposite is true. Even though Rapoport, Schelling, and I have rather different approaches to the conceptualization of conflict, the one thing that we would all agree upon (now or in the past) is that the Cold War did *not* provide a general model of conflict. In their discussion of the "cure approach," they refer to my paper, "Socially relevant science: Reflections on some studies of interpersonal conflict." They manage to present it as though it had a message opposite to what was explicitly communicated by the paper. The theme of the paper was that theoretical research, which had no immediate social relevance, was likely to be of greater social utility than research which was narrowly focused on immediate social concerns. In the paper, I contrasted two early studies of mine, an applied study of interracial housing and a theoretical study of the effects of cooperation and competition upon group process. In my discussion of the theoretical study, I made the point that although my interest had started with a concern about nuclear war, of necessity, in coming to grips with the theoretical issues upon which I focused, the inquiry became transformed and was no longer directly relevant to my initial interest even as, indirectly, it became relevant to a wider spectrum of scientific as well as social concerns.

technologists than like theoretical scientists. Presumably, as a result of doing this, the social psychologist has an unduly narrow conception of the nature of conflict defining it as a "combination of Cold War and cure."

By a somewhat confused use of words, Apfelbaum and Lubek create the image of social psychologists being hired by society to work on its problem of conflict and that their approach was defined and limited by those hiring them. Of course, they know better than this and back away from this formulation, recasting it at one point in terms of "pragmatic questions posed for the most part by the American social milieu," which defined the direction for conflict research. No one will deny that the American social milieu and international events played an important part in influencing American social psychologists as they thought about conflict. One would hope that their ideas would have some connection with the realities of their experience. But Apfelbaum and Lubek seem to have the misconception that the American experience of conflict is rather limited—confined to the experience of the Cold War. I can assure them that the American experience of conflict is very rich and diverse: perhaps too rich and full to digest easily. Most Americans have an almost infinite variety of images of conflict to draw upon—the Revolutionary War, slavery, the Civil War, cowboys and Indians, ethnic conflicts, religious conflicts, racial conflicts, indus- trial strife, sports, political conflict, and all the diverse conflicts that one experiences in one's daily life as a member of a family, as a job holder, as a tenant, etc.

Yes, American social psychologists drew upon their experiences in their social milieu as raw material to stimulate their thinking about conflict. But it is a rich, diverse experience not limited or even dominated by the Cold War. And even when social psychologists such as myself joined in the debate about issues relating to the Cold War, it was largely to show that the justifications being offered for national policy were based on conflict theories that had little empirical support. Some policy makers in the United States were casting the Cold War into badly conceived images of interpersonal conflict. Some of us felt that these faulty conceptions of interpersonal conflict underlying hawkish con- ceptions of international conflict should not go unchallenged.

Apfelbaum and Lubek suggest that social psychologists acted more in the role of consultants and engineers rather than as pure scientists in relation to problems of conflict. I wish it had been so. My own role as a consultant, for example, has been largely confined to working with groups outside the establish- ment—with groups trying to improve the situation of blacks and with peace groups trying to change national policy with respect to arms and also the Vietnam War. My most sustained consulting work with problems of conflict has been as a practicing psychoanalyst dealing with intrapsychic conflict, marital conflict, and family conflict. Research-oriented social psychologists such as myself have had, at most, a very limited consulting role in relation to the important conflicts of our time. Limited as my experience has been, it is evident that their notion of what happens in such a relationship is vastly oversimplified. Rarely does the "client system's" conception of its problem remain unchanged during a consulting relationship and rarely does the consultant find that his own conceptual framework is adequate enough to deal with the details of actual, on-going conflicts. Even if we had been "consulted" by "society" in relation to its problems of conflict, it is absurd to think that there would not have been a rather thorough consideration of the way the problem had been conventionally defined.

(2) Apfelbaum and Lubek express the view that "game theory" has played an important role in the social psychology of conflict. I take it that they do not mean "mathematical game theory" (which has had very little influence)[2] but rather the game situations that have been suggested by game theorists (the PD game, the Battle of the Sexes, the game of chicken, etc.) and widely used in psychological experiments. No one could deny that the game matrices have limitations as tools for studying conflict as do all particular research settings. Nor could one deny that it would be absurd for social psychologists to limit their study of conflict to the game matrix format or to continue to give it the undue emphasis it has received. Yet, having said this, none of their specific statements about the limitations of game theory nor game formats are otherwise correct. I do not have the desire to detail all their misstatements here, but there is nothing inherent in game theory or the game format that implies the protagonists are similar, that their values are identical, that the conflict is momentary and transient, that there is always an "optimal" solution. Nor is there anything inherent in game theory or games that limits them to two-party interaction. I would have supposed that they had heard of coalition theory and the research on coalitions and multiperson games. Moreover, they appear to misunderstand completely that the maximizing gain principle is purely tautological; it is a definitional rather than empirical statement. Of course, many experiments using games conform to their description, but many do not.

If Apfelbaum and Lubek are making the rather obvious point that it is not feasible to study directly large-scale social conflict, with many participants, extending over long periods of time, in the laboratory, who could disagree? If they are making the point that games do not simulate such conflicts, I would certainly agree. Despite the misconceptions of some influential textbook writers (e.g., Jones and Gerard), "games" or laboratory experiments of any kind in social psychology are not miniaturized models or simulations of international or other naturally occurring conflicts. The only relevance that laboratory conflicts

---

[2] Let me digress about "game theory" as it influenced my work. The prestige of "game theory" was being employed by some political scientists—e.g., Herman Kahn, Albert Wohlstetter, T. Schelling—for questionable policy recommendations. My work, in fact, was directed at demonstrating the irrelevance of game theory and at showing that incorrect interpretations would be made if the assumptions underlying the applications of game theory were taken to be valid characterizations of social realities.

have to naturally occurring conflicts (or, for that matter, to other laboratory-induced conflicts)—whether such conflicts be at the interpersonal, intergroup, or international levels—is through the possibility of applying a similar conceptual analysis to the laboratory and nonlaboratory conflicts. The understanding of any specific conflict obviously requires more than knowledge of relevant concepts and propositions; it also entails knowledge of how these concepts and propositions are embodied in the specific historical, economic, and political events occurring in the given conflict. Thus, the relevance of laboratory studies of conflict to large-scale social conflicts is not because they are "models" of these conflicts but rather because they permit an investigation of concepts and propositions that bear upon the naturally occurring large-scale conflicts as well as the artificially induced conflicts of the laboratory. Clearly, we would all agree that if a laboratory study is lacking in ideas or is methodologically unsound it will have no relevance to anything.

(3) Just as Apfelbaum and Lubek have not adequately portrayed the bride (who is falsely alleged to be a relative of game theory), they caricature the groom in their imaginary marriage. In the initial version of their paper, their caricature focused on the term "conflict resolution": they interpreted this term to mean that social psychologists were primarily interested in preventing or eliminating conflict and suggested that this orientation reflected a bias toward preserving the status quo. They now suggest that the bias toward the status quo arises from a fixation on the 1950s' concept of conflict originating from the Cold War, which precludes an awareness of "domination—recognition" conflicts. The earlier version was based upon a gross misinterpretation of the way the term "conflict resolution" had been employed in social psychology; the present one is based upon a somewhat simplistic and grandiose view of social psychological approaches to conflict. The simplism inheres in the assumption that there was a single conception or approach to the Cold War among social psychologists (and among social scientists generally). Anyone who is reasonably well acquainted with the writings of social scientists related to the Cold War should be able to recognize profound differences among their conceptions of its origin, nature, effects, and "cure." Not only was there no single, overriding conception of the Cold War among social scientists, I am confident that those social scientists who had, in fact, made a conceptual analysis of the Cold War would consider the conception presented in the paper by Apfelbaum and Lubek to be a caricature merely serving polemical purposes and not an accurate portrait of any intellectual view of the Cold War which was seriously advanced.

The grandiosity lies in their implicit view of what the social psychology of conflict is or should be. They seem to assume that the experimental studies of conflict were models of the Cold War and its cure; they go on to suggest that since the Cold War is not the only important type of conflict and since it is almost over, we should now model domination—recognition conflicts in our research studies. It is grandiose to suggest that the research on the social psychology of conflict ever modeled the Cold War or that it could now model domination–recognition conflicts. As I have indicated in a preceding paragraph, laboratory experiments in social psychology (of whatever kind) are not properly conceived of as simulations or models of naturally occurring conflicts; they are tools for the investigation and the development of concepts and propositions which bear upon naturally occurring conflicts. The tools and techniques of social psychological investigation, the concepts and propositions of social psychological theory are by themselves not sufficient to characterize adequately large-scale social conflicts such as the Cold War or the domination–recognition conflicts which Apfelbaum and Lubek mention. An adequate characterization of such conflicts requires the diverse methodologies and conceptual apparatuses of the many different social science disciplines. It is grandiose to assume that social psychology, per se, can provide the theoretical analysis or "cure" to war, poverty, racism, sexism, exploitation, crime, or any social problem. We have our role to play in helping to bring about an understanding of complex social problems, but it is only a small role in a complex drama with many actors. Recognition of the inherent limits of our part would not reduce the gap between what is required to solve urgent social problems and what we can do even at our best, but it might alleviate some of the ill-humored frustration associated with unrealistic aspirations.

Although the role of social psychology is small, its part will be inadequately played unless it uses its research tools more thoughtfully. I agree with Apfelbaum and Lubek that too much research in social psychology uses pseudovariables and that insufficient theoretical work underlies many research investigations. Although I agree with their accusation, I object to their paper being so blatantly guilty of the charge they make. They make no theoretical analysis of their own nor do they attempt to give a serious critique of the theoretical ideas of others, such as myself, whose work has always been concerned with ideas that go beyond particular experimental formats—incomplete and inadequate as these ideas may be. What they have done instead is, in effect, to attack the ideas without dealing with them directly. They have done this by proclaiming, rather than demonstrating, that the ideas are guilty of association with "games," with the term "conflict resolution," and with an interest in preventing nuclear war. This is not theoretical analysis, it is criticism by innuendo. I plead guilty to the association but not to the implications which they draw from these associations.

(4) Apfelbaum and Lubek make the charge that social psychologists have concealed from investigation certain types of conflicts that are inconvenient for the maintenance of a certain status quo. The charge is utter nonsense. If they examine the *Journal of Conflict Resolution* and the *Journal of Social Issues*, as well as other social science journals directly concerned with social issues, they will find many research studies and theoretical essays dealing with the issues and problems that they mention. They seem to have the peculiar notion that the work dealing with these issues and problems should always be labeled "conflict";

otherwise, it will be difficult to grasp the links among work labeled as "conflict," "violence," "collective movements," etc. It is precisely because they refuse to see the links and seem intent upon staying at the level of superficial labels, rather than undertaking a theoretical analysis, that they think nothing of relevance has been done by social psychologists (and presumably other social scientists) in relation to the questions they have raised about "invisible" groups.

The questions they raise are clearly important ones but they are hardly new. A substantial portion of my Lewin Memorial Address in 1968 (Deutsch, 1969) was addressed to these questions and many others have raised similar ones. Some of us have even begun the attempt to answer such questions with theoretical analysis and empirical work. In so doing, it is clear that work on such topics as "level of aspiration," "trust," "group formation," "group cohesion," "communication structure," "equity," "bargaining tactics," "power," and "justice" are clearly relevant to these issues. I wonder why Apfelbaum and Lubek can see no linkages among these topics? In a paper of mine, "Awakening the sense of injustice" (Deutsch, 1974), directly dealing with questions similar to those they pose, I found much prior empirical and theoretical work by social psychologists and other social scientists of clear relevance.

None of the foregoing is meant to deny that much more thought has to be given to the questions which are posed by current conflicts; nor is it to deny that current conflicts can suggest new theoretical foci and research emphases. However, the same statements could be as appropriately made about "old" or even past conflicts. The social psychological study of conflict is relatively young; our state of knowledge is rather primitive. Although we are still mainly in the dark, some of the major dimensions and features of this area are beginning to emerge. Let us not be blind to what can be seen even as we seek to extend our vision.

I conclude by paraphrasing Adlai Stevenson[3]: it is time for those who profess to be interested in radical social change to go beyond cursing the darkness and to help light a few candles.

References

Deutsch, M. Productive and destructive conflicts. *Journal of Social Issues*, 1969, **25**, 7–41.
Deutsch, M. *The resolution of conflict: Constructive and destructive processes*. New Haven: Yale University Press, 1973.
Deutsch, M. Activating the sense of injustice, in M. Lerner and M. Ross (eds.), *The quest for justice*. Toronto: Holt, Rinehart, & Winston of Canada, 1974, pp. 19–42.

[3] In a memorial tribute to Eleanor Roosevelt, Adlai Stevenson characterized her as a person who would rather light a candle than curse the darkness.

CRITIQUE
On "Resolution versus Revolution"

PAUL G. SWINGLE

I agree with the thesis of Apfelbaum and Lubek. The question I would like to explore for a few moments, however, is why an area of research which a few years ago held out such great promise is now characterized by senility and irrelevance. The authors conclude that one of the problems associated with present conflict research in social psychology is that the study of such conflict does not take place within the context and perspective of dynamic social change. I agree again with them that this is a problem, but I feel that the principal paradigmatic issue is somewhat more fundamental.

One of the central issues as I see it is that experimental social psychology has become fixated on the linear causal paradigm. Our pursuit of precision, as it finds expression in experimental social psychological research, may encourage what Whitehead termed the fallacy of misplaced concreteness. To understand and describe social events, we abstract from such situations those features which we believe to be essential. These abstractions are then operationalized and varied in highly controlled environments. The problem, of course, is that we tend to attribute to these abstractions a reality which exceeds that which they have in legitimate social situations. Our abstracted independent variables often have demonstrable effects precisely because the experimental design precludes the demonstration of the triviality of such variables.

In its extreme form, the causal fixation gives rise to complete myopia with respect to the reciprocal and circular nature which, as one moment's reflection

PAUL G. SWINGLE · University of Ottawa, Canada.

must indicate, characterizes all social processes. Proshansky, Ittelson, and Rivlin (1970) have offered a similar argument to explain psychology's traditional indifference to the influence of architecture and the physical environment upon behavior.

The literature on social power reflects this error of misplaced concreteness. There is an untoward fixation on linear causal explanations with the attendant deemphasis of the circular and reciprocal nature of all interpersonal situations. Our theories and concepts tend to focus attention upon Source and Targets of influence attempts. The Source is considered the active agent, whereas the Target is a reactive agent. We frequently define power in terms of the change in the probability of the Target performing behavior X following the intervention of the Source. The greater the change in the Target's probable behavior in the direction advocated by the Source, the greater is the Source's power. Power, then, refers to the potential influence that a Source has over a Target, should the former care to exercise that influence. We also recognize in our theories that a Source's power varies from situation to situation and that the cost to the Source of influencing a Target also figures in the calculations of power.

It is interesting to compare theories of power which derive from the experimental social psychological tradition with those which derive from other disciplines. Psychologists generally are given to claiming that power resides in the Source by virtue of that person's ability to marshal greater resources in the eventuality of a conflict. The theories have rather a chief chicken in the barnyard motif. The focus of attention is clearly on the Source as the active agent. And usually there is a deliberate attempt to limit the Target's repertoire of response options in research situations for the purposes of experimental control.

Schattschneider (1960) offers the notion that power resides in the audience or forum of the conflict. In a fight between two men, the physical strength of the bystanders is sufficient to subdue either combatant easily. In any dispute, the winner is likely to be that person who has or wins the support of the forum. Since whoever controls the forum of debate determines the outcome, power results from the relative degree to which protagonists can control the scope or limits of the conflict. Protest that gains wide-scale publicity, for example, changes the forum of the conflict and increases the potential force which various sectors of the public can bring to bear in resolving the situation.

Chadwick (1971), on the other hand, focuses attention on the Target. Every person is being pushed and pulled by society to develop predictable adaptive and nondisruptive life styles that support the status quo. The Target's power, therefore, is defined as one minus the ratio of the distance from his desired state divided by how far away from the pull of society he wants to be, i.e., Power = 1 − (Frustration/Alienation). Or as Bert Raven so well summarized the equation: "a powerful person is one who determines where the stream of society is pulling him and then swims like hell to reach a point which is against the current."

The storm created by Reich's (1970) optimism with regard to the Consciousness III revolution again calls attention to the fact that concepts of power which ignore the Target and focus only upon Source to Target influences are likely to be quite wide of the mark. In Consciousness III, Reich describes a source of power that has been widely recognized but traditionally ignored by both power theorists as well as by many policy makers, namely, the concept that derives from repudiation of values. If Target has limited need for, or value of, resources over which Source has control, Source has limited power. To offer an extreme example: if one does not value one's life, the threat of death is inadequate as a source of influence. Reich maintains that if Targets can avoid acquiring needs and wants which government and business force upon society, then Sources are deprived of the means of influence and control.

It has become fashionable for social psychologists to denounce both experimental methodologies as well as laboratory research. The primal scream for social relevance has encouraged a scramble for new research sanctuaries—stances that provide the comfort of the Zeitgeist. Many, once recognizing that ethnology had become fashionable, went dashing into natural settings with their experimental methodologies. The essential feature of the experimental versus the omnidirectional controversy recently summarized by McGuire, however, is that complete reliance upon linear causal models can seduce us into Ptolemaic systems complete with elegant epicycles which a Copernicus with his 105 IQ (Cox, 1926) can upset.

The problem, however, is deeper yet because reliance upon linear and additive models requires that one accept the faith that building theories, stone by stone, under laboratory conditions or highly controlled field conditions, will permit social scientists to apply these models to other realities such as those mentioned by Apfelbaum and Lubek, with resultant profit in terms of insights gained. This is a linear faith of course; however, the realities may not differ in complexity—they may also be different realities.

References

Chadwick, R. W. Power, social entropy, and the concept of causation in social science. Paper presented at the Albany Symposium on Power and Influence, State University of New York at Albany, October 1971.

Cox, C. M. Early mental traits of 300 genuises, in L. M. Terman *et al.* (eds.), *Genetic studies of genius.* Stanford, Cal.: Stanford University Press, 1926, Vol. II.

McGuire, W. J. The yin and yang of progress in social psychology: Seven koan. *Journal of Personality and Social Psychology,* 1973, **26**, 446–456.

Proshansky, H. M., Ittelson, W. H., & Rivlin, L. G. The influence of the physical environment on behavior: Some basic assumptions, in H. M. Proshansky, W. H. Ittelson & L. G. Rivlin (eds.), *Environmental psychology: Man and his physical setting.* New York: Holt, Rinehart, and Winston, 1970.

Reich, C. A. *The greening of America.* New York: Random House, 1970.

Schattschneider, E. E. *The semi-sovereign people.* New York: Holt, Rinehart & Winston, 1960.

ON "EMANCIPATORY" SOCIAL PSYCHOLOGY

RAGNAR ROMMETVEIT

1. Introduction

The aim of the present paper is not to contribute toward increased social psychological knowledge, but rather to increase our uncertainty with respect to the nature of such knowledge. There seems to be among us an almost unanimous discontent with current "minitheories"; yet at the same time there appears a surprising complacency with respect to tradition-bound philosophical premises for research and theory construction. The novelty of presumedly novel paradigms is hence largely restricted to proposals for improvements and/or eclectic integration of already established theoretical models, and partial empirical corroboration of such minimodels is interpreted as evidence that we are, after all, on the right track. Why shouldn't we, then, continue our trade along the paths we have pursued so far, with sharpened methodological tools and refined theories, yet with an attitude of agnostic innocence or proud independence toward rebels who question its philosophical foundation?

I do not share this complacency, and my faith cannot even be restored by prospects of novel, eclectic, cross-cultural studies accounting for nearly one hundred percent of people's helping-another-person behaviors (see Triandis, 1976, pp. 223). Nor do I believe that hermeneutic–dialectic philosophers of science have provided us with a ready-made novel foundation for our trade. I

RAGNAR ROMMETVEIT · University of Oslo, Oslo, Norway.

would feel very pessimistic, however, if even the younger rebels among us soon join the establishment of tradition-bound researchers, because they are offered more advanced mathematics and "have experimentation in their bones." Their discontent testifies to a genuine feeling of homelessness and an unwillingness to seek safety within narrowly defined fields of academic expertise. And such a feeling of homelessness does not necessarily lead to irrationality and antiscientific attitudes. Epochs of homelessness may also—as suggested by Kuhn (1970) in his analysis of "revolutions" in the history of natural sciences, and by Buber (1962) in his account of Western philosophy—bring about sound and stringent reevaluation of axiomatic components of theories and increased depth and independence of "anthropological thought."

The unique characteristic of anthropological thought is in Buber's opinion its serious concern with Kant's basic question: What is man? Such thought is suppressed during periods of "normal," tradition-bound research and during "epochs of habitation" in philosophy. Its core question is then considered futile or even nonsensical because *some preliminary answer to it is embedded in the prevailing mode of thought and tacitly taken for granted*. Thus, man becomes a comprehensible species along with other species in Aristotle's image of a self-contained and geocentric world of "things," whereas he is made "the horizon and the dividing line of spiritual and physical nature" in the philosophy of Acquinas and Dante's *Divina comedia*. Complacency with such solutions does not last long, however, and various ramifications of the Kantian problem are pursued in novel ways by ardent and genuinely "homeless" thinkers such as Augustine, Pascal, Kierkegaard, and Wittgenstein.

The relevance of Kant's basic philosophical question to humanistic scholars and social scientists—including social psychologists—is brought to the foreground by considering each discipline's contribution toward an understanding of man as a whole. Popper (1974), referring to our increased insight into matter and the merging theoretical unity of physics and chemistry, maintains: ". . . pure knowledge (or 'fundamental research' as it is sometimes called) grows . . . almost in the opposite direction to . . . increasing specialization and differentiation. As Herbert Spencer noticed, it is largely dominated by a tendency towards increasing integration towards unified theories" (p. 262).

Our insight into man appears, in comparison, to be of an extremely fragmentary nature. Novel academic disciplines and subdisciplines such as psychology and social psychology have, indeed, been awarded scientific status only insofar as they could proclaim and legitimize their lack of concern with the Kantian question. They may thus, when considered within Buber's (1962) more inclusive perspective on human self-knowledge, even be interpreted as symptoms of evasion:

> From time immemorial man has known that he is the subject most deserving of his own study, but he has also fought shy of treating this subject as a whole, that is, in

accordance with its total character. Sometimes he takes a run at it, but the difficulty of this concern with his own being soon overpowers and exhausts him, and in silent resignation he withdraws—either to consider all things in heaven and earth save man, or to divide man into departments which can be treated singly, in a less problematic, less powerful and less binding way. (p. 688)

The ramification of what at one time constituted a global and vaguely defined topic for philosophical discourse into conceptually and methodologically encapsulated scientific subdisciplines has within psychology reached its peak in specialties such as measurement of affective word meaning, studies of nonverbal communication, and analysis of deep sentence structure. "Experts" from such subdisciplines, while proudly proclaiming their emancipation from speculative philosophy, have hardly any shared conceptual basis for dialogues across the boundaries between their specialties. Nor can any of them engage in any kind of scientifically meaningful discourse with a friend whose academic expertise pertains, for example, to literary analysis.

This is indeed a rather sad state of affairs, in particular if we keep in mind how the expert on sentence structure and his friend, the expert on poetry, prior to their academic specialization actually may have entered the same university with very similar, though only vaguely apprehended, objectives of deepening their understanding of man and human communication. *Divide et impera* seems to be an essential aspect of scientific knowledge: ignorance can hardly be defeated at all until it can be split up and attacked by research workers who come to know more and more about successively more and more restricted parts or aspects of the entire, initially only vaguely defined field. It is doubtful, however, whether genuine insight follows from such victories unless the resultant fragments of knowledge can be integrated into a coherent picture of the entire field.

A renewed concern with Kant's "anthropological question" implies serious search for a common axiomatic foundation across encapsulated fields of academic expertise. And such a concern is not only expressed by philosophers in search of a novel foundation for social scientific research, but also by the politically engaged and impatient sophomore who feels that we feed him stones instead of bread, and even by the wise layman who—totally unimpressed by our particular professional jargons—asks us *what we have found out* and *how it can be used.* Academic boundaries, as they exist today in the humanities and social sciences, are certainly *not* God-given barriers between mutually exclusive avenues for knowledge. Some of them may upon closer examination actually betray symptoms of a deplorably secular origin, such as the modern academician's needs for professional security and personal achievement within a narrowly defined field of expertise and his institution's docile acceptance and even encouragement of those needs.

2. On Positivism, Hermeneutic–Dialectic Positions, and Agnostic Innocence with Respect to Philosophies of Social Science

American and Western European social psychology are today accused of being dominated by a positivistic bias, and proponents of a hermeneutic–dialectic philosophy such as Apel (1968) argue that positivistic social science is characterized by its technical-manipulatory aim. Progress is assessed in terms of increased control of segments of behavior rather than more profound understanding. Man is made an object of inquiry on a par with matter; his subjectivity is conceived of as an obstacle to "objective knowledge" rather than a phenomenon of significant and legitimate scientific concern; basic epistemological issues such as the reflexivity inherent in man's knowledge of man are evaded or dealt with as embarassing methodological difficulties only. Thus, Feigl (1953) maintains:

> The one remarkable feature in which social-science predictions differ from those in the natural sciences is the well-known fact that once these predictions have been divulged, their very existence (i.e., their being taken congnizance of) may upset the original prediction. It seems at present problematic as to whether it is possible to devise something like a method of convergent successive approximations, in order to take account of the effect of divulged predictions and thus to obviate the notorious difficulty. (p. 418)

The unique characteristics of social scientific research are thus often described in terms of deviance from (ideal) strategies by which the experimental physicist gains knowledge and control of matter. The philosophically agnostic but methodologically conscientious social scientist feels obliged to reduce that deviance to a minimum, and his imitation of the natural scientist makes for a science of man "in the third person." His subjectivity is for artists rather than social scientists to explore, the task of "understanding himself and the environment" in such a way as to affect man's self-image and fate is assigned to "the creators" rather than to social psychologists. The denial of the possibility of a humanistic social science thus often goes together with a faith in two mutually exclusive avenues to knowledge and an admiration of artistic intuition. This is particularly transparent in Hebb's rejection of the very idea of a humanistic psychology. He maintains (1974):

> Humanistic psychology, I think, confuses two very different ways of knowing human beings and knowing how to live with self-respect. One is science, the other is literature. A science imposes limits on itself and makes its progress by attacking only those problems that it is fitted to attack by existing knowledge and methods. . . The other way of knowing about human beings is the intuitive artistic insight of the poet, novelist, historian, dramatist, and biographer. This alternative to psychology is a valid and deeply penetrating source of light on man, going directly to the heart of the matter. (p. 74)

The same faith in mutually exclusive avenues to knowledge is also expressed by outstanding humanistic scholars. Thus, Wellek (1966) maintains about literary analysis:

In reading with a sense for continuity, for contextual coherence, for wholeness, there comes a moment when we feel that we have "understood," that we have seized on the right interpretation, the real meaning. The psychologists might say that this is a mere hunch, a mere intuition. But it is the main source of knowledge in all humanistic branches of learning, from theology to jurisprudence, from philology to the history of literature. It is a process that has been called "the circle of understanding." It proceeds from attention to a detail to an anticipation of the whole and back again to an interpretation of that detail. It is a circle that is not vicious, but a fruitful circle. It has been described and defended by the great theorists of hermeneutics, by Schleiermacher and Dilthey, and recently by one of the best living practitioners of stylistics, Leo Spitzer. (p. 419)

The point of departure for some novel programs for an emancipatory and hermeneutic–dialectic social science is precisely this dichotomy between natural scientific explanation and humanistic understanding. Thus, Apel sets out to outline a general theory of science within the context of "an anthropology of knowledge." And some of his central theses may be summarized as follows (see Apel, 1968, p. 38): Natural sciences originate from subject–object relations and describe or "explain" events according to laws. "Sciences of the mind," on the other hand, stem from an interest in understanding (communication) within the intersubjective dimension of the human "community of interpretation." The latter is also presupposed in our constitution of objects, and the problem of understanding can for that reason not even in principle be reduced to a problem of objective "explanation." The two mehotds of knowledge are in fact complementary, the one (intersubjectivity and "understanding" within the human community of interpretation) being a *sine qua non* for the other. The methods of modern social science cannot, according to Apel, be reduced to either those of the explaining natural sciences or those of the understanding sciences of the mind. The aim is a synthesis: the explaining social sciences of human beings. The results of the latter, which as objects are also potentially the subjects of these sciences, can be transformed into deepened self-understanding. This appears to be the goal in psychoanalysis: The patient's symptoms are made the object of causal explanation, made intelligible to him—and overcome. Both Apel and Habermas (1968) hence refer to successful psychoanalytic therapy as a paradigm case of "dialectic mediation of explanation and understanding." A distinctive and basic difference between positivistic social science on the one hand and hermeneutic–dialectic social science on the other is thus revealed in their approaches to the issue of reflexivity: What from one perspective is encountered as a notorious difficulty is from the other conceived of as an asset and a prerequisite for emancipatory effects. Apel and Habermas are accordingly both very much concerned with the possibilities of changing human conditions and conduct by unraveling "quasi-causal" relationships. The unique characteristic of such regularities is that they resemble "laws of nature" only as *long as they remain unknown*, since taking congnizance of them may in principle be conducive to their negation as laws of nature.

Apel and Habermas are thus modern proponents of the gospel of enlightenment. Implicit in their recipe for emancipation is the assumption that man is
rational and that his domain of rational choice can be expanded by increased
self-knowledge. Aspects of his conduct that must be conceived of as embedded
in a causal texture and therefore "part of nature" as long as he remains ignorant
about them may, once that causal texture is revealed and transformed into
self-insight, become accessible to self-control. The notion of an emancipatory
social science is for that reason in accordance with Nietzsche's answer to the
Kantian question (see Buber, 1962, p. 713): Man is "the animal that is not yet
established," he "suffers from himself and the problem of what life means." This
is also a central theme in a dialectic philosophy of *becoming* with its origin in
existentialistic thought. Laing and Cooper (1971, pp. 50, 130) speak of prerequisites for human choice of fate in terms of "becoming conscious of oneself"
and "becoming a historical subject," and reality is from such an existentialistic–
dialectic position conceived of as a "coefficient of resistance to my practicee".
Such ideas are mediated primarily via works of fiction and only partially
comprehensible philosophical essays, however, works whose ethical pathos and
appeal are at variance with, or even inversely related to, their contributions
toward sober elucidation of biological and social constraints pertaining to change
of man's conduct and social conditions. The existentialists are, unlike the
positivistic social scientists, submerged in speculations concerning man's subjectivity, so much so that Lévi-Strauss (1971, p. 164) accuses them of preferring a
subject devoid of rationality to a rationality that leaves out the subject. They
are, therefore, if we endorse the proposal concerning boundaries suggested by
Hebb, "creators" or "intuitive artists" rather than social scientists. It is surprising, however, how psychologists subscribing to different philosophies tend to
converge when issues of rationality and self-control are discussed within more
narrowly and pragmatically defined contexts. Consider, for instance, Carl Rogers
and Donald Hebb, who recently have announced very different positions with
respect to humanistic psychology. Hebb (1974) maintains

> Mind . . . is the capacity for thought, and thought is the integrative activity of the
> brain—that activity in the control tower that . . . overrides reflex response and frees
> behavior from sense dominance . . . Free will is not a violation of scientific law; it
> doesn't mean indeterminism, it's not mystical. What it is, simply, is a control of
> behavior by thought process (p. 75).

And Rogers (1974) approaching closely related issues in a retrospective account
of his experiences from nondirective counseling, concludes

> the individual has within himself vast resources for self-understanding, for altering his
> self-concept, his attitudes, and his self-directed behavior—and . . . these resources can
> be tapped if only a definable climate of facilitative psychological attitudes can be
> provided (p. 116).

Both Rogers and Hebb are thus proponents of emancipatory social science in the
sense that they assume that *the domain of man's self-control and rational choice*

can be expanded. Rogers is also in agreement with the Frankfurt philosophers with respect to the role of communication and increased self-understanding. Insight in the other is to be achieved by "emphatic listening"; the dialogue between the psychotherapist and his client presupposes some commonality with respect to interpretation; psychological knowledge is in part conceived of as an explication of meaning of a kind resembling the "circle of understanding" in hermeneutic analysis of texts.

I have argued elsewhere, in a critical analysis of parts of the program advocated by Apel and Habermas, that their request for emancipatory and *only* emancipatory knowledge may possibly be rephrased in terms of a novel, anti-positivistic commandment (Rommetveit, 1972) "Thou shalt not seek knowledge about thine Brother that cannot be converted into self-insight in Him" (p. 227). Rogers may possibly even agree to such a directive, at least as a recommendation for social psychological and personality research geared toward improved counseling and individual and group therapy. Hebb, on the other hand, will probably strongly object to such constraints. He may argue that they confuse two very different ways of knowing human beings, that psychological knowledge about man's self-control is achieved by imagination and strict experimentation rather than by emphatic listening; and that such knowledge, in order to be scientific, must be formulated in terms of abstract models of brain activity rather than in concepts intelligible to his lay brother by virtue of their firm foundation in that shared and only intuitively accessible *Lebenswelt* which constitutes the basis for humanistic inquiries. Hebb's rejection (Hebb, 1974) of the idea of a humanistic psychology is based upon the conviction that "Science is the servant of humanism, not part of it" (p. 74). Apel (1968), on the other hand warns against the danger that a science of man "in the third person" may be applied as fragmentary expert knowledge in such a way that man and society are degraded into something that can be manipulated. And this is precisely what most likely will happen according to the prognosis of many futurists. Geneticists will by then be serving mankind by breeding an intellectual elite; man's personality will be reshaped by means of the technological fruits of psychopharmacological research; scientific knowledge of brain activity will have reached a stage that allows for an extension of human intelligence via symbiosis of brain and computer. In other words, man will have drastically changed his own "nature" and existential onditions via implementation of expert biological and social scientific knowledge without ever having pondered the Kantian question of what he is or wants to be. Some of our colleagues seem to adopt the position that we as social psychologists are and should be primarily observers of such large-scale social change and innovation. From this point of view, social change (rather than, e.g., novel and philosophically significant social scientific insight into human conditions) will generate philosophical change, and finding order in chaos will be a task for "creators" (artists and intellectuals) rather than for social scientists. We shall thus as professional social psychologists, if we have faith that affairs will turn out as predicted by the futurists, dedicate our improved mathematical and statistical sophistication to the preparation of "social indicators," scales for assessing "happiness" and "quality of life." We shall feel that it is by no means our duty to provide man with self-understanding of a kind that may significantly affect his future. Such a fatalistic outlook, when considered from the perspective of Apel's "anthropology of knowledge," is based upon agnostic innocence with respect to some of the central themes within his philosophy of emancipatory social science. Quantification is always based upon a qualitative foundation: "facts" about man and society can be converted to numbers only via interpretation; and options of interpretation have in turn to do with man's "understanding himself and the environment" and hence with *explicitly stated or tacitly and unreflectively endorsed assumptions of a philosophical nature.* The professional social psychologist who claims independence from philosophy and denies coresponsibility for large-scale social change is accordingly a blindfolded "creator" from the point of view of Apel's philosophy. He may justly, and with the appropriate scientific modesty, insist that *his* particular minitheory is hardly of any significance whatsoever to humanity at large, and he may conceive of practical implementations of that fragment of novel knowledge which constitutes *his* particular contribution as a minor technological affair. The combined net results of all such minor implementations of social psychological knowledge may, however, nevertheless contribute more to the states of affairs in the year 2000 than the combined efforts of all presumedly far more influential "creators."

3. On Kantian Themes in Social Psychological Research and Potential and Indirect Emancipatory Effects

The formula of "dialectic mediation of explanation and understanding" with its reference to classical psychoanalytic therapy may appear somewhat esoteric to nondirective counselors as well as to social psychologists. Neither Rogerian therapists nor applied social psychologists are very much concerned with expansion of "ego control" to domains ruled by "the id." Options with respect to interpretation of human conduct and social conditions are revealed in alternative conceptual models and coding systems, however, and eating the fruits of knowledge from some psychological tree implies adopting *schemata for categorization* characteristic of that particular theory. Conversion of such knowledge to self-understanding, moreover, implies that the informed layman comes *to size up his own social situation and action alternatives in accordance with those schemata.* Impact of social psychological knowledge upon action via revised self-understanding, including potential "emancipatory" effects, may hence possible be further illuminated by an excursion into decision theory.

Consider the following case: An individual is faced with a choice between three actions, $a_1 - a_3$. Whatever he does, he runs the risk of losing some money.

The magnitude of his loss, however, is dependent upon his choice and a future state of nature. He knows that one of two different states of nature S_1 and S_2 may occur, but he is entirely ignorant with respect to the probabilities of S_1 and S_2. Let us assume then that he is faced with the loss matrix below. If he chooses action a_1 and S_1 occurs, he will lose \$200. If a_1 is chosen and S_2 occurs, he will lose nothing at all, etc.:

	S_1	S_2
a_1	200	0
a_2	168	48
a_3	120	120
(a_4)	(0)	(300)

Let us assume, furthermore, that the individual's major aim is simply to safeguard himself against regret afterward. In other words, he wants to choose a mode of behavior "minimizing maximal regret." For that purpose, the loss matrix is transformed into a regret matrix. If he chooses a_1 and S_1 occurs, the regret will be \$80, i.e., his regret will then be that of having lost \$80 more than if he had chosen a_3, which is the optimal behavioral choice provided S_1 occurs. The regret matrix under conditions of these behavioral choices will therefore be as described below, and his aim of safeguarding himself against great regret is securely achieved by choosing action a_2. By that choice he does not risk a regret greater than \$48 at all, whereas a_1 and a_2 imply risks of regrets of \$80 and \$120, respectively:

	S_1	S_2
a_1	80	0
a_2	48	48
a_3	0	120

If now our individual has been misinformed in the sense that he believes that a fourth behavioral choice (a_4 in the loss matrix) is available, his regret matrix will be significantly changed. The amounts of postdecision regret he is now faced with will be as shown in the following regret matrix:

	S_1	S_2
a_1	200	0
a_2	168	48
a_3	120	120
a_4	0	300

Under these conditions, therefore, a_3 will be his logical choice. In other words, his choice among three possible actions has been influenced by the introduction of an additional irrelevant alternative, even though the latter is not chosen at all.

This paradigm may serve to explain the intentionally creative impact of some forms of science fiction: the socially engaged writer may affect our choice between alternative realistic action programs by visualizing some particular combination of an additional irrelevant alternative and a future state of nature he knows that we want to avoid. And formally analogous situations may arise in counseling and social psychological action research, even though the creative or conserving impact in the latter case often is camouflaged by quantification and for that reason very seldom recognized. Options with respect to interpretation and categorization of alternative courses of action are in action research revealed in *alternative models of social realities*, however. This has recently been cogently pointed out by Campbell (1974), who maintains "recording of responses and the coding of free response answers achieve quantification only as the end product of a qualitative judgmental process . . ." (p. 13). "If we are truly scientific, we must re-establish . . . qualitative grounding of the quantitative in action research" (p. 30). Let us at this stage leave problems of applied social psychology, however, and consider potentially "creative" or "emancipatory" effects inherent in dissemination of social psychological theory. What kind of an image of man and his action alternatives is conveyed to people via popularization of social psychology, and in what manner may such large-scale dissemination affect social planning, policy making, and legislation?

Apel and Habermas argue that dissemination of positivistic minitheories makes for alienation and apathy because such theories, unlike dialectic approaches, deal with reflective self-control and self-initiated change as "notorious difficulties" rather than basic human phenomena of legitimate scientific concern. Social psychological theory is today a collection of partially competing theoretical paradigms with hardly any shared axiomatic foundation. The common denominator of the positivistic part of that collection, moreover, is, according to hermeneutic–dialectic philosophers, its imitation of natural sciences and programmatic evasion of issues having to do with meaning and human subjectivity. The popularized version of such a science makes for a peculiar "self-understanding" that, in caricature, resembles an enlightened state of paralysis: the "well-informed" layman feels relieved from assuming responsibility and offering reasons for his conduct because the latter is "explained" as a necessary consequence of antecedent conditions. This is the kind of opportunistic determinism advocated by the young people in "West Side Story," and different versions of such a vulgar social scientific fatalism are exploited by "creators" of social satire. The invariant and central theme, though, appears to be the dilemma of perfect self-knowledge versus freedom of will. We may therefore cautiously conclude that social psychological theory has at least an indirectly creative impact by providing themes for creators of satire. This would hardly be the case, however, unless it were misunderstood by the satirist and his audience in terms of some absurd form of determinism. The immediate effect of dissipation of social psychological knowledge formulated in terms of "laws" and deterministic models on the layman is a feeling of being imprisoned within some causal texture rather than an experience of being offered an enriched menu of action alternatives. Russell (1953) warns against the very terminology of causation, in natural as well as in social sciences: "The reason why physics has ceased to look for causes is that, in fact, there are no such things. The law of causality, I believe, like much that passes muster among philosophers, is a relic of a bygone age, surviving, like the monarchy, only because it is erroneously supposed to do no harm" (p. 387). Further, "what science does, in fact, is to select the *simplest* formula that will fit the facts. But this, quite obviously, is merely a methodological precept, not a Law of Nature" (p. 401). Popper (1974) claims: "In my view, aiming at simplicity and lucidity is a moral duty of all intellectuals: lack of clarity is a sin, and pretentiousness is a crime" (p. 44).

A methodological precept in natural science does not necessarily preserve its epistemological innocence when adopted by social scientists, however, and it is easily interpreted as something else by those who are concerned with implementation of the results rather than with the methods of inquiry. Simplicity, moreover, may sometimes border on simplemindedness, and our urge for lucidity may at times become so strong that it makes us search only in well-illuminated areas for something we know we lost where it is dark. The simplicity of the "behavioral laws" from the "age of theory" within psychology may thus in view of recent open systems approaches appear as simplemindedness. And systematic evasion of problems of meaning, *even in psychological research on language and communication*, indicates that we often prefer elucidating trivialities to groping for significance in the dark (see Rommetveit, 1972, p. 214; 1974, pp. 95–101).

The notion of *causal explanation* is intimately related to that of *prediction*, but scientific explanation is nevertheless perfectly possible even when prediction is precluded. Scriven (1969, p. 118) therefore advises us social scientists to replace our favorite myth of the Second Coming (of Newton) with the recognition of the reality of the Already Arrived (Darwin). Life may be understood— and explained—*backward*, and its continuation may also be affected by such understanding. Moreover, experimentation within the social sciences may serve the purpose of explanation even when its immediate goal is purely diagnostic. Psychologists like Michotte and Piaget may thus actually be conceived of as true descendants from Kant. A major aim of their experimentation is to reveal *what man is*—how he reasons and experiences events—under conditions transcending both everyday life situations and those imagined by the speculative philosopher.

The idealized paradigm of the "hard" natural sciences is the hypothetic-deductive method, whereas that of the "soft" humanities is the hermeneutic circle. The former aims at knowledge of nature in terms of an axiomatically organized set of "laws," the latter aims at explication of human meaning. Many social scientific inquiries, however, appear to be characterized by some mixture of the two. Sociological and social psychological "explanation" of some social reality, for instance, is in part a matter of defining that reality in terms of its locus within some more inclusive network of social insttitutions and human attribution. *Crime* is thus in part "explained" by comparing it to *sickness*, and a careful analysis of borderline cases shows that *attribution of personal responsibility* is crucial for the decision as to whether some deviant conduct is to be handled by the legal or the medical institution (Aubert, 1958). Such a systematic explication may even become part of a revised public notion of what crime is. This in turn implies an enriched rational basis for decisions concerning institutional reactions to social deviance.

Aubert's analysis of the criminal and the sick is thus in a way a Kantian analysis: Some state of affairs which traditionally has been conceived of as a reality is explicated in such a way that its social reality component is clearly revealed. Revised "self-understanding" implies, therefore, recognition of novel action alternatives which, even if they turn out to be unrealistic, may affect political decisions and be conducive to institutional innovation. The same general formula seems to apply to dissemination of sociological and social psychological role theory: the latter provides for a novel perspective on well-known "facts," and inherent in that perspective are possibilities of change that were not clearly recognized before. A "scientifically founded" program for women's emancipation may thus be formulated as a deliberately planned transcendence of a formerly taken-for-granted "female nature" via removal of man-made constraints and self-fulfilling prophecies inherent in prescientific notions.

Kantian themes in social psychology have to do with the social nature of man and the subtle interrelationships between man and man-made social realities. They are particularly visible in inquiries into symbolic interaction, cognitive dissonance, and attributions. They may be pursued in macro- as well as in microanalysis of social behavior, and by scholars with definite philosophical orientations as well as by experimentalists whom hardly anybody would accuse of criminal philosophical pretentiousness. Significant aspects of man's social nature are thus elucidated in small group experiments on social comparison processes (Festinger, 1954) and cognitive and social determinants of emotive states tend to seek company with others who are assumed to resemble them or to have suffered a similar fate (Schachter and Singer, 1962). Conditions of subjective uncertainty may then be transformed to self-knowledge anchored in a social reality. What seems to emerge from experimental analysis of verbal communication, moreover, is hopefully a more and more intelligible picture of man as a creature capable of transforming part of his subjectivity into states of intersubjectivity (Rommetveit, 1976).

Polanyi (1968) has analyzed various kinds of indeterminacy of scientific knowledge, and in particular its dependence upon prescientific "tacit knowledge." Positivistic social psychology tries to eliminate such indeterminacy by systematic evasion of human meaning. Explication of personal versus impersonal causality, of crime versus sickness, and of the nature of social reality is on the other hand bound to contain some residual indeterminacy. And such a residual is possibly the price we have to pay if we want to preserve some sort of bridge between our scientific knowledge and what we "tacitly knew" prior to our professional training. It may hence provide a basis for emancipatory self-understanding, and possibly also for rewarding dialogues with philosophers concerned with ontological and epistemological issues.

References

Apel, K. O. Scientifik, Hermeneutik, Ideologie–Kritick: Entwerf einer Wissenschaftslehre in erkenntnisanthropologischer Sicht. *Man and the World*, 1968, 1, 37–63.

Aubert, V. Legal justice and mental health. *Psychiatry*, 1958, 21, 101–13.

Buber, M. What is man?, in W. Barrett and H. E. Aiken (eds.), *Philosophy in the twentieth century*, Vol. 4, pp. 688–719. New York: Random House, 1962.

Campbell, D. T. Qualitative knowing in action research. Kurt Lewin Award Address at A.A.A. meeting in New Orleans, September 1974.

Feigl, H. Notes on causality, in H. Feigl and M. Brodbeck (eds.), *Readings in the philosophy of science*, pp. 408–18. New York: Appleton-Century-Crofts, 1953.

Festinger, L. A theory of social comparison processes. *Human Relations*, 1954, 7, 117–40.

Habermas, J. *Erkenntnis und Interesse*. Frankfurt: Suhrkamp, 1968.

Hebb, D. O. What psychology is about. *American Psychologist*, 1974, 29, 71–79.

Kuhn, T. S. *The structure of scientific revolutions*. Chicago: University of Chicago Press, 1970.

Laing, R. D., and Cooper, D. G. *Reason and violence. A decade of Sartre's philosophy 1950–1960*. New York: Random House, 1971.

Lévi-Strauss, C. L'homme nu. Paris: Plon, 1971.

Polanyi, M. Logic and psychology. *American Psychologist*, 1968, 23, 27–43.

Popper, K. R. *Objective knowledge. An evolutionary approach*. Oxford: Clarendon Press, 1974.

Rogers, C. R. In retrospect. Forty-six years. *American Psychologist*, 1974, 29, 115–29.

Rommetveit, R. Language games, deep syntactic structures, and hermeneutic circles, in J. Israel and H. Tajfel (eds.), *The context of social psychology: A critical assessment*. London: Academic Press, 1972.

Rommetveit, R. Language games, deep syntactic structures, and hermeneutic circles, in J. Israel and H. Tajfel (eds.), *The context of social psychology: A critical assessment*. London: Academic Press, 1972.

Rommetveit, R. *On message structure. A conceptual framework for the study of language and communication*. London: Wiley, 1974.

Rommetveit, R. On the architecture of intersubjectivity in L. H. Strickland, K. J. Gergen, and F. J. Aboud (eds.), *Social psychology in transition*, pp. 201–214. New York: Plenum Press, 1976.

Russell, B. On the notion of cause, with application to the free-will problem, in H. Feigl and M. Brodbeck (eds.), *Readings in the philosophy of science.* pp. 387–407. New York: Appleton-Century-Crofts, 1953.

Schachter, S., and Singer, J. E. Cognitive, social and physiological determinants of emotive state. *Psychology Reviews,* 1962, 69, 379–99.

Scriven, M. Explanation and prediction as non-symmetrical, in L. I. Krimerman (ed.), *The nature & scope of social science: A critical anthology.* New York: Appleton-Century-Crofts, 1969.

Triandis, H. Social psychology and cultural analysis in L. Strickland, K. J. Gergen, and F. J. Aboud (eds.), *Social psychology in transition.* New York: Plenum Press, 1976.

Wellek, R. From the point of view of literary criticism. Closing statement, in A. Sebeok. (ed.), *Style in language.* Cambridge: M.I.T. Press, 1966.

POSSIBLE LIMITS ON A SCIENCE OF SOCIAL BEHAVIOR

WARREN THORNGATE

About a quarter of a century ago Edmund Whittaker (1949) wrote a fascinating series of lectures on the history and implications of recent developments in theoretical physics. Almost parenthetically, he outlined therein a means of viewing scientific progress which is at once both unorthodox and profound. It is a means founded on what Whittaker terms "postulates of impotence," which he defines as assertions of "... the impossibility of achieving something, even though there may be an infinite number of ways of trying to achieve it." He continues:

> A postulate of impotence is not the direct result of an experiment or of any finite number of experiments; it does not mention any measurement, or any numerical relation or analytical equation; it is the assertion of a conviction that all attempts to do a certain thing, however made, are bound to fail. (p. 59)

To illustrate, Whittaker cites many examples of such postulates that occur in physics—the Heisenberg uncertainty principle and the second law of thermodynamics being two. It is Whittaker's contention that postulates of impotence (hereafter called impostulates) may occur with increasing frequency as any branch of science develops and, as in the case of thermodynamics, that they may

WARREN THORNGATE · University of Alberta, Edmonton, Alberta, Canada. Whatever merit is to be found in this paper is to a large extent due to the following people: Sharon Batt, Hillel Einhorn, Johanna Filp, Robert Knox, Ronald Savitt, Lloyd Strickland, Godfried and Ninoska Toussaint. I deeply appreciate their comments and support.

increasingly come to form the *a priori* axioms of hypothetico-deductive theoretical systems.

Whittaker's contention may indeed be correct. Hardin (1961) has shown how much of evolution theory is based upon two impostulates: Weismann's principle (the separation of soma and germ plasm; the so-called anti-Lamarckian postulate) and Gause's law [or the principle of competition exclusion; "no two organisms that complete in every activity can coexist indefinitely in the same environment" (p. 265)]. Fein (1968) and Nievergelt and Farran (1973) discuss the development of various impostulates in automata theory, while Dreyfus (1972) gives a provocative account of some implications of those impostulates for the limits of artificial intelligence. Dahl (1956) has shown how many problems in democratic theory can be traced to a delightful impostulate, Arrow's (1951) possibility theorem (a general account of the paradox of voting). Even Abraham Lincoln's assertion of the impossibility of fooling all of the people all of the time may be regarded as an impostulate, though the behavior of many contemporary politicians suggests that the assertion, however true, is still not universally accepted.

Do impostulates exist in social psychology? If so, what might they be, and what might they imply for the future of the discipline? These questions seem particularly germane to the issues raised in this book and elsewhere (e.g., Israel & Tajfel, 1972). In what follows, I shall present what I believe to be one social psychological impostulate and discuss some of its implications for social psychological research. Since the impostulate by definition constitutes a statement of what cannot be done, it may easily be construed as cynical or nihilistic. I do not think it should be interpreted in this way. Impostulates, as Whittaker suggests, may serve to organize heretofore unrelated theoretical statements or empirical findings. They may also serve to temper otherwise dogmatic philosophical propositions and to redirect or terminate otherwise misguided or fruitless research efforts.[1] Finally, they may provide the foundation for alternative conceptions of research relevance which I believe to be far more sensible than those now inflicted upon us. Limits define potentials; statements of what cannot be done will give us a better understanding of what can and should be.

It should be noted that numerous impostulates already exist in psychology, though they are generally not recognized as such. Most appear as tacit assumptions, and our adherence to or rejection of them largely defines our personal orientations toward the discipline. The beginnings of the psychoanalytic tradition in psychology, for example, can be traced to an acceptance of the belief that *it is impossible to account for all physical maladies on the basis of physiological*

---

[1] Attempts to construct perpetual motion machines, for example, have declined noticeably with general acceptance of the second law of thermodynamics.

disfunction.[2] The behaviorist credo appears to stem from a love of parsimony and a belief that *it is impossible to assess any "mental state" of an organism without the use of one or more behavioral measures.* Much of the gestalt tradition has emerged from the contention that *it is impossible to account for the responses to all composite stimuli on the basis of previously determined responses to their elements.* And recent interest to experimenter effects and demand characteristics of the laboratory has led to the belief that *it is impossible to eliminate the effects of the laboratory setting on a subject's responses by instituting experimental controls with the laboratory.*

Judging from the above examples there is reason to believe that most, if not all, schools or traditions of psychology which began as a reaction to some existing theoretical or methodological orientation have been founded upon one or more impostulates. On these foundations were constructed the "conceptual frameworks" which characterize each tradition (Brunswik, 1952). Until recently, it has been generally felt that the facts or research findings which are laid over, or discovered within these conceptual frameworks, are the most important measure of our scientific prowess. The facts or findings of psychology are usually the only artifacts of our discipline to which the nonscientific community is exposed. It is thus easy to see why their importance might commonly be judged so high. However, Kuhn (1962) has cogently argued that the conceptual frameworks or "paradigms" themselves rank as our most important scientific contribution. To the extent that the frameworks are in turn based upon impostulates, we may extend Kuhn's argument one step further: Scientific psychology advances only with the discovery of its limits.

There are undoubtedly numerous impostulates in social psychology. Alas, they do not lay themselves in our laps; we must ferret them out in a forest of conflicting observations. It may help, however, to realize that most impostulates are simply formal statements of an existing dilemma, and that when persons are confronted with dilemmas they tend to exhibit predictable (usually maladaptive) behavior. Research on the prisoner's dilemma and other forms of conflict, for example, has demonstrated that when individuals are confronted with such situations their behavior becomes uncoordinated, repetitious, and extreme (see Mintz, 1951; Gamson, 1964; Deutsch & Krauss, 1960). Some persons will hit upon one of many arbitrary "solutions" and pursue it doggedly; others will vascillate between arbitrary solutions; still others will attempt to leave the situation altogether, either by flight or by denial (Lewin, 1935; Abelson, 1959; Asch, 1951).

The history of social psychology is a chronology of analogous behaviors. Theoretical positions have been, and still are, pursued and defended with notable

---

[2] The statement of this impostulate and others that follow it are my own. They represent only first approximations and are therefore subject to change without notice.

doggedness (see, for example, Deutsch & Krauss, 1965). New mutations of old concepts are born with remarkable regularity and increasingly appear to survive more on their cuteness than their content (see Dunnette, 1966; Ring, 1967). The flight to humanism has approached, in both popularity and profundity, the North American college students' recent craze for a summer in Europe. For those who choose to remain on more traditional territory, larger issues are ignored or denied in the thoughtless pursuit of "Just One More Experiment."[3]

It is difficult not to suspect that these behaviors are symptomatic of some underlying dilemma. What is the dilemma? How may we formulate it in terms of an impostulate?

The Impostulate of Theoretical Simplicity

Let us begin with a simple observation: psychologists differ widely in their preferences for explanations about various human behaviors, but the preferences of any one psychologist do not fluctuate widely from day to day. This implies that there exists a set of relatively stable characteristics on which individual preferences for these explanations are based. Little if any research has attempted to dilineate what these characteristics are, but there is a considerable body of speculation, usually referred to as philosophy of science, which attempts to dilineate what these characteristics should be (see, for example, Mandler & Kessen, 1959; Becker & McClintock, 1972). Some of the characteristics are subsumed under the catch-all title of heuristics. While important, they are usually judged in more traditional philosophy of science as too informal or subjective to constitute any ultimate basis for preference (but see Polanyi, 1964). The remainder are traditionally considered to be more objective or formal and hence more important. Included here are such characteristics as (1) the generality or specificity of an explanation's domain, (2) the simplicity (parsimony) or complexity of its syntax, and (3) the accuracy (precision, validity) or inaccuracy of its predictions.

In psychology, the generality of an explanation is assumed to be a function of the number of subjects, situations, or responses for which accurate predictions can be made. Other things being equal, we should prefer a general explanation to a more specific one. Thus, if theories A and B can each explain

---

[3] There is much truth in the comment that interest in any social psychological phenomenon reaches a peak about the time the first research review is published and begins to decline shortly thereafter. The reviews invariably delineate numerous inconsistent research results, then plead for more theory and research to patch things up. What research is subsequently produced is almost always as confusing as the original. Theoreticians cannot account for the discrepancies. Enthusiasm falters. The phenomenon is put to pasture. In memorium, the first few experiments are embalmed and stuffed into introductory textbooks and Graduate Record Exams. The remainder are buried in a mass grave: our libraries.

the learning of foreign language vocabulary equally well, while only theory A can also explain the course of improvement in a game of horseshoes, then A should be preferred to B.

The simplicity or complexity of an explanation is somewhat more difficult to define. Complexity is generally assumed to increase in direct relation to the number of free parameters or variables in an explanation. Other things being equal, we should prefer a simple explanation to a more complex one. Thus, if a three-factor theory of connotative meaning can account for as much of the variance in subjective reactions to symbols and objects as a theory having four or more factors, then it should be preferred as well. The complexity of an explanation can also be assumed to vary as a function of its operations; linear operators, for example, are generally considered to be more "simple" than nonlinear operators; additive relations are generally considered to be less complex than configural ones, etc. (see Thorngate, 1971). This form of complexity is more difficult to quantify, though recent work suggests that it may be accomplished by measuring various properties of representative algorithms (see, for example, Einhorn, 1970). Regardless of the ultimate measure, however, our preferences should still lie with the simple operators as they are, in a word, more "elegant."

The accuracy of an explanation is assumed to be directly related to the goodness of fit between the predictions derived from it and the actual state of nature about which the predictions are being made. Other things being equal, the more accurate an explanation—that is, the better the fit between its predictions and the relevant data—the greater should be our preference for it. Of course, the precision of a prediction places an upper limit upon the accuracy or goodness of fit that can possibly be attained, much like the reliability of a measurement places an upper limit upon its validity. Precision, in turn, is dependent upon the nature of the variables, constructs, parameters, and operators of an explanation. For example, constructs or variables with rigid operational definitions have the potential of being more precise than those which are not. Operators that generate point predictions are more precise than those which generate directional predictions, and these in turn are more precise than those which only generate predictions of a nominal nature. The increasing popularity of attempts to quantify and mathematize theories of psychological phenomena is indicative of the desire to provide the necessary, but not sufficient, conditions for accurate explanations (see, for example, Atkinson, Bower, & Crothers, 1965; Blalock, 1969).

It is tempting to believe that by successively generating explanations and applying the preferential criteria of generality, simplicity, and accuracy to them we should inexorably progress toward an "ideal" explanation, which is at once general, simple, and accurate. It is also difficult to believe that we have made significant headway to date (see Koch, 1961; McGuire, 1973; Smith, 1972; Tajfel, 1972; Von Bertalanffy, 1962). Some have attributed our floundering to the current *Zeitgeist*, which is thought to emphasize behavior over conscious-ness, molecular over molar problems, or the pursuit of "academic" over mean-ingful" goals (see Burt, 1962; Moscovici, 1972; Rogers, 1965, 1973; Tajfel, 1972). Others have attributed our floundering to an underemphasis of the same (see, for example, Schlenker, 1974; Skinner, 1953, 1971). Still others have attributed it to a lack of understanding about the multifaceted nature and functions of explanations themselves (see Marx, 1963; Rogers, 1965). There is considerable disagreement about the form an ideal explanation should take and about the means by which it should be achieved (see, for example, Gergen, 1973; Katz, 1972; Maslow, 1946; McGuire, 1973; Schlenker, 1974; Smith, 1972). Yet the disagreement itself appears to be based upon a tacit and widespread acceptance of the underlying assumption that such an explanation is both desirable and ultimately possible.

The assumption has rarely been challenged. Ritchie (1965) has argued that all psychological theories are incurably vague. Karl Lashley is said once to have remarked that theories in psychology must be either vague or wrong (see Wertheimer, 1972, pp. 217–219). Coombs (1962) has argued that "we buy konwledge with the assumptions we make—the more assumptions made the more knowledge obtained" (p. 284). Gardiner (1970) has observed that "psy-chological research seems to be constrained by the iron-clad law that rigor times relevance is a constant" (p. 18). Each of these statements can be seen as an indirect indictment of the validity of the assumption. But they are all too easily dismissed as mere cyncial aphorisms or are grudgingly acknowledge and quickly forgotten.

Taken together, however, these aphorisms point directly to the dilemma underlying the current disarray of our discipline and lack of progress toward a general, accurate theory of social behavior. The dilemma may be summarized in what I shall term the impostulate of theoretical simplicity, which can be stated as follows: *It is impossible for an explanation of social behavior to be simul-taneously general, simple, and accurate.*

The implications of this impostulate are far reaching and profound. We may formulate explanations of human behavior that are simple and accurate, but to do so we must necessarily restrict our explanations to a limited domain of persons, situations, or responses. This "solution" to our dilemma has tradition-ally been preferred by experimentally oriented social psychologists (see Gergen, 1973; Tajfel, 1972). Pursued to its extreme, the solution produces explanations which say everything about nothing (see Kretch, 1970; Rudin, 1959). Alterna-tively, we may formulate explanations of human behavior which are simple and general, but to do so we must relinquish accuracy, either by becoming vague in our definitions or by maintaining their precision and decreasing goodness of fit. This solution to our dilemma has traditionally been preferred by experientially oriented social psychologists (e.g., Goffman, 1959, 1961). Pursued to the ex-treme, it leads to explanations which say nothing about everything (see Kretch,

1970; Rudin, 1959). The relative simplicity of our explanation sets an upper limit upon their generality or accuracy. General, accurate theories of social behavior must necessarily be complex.

Why should anyone believe the impostulate of theoretical simplicity? And even if believed, so what? Is there anything wrong with complex theories? Let us consider these questions in turn.

Evidence for the Impostulate

Though impostulates are assertions of convictions rather than statements resulting from inductive inference, we need not accept or reject them on blind faith. I believe the most convincing arguments in support of the impostulate of theoretical simplicity are beginning to emerge from two disciplines: automata theory and theoretical biology. They are arguments by analogy and admittedly speculative, but they are at least worthy of exposition.

Studies of automata and artificial intelligence have provided much insight into the futility of constructing a unified theory of social behavior. Virtually all social behavior is mediated by some form of cortical activity. The brain possesses all the formal properties of a universal Turing machine (see Kleene, 1956; McCulloch & Pitts, 1943). It may be impossible to program an electrical Turing machine, e.g., a computer, to mimic all human behavior (see Dreyfus, 1972; Turing, 1964). However, there can be little doubt that the brain can mimic any behavior of a Turing machine. This fact has an interesting implication: All computable predictions of any theory of social behavior can theoretically be supported (or refuted) by the individuals whose behavior they are attempting to predict (see Scriven, 1965). The brain—to use a homey analogy—is much like silly putty; it can, in principle, form itself to fit any theoretical container.

What can occur in principle may not occur in fact. Even so, three decades of social psychological research have clearly demonstrated that the cortical or cognitive processes governing social behavior are sufficiently plastic or diverse that no theory of social behavior derived from them has failed to gain at least some empirical support. Robert Knox (1969), in one of his delightful fits of humourous insight, once proposed the law of wishy-washy results, which I think nicely summarizes the situation. Knox's law asserts that any series of experiments designed to test two or more social psychological theories will tend to give wishy-washy support to them all. It may be formally stated as follows: If n experiments are conducted to test any t theories of social behavior, the number of experiments supporting any one theory will approach $1/t$ as n approaches infinity.

Why should the processes underlying social behavior be so diverse or varied? The answer may lie in the parallels between social and biological systems (see Holling, 1968; Pringle, 1951; Slobodkin, 1965). Both intra- and interindividual systems, like biological systems, can be seen as self-regulating and hence subject to the law of requisite variety (Ashby, 1963, Chapter 11). This law states, in essence, that in order for a system to be self-regulatory, "the variety within a system must be at least as great as the environmental variety against which it is attempting to regulate itself" (Buckley, 1968, p. 495). The maximum variety of a system can only be increased by increasing the complexity of the processes that define it. Increased complexity may be achieved in several ways. Pringle (1951), for example, has shown that a learned response always increases the complexity of the organism that learns it. Since the processes governing social behavior are almost always learned, and since they are learned in diverse situations, their diversity is to be expected.

The law of requisite variety implies that the complexity of a cognitive system or a social system will reflect the complexity of the environment in which it operates. We often limit environmental complexity in hopes of reducing behavioral variety and hence the complexity of the processes which govern the behavior. To do so we design our laboratories to be as stark as possible, keep our stimuli simple, and truncate the admissible range of our subjects' responses. Simple theories may then be constructed which often will accurately predict (or postdict) the resulting stimulus–response relations (e.g., Anderson, 1965, 1968; Atkinson & Estes, 1963; Meesick & McClintock, 1968). But as generalizations of these theories are made to more complex nonlaboratory environments, their accuracy becomes much diminished.

There are, to be sure, a few simple models that are sufficiently "robust" to account accurately for behavior in a wide variety of situations. For example, a rather simple model of information integration has been shown to do a remarkable job of mimicking the responses of subjects in a number of different attitude change and impression formation tasks (see Anderson, 1965, 1971). However, the parameter values of such models vary markedly as a function of any number of situational and personal factors (see Anderson, 1971). As a result, the models tend to become little more than rules for generating "derived measures" (see Suppes & Zinnes, 1963) and their status as a theory becomes highly suspect. Chomsky (1963) and Wilson (1974) have shown that models of minutiae represent context-free grammars in a context-sensitive universe. Parameter variance of models at one level of abstraction may be accounted for by constructing metamodels, but the inclusion of metamodels in theories of social behavior necessarily complicates them.

If the analogy between behavioral and biological systems is valid, we might expect the impostulate of theoretical simplicity to have a biological sister. The sister does, indeed, exist. Richard Levins (1968) has argued that the fragmentation of environmental biology shall never be reversed by applying some simple metatheoretical adhesive, simply because such an adhesive is impossible to concoct. In particular, it is Levins' contention that ". . . it is not possible to maximize simultaneously generality, realism, and precision" (p. 7) in a theory of ecological systems. Precision is, of course, equivalent to accuracy in the impostulate of theoretical simplicity. Realism is implied to be a direct function of the correspondence between theoretical and biologically identifiable variables. Identifiable variables in ecological systems abound. As a result, a realistic theory of these systems must also be a complex theory.[4]

In sum, there is greater reason to believe that a general, simple, accurate theory of social behavior does not exist than there is reason to believe otherwise. Attempts to develop more general theories of social behavior—for example, ones which would integrate the findings of various subareas of social psychological research—must result in a proliferation of variables or parameters. Of course, theories in many areas of psychology have been evolving in this direction. Single-cause or single-parameter theories have given way to dual-parameter theories and these in turn are being replaced by theories with three or more parameters. The immense growth in the number of experimenters and experiments has accelerated the pace of evolution. Markov learning models, for example, have shown rapid growth in complexity in recent years (see Millward & Wickens, 1974). Social psychological theories have grown more slowly in complexity, perhaps because of our tendency to explore, rather than settle, new corners of our domain. However, many have concluded that increased complexity is inevitable and have advised us to get on with it (see, for example, McGuire, 1973, Von Bertalanffy, 1970).

The Curse of Complex Theories

What is wrong with complex theories? Perhaps nothing. If we wish to pursue them, however, we must be aware of at least two assumptions on which our pursuit is based. The first assumption is merely an extension of the assumptions of logical positivism, which may be stated thus: *The complexity of social behavior is organized* (see Weaver, 1948; Frank, 1970). From this assumption follows a fundamental corrolary: The more complex a theory of social behavior, the greater the chances that it will "explain," or account for, the organized complexity of social behavior at any given level of accuracy. The second assumption is equally important and is firmly fixed in the tenets of science: *Complex theories can be subjected to empirical tests.* From this assumption follows another fundamental corollary: Given a set of two or more complex theories of social behavior, we may measure their relative validity or accuracy by

---

[4] It is interesting to note, in passing, that the solution that Levins prefers in resolving this dilemma is "the sacrifice of precision for generality and realism" (p. 7). Though Levins may have anticipated the impostulate of theoretical simplicity in social psychology, his solution to the dilemma it summarizes has existed in psychology for some time. The ideas subsequently presented in his book bear a striking resemblance to Lewin's (1951) field theory.

execution of complex experiments. Let us call these two assumptions the assumption of *organization* and the assumption of *verification*, and critically examine each.

The Assumption of Organization. Consider first the assumption of organization. At least two important questions may be raised with respect to this assumption: Is it ever advantageous for an individual to be unorganized? If so, how common might these occasions be? Von Neumann and Morgenstern (1944) give perhaps the earliest formal answer to the first question. They have shown that social situations exist in which it is most rational for an individual to emit the least organized sequence of behavior possible. According to the minimax criterion of rationality, the optimal strategy to pursue in zero-sum games without a saddle point is to behave randomly. This will ensure that one's opponent or opponents will be unable to detect any behavioral regularities and hence construct any theory of one's behavior having a finite number of parameters which will increase the accuracy of their predictions beyond the level of chance. Both Scriven (1965) and Gergen (1973) have argued that the subjects in our experiments may come to interpret our experiments as such a game and behave accordingly (or refuse to play). If this were to occur, laboratory tests of any theories, complex or simple, would become impossible.

Perhaps the reasoning of Scriven and Gergen is farfetched. The skeptic, however, should ponder a second source of disorganization, which I believe to be much more common than certain zero-sum games and hence a more serious problem for the assumption of organization.

Social norms have the net effect of organizing intra- and interpersonal behavior. They are also, by definition, rules that are shared by the majority of members of a group. For this reason, most or all social psychological research may be viewed as an attempt to uncover and codify norms, be they norms of behavior or norms of thinking, motivation, etc.

Many, if not most, norms exist as a result of historical accident; they are arbitrary and only coincidentally related. Even so, we adopt them readily; seven decades of research in verbal learning have demonstrated that, when the occasion warrants it, individuals are quite capable of learning arbitrary relationships. Thus, even though we observe organized patterns of behavior within situations, there is little reason to believe that differences in behavior patterns across situations are also organized. In short, local organization may be observed within general disorganization; the former does not necessarily imply the latter.

A fine example of the arbitrary nature of social norms can be found in the very words you are now reading. Norms governing the spelling and pronunciation of the English language represent some of the most absurd and arbitrary ever created by the human mind. Bernard Shaw, I believe, has already commented on the curious problem of pronouncing the suffix of through, thorough, and tough. I myself have been severely criticized for spelling judgment as judgement even though other words which end in "e" retain it when the suffix "ment" is added. Violation of spelling norms usually evokes ridicule: as a result it is advantageous to learn to be reliably unorganized. A theory relating English phonemics to English spelling would at best be extremely complex. More likely, as Bar-Hillel (1964) might argue, it would be impossible to construct.

Some social behavior may exhibit transsituational organization. It may therefore be argued that only this behavior should define the domain of social psychology and that the rest should be classified as outside the realm of science. Unfortunately, it is impossible to stipulate a priori which behavior lies within the domain. In addition, there is no a priori reason to believe the organization will not itself be complex. Levins (1968), in his discussion of theories of biological systems, makes a point worth quoting:

> An attempt to consider genetic, demographic, environmental and interspecific differences [in biological systems] simultaneously immediately runs into technical difficulties. A precise mathematical description may involve hundreds of parameters, many of which are difficult to measure, and the solution of many simultaneous non-linear partial differential equations, which are usually insoluble, to get answers that are complicated expressions of the parameters which are uninterpretable. (p. 5)

The Assumption of Verification. Consider now the assumption of verification. Judging from the history of science, complex theories are far easier to construct that simple ones; science bestows fame and prestige on those who generate simple, accurate theories for this very reason. In addition, the more free parameters and operators one allows in a given set of theories, the greater the number of alternative theories may be included in the set. From these two premises, a simple conclusion may be derived: As theories of social behavior become more complex they will also become far more numerous.

The goal of experimentation is to eliminate all but the "best" theory or explanation. However, as the number of possible explanations increases, so too must the channel capacity or resolving power of the experiments sufficient to reach this goal. We may reduce the number of contending explanations by lumping subsets of explanations into equivalence classes according to any of a number of criteria. Explanations may be "nested," for example, by demonstrating how some are special cases of others. But nesting merely subsumes simple explanations under more complex ones. Though we can eliminate simple explanations by demonstraging the inadequacy of its own complex parent to account for experimental results, we cannot do the converse. Complex explanations must ultimately be put to experimental tests. Alternatively, we may amalgamate explanations by "linking" their variables with one or more hypothetical constructs (e.g., the construct of "anxiety"). But unlike nesting, linking is not the result of any a priori logical derivation. The rules which govern the linking of variables are themselves parts of explanations and thus subject to the same degree of proliferation as the theories that subsume them.

A number of statistical techniques are available under the titles of factor analysis and multidimensional scaling which claim to help us uncover some of the constructs linking variables. But the techniques in no way constitute an explanation unto themselves (see Shepard, 1968; Eacker, 1972; Green, 1968). Indeed, the use of these techniques may lead us astray by smothering or covering up important features of the phenomena under investigation (see Armstrong, 1967; Boyd, 1972). To illustrate, recent investigations by Thorngate and Mitchell (1972) have shown that subjects use qualitatively different processes for integrating idiographic as opposed to nomothetic information. When analyses of variance are employed to represent these processes, their differences appear as small but highly significant higher order interactions; subjects search for patterns of all kinds when integrating idiographic information, but do not when integrating nomothetic information. Such interactions could not be uncovered by most factor-analytic or multidimensional techniques, though these techniques would account for the vast majority of nonerror variance in subjects' responses. The account may be sufficient for many practical applications (see Goldberg, 1968). It is not, however, sufficient for scientific ones. Had astronomers judged explanations of celestial movement by the criterion of practicality, it is doubtful they ever would have abandoned the Ptolemaic model of the universe.[5]

The resolving power of our experiments places an upper limit upon the complexity of alternative explanations which can, at any given level of accuracy, be reliably differentiated (see, for example, Greeno & Steiner, 1964). Resolving power in turn, is a function of the size or complexity of an experiment, since the size places an upper limit upon the resolution that can be attained. Because of this fact, the complexity of explanations we wish to test dictates the complexity of experiments necessary to test them. This is nicely illustrated in terms of factorial designs. Factorial designs represent one of our most powerful means of determining the relative accuracy of any given set of alternative explanations (see Anderson, 1970). But their size increases exponentially with the number of variables in the explanations being tested; each time we add a variable to a factorial design its size is at least doubled. Here again we may shrink the size by invoking such shortcuts as fractional replication or nesting. But we pay for these shortcuts, as Coombs (1964, p. 284) suggests, with the assumptions we make in order to invoke them. The assumptions generally concern the lack of "large" interactions. Yet, as stated above, the presence of even "small" interactions is often crucial in distinguishing the relative validity of alternative theories.

By increasing the complexity of our theories we quickly encounter what may be termed the "problem of free parameters." Complex explanations, by definition, have lots of them. As long as their number is finite we can—in

[5] Ptolemy's epicyclic model is not dead. It is alive and well living under an assumed name: the analysis of variance (which, of course, conceives interactions as epicycles or perturbations of row—column means). There is good fun in speculating that the abandonment of this analysis may do for social psychology what it did for astronomy. The problem is to find an alternative to replace it.

theory—design an experiment which will reliably estimate their values and map their relationships. But for any given level for resolving power, the size or complexity of the experiment will increase far more rapidly than the number of parameters in the explanations under test.

There can be little doubt that there is a practical limit to the size or complexity of the experiments which we can ever hope to execute within our discipline. Anyone who, in a burst of naive enthusiasm, has ever attempted to execute an experiment involving, say, a six-way factorial between-subject design or administer a large battery of psychological tests should be painfully aware of these limits. We are certainly limited by logistic considerations, for example, by the cooperation or availability of subjects, space, equipment, and time. We are also limited by a host of ethical considerations which often prevent us from measuring explanatory variables defined in terms of unpleasant operations (e.g., castration anxiety) or measuring them without the subjects' consent. We are also limited, paradoxically, by the power of our own statistics which all but guarantee that our results will be more confusing than we desire (see Meehl, 1967; Rozeboom, 1960). Finally, and perhaps most important, we are limited by our own native abilities to comprehend complex experiments and the import of the results they accrue. Donald Norman's (1973) statements in this regard is well worth quoting. In a discussion of the impact of computers in the psychology laboratory he states,

> More complex experiments will certainly become possible when [computers] start becoming commonplace components in laboratory equipment, but these complexities may be detrimental: they may simply make the understanding of experiments much more difficult. (p. 86)

Have We Reached Our Limits?

What remains contentious is where our limits lie. It is my contention that the practical limit to the size of experiments which are possible to conduct in social psychology is relatively small. Indeed, I strongly suspect that we have already reached it or, if not, that we are very close. During the last quarter century there has been a trend in social psychological research from single- to multifactor designs (see, for example, Highbee & Wells, 1972). But growth in the size of the multifactor designs has leveled off considerbly. It is still rare to find a report of social psychological research which manipulates, at once, more than four variables. The pragmatics of research will, I believe, ultimately limit us to designs which can test explanations with nor more than five or six free parameters.

To illustrate, consider the growth of the size of factorial designs reported in the *Journal of Personality and Social Psychology* over the last decade. Random samples of 20 such designs were taken from this journal for each of the years 1962, 1965, 1968, and 1971. The average number factors in these designs, including repeated measures, were computed for the sample and were found to be 2.10, 2.15, 2.05, and 2.45, respectively. Alas, these means were not significantly different ($F = .76, df = 3.76, p > .5$).

Social psychologists may have long ago realized the practical limits to the complexity of their experiments. Contemporary research in social psychology appears to be characterized by a mad rush to explore every conceivable combination of two, three, or four independent, correlational, and dependent variables.[6] Even if we conservatively estimate that only 30 or 40 of each of these variables have been isolated to date and that no more shall henceforth appear, hundreds of thousands of such combinations are possible. Since the number explored to date does not begin to approach this figure, we can be assured of virgin territory long into the future. Of course, many of the more interesting combinations have already been claimed, but many remain, especially in the so-called cross-disciplinary areas. We may well look forward to such scintillating cross-disciplinary dissertation titles as *The effect of authoritarianism, race, sex, and room size upon attributions of causality following a risky shift.* Our intellectual atrocities are only limited by our imagination. A few are appearing now; the future awaits their sequels.

Variables may be fruitfully studied in isolation only by assuming they do not interact. But even when only a few variables are studied in combination, interactions are common. The shift from univariate to multivariate designs was presumably motivated by this observation. The use of multivariate experiments made it possible to determine why many of the results of isolated univariate experiments were contradictory: Multivariate designs provided a means of demonstrating how unmeasured variables of univariate experiments could interact with the measured variables to produce the divergent results. Social psychology is now faced with increasingly contradictory results of isolated multivariate experiments. To account for their contradictions we have no recourse but to deploy even larger multivariate designs. Yet, for all practical purposes, their sheer bulk guarantees that they shall never reach fruition in the laboratory (or out of it).

Let us summarize. The impostulate of theoretical simplicity dictates that we shall never see a general, simple, accurate theory of social behavior. In order to increase both generality and accuracy, the complexity of our heories must necessarily be increased. Complex theories of social behavior will be viable only to the extent that the complexities of social behavior are organized. However, there is reason to believe that much social behavior is not organized beyond a "local," or situation-specific, level. Even if it is organized beyond this level, there is faint reason to believe that the organization is simple. Complex theories of social behavior may be easily constructed in an attempt to describe this organization,

---

[6] A cursory glance at any psychology convention calendar should quickly convince you of this.

but the ethics and pragmatics of research set severe limits on the complexity of theories that can be subjected to empirical test. Herein lies the ultimate irony of our discipline: Precise and complex theories may hold the promise of being general and accurate, but in the end they are as untestable as those which are simple and vague.

Implications for Future Social Psychological Research

Social psychology could be an organized comprehensive science were it not for its subject matter. The disorder of our discipline is far more a reflection of the nature of the phenomena we study than it is of ourselves. As a result, anyone who views social psychological research as a means of uncovering generalizations fails to perceive its most important function: the delineation of limits or boundaries. Levins (1968) makes the same point: "Given the essential heterogeneity within and among complex biological systems, our objective is not so much the discovery of universals as the accounting for differences" (p. 6).

Bertrand Russell spent much of his life arguing that the problems of mankind stem far less from ignorance than from arrogance. From his thesis the truly important contribution of social psychological research becomes clear. Experimental social psychology has emerged as our culture's most sophisticated method of arresting arrogance by deflating generalizations and debunking social myths. As a result, we have—for the first time in history—provided empirical support for a social ethos, one based on humility, flexibility, and tolerance. Our support could not have come in a more crucial era; to preserve the species, this ethos needs all the support it can get (see Hardin, 1972).

The full impact of this research contribution has yet to be witnessed. Members of the public continue to expect social psychological research to cater to their biases, not to challenge them (see Looft, 1971). Social psychology has unfortunately been sold with promises of social bandaids constructed from the assumptions that one's failures are the fault of others, and one's successes, the result of oneself (see Miller, 1969). We are too often expected to cut up society's blame pie and serve the biggest slices to the "enemy." When we fail to meet these expectations we please no one and unless the expectations change, we ourselves stand a good chance of becoming, as Ibsen's play suggests, "An Enemy of the People."

Public expectations of social psychology are, to a large extent, the product of social psychologists. We have extracted large amounts of money from the public by catering to their whims, much like the geisha. By allowing the media to disseminate gross oversimplifications and biased representations of our work, we have helped perpetuate falsehoods. Social psychologists have for too long been apologetic for their learned ignorance. We should, instead, flaunt it. In our midst are found some of the most intelligent, creative, and dedicated individuals our society has produced. Though we may curse the relative crudeness of our research techniques, they are immensely sophisticated in comparison to those employed by self-proclaimed social philosophers. For better or worse, our flounderings represent the threshold of knowledge. We must take pride in them and seek to publicize their merits.

I do not wish to imply that, as social psychologists, we should smugly rest on our failures. There is much to be said for the argument that our discipline faces stagnation unless we begin to develop new approaches to it. Prescriptions concerning the future direction of social psychology are numerous and varied (see, for example, Israel & Tajfel, 1972). Most appear to be tedious to pursue, though all appear to be worthwhile. Each of us must have our favorite, and I look forward to inflicting mine upon the social psychology community in the near future (Thorngate, in press).

Regardless of the future directions which our discipline shall take, I am confident that none shall overcome the limits I have outlined above. Social behavior is too complex, too fluid, ever to be comprehended as a whole. I am grateful it is such; if social behavior were simple and regular, it would be frightfully dull. We are fortunate that social phenomena are sufficiently predictable to intrigue us with their transient patterns and sufficiently irregular to provide us with constant and joyous surprise. Social psychological research can reveal the wonderous interplay of these patterns and irregularities to a degree unmatched by any other endeavor. It is, in the end, a delightful exercise in the esthetics of human interaction. No endeavor could serve a more noble function.

References

Abelson, R. Modes of resolution of belief dilemmas. *Journal of Conflict Resolution*, 1959, 3, 343–352.

Anderson, N. Averaging versus adding as a stimulus combination rule in impression formation. *Journal of Experimental Psychology*, 1965, 70, 394–400.

Anderson, N. Functional measurement and psychophysical judgment. *Psychological Review*, 1970, 77, 153–170.

Anderson, N. Integration theory and attitude change. *Psychological Review*, 1971, 78, 171–206.

Armstrong, J. S. Derivation of theory by means of factor analysis or Tom Swift and his electric factor analysis machine. *The American Statistician*, December 1967.

Arrow, K. *Social choice and individual values.* New York: Wiley, 1951.

Asch, S. Effects of group pressure upon the modification and distortion of judgment, in H. Goetzkow (ed.), *Groups, leadership and men.* Pittsburgh: Carnegie Press, 1951.

Ashby, R. *Introduction to cybernetics.* New York: Wiley, 1963.

Atkinson, R., Bower, G., and Crothers, E. *An introduction to mathematical learning theory.* New York: Wiley, 1965.

Atkinson, R., and Estes, W. Stimulus sampling theory, in R. Luce, R. Bush, and E. Galanter (eds.), *Handbook of mathematical psychology*, Vol. II. New York: Wiley, 1963.

Bar-Hillel, Y. The present status of automatic translation of language, in F. L. Alt (ed.), *Advances in Computers*. New York: Academic Press, 1964.

Becker, G. M., and McClintock, C. G. Scientific theory and social psychology, in C. G. McClintock (ed.), *Experimental social psychology*. New York: Holt, 1972.

Blalock, H. *Theory construction*. Englewood Cliffs, New Jersey: Prentice-Hall, 1968.

Boyd, J. Information distance for discrete structure, in A. Romney, R. Shepard, and S. Nerlove (eds.), *Multidimensional scaling, Vol. I*. New York: Seminar Press, 1972.

Brunswik, E. The conceptual framework of psychology, in O. Neurath (ed.), *International encyclopedia of unified science*, Vol. 1. Chicago: Univ. of Chicago Press, 1952.

Buckley, W. Society as a complex adaptive system, in W. Buckley (ed.), *Modern systems research for the behavioral scientist*. Chicago: Aldine, 1968.

Burt, C. The concept of consciousness. *British Journal of Psychology*, 1962, 53, 229–242.

Chomsky, N. Formal properties of grammars, in R. Luce, R. Bush, and E. Galanter (eds.), *Handbook of mathematical psychology, Vol. II*. New York: Wiley, 1963.

Coombs, C. *A theory of data*. New York: Wiley, 1964.

Dahl, R. *A preface to democratic theory*. Chicago: Univ. of Chicago Press, 1956.

Deutsch, M., and Krauss, R. The effects of threat on interpersonal bargaining. *Journal of Abnormal and Social Psychology*, 1960, 61, 181–189.

Deutsch, M., and Krauss, R. M. *Theories in social psychology*. New York: Basic Books, 1965.

Dreyfus, H. *What computers can't do*. New York: Harper & Row, 1972.

Dunnette, M. Fads, fashions and folderol in psychology. *American Psychologist*, 1966, 21, 343–352.

Eacker, J. Some elementary philosophical problems of psychology. *American Psychologist* 1972, 27, 553–565.

Einhorn, H. The use of nonlinear, noncompensatory models in decision making. *Psychological Bulletin*, 1970, 73, 221–230.

Fein, L. Impotence principles for machine intelligence, in L. N. Kanal (ed.), *Pattern recognition*. Washington: Thompson, 1968.

Frank, L. K. Organized complexities, in J. Royce (ed.), *Toward unification in psychology*. Toronto: Univ. of Toronto Press, 1970.

Gamson, W. Experimental studies in coalition formation, in L. Berkowitz (ed.), *Advances in experimental social psychology, Vol. 1*. New York: Academic Press, 1964.

Gardiner, W. *Psychology: A story of a search*. Belmont, California: Brooks-Cole, 1970.

Gergen, K. Social psychology as history. *Journal of Personality and Social Psychology*, 1973, 26, 309–320.

Goffman, E. *The presentation of self in everyday life*. Garden City, New York: Doubleday, 1959.

Goffman, E. *Encounters*. Indianapolis: Bobbs-Merrill, 1961.

Goldberg, L. Simple models or simple processes? Some research on clinical judgments. *American Psychologist*, 1968, 23, 483–496.

Green, B. Descriptions and explanations: A comment on papers by Hoffman and Edwards, in B. Kleinmuntz (ed.), *Formal representation of human judgment*. New York: Wiley, 1968.

Greeno, J., and Steiner, T. Markovian processes with identifiable states: General considerations and application to all-or-none learning. *Psychometrika*, 1964, 29, 309–333.

Hardin, G. *Nature and man's fate*. New York: New American Library, 1961.

Hardin, G. *Exploring the new ethics for survival*. New York: Viking, 1972.

Highbee, K., and Wells, M. Some research trends in social psychology during the 1960s. *American Psychologist*, 1972, 27, 963–966.

Holling, C. S. Stability in ecological and social systems, in G. M. Woodwell and H. H. Smith (eds.), *Diversity and stability in ecological systems*. Upton, New York: Brookhaven National Laboratory, 1969.

Israel, J., and Tajfel, H. *The context of social psychology*. London: Academic Press, 1972.

Katz, D. Some final considerations about experimentation in social psychology, in C. G. McClintock (ed.), *Experimental social psychology*. New York: Holt, 1972.

Kleene, R. C. Representation of events in nerve nets and finite automata, in C. Shannon and J. McCarthy (eds.), *Automata studies*. Princeton: Princeton Univ. Press, 1956.

Knox, R. Personal communication, 1968.

Koch, S. Psychological science versus the science–humanism antinomy: Imitations of a significant science of man. *American Psychologist,* 1961, **16**, 629–639.

Kretch, D. Epilogue. In J. R. Royce (ed.), *Toward unification in psychology*. Toronto: Univ. of Toronto Press, 1970.

Kuhn, J. *The structure of scientific revolutions*. Chicago: Univ. of Chicago Press, 1962.

Levins, R. *Evolution in changing environments*. Princeton: Princeton Univ. Press, 1968.

Lewin, K. *A dynamic theory of personality*. New York: McGraw-Hill, 1935.

Lewin, K. *Field theory in social sciences*. New York: Harper, 1951.

Looft, W. The psychology of more. *American Psychologist*, 1971, **26**, 561–565.

Mandler, G. and Kessen, W. *The language of psychology*. New York: Wiley, 1959.

Marx, M. The general nature of theory construction, in M. Marx (ed.), *Theories in contemporary psychology*. New York: Macmillan, 1963.

Maslow, A. Problem centering vs. means centering in science. *Philosophy of Science*, 1946, **13**, 326–331.

May, R. *Stability and complexity in model ecosystems*. Princeton: Princeton Univ. Press, 1973.

McCulloch, W., and Pitts, W. A logical calculus of the ideas immanent in nervous activity. *Bulletin of Mathematical Biophysics*, 1943, **5**, 115–133.

McGuire, W. The yin and yang of progress in social psychology: Seven Koan. *Journal of Personality and Social Psychology*, 1973, **26**, 446–456.

Meehl, P. Theory-testing in psychology and physics: A methodological paradox. *Philosophy of Science*, 1967, **34**, 103–115.

Messick, D. M., and McClintock, C. G. Motivational bases of choice in experimental games. *Journal of Experimental Social Psychology*, 1968, **4**, 1–25.

Miller, G. Psychology as a means of promoting human welfare. *American Psychologist*, 1969, **24**, 1063–1075.

Millward, R., and Wickens, T. Concept-identification models, in D. Krantz, R. Atkinson, R. D. Luce, and P. Suppes (eds.), *Contemporary development in mathematical psychology, Vol. I*. San Francisco: Freeman, 1974.

Mintz, A. Non-adaptive group behavior. *Journal of Abnormal and Social Psychology*, 1951, **46**, 150–159.

Moscovici, S. Society and theory in social psychology, in J. Israel and H. Tajfel (eds.), *The context of social psychology*. London: Academic Press, 1972.

Nievergelt, J., and Farrar, J. C. What machines can and cannot do. *American Scientist*, 1973, **61**, 309–315.

Norman, D. A. The computer in your briefcase. *Behavioral Research Methods and Instrumentation*, 1973, **5**, 83–87.

Polanyi, M. *Personal knowledge*. New York: Harper-Row, 1964.

Pringle, J. On the parallel between learning and evolution. *Behaviour*, 1951, **3**, 174–215.

Ring, K. Eperimental social psychology: Some sober questions about some frivolous values. *Journal of Experimental Social Psychology*, 1967, **3**, 113–123.

Ritchie, B. F. Concerning an incurable vagueness in psychological theories, in B. Wolman (ed.), *Scientific psychology*. New York: Basic Books, 1965.

Rogers, C. Some thoughts regarding the current philosophy of the behavioral sciences. *Journal of Humanistic Psychology*. 1965, 5, 182–194.

Rogers, T. Notes and comments on building bridges. *Canadian Psychologist*, 1973, 14, 212.

Royce, J. Prologue, in J. Royce (ed.), *Toward unification in psychology*. Toronto: Univ. of Toronto Press, 1970.

Rozeboom, W. The fallacy of the null-hypothesis significance test. *Psychological Bulletin*. 1960, 57, 416–428.

Rudin, S. Book reviews: Two typical books from American psychologists. *Psychological Reports*, 1959, 5, 113–114.

Schlenker, B. Social psychology and science. *Journal of Personality and Social Psychology*, 1974, 29, 1–15.

Scriven, M. An essential unpredictability in human behavior, in R. Wolman (ed.), *Scientific psychology*. New York: Basic Books, 1965.

Shepard, R. Introduction, in A. Romney, R. Shepard, and S. Nerlove (eds.), *Multidimensional scaling*, Vol. I. New York: Seminar Press, 1972.

Skinner, B. F. *Science and human behavior.* New York: Macmillan, 1953.

Skinner, B. F. *Beyond freedom and dignity.* New York: Knopf, 1971.

Slobodkin, L. On the present incompleteness of mathematical ecology. *American Scientist,* 1965, 53, 347–357.

Smith, M. B. Is experimental social psychology advancing? *Journal of Experimental Social Psychology,* 1972, 8, 86–96.

Suppes, P., and Zinnes, J. Basic measurement theory, in R. Luce, R. Bush, and E. Galanter (eds.), *Handbook of mathematical psychology, Vol. I.* New York: Wiley, 1963.

Tajfel, H. Experiments in a vacuum, in J. Israel and H. Tajfel (eds.), *The context of social psychology*. London: Academic Press, 1972.

Thorngate, W. *On the learning and transfer of multi-cue judgement processes*. Report 71-3, Social Psycyhology Labs., Department of Psychology, Univ. of Alberta, 1971.

Thorngate, W. Must we always think before we act? *Personality and Social Psychology Bulletin*, in press.

Thorngate, W., and Mitchell, G. *Judgmental processes and the prediction of behaviour from historical and coincidental information*. Report 72-3, Social Psychology Labs., Department of Psychology, Univ. of Alberta, 1972.

Turing, A. M. Computing machinery and intelligence, in A. R. Anderson (ed.), *Minds and machines*, Englewood Cliffs, New Jersey: Prentice-Hall, 1964.

Von Bertalanffy, L. General systems theory—a critical review. *General Systems*, 1962, 7, 1–20.

Von Bertalanffy, L. General systems theory and psychology, in J. Royce (ed.), *Toward unification in psychology*. Toronto: Univ. of Toronto Press, 1970.

Von Neumann, J., and Morgenstern, O. *Theory of games and economic behavior*. Princeton: Princeton Univ. Press, 1944.

Weaver, W. Science and complexity. *American Scientist*, 1948, 36, 536–544.

Wertheimer, M. *Fundamental issues in psychology*. New York: Holt, Rinehart & Winston, 1972.

Whittaker, E. *From Euclid to Eddington.* Cambridge: Cambridge Univ. Press, 1949.

Wilson, K. V. Linear regression equations as behavior models, in J. Royce (ed.), *Multivariate analysis and psychological theory*. New York: Academic Press, 1973.

Woodwell, G. M., and Smith, H. H. (eds.), *Diversity and stability in ecological systems.* Upton, New York: Brookhaven National Laboratory, 1969.

SOME METATHEORETICAL ISSUES IN SOCIAL PSYCHOLOGY

CHARLES A. KIESLER AND JOSEPH LUCKE

Recently, there has been a great deal of dissatisfaction expressed about social psychology as a field. As described by Shaver (1974), the crisis "... was that despite the development of an impressive methodology, many American social psychologists felt they had neither contributed substantially to the improvement of social life nor succeeded in developing a coherent scientific discipline" (p. 356). Jahoda (1974) describes it as a "failure of nerve" that "many people no longer fully believe in what they are doing, feeling that they may be on the wrong track" (p. 105). Jahoda describes the current split among social psychologists as developing "between those who wish to press on along the same well established route of empirical research and those who felt it was not getting us anywhere" (p. 105).

There are both some attractive and unattractive features of the current conflict. On the positive side, a periodic reexamination of one's assumptions, methodology, and theory is necessary and desirable in any field. Usually such reexamination reflects dissatisfaction with the field and dissatisfaction in science is a sign of impending change. Almost surely at least some of social psychology will be reconstrued in the near future and that prospect is very exciting. Such potential for revolutionary thought has not existed for some time.

CHARLES A. KIESLER AND JOSEPH LUCKE · University of Kansas, Lawrence, Kansas. A preliminary version of this paper was presented at the meeting of the Society of Experimental Social Psychology, October 1974, Champaign, Illinois. Preparation of the paper was facilitated by NSF Grant GS-29722X2.

On the other hand, depending on how one represents the conflict, it can have potentially negative overtones. In the shuffle to see the future, the past is often decried. In our collective search for the future of social psychology, we need not be ashamed of our past. For example, the progress of the average social psychologist in research design and data analysis in the last twenty years is extraordinary. Students receiving Ph.D.s in social psychology these days are as sophisticated about design, methodology, and statistics as those in any substantive area of psychology. It is true that our field has perhaps trod an increasingly narrow path over those same years, but narrowness in selection of problems for study can be corrected quite easily, and by a relatively small number of people. Naivete in methods of solving scientific puzzles and a degradation in scientific rigor are not so easily coped with.

Dissatisfaction with the state of social psychology has been evidenced by the Europeans for years (for example, cf. Moscovici, 1972), but many Americans have also recently expressed concern. For example, Gergen (1973) claims that social psychology can not be a science "because the facts on which it is based do not generally remain stable" (p. 310). He suggests that theories are primarily a reflection of contemporary history; that science and society form a feedback loop such that science affects society and is thereby itself changed. In a somewhat different vein, McGuire (1973) has recently criticized both theory-derived hypotheses and current research in the field. He emphasizes hypothesis generation rather than hypothesis testing and suggests that we should move methodologically more toward systems theory and multivariate correlational designs. What McGuire implies without actually saying so is that the historical emphasis upon hypothesis testing and laboratory research has led to a relatively narrow data base. As a result, the generality and representativeness of our hypotheses are left unchecked against a broader reality. Perhaps this point most of all underlies the current dissatisfaction: the feeling that our collective and cumulative research efforts do not have important and clear-cut implications for the significant social problems of the day.

Many social psychologists are apparently uneasy about both what we know and what we are trying to learn. In that sense, the crisis in social psychology rests upon a dissatisfaction with the current state of theory and experimental paradigms. While much of the criticism of social psychology has merit, the prescriptions suggested to remove these criticisms are often misguided, and the discussion has missed some major points. Some perspective on the controversy might be gained by a consideration of the following questions:

1. If our field is indeed a science, how may we place our present dilemma in a broader historical context and what implications does the history of social psychology as a science have for the future?

2. In our approach to theory, have we leaned too heavily on strict hypothesis testing and what alternative conceptualizations of theory might be most stimulating and provocative, at this stage in our history?

3. How sophisticated is social psychological theory from the viewpoint of philosophy of science?

4. If we are indeed a science, and if we are making respectable empirical and theoretical progress, why do we seem to be so dissatisfied as a collectivity of presumably scientific psychologists?

5. If social psychology as a field is drifting, then what prescriptions and proscriptions will help correct the system as a whole, and how may individual researchers relate to this overall approach?

People have criticized how little we know about important social processes. However, what we "know" about social processes is really a reflection of our theoretical understanding of those processes. Hence, the criticism of the extent of our knowledge is a criticism of the quality of current theories. Although also implicit is the criticism of the integrity of our experimental paradigms, some sort of overall analysis of the current role of theory in social psychology is needed, and some suggestions derived from that analysis for a heterogeneous approach to solve problems in the future. Such an analysis is the topic of this paper.

Much of what follows builds upon current work in philosophy of science but goes one step beyond it. One of the major problems social psychology has had relating to philosophies of science is the passive acceptance of what such philosophers say. We have often turned to the philosophy of science in the past to alleviate anxieties about the scientific status of social psychology. There we had hoped to find some kind of advice on what to do in order to eliminate crises of the current type and to get on with research secure in the knowledge that we were indeed doing science. We have sought and obtained such advice throughout all of social psychology's short history. Yet, after following the advice for a number of years, the feeling of having arrived at a level of "true" science did not occur and once again the philosophical crises have ensued. At present we are told by some philosophers of science that our discipline is still in a preparadigmatic and prescientific stage. As a consequence, a large number of people are wholly or partly engaged in trying to accelerate the "coming of our paradigm." A large number of other people reject the notion that such a paradigm is ever forthcoming.

However, the concept of a single paradigm for social psychology is outdated and inadequate and does not grant us sufficient control of our scientific future. Much of the discussion about theory in social psychology appears to be based on the well known Popperian hypothetico-deductive sequence of creating theories, deriving prediction, subjecting them to experimental test, and rejecting the theory if predictions are disconfirmed. This procedure once was considered to be objective and rational and not influenced by psychological or social psychological variables. However, it is commonly acknowledged these days that psychological and sociological processes are quite influential in the process of scientific discovery and everyday scientific activities. Originally based mainly on an analogy with great historical discoveries, the very rational and objective sequence described by Popper is now thought to describe adequately neither the process of scientific revolution nor scientific activities between revolutions. As Kuhn (1970) says,

> Sir Karl has erred by transferring selective characteristics of everyday research to the occasional revolutionary episodes in which scientific advance is most obvious and by thereafter ignoring the everyday enterprise entirely. In particular, he has sought to solve the problem of theory choice during revolutions by logical criteria that are applicable in full only when a theory can already be supposed. (p. 19)

Kuhn has also said (and this is an important point for us), "It should be clear that the explanation (of scientific progress) must, in the final analysis, be psychological or sociological" (p. 21).

Kuhn has criticized philosophers because their prescriptions had little resemblance to the actual practice of science by scientists. It is our view that scientific progress and discovery are heavily influenced by social psychological processes, and therefore social psychologists should be able to use their own research findings to consider alternative systematic approaches for their field. As psychologist-logicians we might accept Kuhn's description of "normal science" and then building upon previous work in social psychology, such as problem solving and group interaction, we can suggest how the process might be improved or made more efficient. If the aim of science is to overturn paradigms (in the Popperian sense) or solve puzzles (in the Kuhnian sense), the issue is still how quickly or how efficiently we are able to do either one. As the physicist Wheeler (cf. Watkins, 1970) put it, "Our whole problem is to make the mistakes as fast as possible." As experts in group problem solving, we are as able or more able to make recommendations for the advance of social psychology as any philosophers of science.

The major question of the present paper is, given the point in time in the history of social psychology, what should the collectivity of individual research investigators do to move social psychology off this unsatisfying plateau? Much of what follows builds upon recent work by Feyerabend (1965, 1970a–c), an ex-Popperian who, stimulated by Kuhn, has conducted illuminating inquiries into the history of scientific progress.

Many critics contend that we do too much theorizing in social psychology. Quite the contrary, we suggest that we do not do enough and we are insufficiently critical of what we do. We should, to paraphrase Chairman Mao, "Let a thousand theoretical flowers bloom," and further not prune them too quickly. We should intentionally promote more theories, hopefully of varying breadth and depth, cutting across current areas of social psychology.

Our recommendation then is that social psychology should intentionally encourage more theories and nurture them in their developing stages—irrespective of the number or perceived adequacy of existing theories. Feyerabend's two principles of tenacity and proliferation provide the basis for our recommendation.

The Principle of Tenacity.   This is essentially the claim that it is reasonable to take a theory that appears fruitful and develop it, in spite of such obvious problems as empirical counterexamples, absurd interpretations of reality, logical difficulties, and the presence of better theories. Feyerabend's point is that it takes time to develop theories, and therefore means must be developed to retain theories so that their full potential may be developed. If a theory is discarded too quickly we may never discover what explanatory power it may have had. New underdeveloped theories, in particular, may be forced through premature attack to regress to the point of accounting for only a small domain of phenomena, and perhaps dealing with alleged refutations on an ad hoc basis. Further, there may not exist the proper techniques or instruments for adequately testing a theory; in fact the theory itself may play a major role in developing those techniques and instruments. In clinging to a theory in the beginning stages, the theorist should be allowed to employ ad hoc adjustments to his theory, ignore refutations, or even engage in propagandistic defense. These "defense mechanisms" have historical roots and have been employed by successful theoreticians in the past (e.g., Galileo). From historical analyses, such dogmatism appears necessary for scientific progress.

The Principle of Proliferation.   The success or failure of a theory appears to be largely determined by the relative persuasiveness of the critical alternative theories. It is the principle of proliferation which provides for these critical alternative theories. This principle holds that it is reasonable to propose theories that are inconsistent with well-confirmed theories or accepted observations, even if there is no hint of trouble within the established theory. Since criticism of dominant theories proceeds best from developed alternative theories, the latter are necessary for maximum criticizability. Indeed, one could even go further and within the principle of proliferation suggest a procedure of intentional counter-induction that aims precisely at developing those theories and data sets which will enlarge the number of counterexamples to the dominant theory.[1] For example, dissonance theory for years held sway as the dominant theory in a substantial area of social psychology. Even at the peak impact of dissonance theory, we all were aware of several counterexamples: studies in which, for example, greater attitude change was produced by the larger incentive, or less volition. We think it is fair to say that many of these studies were shunted aside and their authors often settled for a less prestigious publishing source and less financial research support. A procedure of intentional counterinduction would

---

[1] If one wishes to promote and nurture counterinduction, then one searches for counterexamples on which to build and understand. This implies that criticisms per se of either existing theory or the counterexamples do not play as productive or important a role as currently believed. Thus current criticisms of existing paradigms are not especially productive. These critics would be better to provide counterexamples or examples of new paradigms. Thus analytical, theoretical, or empirical work is desperately needed—as always. Criticism per se is a small step.

have cherished these examples and encouraged the investigators to develop them further. Attribution theory is probably the dominant theoretical perspective today (Kiesler and Munson, 1975), and we all should be encouraging counterexamples to that theoretical approach. To do so would not only enhance the criticizability of attribution theory but also provide the underpinning for long-term theoretical development in social psychology.

Unfortunately, social psychologists, like other scientists, have a tendency to reify theory, to assume its eternal dominance. However, at this point in our history it would be naive to assume that any extant social psychological theory will not be seriously modified in the next 10–20 years, if not discarded altogether. It should be our collective plan to hasten that process of modification and to discard—to make our mistakes as fast as possible. It is our contention that adherence to the principles of tenacity and proliferation would speed up and enhance the process of theory development, modification, and discarding in the field of social psychology. However, this approach brings to mind several problems regarding comparisons of theories. We note that these problems of comparisons of theories exist now in the field and should be faced directly; our approach merely makes them salient. One such problem is the issue of the incommensurability of theories.

Incommensurability. It is often assumed that there is a body of core facts that could be accounted for by a theory. It is further assumed that the better of two theories should account for all of the facts accounted for in the lesser theory plus some additional novel facts. However, it must be emphasized that the language used in theories is itself implicitly laden with theoretical concepts and it is often quite difficult to translate from one theory to another. It is quite possible in fact that a new theory may propose a decidedly different ontology; it may partition the world in a manner radically different from the old theory. Thus from the new theory's perspective, descriptions of the world formulated by the old theory may now be seen to be inadequately formulated, entities assumed to exist in the old may be considered not to exist in the new, or vice versa. In short, the theories may be incommensurable.

In social psychology, there are three main theoretical approaches and they are basically incommensurable. One approach is Lewinian. The dominant approach in social psychology for decades, Lewinian theory is ahistorical and places emphasis on phenomenology (at least in the sense of the subject's interpretation of contemporaneous events). Various Lewinian formulations emphasize cognitions, inconsistencies or balance among cognitions, attitude change, perceived choice, and so on. The second approach is the learning approach, which is historical and emphasizes behavior without regard to phenomenology (although the research based on this approach in social psychology tends to be largely ahistorical, which is peculiar). There are really several viable theories based on general learning theory, ranging from the radical behaviorist variety, eschewing reference to internal constructs (e.g., Bem, 1967) through

broad eclectic models (e.g., Bandura and Walters, 1963), to rather literal interpretations of Hullian theory (e.g., Weiss, 1968). These various theories talk
about reinforcing events, contingencies, mands, tacts, discriminative stimuli, and
the like. Yet a third approach is the information-processing one, which like
Levinian theories is cognitive but tends to be less ahistorical. In this approach,
the subject's psychological processes are often represented in some detail theoretically, as in simulations, but the theoretical underpinnings of this approach
have not really been tested. Most of the theorizing in the information-processing
approach has been by analogy from some other area of psychology or from
computer science.

These three theoretical approaches applied to the same event (assuming they
can agree upon the "sameness" of an event) isolate different properties as
entering into explanations. It should be clear that there is no straightforward
method of translation among the theories. Indeed, some of the radical principal
entities assumed to exist in cognitive theories (e.g., attitudes) are often explicitly
denied existence in some behaviorist theories.

Given that the observations obtained within a theory are often dependent on
the theoretical language itself, it may be felt that this renders theories tautological and untestable, since the theory defines both the main terms and the
relationship among them. However, it must be pointed out that while the
meanings of the terms used within a theory and the theoretical observation
language are dependent conceptually on the theory, predictions derived from the
theory involve both the general laws postulated by the theory plus a statement
of the initial conditions. It is quite possible that a prediction or observation
statement derived from the general laws and initial conditions will give an
incorrect description of reality, and thus provide a basis for refutation. However,
without alternative theories, such within-theory refutations may not have much
impact. Indeed, the disconfirmation of a prediction may be as indicative of a
faulty observation terminology (e.g., inappropriate attitude scales) as it is of a
faulty theory. The process of theory testing is far more complex than is typically
presented in social psychology.

From this concept it should be apparent that one cannot list strict rules
regarding whether a theory should continue to be developed or abandoned. That
is, we are saying that theories should be allowed time to develop, and theorists
allowed to grind their own axes in the interim period. However, it is a judgment
at best whether sufficient time has been allowed for development and, if so, the
full force of potential criticism unleashed. Of course, the initiator of a developing theory is probably all too painfully aware of its inadequacies, and so very
critical responses to the theory might not be fruitful. On the other hand, a
hypercritical response from a competing theorist might well provide a useful
psychological index for having hit upon a theoretical weakness previously
ignored.

At some point, of course, theories must deliberately be brought into confrontation. Such confrontation among theories almost surely would involve a number of instances of comparison. At this point in our history, it is likely that an individual "critical experiment" cannot provide much impact for or against a theory. Our theories are too vaguely formulated and our procedures insufficiently tested for a single experiment to have critical exclusionary impact. However, these empirical counterexamples are cumulative over time. For example, there is some evidence that the manipulations used in dissonance experiments are physiologically arousing (cf. Kiesler and Pallak, 1976). Assuming this is true, it is an observation inconsistent with some of the basic tenets of attribution theory. However, the fact that attribution theory cannot easily handle the arousal aspect of inconsistency, and dissonance theory in some vague sense can, is neither disproof of the former or proof of the latter, but merely a "puzzle" to use Kuhn's term—a puzzle that requires further investigation before its meaning becomes clear. The fact that the puzzle exists dictates no specific or necessary theoretical conclusion. However, this particular puzzle is still an important problem for social psychology with rather broad implications, and if these two theoretical approaches are not brought into confrontation, the problem may remain unaddressed.

Summary and Implications. The current crisis in social psychology is not an unusual stage in the development of science. Part of the crisis is in reaction to the relatively narrow data base we have accumulated in recent history. Our theories, inextricably intertwined with our data, are seen by many to be narrowly focused and consequently lacking in plausible applicability to significant problems of the day. We have suggested that part of the problem is due to our collective lack of encouragement of development of theories. We propose an endorsement of Feyerabend's principles of tenacity and proliferation, implying both more theories and a tolerance for ambiguity in the initial stages of their development. Further we suggest that the development of intentional counterexamples to current theory be nurtured. With these general comments and building upon Feyerabend's principles of tenacity and proliferation and his concept of theoretical incommensurability we can make some statements about some current problems of interest in social psychology.

1. McGuire's recent statement in favor of systems theory, multivariate correlation designs, and an emphasis upon hypothesis generation would be wholly endorsed by the approach outlined in this paper. The principle of proliferation and that of tenacity both require data to build upon. McGuire's approach would surely provide new challenges both to current theory and to our observation language. We should note, however, that McGuire's dictum against hypothesis testing is less favorably interpreted by the current approach since it is a violation of the principle of proliferation. Proliferation of theories enhances the criticizability of current theory by providing counterexamples and perhaps leading to a better account of the phenomena. Techniques emphasizing hypothesis genera-

tion would be a welcome addition to, but not a replacement for techniques emphasizing hypothesis testing.

2. An issue implicit in many discussions in social psychology today is comparative advantages of inductive and deductive theorizing. Though there are no perfect examples of either theoretical approach, perhaps attribution theory comes closest to inductive and dissonance theory to deductive theorizing. To the question of which approach social psychology should lean on, the answer is quite clearly "both." At the moment each approach presents an incomplete picture, and with the principle of tenacity we can encourage both to grow and develop. Deductive theory has the several advantages of Popperian scientific thinking. For example, the assumptions are openly stated and therefore easily subject to criticism and discussion; the theory could make nonobvious and hence conceptually unique predictions; and the relationship among terms must be openly stated. Since the major components of the theory are clearly and openly stated, its criticizability is thereby enhanced. However, perhaps the major advantage of deductive theorizing is that it forces the theorist to inspect his own thinking in some depth and to specify the theoretical elements exactly. The process of deductive theorizing is probably more important for a field than the specific theoretical outcome. A major disadvantage for a field is that deductive theorizing can be quite narrow and self-contained. One could argue that, *ceteris paribus*, inductive theorizing casts a broader empirical net and more easily incorporates new findings. Both approaches should be encouraged if one is to seek both the rigor and precision of scientific thinking and dynamic potential for change in science. The process and effect of the generation and criticism of theories on the testing of them is not entirely logical (although logic is obviously employed). Taken alone, the inductive and deductive approach each overemphasizes the logic of science and underemphasizes its social psychological underpinnings.

3. Theoretical confrontation versus axe grinding. As mentioned, we cannot be very specific about when theories have been allowed enough time to develop sufficiently so that they should be brought into confrontation with each other. One suspects though that as theoretical approaches develop, the theorists will desire to address similar batches of data. As theories become more strongly competitive, each may make attempts to account for the opponent's data, and provide further criticism if at all possible. Thus, there will be stronger and stronger attempts to provide translations between theories over certain empirical areas so that theory conflict, criticism, "crucial" experiments, and persuasion can have more impact. Hence the problem about when theories should be brought into conflict will partly be resolved by their increasing conflict over a similar data base. Of course, the appetite of certain individuals for theoretical conflict may play a major role in this arena.

4. Is social psychology a science? Although philosophers of science differ somewhat on this point, we have nothing to be defensive about. Feyerabend

(1970) says for example that "... certain parts of psychology are far ahead of contemporary physics in that they manage to make the discussion of fundamentals an essential part of even the most specific piece of research. The concepts are never completely stabilized but are left open and are elucidated now by one, now by the other theory" (pp. 198–199).

5. Field versus laboratory research. To encourage a proliferation of theories implies that we must also encourage a proliferation of observations on which to base and check theories. We supported McGuire's idea of hypothesis generating research on those very grounds. The important ingredient in this recommendation is the interplay between laboratory and field observations. Field observations both provide a check on the predictive power and explanatory adequacy of our theories and provide as well the basis for further theory building. Over the field as a whole, we should have some balance between laboratory and field research. However, what we seem to have accomplished instead is some sort of cycle between laboratory and field research. In one decade we emphasized laboratory research to the exclusion of field research. Now we have many people advocating field research to the exclusion of laboratory research. The advocacy of one approach over the other is silly.

6. Should we "press on with empirical research" and strive to uphold those principles considered "scientific," i.e., objectivity, prediction, etc.? The reply is obviously "What is the alternative?" If our goals as scientists are to provide knowledge that will withstand the test of criticism, to appraise our knowledge critically and make radical changes if warranted, to remain open and responsive to criticism and new developments—if these are our goals, and if the methods of science are designed to maximize those goals—then to ask us not to be "scientific" is tantamount to asking us to be less critical and more dogmatic. We are in a very real sense being asked not to think as deeply as we can about our field. On the other hand, we need not be philosophers of science to be scientists. As Lakatos (1970) remarked, "My pet thesis [is] that most scientists tend to understand little more about science than fish about hydrodynamics" (p. 148). Scientific progress is not necessarily enhanced by a continuous discussion about our scientific status.

Feyerabend (1970) suggests a very open view of science:

> The scientific method as softened up by Lakatos has been an ornament which makes us forget that a position of "anything goes" has in fact been adopted ... Such a development, far from being undesirable, changes science from a stern and demanding mistress into an attractive and yielding courtesan who tries to anticipate every wish of her lover. Of course, it is up to us to choose either a dragon or a pussycat for our company. I do not think I need to explain my own preferences. (p. 229)

We suggest that social psychology be openly scientific. We have urged that we all evaluate the potential outcomes of our current approach (as well as those approaches suggested by others in this volume) and consider changes necessary to affect the system as a whole. We have proposed that much of the current conflict within social psychology is related to the notion that social psychology has been too narrowly scientific. The lack of a monotheoretical paradigm has been interpreted by some as a weakness rather than a strength. We should encourage instead, adapting the principles of tenacity and proliferation and thereby opening up our scientific approach to social psychology.

References

Bandura, A., and Walters, R. *Social learning and personality development.* New York: Holt, Rinehart & Winston, 1963.

Bem, D. J. Self-perception: An alternative interpretation of cognitive dissonance phenomena. *Psychological Review*, 1967, 74, 183–200.

Feyerabend, P. K. Problems of empiricism, in R. G. Colodny (ed.), *Beyond the edge of certainty.* Englewood Cliffs, New Jersey: Prentice-Hall, 1965.

Feyerabend, P. K. Problems of empiricism, II, in R. G. Colodny (ed.), *The nature and function of scientific theory.* Pittsburgh: Univ. of Pittsburg Press, 1970a.

Feyerabend, P. K. Against method, in M. Radner and S. Winokur (eds.), *Minnesota studies in the philosophy of science*, Vol. 4. Minneapolis: Univ. of Minnesota Press, 1970b.

Feyerabend, P. K. Consolations for the specialist, in I. Lakatos and A. Musgrave (eds.), *Criticism and the growth of knowledge.* Cambridge: Cambridge Univ. Press, 1970c.

Gergen, K. Social Psychology as history. *Journal of Personality and Social Psychology*, 1973, 26, 309–320.

Jahoda, G. The context of social psychology: A critical assessment, edited by Joachim Israel and Henri Tajfel. *European Journal of Social Psychology*, 1974, 4-1, 105–112.

Kiesler, C. A., and Munson, P. A. Attitudes and opinions, in M. R. Rosenzweig and L. W. Porter (eds.), *Annual Review of Psychology*, 26, 1975, 415–456.

Kiesler, C. A., and Pallak, M. S. The arousal properties of dissonance manipulation. *Psychological Bulletin*, 1976.

Kuhn, T. S. Logic of discovery or psychology of research? In I. Lakatos and A. Musgrave (eds.), *Criticism and the growth of knowledge.* Cambridge: Cambridge Univ. Press, 1970.

Lakatos, I. Falsification and the methodology of research programmes, in I. Lakatos and A. Musgrave (eds.), *Criticism and the growth of knowledge.* Cambridge: Cambridge Univ. Press, 1970.

McGuire, W. J. The yin and yang of progress in social psychology. *Journal of Personality and Social Psychology*, 1973, 26, 446–456.

Moscovici, S. Society and theory in social psychology, in J. Israel and H. Tajfel (eds.), *The context of social psychology: A critical assessment*, pp. 17–68. London: Academic Press, 1972.

Shaver, P. European perspectives on the crisis in social psychology. *Contemporary Psychology*, 1974, 19, 356–359.

Watkins, J. W. Against normal science, in I. Lakatos and A. Musgrave (eds.), *Criticism and the growth of knowledge.* Cambridge: Cambridge Univ. Press, 1970.

Weiss, R. F. An extension of Hullian learning theory to persuasive communication, in A. G. Greenwald, T. C. Brock, and T. M. Ostrom (eds.), *Psychological foundations of attitudes.* New York: Academic Press, 1968.

SECTION IV

RESEARCH RESPONSE

PREFACE

Emergence of Individual Differences in Social Context

ROBERT B. ZAJONC

A priest who was a heavy smoker once asked his bishop if it was all right if he smoked while praying. Appalled, the bishop chastised the priest for the very thought of soiling the solemn moment of prayer with such a filthy habit.

Some years passed and the bishop came again through our priest's parish. And our tormented priest asked again about his predicament. But he asked a somewhat different question: "Your excellency," he said, "is it all right to pray while smoking?" There was no hesitation in the bishop's answer. "Of course!" he said. "There is nothing in the world that should keep you from praying. You can always pray, my son. You should miss no opportunity to pray. Whenever you wish to pray, by all means pray!"

The relationship between individual differences and social psychology is roughly the same as between smoking and praying. Many social psychologists, and especially experimental social psychologists, are openly disdainful of individual difference variables. They avoid them in their studies and refuse to incorporate them in theories. The reasons for their (and we really should say "my" because the author is no exception in this matter) attitude are not obvious.

It is claimed, perhaps not without some grounds, that individual difference measures are not sufficiently reliable to be employed as independent or mediating variables in experimental research. But one gets the feeling that even if they were reliable there would be a great deal of resistance against giving them

ROBERT B. ZAJONC · University of Michigan, Ann Arbor, Michigan.

some sort of significant and legitimate status in social psychology. This resistance stems from the belief that individual differences are not very informative to begin with.

But let us ask our favorite experimental social psychologist another question: How do individual differences arise? Without much hesitation he will acknowledge that (apart from some genetic factors that might account for a small portion of variance) different social environments produce different people. People who are brought up in competitive societies are quite different from people brought up in cooperative societies. A child reared by strict parents is going to develop in different ways than one who grew up with permissive parents. In fact, the social psychologist would assert that the influence of early social environment cannot be overstressed. It leaves profound marks on the person that stay with him for a lifetime.

The parallel is obvious. Should we study individual differences when we concern ourselves with social psychology? No! Can we concern ourselves with social psychology when we study individual differences? We must!

But, while we might agree that social environment often has pronounced and lasting effects, very few of us experimental social psychologists are about to embark on this sort of research. We leave it to developmental psychologists.

Even though we are social psychologists we shall discuss individual differences, and we shall discuss the most controversial among them, namely, individual differences in intelligence. Moreover, we may have something rather positive to say about them. It is our hope that we can convince some readers that legitimate research can be done in this area, even by social psychologists. In fact, social psychologists, because of their particular orientation, might have something useful to contribute to the study of individual differences. The sort of individual differences that we shall discuss emerge, at least in part, as a result of exposure to what we might want to call intellectual environment, which after all is but an aspect of social environment. We have a number of people: a family. Some of us would not be averse to calling it a "group." The members of this group are not identical—some have reached a higher level of intellectual development than others—and because at any given time different families represent different configurations of age and of intellect, they represent a different intellectual environment. As he grows up, the individual is under the influence of his environment. But he is also a part of it. He is therefore both a *source* and a *target* of the powerful effects such an environment might have. Except that we deal here with long periods of time (certainly longer than fifteen minutes, which is the modal duration of experimental manipulation of influences in social psychology), there is little in this paradigm that should be alien to a social psychologist. And nothing alien should be found in our attempt to bring in birth order effects. In fact, we are all too familiar with these data, which have made many social psychologists shy away from individual differences as independent variables. It is not without some restraint, therefore, that we are broaching the subject.

BIRTH ORDER AND
INTELLECTUAL DEVELOPMENT

ROBERT B. ZAJONC AND GREGORY B. MARKUS

A confluence model is developed that explains the effects of birth order and family size on intelligence. Intellectual development within the family context is conceived of as depending on the cumulative effects of the intellectual environment, which, for the purposes of the model, consist primarily of the siblings' and parents' intelligence. Mutual influences, through time, on the intellectual development of the siblings are described by the growth parameter α. The confluence model predicts positive as well as negative effects of birth order, a necessarily negative effect of family size, and a handicap for the last born and the only child. The model explains several features of a large birth order study carried out on nearly 400,000 19-year olds. A number of implications of the model are discussed, among them the effects of age separation between successive children. In agreement with the implications, data on the relatively low IQ of twins and triplets are cited. Extensions of the confluence model to other social processes are discussed. The confluence model is examined for its usefulness in explicating a general class of social-psychological problems: the emergence of individual differences in a social context.

ROBERT B. ZAJONC AND GREGORY B. MARKUS · University of Michigan, Ann Arbor, Michigan. We wish to thank Hazel Markus, Michal Bester, and David Krantz for their suggestions and critique in the preparation of this manuscript.

Reprinted from *Psychological Review*, 1975, **82**, 74–88. Copyright 1975 by the American Psychological Association. Reprinted by permission.

A recently published review on birth order effects (Schooler, 1972) has all but put this field of research to rest. That article, entitled "Birth order effects: Not here, not now!" concludes that "The general lack of consistent findings revealed by this review leaves real doubt as to whether the chance of positive results is worth the heavy investment needed to carry out any more definitive studies" (p. 174). While the general tone of the article and of its conclusion is that of understated skepticism, the author ends the article on a cryptic, but as it turns out, rather prophetic note:

> On the other hand, I suspect that other investigators, including myself, will not be able to resist the temptation of taking a cheap bet on a long shot by collecting birth order data on their subjects as they pursue studies more central to their interests. And that is how we got into this trouble in the first place (N. B. Schachter, 1959). (p. 174)

Schooler's forecast about the continued fascination with birth order found solid confirmation in an extensive series of studies concerned with the effects of malnutrition on the intellectual performance of children born in the Netherlands at the end of the second World War (Stein, Susser, Saenger, & Marolla, 1972). As an unanticipated by-product of these studies, Belmont and Marolla (1973) discovered a strong relationship between birth order and intellectual performance. Even the most skeptical of birth order researchers will find it difficult to ignore these findings, which exhibit most interesting patterns and which are based on no fewer than 386,114 data points, the entire male population of the Netherlands who attained 19 years of age in the years 1963 to 1966. The Belmont–Marolla results are reproduced in Figure 1, which reveals the five following features: First, intellectual performance as measured by Raven Progressive Matrices declines with family size. Second, within each family size ($j \geq 2$, where j is the number of children), Raven scores also decline with birth order. Third, within each family size ($j > 2$), the last born shows a greater decline in intellectual performance than any other birth rank. For a given family size ($j > 2$), the decline from the jth -1 to the jth child is about three times greater than the average intellectual difference between adjacent siblings. Fourth, excluding last borns, intelligence and birth order are related by a quadratic function: There is a clear indication of a reduction in the rate of intellectual decline with higher birth orders, and there is an upswing for families of eight and nine. Fifth, the only child scores at about the same level as the firstborn of a four child family. The magnitude of these effects is revealed in the fact that the highest (firstborn of two) and the lowest (last born of nine) scores in the Belmont–Marolla data are separated by about two-thirds of one standard deviation.[1]

---

[1] Note that in the course of transformation, a constant of over 100 was added to the original Raven scores. Hence, the difference between the highest and the lowest mean in Figure 1 is equivalent to 17% of the maximum possible difference.

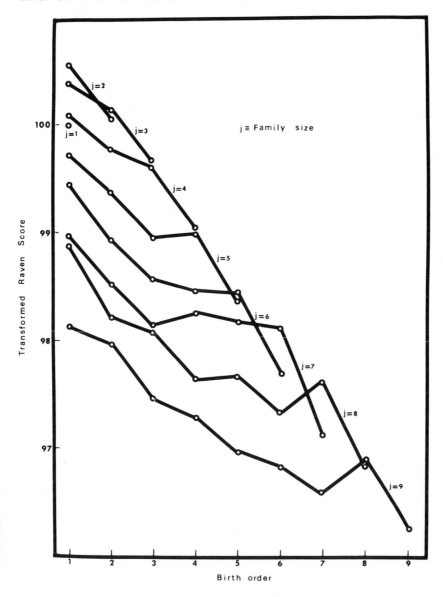

Figure 1. Average transformed Raven scores as a function of birth order (i) and family size (j), recalculated from Belmont and Marolla (1973). (The Raven scores were reported by Belmont and Marolla in terms of six categories from 1, high, to 6, low. For the purposes of the present analysis a linear transformation, $X_{tr} = 113.45 - 5.0047X$, was performed on these scores, inverting the scale so that increasing values now indicate increasing intelligence and setting the score of the only child at 100.)

There has been much theorizing about birth order effects in the past. Speculations about birth order effects range from ideas about uterine fatigue to economic factors (Clarke, 1916). Psychological explanations of birth order effects (Schachter, 1959; Sears, 1950) invariably invoke the relationship of the child to its mother. Since Schachter's (1959) work on affiliation, a vast array of consequences have been imputed to birth order. Studies can be found that relate birth order to visual acuity (Becker, 1965), artistic creativity (Eisenman, 1964), schizophrenia (Farina, Barry, & Garmezy, 1963; Schooler, 1964), pain tolerance (Gelfand, 1963), tolerance of frustration (Glass, Horwitz, Firestone, & Grinker, 1963), suicide (Lester, 1966), marital adjustment (Levinger & Sonnheim, 1965), conformity (Sampson, 1962), sociometric choice (Schachter, 1964), alcoholism (Smart, 1963), volunteering for experiments (Ward, 1964), social facilitation (Innes & Sambrooks, 1969), juvenile delinquency (Sletto, 1934), and even extrasensory perception (Green, 1965).

Most recent reviews of the subject matter, however, doubt whether birth order data, with their instability, warrant any theorizing at all. One investigator (Bradley, 1968) writes that,

> After a century of research on birth order it still appears necessary to know *what* differences occur before a theoretical model can be augmented. Once outcome variables are identified, explorations can turn to *why* differences occur. (p. 50)

The last paragraph of another article (Altus, 1966) is no more encouraging:

> The viewpoint embodied in this paper may be fairly summarized by a single sentence: Ordinal position at birth has been shown to be related to significant social parameters, though the reasons behind the relations are as yet unknown or at best dimly apprehended. (p. 48)

Belmont and Marolla (1973), with their large data set, were able to rule out socioeconomic status as a significant factor in birth order effects, but they did not suggest factors or processes that might have explained their interesting results.

This article offers an explanation of the five features of the Belmont–Marolla findings and of other data relating birth order and family size to intelligence. The explanation, which can be called the "confluence model," is based entirely on the mutual intellectual influences among children as they develop in the family context. The major emphasis is on the intellectual environment of the individual during the course of his development: more specifically, on the intellectual level of the individual's siblings and parents. The discontinuities associated with the lastborn and the only child are also explained.

Consider the intellectual environment in a given family at the birth of the first child. If we average the absolute intellectual levels in this family (assuming 100 arbitrary units for each of the parents and a value near zero for the newborn child), we obtain a value of 67. As the child grows, its intellectual level increases, and it contributes more and more to the intellectual environment within its family.

When a second child is born, there is a change in the intellectual environment. Suppose that the older child has by this time attained an intellectual level of 40; the second born then enters into an intellectual environment of (100 + 100 + 40 + 0)/4 = 60. (Note that the individual is included as part of his own environment.) Suppose a third child is born when the intellectual level of the firstborn reaches 50. If the second born is now at 30, the intellectual environment for the third born and for the remainder of the family is reduced to 56. In general, if such a pattern continues, successive children may be born into an increasingly inferior environment. But this consequence is not a necessary one. It will be shown that under some conditions the reverse is true. Regardless of what may be the relationship between intellect and birth order, however, it should be clear that, to the extent that some portion of the intellectual growth of children is determined by an interaction with the intellectual levels of their parents and siblings, larger families will be associated with lower intellectual levels because the larger the family, the larger is the proportion of individuals with low absolute intelligence.

We shall show that the five features of the Belmont–Marolla data can all be explained, that, with one specific exception, family size must have a depressing effect on intellectual level, that intellectual ability may under some circumstances decrease and under others increase with birth rank, and that age gaps between successive children play an exceedingly important role in the birth order effects found by Belmont and Marolla and by others.

The absolute intellectual level of a child, M_t, can be represented as a function of age. The sigmoid function

$$M_t = 1 - e^{-k^2 t^2} \tag{1}$$

(where t is age in years, and k is an arbitrary constant that varies with the type of intellectual ability involved) seems to represent intellectual growth quite well. The constant $k = .1$ characterizes intellectual growth measured by perceptual tests, while $k = .07$ characterizes the growth of verbal abilities, which develop more slowly. The constant k may also be used to reflect individual differences. Let us assume that this function changes with new additions and departures from the family, an effect which is summarized by a parameter α. Whenever the family configuration changes, thus altering intellectual environment, the intellectual growth functions of all family members also change. Thus, the only child grows until adulthood, according to the function $f(t) = \alpha_0(1 - e^{-k^2 t^2})$, and the firstborn in a family of j children develops intellectually by the same function until a sibling is born. When a brother or sister joins the family, the firstborn will shift from $f(t)$ to some other function $g(t) = \alpha_1(1 - e^{-k^2 t^2})$. A shift to yet another function, $h(t) = \alpha_2(1 - e^{-k^2 t^2})$, will occur when a third child is born, and so on until there are no more acquisitions to or departures from the family.

Figure 2 depicts this process of intellectual development for the oldest of two children. In this example the parameter α_0 for a child born into a childless

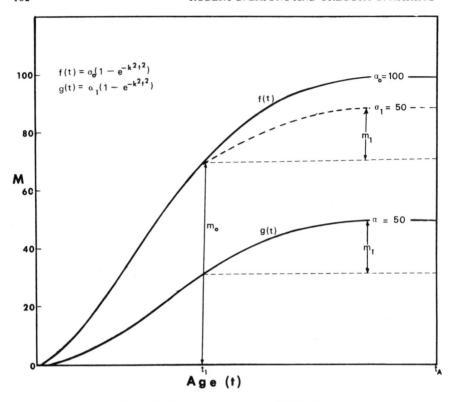

Figure 2. The α process in a two-child family.

family is assumed to equal 100; had individual i remained an only child until adulthood, t_A, he would develop according to $f(t)$, and his intellectual level would reach $f(t_A)$. When i is t_1 years old, however, there is a change in the family configuration, and because of the changed intellectual environment, i henceforth will develop according to $g(t)$, where $\alpha_1 = 50$ in this example.

The individual's absolute intellectual level M_{it_A} at maturity can be expressed as the sum of the two ordinate segments m_0 and m_1, as seen in Figure 2. The person's level at maturity cannot be estimated from $g(t_A)$ because $g(t)$ describes his growth only past the age t_1. The intellectual increment that accrues thereafter must be added to the accumulation at t_1. Hence, $g(t)$ must be adjusted for its intercept, and we have

$$M_{it_A} = m_0 + m_1 = f(t)|_{t_o}^{t_1} + g(t)|_{t_1}^{t_A} \tag{2}$$

$$= \alpha_0(1 - e^{-k^2 t_1^2})$$

$$+ [\alpha_1(1 - e^{-k^2 t_A^2}) - \alpha_1(1 - e^{-k^2 t_1^2})]$$

The growth parameter α represents an important aspect of this analysis, for it reflects the significant changes in the individual's intellectual environment. But it also reflects the interdependent nature of intellectual development within the family context. Because he is part of the given environment, the individual (with his changed intellectual growth rate) affects the intellectual environment of the siblings. The various α's within the given family are, therefore, interdependent and show the mutual intellectual influences among family members. It may be noted that the later these influences come in the individual's life, the smaller will be their effect—a feature of intellectual development that is also reflected by the variable asymptote formulation. For, given $M_i = m_0 + m_1$, the older the individual, the larger proportionally is m_0. And therefore m_1, which denotes the proportion of growth *after* a change in the intellectual environment, makes less and less of a contribution.

Figure 3 shows graphically how the intellectual levels M of the ith child in a family of j children change as new siblings are introduced at different times. The first child is born in 1950 and grows at a rate characterized by the parameter α_0. In 1956 a new sibling arrives, and the firstborn's growth parameter changes to α_1. Since, at that time the firstborn ceases to be an only child, the change from α_0 to α_1 is positive. This phenomenon will be discussed fully below. In 1961 a third sibling is born, causing a decline in the intellectual environment. In 1967 a fourth sibling arrives, reducing the level even further. The growth parameter in the function describing the intellectual development of the first child has thus changed from α_0 to α_1 (in 1956), to α_2 (in 1961), and finally to α_3 (in 1967). The firstborn continues to develop to maturity at the latter rate. Corresponding

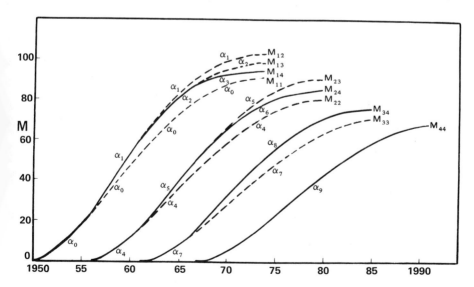

Figure 3. Changes in the intellectual development of siblings in a four-child family.

changes occur in the intellectual development of the other siblings in the family. Should some of the children leave home, or should the family acquire other members, for example, should grandparents join the family, the growth rates of all family members would be adjusted according to the new intellectual environment thus created.

Estimates of the α's may be obtained from information about individual adult intellectual levels and age gaps between siblings. To give an example using the aggregate Belmont–Marolla data, we know that the transformed Raven scores for M_{11} (the only child) and for M_{12} (firstborn of two) were 100.00 and 100.57, respectively, when they reached 19 years of age. Assuming a k value of .1 and a mean gap between firstborn and second born of 2 years, we obtain the following simultaneous equations:

$$M_{11} = \alpha_0(1 - e^{-(.1)^2 (19)^2}) = 100.00$$

$$M_{12} = \alpha_0(1 - e^{-(.1)^2 (2)^2})$$
$$\qquad + [\alpha_1(1 - e^{-(.1)^2 (19)^2}) \qquad (3)$$
$$\qquad - \alpha_1(1 - e^{-(.1)^2 (2)^2})] = 100.57$$

which yield the solution $\alpha_0 = 102.780$ and $\alpha_1 = 103.383$.

Different sets of α's would be found by assuming different gaps between siblings. Moreover, with true individual level data on intelligence and sibling age separation, a least squares estimation procedure would be employed.

The precise nature of the relationship between the growth parameter α and the pattern of gaps can be determined only if empirical information is available about adult intelligence levels of a large population for which gaps are also known. On the theoretical level, however, the confluence model predicts different birth order effects for different gaps. Figure 4 illustrates the significance of gaps between successive siblings. The gaps in Figure 4, top, are small, and each successive child comes into a severely impoverished intellectual environment (indicated by the thin broken line). If, however, the gaps are substantial, the intellectual level of the entire family is allowed to rise and the newborn comes into a more favorable environment. If the gaps are sufficiently large, as they are in Figure 4, bottom, the intellectual level actually might show an increase with birth order. This consequence of the confluence model is quite important because there are data that do, in fact, show a positive relationship between birth order and IQ (Thurstone & Jenkins, 1929; Willis, 1924). Because they constitute a major inconsistency with other results, data like these discouraged theorizing about the nature of birth order effects. Unfortunately, nothing is known about age separations between siblings in these studies.

Each graph in Figure 4 has been intersected at a point on the abscissa where the third born had reached some fixed age, the same in both graphs. In Figure 4, top, where the gaps are small, intellectual environment at birth of this third child is approximately equal to 50. In the bottom portion of the figure, with the gaps

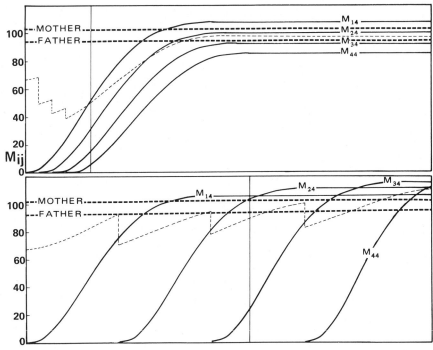

Figure 4. Intellectual environment (thin broken line) in a four-child family with small age separations (above) and large age separations (below).

extended, it is 85. It is also obvious in the top portion that the declines in the quality of the intellectual environments for each successive child are smaller and smaller. Had the number of children been extended and the small gaps preserved, eventually the newly born child would come into a *more* favorable environment than his immediate predecessor. Assuming 1-year and 2-year gaps, and, for illustrative purposes, setting the α parameters to be constant at 100, the environments at birth of nine successive children were calculated, and they are shown in Table 1. It is clear that these environments decline for the first seven children but that they begin to improve thereafter, revealing the quadratic trend that characterizes the Belmont–Marolla data. This is evident for gaps equal to 1 year as well as for gaps equal to 2 years, although in the second case the upswing comes somewhat sooner. Also, as already noted, the absolute levels of intellectual environment are higher when the gaps are 2, rather than 1, years. Note that the environmental patterns shown in Table 1 were obtained with α held constant. These examples, therefore, illustrate the fact that temporal configurations of intellectual levels within the family are in themselves capable of explaining much of the Belmont–Marolla data. Thus, seen in that table is a quadratic decline with birth order, and a decline with family size can be readily inferred. A more complete account of the birth order data, however, requires the

Table 1. Intellectual Environment at Birth

Mother	Father	Intellectual level of sibling									Intellectual environment
		1	2	3	4	5	6	7	8	9	
					1-year gap						
100	100	0									66.7
100	100	1	0								50.2
100	100	4	1	0							41.0
100	100	9	4	1	0						35.7
100	100	15	9	4	1	0					32.7
100	100	22	15	9	4	1	0				31.4
100	100	30	22	15	9	4	1	0			31.2
100	100	39	30	22	15	9	4	1	0		32.0
100	100	47	39	30	22	15	9	4	1	0	33.4
					2-year gap						
100	100	0									66.7
100	100	4	0								51.0
100	100	15	4	0							43.8
100	100	30	15	4	0						41.5
100	100	47	30	15	4	0					42.3
100	100	63	47	30	15	4	0				44.9
100	100	76	63	47	30	15	4	0			48.3
100	100	86	76	63	47	30	15	4	0		52.1
100	100	92	86	76	63	47	30	15	4	0	56.6

growth parameter α, which serves three functions: It allows for scale-congruent numerical predictions; it can reflect the handicap of the last born; and when calculated from data having gap information, it can be used as an empirical index of growth changes that are brought about by changed family configurations.

This theoretical result that gaps between children affect their intellectual level leads to the prediction that IQ scores of twins and of triplets should be generally lower than the population average. This is in fact so (McCall, Appelbaum, & Hogarty, 1973; Mehrotra & Maxwell, 1949; Thurstone & Jenkins, 1929). In agreement with previous studies, Record, McKeown, and Edwards (1970), for instance, report an average verbal reasoning score of 95.7 for 2,164 twins and 91.6 for 33 triplets. A comparison group of single-birth individuals earned an average score of 100.1. Admittedly, other factors may influence intellectual attainment of children of multiple births (Churchill, 1965; Lewis, 1963; Wilson, 1972). However, it is also a reasonable hypothesis that to the extent that a family with two nontwin siblings and a family with twins represent different intellectual environments, the intellectual growth of twins and nontwin siblings should reflect these differences. For families with two children, the intellectual environment at birth of twins is $(100 + 100 + 0 + 0)/4 = 50$. For nontwin siblings, this environment is $(100 + 100 + 0)/3 = 67$ for the firstborn, and it is obvious that it must be higher than 50 for the second born, regardless of how short the gap and how close to zero the intelligence level of the firstborn when the second child is born. Moreover, each twin constitutes a large portion of the other's environment, and hence twins are less likely than other children to interact with their parents or other siblings.

It should also be clear from the above illustrations that the level of mental development decreases with family size. Regardless of the size of gaps, the overall intellectual environment declines as family size increases because in larger families the proportion of individuals with relatively low intellectual development must be necessarily high. Large gaps help younger children surpass older children, and they may cause a reversal in the relationship between birth order and intellect.

Let us return to last and only children. It was clear from Figure 1 that intellectual ability declines systematically with birth order. But the last child constitutes a departure from this pattern showing a decline that is substantially greater than that of the intermediate children. This discontinuity can be seen better in Table 2 in which linear regression slopes were computed for the Belmont–Marolla data. In nearly every case the decline from the jth $-$ 1 to the jth child is considerably greater than the average decline for other consecutive siblings. Because of their small numbers in the population, birth ranks below five or six are often collapsed in birth order studies. Hence, the sharp decline for the last born as well as the quadratic trend, such as seen in the Belmont–Marolla data, may have been inadvertently concealed in past birth order research. There are some indications that the decline of the last born is not limited to the Dutch data. Altus (1965), for example, reports Scholastic Aptitude Test data that fit

Table 2. Decline in Transformed Raven Scores with Birth Order for Last-Born and Earlier-Born Children

Family size	1 to $(j-1)$	$(j-1)$ to j
2	–	.520
3	.270	.435
4	.257	.541
5	.253	.666
6	.250	.756
7	.146	1.056
8	.221	.811
9	.212	.625
Average	.230	.677

the above pattern. In a two-child family the decline from the first to the second (i.e., last) born is 10 for males and 20 for females. But in a three-child family, the decline from the first to the second child is only 1 and 3 for males and females, respectively. But again, the decreases in Scholastic Aptitude Test scores are 31 for males and 13 for females when the second and last children are compared in three-child families.

There is another interesting finding in the Dutch data. Consistent with other research on birth order (Damrin, 1949; Maller, 1931; Schachter, 1963; Breland, Note 1) the only child does not fit the general pattern: Rather than occupying the dominant position, he seems to reach a level of intellectual ability comparable to that of the firstborn of a four-child family. Breland (1974) wrote recently:

> Belmont and Marolla note that the mean score for only children does not follow a family size gradient. I have also observed this phenomenon . . . , but I have found no adequate explanation for it. That is, if scores tend to decline with both birth order and family size, why doesn't an only child follow this same rule and thus have the highest mean score of all? (p. 114)

Were we to extrapolate from the curve of the firstborns of families of various sizes, the expected transformed Raven score of the only child should have been 101.039. Hence, the score of 100.000 (see Figure 1) obtained by only children in the Belmont–Marolla study represents a decline of 1.039, similar to the declines of last children shown in Table 1.

The failure of only children to conform to the pattern of birth order results in the Belmont–Marolla research and in other studies has never been understood. Generally, the only child has been regarded as an anomaly among firstborns (Altus, 1966; Belmont & Marolla, 1973; Schachter, 1963). It has been suggested, for example, that many only children come from parents who either cannot or will not have more children. Neither condition, however, necessarily implies that the child will be handicapped. Many parents who cannot have more children give their only offspring more attention and affection than would otherwise be the case. And it is not a foregone conclusion that those who want no more than one child have a necessarily depressing effect on its intellectual growth. This leaves parents who cannot have more than one child because of a specific physiological or somatic cause that had detrimental consequences for the intellectual development of the first child, parents whose first child was such an intellectual disappointment that they were unwilling to have another, and parents whose first child was an unwanted one to begin with. It is simply not known what proportions of only children come from these various types of parental environments, and there is no good evidence that only children differ in their personality from other children.

There is, however, another explanation—not necessarily contradictory—that accounts for the depressed levels of intellectual performance not only of only children but also of *all* last children. Note that we are treating the only child as a last born and ignore that he is also the firstborn. The particular circumstance that accompanies the intellectual growth of last and only children is the fact that they do not serve as intellectual resources to their siblings. If a child does not know how to solve a particular problem, he is not likely to ask the youngest; if he is missing a word, it is not the youngest who will supply it; if there is an ambiguity about the rules of a game or a pattern of play, it will not be resolved by the youngest. In short, the last born is not a "teacher" and neither is the only child. It would be quite surprising if the opportunity to perform such a "teaching" function did not have beneficial effects for intellectual development. It appears from data reported by Belmont and Marolla that there is a fairly high penalty for being last and that the removal of this penalty augments intellectual growth even under otherwise relatively unfavorable circumstances.

The last born's handicap is, of course, reflected by the α's, which change with the changing family configuration. In fact, all changes in the intellectual environment are captured by the parameter α. Important new information may be obtained when we inquire about the way in which the parameter α relates to the manifest variables of birth order data. For example, the Belmont–Marolla results represent clear effects of at least three variables. It was noted in Figure 1 that the major factors of the Belmont–Marolla data were birth order (i) and family size (j). However, it was also evident that the last born and only children exhibited a decrement larger than expected from the overall pattern. Hence a third variable, λ, the last born's handicap (including the only child as a last born), also had an influence on the data. Finally, it will be recalled that the Dutch data were characterized by a quadratic trend. Given these three variables (i, j, and λ) and the quadratic trend, the transformed aggregate Raven scores of the Belmont–Marolla study are accurately described by the following regression equation, which accounts for 97% of the variance:

$$M_{ij} = 101.31 - .31i + .01i^2 - .37j + .48\lambda. \qquad (4)$$

The variable λ is equal to 0 for last children and to 1 otherwise. Once obtained, the α's may be examined for the relationship to these variables, allowing us to evaluate the relative influence of these factors on intellectual growth within the family.

In order to obtain the α's, we posited a demographically reasonable gap pattern to be used for heuristic purposes, in conjunction with the Belmont–Marolla aggregate data. The pattern assumed an average separation between siblings of 2 years except for the last born, who is separated from his closest sibling by 4 years. Since there are $1 + 2 + \cdots + 9 = 45$ α's to be evaluated and, in the aggregate data, 45 Adult Raven scores, the growth parameters are obtained exactly by means of simultaneous equations.

With 2- and 4-year gaps, when the 45 α's are regressed upon the four independent variables in Equation 4, 69% of the total variance in the α's is accounted for. Of the four variables, family size (j) was significant at the .001 level ($t = 8.16$) and the last born's handicap (λ) at the .02 level ($t = 2.46$). Of greatest interest, however, is the fact that the contributions of i and i^2, the two birth order variables, were not significant in this multiple regression analysis. Recall in this context that, according to the confluence model, the simple relationship between birth order and intellect may be either positive or negative, depending on the gap pattern among siblings (see also Figure 4). It is less important to know what birth rank the individual occupies than how many years separate him (or her) from older and younger siblings. Family size, however, is not an artifactual variable, and it *necessarily* depresses intellectual environment. As j increases, so does the proportion of family members with low absolute intellectual levels. Hence the intellectual environment is necessarily diluted. Within a given sibship, large age separations between successive siblings may partly mitigate the negative effects of family size. While it is for future studies to determine what might be the trade-off between family size and age separation, it is obvious that the counteraction of the ill effects of family size by age gaps is severely limited by the physical constraints of mother's age. The larger the sibship the greater need be the separation between successive siblings. But with the size of sibship held constant, the sum of age separations between children cannot exceed the mother's fecund years. And moreover, with large gaps the overall intellectual level in the family will suffer because each successive child must spend relatively long periods of his growth as the youngest of the family and suffer the handicap of the "last" child.

Conclusions

The model developed in this article was based on data collected from individuals who had been born during the Dutch famine of 1944. Apparently, no ill effects of malnutrition were found from these subjects when comparisons of intellectual performance were made between them and other cohorts whose nutritional resources were satisfactory (Stein, Susser, Saenger, & Marolla, 1972). It is, nevertheless, possible that the substandard nutritional conditions under which the Belmont—Marolla subjects, many of whom are from the above sample, were reared may have intensified birth order and family size effects without changing the overall intellectual level of the entire population. It is also possible that because the Belmont—Marolla data cover the *entire* Dutch population of 19-year-olds, socioeconomic biases may have contributed to the results. However, Belmont and Marolla do break down their results by socioeconomic class and still find significant birth order and family size effects. Moreover, Breland (1974) reports that the Belmont—Marolla results, which include males alone, are "remarkably similar to [his] observations in a study of almost 800,000 National Merit Scholarship participants" (p. 114) of both sexes. Since these applicants presumably come from a more homogeneous socioeconomic background, they constitute added support for the Dutch findings.

Second, the data on which the present analysis was made are scores of the Raven Progressive Matrices test, which is reported to be fairly free from cultural and environmental influences. We would expect, therefore, that verbal tests would reveal patterns of results that would be even more pronounced than those of Belmont and Marolla. The data analyzed by Breland (Note 1) are verbal in nature and they seem to be "remarkably similar." Interestingly, Altus (1965) found birth order effects in verbal but not in the quantitative scores of the Scholastic Aptitude Test given to University of California students.

With these cautions in mind, some answers to the puzzling questions of the relationship between birth order and family size on intelligence may be summarized. A parsimonious explanation of birth order and family size effects is obtained when we consider the nature of the intellectual environment within which children develop. This "intellectual environment" may be assessed simply by averaging the absolute intellectual levels in the given family. For particular cases, of course, we may wish to know the precise nature of the social interaction between the child and his siblings and parents. But for the purposes of gross analysis, it suffices to consider the interdependence among the children's intellectual levels and nothing more. This interdependence need not exclude parents, whose intellectual level may also be affected, however little, by the presence of children. Casual observations suggest that kindergarten teachers seem to regress in their verbal habits to the level of their charges, and parents of large families whose major interaction is with intellectually immature individuals may suffer a similar intellectual decrement. Note that had intellectual environment been represented not as an average but as a sum, family size would necessarily have *positive* effects on intelligence, a result that is contrary to the typical data in this area, including of course the Belmont–Marolla study. It is also counterintuitive to treat intellectual environment as a sum. An environment consisting of one person with an IQ of 150 is surely superior to one consisting of five persons each with an IQ of 30. It is nevertheless true that an environment of five adults each with an IQ of 150 is superior to an environment of just one adult with an IQ of 150, because a newly born child enjoys an average intellectual level of 125 in the first case and of 75 in the second.

This analysis leads to the conclusion that there are two primary determinants of intellectual growth, both embedded in the individual's intellectual development: One is the spacing between children and the other is family size. Large spacing is beneficial to the younger and detrimental to the older sibling, small spacing is less detrimental to the older but more harmful to the younger. Family size is damaging to all. In addition, the opportunity to serve as an intellectual resource is a factor that explains the only-child and the last-child syndrome. Neither has an opportunity to be a "teacher" of others.

The five features of the Belmont–Marolla data can be explained as follows: First, intellectual performance decreases with birth order but only when there is close spacing between successive children. Under these conditions each successive child has access to a less favorable intellectual environment. With larger gaps between children, this pattern can be arrested and even reversed. Second, according to the confluence model, intellectual ability decreases with family size because the larger the sibship the poorer the intellectual environment. Excluded from this generalization, of course, are cases where family size is increased by adoption of nearly adult children or by the inclusion of adult relatives (grandparents, aunts, uncles, etc.). However, when the family increases as a result of new births, the relationship between intellectual environment and family size will be *necessarily* negative. In contrast to their capacity of modifying birth order effects, gaps, however large, cannot overcome the negative effects of sibship size. Third, the last child shows a larger drop in intelligence scores because of a lack of opportunity to "teach." Fourth, the only child also suffers from the "last-child" handicap. Finally, the upswing in the Raven scores which were found for the lower ranks in larger families is a feature of combining exponential functions, and it occurs because lower ranks have an environment that includes fewer individuals with an intelligence level lower than their own, while this is not the case for higher birth ranks.

If the Belmont–Marolla data represent a general pattern—and Breland's (Note 1) data suggest that they may indeed do so—then it is clear from the above analysis that if one had a choice, one would want to be the firstborn of a family of two, with the younger sibling following closely in time. The sooner one acquires a younger sibling, the sooner one acquires the role of "teacher." If there already happens to be a firstborn in the family, then one would want to postpone another birth for a period of time, allowing the older sibling to gain a substantial level of intellectual maturity. If we ignore other factors that influence intellectual growth, then under the constraints of the confluence model, the parents' dilemma can be formulated. How should they select the spacing of children which is optimal (or fair) according to some criterion? If the gap is small, the firstborn benefits because he loses the "last-child" handicap early. But, the second born is brought into an inferior environment because of his older sibling's intellectual immaturity. The second can only benefit by a longer gap. But then the firstborn is at a disadvantage because he must spend a long period of his growth as the last born. Ignoring other factors, it is possible, in principle, to select a separation between children that minimizes (or maximizes) intellectual differences. It is equally possible to select a gap that maximizes the *average* intelligence level. The dilemma may be exacerbated by the fact that a high *average* intelligence may be obtained only at the expense of large differences between siblings. These speculative implications, however, must be substantiated by empirical information about the true effects of gaps. While the confluence model developed here leads to the derivation that, other things equal, gaps are beneficial, other things are seldom equal, and in reality the greater the gap the less the time siblings spend together—not only because the older is likely to leave home sooner but also because he engages in activities in which the younger cannot share. Hence, in practice gaps have optimal lengths. Studies that relate intelligence to gaps (Cicirelli, 1967; Koch, 1954; Thurstone & Jenkins, 1929) are based on samples that are small and do not control for family size and birth order. Hence, they do not allow clear interpretation. They do, however, show a trend that agrees with the suspicion that the relationship between gap length and intelligence is not monotone but that there is an optimal separation between children's ages.

The confluence model shows that environment, even in the restricted sense used here, may have powerful effects on the intellectual development of the individual. It goes without saying that other factors, such as genetic background and other environmental processes not considered here (such as child-rearing practices, unique experiences, etc.), all contribute to that development as well. But, although it is beyond the present means to determine just how much variation in intellectual growth is contributed by these factors and by those considered here, it is nevertheless worth noting that much of the birth order data can be parsimoniously explained by considering no more than absolute intelligence levels of siblings during the course of their development.

The confluence model need not be restricted to the growth of intelligence. Other processes that develop over time may very well have a similar form. The confluence model formulates an analysis of a social process in a way that resembles a river. It is a somewhat unusual river because even after having joined the general flow, its tributaries are distinguishable and do not lose their identities. As the separate currents, one after another, join the mainstream, they affect the general flow of the river and are themselves affected by uniting with it. The main feature of the formation is that *the individual is considered to be a part of his own environment.* And this environment is conceived of not as a static and stable background condition, but as one that changes over time, and one that is dynamically interdependent with its components. The individual is continually influenced by his own environment, and being thus influenced and changed, himself brings about changes in his environment *by virtue of his very own change.* These mutually dependent changes in the individual and in the environment occur instantaneously.[2] This interdependence is reflected in the simultane-

---

[2] It is possible to let α vary continuously instead of having it remain constant between successive births, as we did earlier. Let α be equal to some average of the intellectual levels of all of the children and adults in the given family at a given time t. Then the rates of intellectual growth, according to the function $f(t) = \alpha(1 - e^{-k^2 t^2})$, can be expressed by the differential equation $df/dt = 2k^2 t(\alpha - f)$. For a given intellectual level, M_i, we have $dM_i/dt = 2k^2 t[\alpha(t) - M_i(t)]$. Note that the last born's handicap would have to be represented by a separate parameter. The obvious advantages of a variable α formulation are offset by the fact that because α's now vary continuously, they can no longer be evaluated in relation to birth order, family size, and other variables that affect intellectual growth within the family if repeated measures of all individuals in the sample are not available. Since there are no such birth order data at present and since longitudinal information was not available for the Belmont–Marolla results, a continuously changing α was approximated by a step function where α changed whenever family composition changed.

ous equations employed in the analysis. Quantification of this process involves the assessment of the individual at each point of time along a specified dimension, for example, intellectual level, and of the ever-changing environment that emerges. What we mean by "environment" is the surrounding intelligence whose level varies as the participants enter, leave, and change. As we have seen, these temporal changes follow a *dilution* pattern.

To carry out this sort of analysis one requires a reliable measure of the individual quality under examination and a knowledge of changes in this quality over time. Intelligence satisfies these requirements, and hence a confluence analysis can be carried out. If growth rates or changes over time are *not* known, an analysis is still feasible if a suitable assumption is made.

What would the application of the confluence model look like in traits other than intelligence? Clearly, the relationship between birth order and personality development constitutes a more complex problem than the development of intellectual ability. One can, however, make some speculations. With regard to traits such as dependency, for example, it is a fair hypothesis that if the first child is in fact likely to be quite dependent on its mother (Sears, 1950), the access to the mother by children born later may thereby become restricted. Later-born children may, therefore, become less dependent than the firstborn because when young they learn to seek support from a greater variety of social sources, including other siblings. The development of dependency in the family context represents what seems to be a "preemptive" pattern: If earlier children are dependent, they force younger children into a situation that requires independence because the major social targets of dependence have been preempted. Other traits may show other patterns. Intelligence produces a "dilution" pattern. Affiliation, on the other hand, may be "cumulative," with each successive child having a greater variety of affiliative targets and developing, therefore, greater affiliative skills. Gaps may influence the development of affiliative behavior, since dissimilarity of ages may tend to reduce social contact. Status needs and dominance behavior are more likely candidates for a systematic relationship to birth order. If intellectual level tends to promote assertive behavior, and to the extent that earlier-born children are treated as "teachers" by younger siblings (and often given this responsibility quite explicitly by their parents), they are more likely to develop leadership skills.

Not only permanent personality traits but also temporary individual differences that characterize the individuals' relations to a group might also be analyzed as they emerge in a social context. Take group cohesiveness, which has been conceptualized traditionally as some function of the attraction of the individual members to the group. A group is formed. It has some goal. The original founders are naturally very committed to the group goal and are very attracted to each other. New members are recruited. At the time of joining, their attraction for the group is lower than that of the founding fathers. Therefore, by joining, the new member dilutes the "cohesiveness" environment of the group.

The average attraction in this group is now lower than previously, and if there is a second recruit, he shall join a "different" group than the first. And so on. We have a similar situation here as with intelligence and the family. To the extent that attraction to the group depends on all the attractions in that group in the same way that intelligence depends on intellectual environment, and if we know the rate at which attraction grows and what is the pattern of entries, we can make predictions about differences in attraction of individual members to the group and about overall group cohesiveness. The study of changing norms and of conformity in groups with changing memberships may also benefit from the use of the confluence model. In fact, Jacobs and Campbell (1961) report experimental data on the transmission of a norm over "generations" of subjects that show a dilution pattern. However, for none of these illustrations, except perhaps for the last, is it possible at present to perform an analysis such as was done for intelligence, birth order, and family size. Large sample data, together with solid information about rates of change, are required.

Reference Note

Breland, H. M. Birth order, family configuration, and verbal achievement (Research Bulletin No. 72-47). Princeton, N.J.: Educational Testing Service, 1972.

References

Altus, W. D. Birth order and scholastic aptitude. *Journal of Consulting Psychology*, 1965, **29**, 202–205.

Altus, W. D. Birth order and its sequelae. *Science*, 1966, **151**, 44–49.

Becker, G. Visual acuity, birth order, achievement versus affiliation and other Edwards Personal Preference Schedule scores. *Journal of Psychosomatic Research*, 1965, **9**, 277–283.

Belmont, L., and Marolla, F. A. Birth order, family size, and intelligence. *Science*, 1973, **182**, 1096–1101.

Bradley, R. W. Birth order and school-related behavior: A heuristic review. *Psychological Bulletin*, 1968, **70**, 45–51.

Breland, H. M. Birth order, family size, and intelligence. *Science*, 1974, **184**, 114.

Churchill, J. A. The relationship between intelligence and birth weight in twins. *Neurology*, 1965, **15**, 341–347.

Cicirelli, V. G. Sibling constellation, creativity, IQ, and academic achievement. *Child Development*, 1967, **38**, 481–490.

Clarke, E. L. *American men of letters, their nature and nurture.* New York: Columbia Univ. Press, 1916.

Damrin, D. E. Family size and sibling age, sex, and position as related to certain aspects of adjustment. *Journal of Social Psychology*, 1949, **29**, 93–102.

Eisenman, R. Birth order and artistic creativity. *Journal of Individual Psychology*, 1964, **20**, 183–185.

Farina, A., Barry, H., and Garmezy, N. Birth order of recovered and nonrecovered schizo-phrenics. *Archives of General Psychiatry*, 1963, 9, 224–228.

Gelfand, S. The relationship of birth order to pain tolerance. *Journal of Clinical Psychology*, 1963, 19, 406–407.

Glass, D. C., Horwitz, N., Firestone, I., and Grinker, J. Birth order and reactions to frustration. *Journal of Abnormal and Social Psychology*, 1963, 66, 192–194.

Green, C. E. The effect of birth order and family size on extra-sensory perception. *Journal of the Society for Psychical Research*, 1965, 43, 181–191.

Innes, J. M., and Sambrooks, J. E. Paired-associate learning as influenced by birth order and the presence of others. *Psychonomic Science*, 1969, 16, 109–110.

Jacobs, R. C., and Campbell, D. T. The perpetuation of an arbitrary tradition through several generations of a laboratory microculture. *Journal of Abnormal and Social Psychology*, 1961, 62, 649–658.

Koch, H. L. The relation of "primary mental abilities" in five- and six-year-olds to sex of child and characteristics of his siblings. *Child Development*, 1954, 25, 209–223.

Lester, D. Sibling position and suicidal behavior. *Journal of Individual Psychology*, 1966, 22, 204–207.

Levinger, G., and Sonnheim, M. Complimentarity in marital adjustment: Reconsidering Toman's family constellation hypothesis. *Journal of Individual Psychology*, 1965, 21, 137–145.

Lewis, M. M. *Language, thought and personality in infancy and childhood*. London: Harrap Press, 1963.

Maller, J. B. Size of family and personality of offspring. *Journal of Social Psychology*, 1931, 2, 3–27.

McCall, R. B., Appelbaum, M. I., and Hogarty, P. S. Developmental changes in mental performance. *Monographs of the Society for Research in Child Development*, 1973, 38 (3, Serial No. 150).

Mehrotra, S. N., and Maxwell, J. The intelligence of twins. A comparative study of eleven-year-old twins. *Population Studies*, 1949, 3, 295–302.

Record, R. G., McKeown, T., and Edwards, J. H. An investigation of the difference in measured intelligence between twins and single births. *Annals of the Human Genetic Society*, 1970, 34, 11–20.

Sampson, E. E. Birth order, need achievement, and conformity. *Journal of Abnormal and Social Psychology*, 1962, 64, 155–159.

Schachter, S. *The psychology of affiliation*. Stanford, Calif.: Stanford Univ. Press, 1959.

Schachter, S. Birth order, eminence and higher education. *American Sociological Review*, 1963, 28, 757–768.

Schachter, S. Birth order and sociometric choice. *Journal of Abnormal and Social Psychology*, 1964, 68, 453–456.

Schooler, C. Birth order and hospitalization for schizophrenia. *Journal of Abnormal and Social Psychology*, 1964, 69, 574–579.

Schooler, C. Birth order effects: Not here, not now! *Psychological Bulletin*, 1972, 78, 161–175.

Sears, R. R. Ordinal position in the family as a psychological variable. *American Sociological Review*, 1950, 15, 397–401.

Sletto, R. F. Sibling position and juvenile delinquency. *American Journal of Sociology*, 1934, 39, 657–669.

Smart, R. G. Alcoholism, birth order, and family size. *Journal of Abnormal and Social Psychology*, 1963, 66, 17–23.

Stein, Z., Susser, M., Saenger, G., and Marolla, F. Nutrition and mental performance. *Science*, 1972, 178, 708–713.

Thurstone, L. L., and Jenkins, R. L. Birth order and intelligence. *Journal of Educational Psychology*, 1929, **20**, 641–651.

Ward, C. D. A further examination of birth order as a selective factor among volunteer subjects. *Journal of Abnormal and Social Psychology*, 1964, **69**, 311–313.

Willis, C. B. The effects of primogeniture on intellectual capacity. *Journal of Abnormal and Social Psychology*, 1924, **18**, 375–377.

Wilson, R. S. Twins: Early mental development. *Science*, 1972, **175**, 914–917.

POSTSCRIPT

To
Birth Order and Intellectual Development

ROBERT B. ZAJONC

Since this symposium is concerned with priorities and paradigms, some remarks about these matters are in order. We should also, in conclusion, return to smoking and praying.

We are afraid that we have little wisdom to contribute about priorities. There are two sources of scientific priorities. Priorities may be dictated by the needs of society. But science also has its own needs, and therefore its own priorities. We are not really qualified to speak about the first source of priorities, nor are we able to generate a great deal of enthusiasm about the second. We do not have as yet a sufficiently well articulated theory in social psychology that can point to *the* next step in our research. We simply do not know what must be known in order to move ahead. The most that can be now said is that the top priority should be assigned to constructing a theory. We would also assign a high priority to a form of restraint that may be extremely difficult to exercise: research that does not resolve or clarify conceptual or theoretical problems, but seeks only to acquire new empirical information, should be suspended until there is some reasonable likelihood that a fairly general theoretical framework is in the making. There seems to be little purpose in flooding the journals with data that in 99% of the cases will turn out redundant, theoretically barren, or meaningless.

ROBERT B. ZAJONC · University of Michigan, Ann Arbor, Michigan.

In a way, the analysis we have presented here might well represent a paradigm, if by "paradigm" we understand a way of formulating a class of problems. What we have called the confluence model might legitimately be termed for the purposes of this volume, the *confluence paradigm*.

This paradigm helps illustrate, we hope, what social psychology (praying) can do for individual differences (smoking). It shows that it is quite all right, even fruitful, one might say, to pray while smoking. Here we agree with the bishop. Let us remind you, in contrast with the confluence analysis, about the typical approach in research and theory on the development of individual differences. What we typically have is a truncated paradigm, $y = f(x)$, which leaves a great deal out of what we all know to be a complex and extensive social process. The truncated paradigm of individual differences asserts that there exists some antecedent condition that extends over a lump of time and that can vary in "quantity" or "degree," and that the cumulative effects of this condition result in the development of the particular personality trait. For example, a lot of independence training (x) leads to high need achievement (y), or strict upbringing (x) produces authoritarianism (y), etc.

But what about smoking while praying? What can individual differences do for social psychology?

When the two assertions of the bishop are examined more carefully, we shall find no real contradiction there after all. Let us return to priorities. If the activity highest in priority happens to be praying, then the bishop is absolutely right in insisting that something may be lost in the piety and solemnity of the moment by lighting a cigarette. But if, on the other hand, smoking is the activity that is highest in priority, then the interference in smoking caused by prayer will surely be negligible. In fact, there may not be any interference at all, and the cigarette might even taste better, the smoker experiencing a feeling of safety that derives from prayer.

Similarly, there is no real contradiction between the assertion that individual differences have no *significant* contribution to make in explicating *basic* social processes and the assertion that these very social processes are sources of profound differences between people. If your priority is *basic* concepts in social psychology then we would certainly not turn to individual differences. This is not to imply that these variables are incapable of making any contribution to a social-psychological analysis. They can, but their role is secondary. An analogy can be made here to the properties of chemical elements such as melting point or expansion factor of metals, for example. These properties have no *basic* status in the analysis of matter. Yet they can be inferred from the basic knowledge of subatomic structure. Nevertheless, they are useful, especially in engineering, and they would be useful even if we knew nothing about the basic nature of these properties. Of course, with the knowledge of the subatomic structure underlying these "individual differences" among metals, their application becomes considerably richer and more efficient.

Hence, we are not going to knock applied smoking. No doubt, individual differences are quite useful in industrial, engineering, personnel, educational, clinical, and other varieties of applied psychology. In social psychology they have sometimes been employed as modifying variables or as parameters that set limits or qualifications on more general relationships. For example, suppose we have a hunch that there is a clear relationship between some social-psychological variables. But the function revealed by our data shows quite a bit of wobble. Sometimes this wobble can be reduced by plugging in individual differences.

Enough has been said thus far about individual differences. We imagine that there are differences of opinion about the role of individual differences in social psychology and about the ways of analyzing their development. So be it. Should you, however, wish to evaluate the opinions expressed here you shall make a more sophisticated judgment if you know that (a) Robert Zajonc was an only child, (b) Gregory Markus was a firstborn of two, and (c) Neither smokes.

CRITIQUE
Zajonc and Science: A Case Study

ALAN MOFFITT

Psychologists have spent the better part of this century legitimizing a scientific approach to the study of man, an approach that was supposed to clarify those questions which are answerable and exclude from analysis those which are unanswerable given current technological skills or fundamentally metaphysical. A number of forces both outside and inside the discipline produced this legitimization, such as the operationism of Bridgeman in physics, the philosophical and analytic sophistication of the logical positivists, the application of mathematical formalism to human behavior (for example, Estes' work), and the theoretical sophistication of learning theorists such as Hull and Spence. By means of a general commitment to empiricism and to thematic physicalism (Brunswick; see Postman and Tolman, 1959), psychology was able to achieve formal, substantive, and institutional independence from philosophy. It is now becoming apparent, however, that the gratifying sense of independence may have been premature. A number of recent events are pushing the community of scientific psychologists into varying degrees of realization that our traditional approaches to problems of theory and method have serious limitations, if indeed they are not fundamentally flawed (see, for example, Levine, 1974). These recent events like those earlier events which led to the legitimization of psychology as a science have come from both inside and outside the discipline. From outside the discipline psychologists have had to deal with Kuhn's (1970)

ALAN MOFFITT · Carleton University, Ottawa, Canada.

analysis of the sociology of science, with Chomsky's (1959, 1972) analyses of the adequacy of traditional forms of behaviorism and associationism as these have been applied to the analysis of human language, and with Wheeler's (1973) analysis of the applicability of empiricist behaviorism to large classes of social problems. From within the discipline of psychology, one particular sequence of events has an important bearing on the present discussion and involves the apparent failure of the scientific study of human behavior to produce fruitful results when applied to a particular area of concern within society. This sequence of events involves the optimizing or maximizing of human development through the practical application of developmental psychology during infancy and early childhood. During the last decade and a half, the study of infancy and early childhood has undergone explosive development, resulting in the creation of programs for infant and early childhood education that attempt to ameliorate the known and presumed effects of poverty (Gordon, 1972). These developments, of course, did not occur independently of an historical context. The history of the scientific study of human development during this century has been dominated by three major approaches, the psychometric approach during the early part of the century, the learning theory approach during the middle part of the century, and during the last decade a growing interest in cognitive development influenced both by the work of Piaget and Hunt and by comparative developmentalists interested in the behavioral and neurophysiological effects of early experience (see Mussen, 1970, for a review of the "current state" of developmental psychology). All of these approaches in one form or another have been concerned with the development of intelligence or adaptive functioning during infancy, early childhood, and later life. For example, the overwhelming response (positive and negative) to Jensen's (1969) claims concerning the genetic basis of intelligence bears witness to the continuing vitality of this topic and to the lack of consensus in virtually any area of debate, theoretical, methodological, or empirical (see Harvard Educational Review, 1969). Thus it is of no small interest that there seems to be reasonable agreement among developmental psychologists that nearly a decade after the initiation of Project Head Start we are only now beginning to understand some of the complexities involved in "promoting human development" through early childhood education (see Gordon, 1972). To put it more bluntly, American society decided to cash the blank check which was issued to scientific psychology earlier in this century in an area of major social concern, the psychological development of its children. Ten years after the event it is fair to say that the check bounced and we are still trying to find out why. It is obvious now, of course, that it was naive to expect that scientifically based early childhood education programs could "solve" a problem as complex as that of the psychological effects of poverty, in the normative sense of promoting adaptive functioning. By any measure, however, it is equally clear that these programs failed to produce lasting intellectual changes in children, or to produce differential changes in intellectual functioning in children when we had every scientific reason to expect differential development (Gordon, 1972). The recent development of interest in evaluation research is a testimony to the limitations of our earlier approaches, as are the attempts of numerous people to develop alternative approaches to the general nature of the scientific inquiry in psychology (Levine, 1974; Guttentag, 1971; Weimer, 1973).

It is with these considerations in mind that I would like to turn to a discussion of Zajonc's paper. Because it is an intellectual *tour de force*, it merits careful consideration. The discussion which follows is offered in the hope of initiating a consideration of the limitations of "doing science" in the manner exemplified by Zajonc's paper and during this process to indicate other options that appear to be under investigation at this juncture in the development of the science of psychology. The discussion will be organized in the following manner: first, a short sketch of Zajonc's model will be presented, followed by a critical consideration of his paper, both formally and substantively. Finally, some recommendations will be made concerning the development of alternative paradigms and priorities.

Zajonc's paper is both comprehensive and provocative. His intent is to systematize an area of research which he correctly notes has almost been put to rest (Schooler, 1972), the relationship of birth order to the development of intelligence. He develops a mathematical formalism which with a few basic assumptions is able to account for a massive data base (the standardized test scores on the Raven's Progressive Matrices of the entire male population of the Netherlands reaching 19 years of age between 1963 and 1966, or 386,114 data points). In addition, the model is intended as a characterization not only of the development of intellectual abilities within a social context but also holds promise as a general paradigm, which with different sets of assumptions can serve the development of theoretical models in such diverse areas as dependency, affiliation, assertive behavior, and group cohesiveness. Zajonc's model attempts to account for the following facts:

(1) Intellectual performance declines with birth order (as measured by the Raven's). [Presumably other measures of intellectual status might show a different pattern, but this difficulty is dealt with in terms of the value assigned the value of the parameter k in Equation 1 (see Zajonc's paper) describing the growth of intelligence as a function of age.]

(2) Intelligence scores also show a decline with family size.

(3) The lastborn shows a greater decline in intellectual performance than any other birth rank (about three times greater than the decline between adjacent siblings.)

(4) Excluding lastborns, the relation of birth order to intelligence is quadratic.

(5) Intelligence scores of first and last borns are depressed by approximately the same amount.

To account for these facts, Zajonc proposes an explanatory framework that is based ". . . entirely on the mutual intellectual influences among children as they develop in the family context." The theoretical construct Zajonc employs to represent these influences is "an average intellectual environment," represented by the parameter a in his model. As successive children are added to the nuclear family the average intellectual environment changes and a new growth function for intellectual development must be computed. The additional assumption that both first- and lastborns are denied the opportunity to experience the beneficial effects of acting as a "teacher" to other siblings is required in order to account for the intellectual status of these particular ordinal positions. As Zajonc points out, his model follows a dilution pattern, meaning that adding a sibling to a family dilutes or degrades the average intellectual environment. The result is that the intellectual development of all concerned is depressed (subject to certain limiting conditions related to point 4, above, having to do with the spacing of siblings). On the basis of the development of a mathematical formalism embodying these general assumptions, Zajonc quite successfully accounts for the data of Belmont and Morolla (1973), discusses the possibility of "optimizing" (maximizing or minimizing) the average intellectual environment, and at least tentatively suggests the possibility of extending the model and its assumptions to different substantive areas (as indicated above), subject to the availability of certain empirical information (estimates of the numerical values of certain parameters, which are necessary for the formalism to have valid empirical reference).

These accomplishments constitute a theoretical *tour de force* of a scope not often found in contemporary psychology. It is hard to give credence to Zajonc's disclaimer that he has little to contribute to a discussion of priorities for research when the very power of his example appears so fruitful. Thus, we will examine what Zajonc does when doing science rather than what he says about what he does. I would claim, in fact, that his approach exemplifies very clear research priorities and is paradigmatic of a particular approach to scientific psychology. It follows a clearly discernible pattern. First, one starts with a substantive area that has resisted coherent explanation. Second, one finds a sufficiently good set of data that meets certain formal constraints. These constraints are as follows: (a) the data domain must be empirically quantified in a particular way; (b) the data must be based on a large sample. Third, one establishes a mathematical formalism which satisfies certain conditions in order to account for the data domain. These conditions are: (a) the formalism must exhibit power in terms of the scope and efficiency of the primitive assumptions necessary to make it work; (b) it must exhibit parsimony in the sense of making no more assumptions than are necessary to account for the data domain; (c) it must exhibit fruitfulness (i) in terms of the possibility of extending the formalism to account for other substantive areas (that is, fruitfulness for future research), and (ii) in terms of implications for social policy.

A final characteristic of the paper under discussion that also seems to be a characteristic of the paradigm (although obviously not an essential component) is that of tone or "clout." Each one of these features will be examined in turn, and suggestions will be made concerning alternative ways of conducting a scientific study of human development.

The first issue of empirical quantification will be examined from two points of view, formal and substantive. Presumably Zajonc (and Belmont and Morolla, and the Dutch Army) feel that a meaningful index of intellectual ability must have the property of being quantifiable, and quantifiable in a way which represents very strong constraints on the notions of an empirical datum, and of intelligence. Specifically, the constraint is that the quality or dimension must be quantifiable as a ratio scale and thus capable of representation within the operations of an Abelian group (that is, the operations of addition, subtraction, multiplication, and division can be applied over the data domain). It must be suggested, however, that other approaches to the issue of quantification and scaling are possible. For example, much of the current debate concerning the validity of a developmental stage analysis of the course of cognitive-intellectual development revolves around whether an ordinal scale is an appropriate representational procedure (see, for example, Flavell and Wohwill, 1969). Zajonc's approach to intelligence, however, simply assumes a continuously varying underlying dimension as did much of the earlier literature in developmental psychology dealing with psychometric approaches to intelligence (Hunt, 1961). It is precisely these assumptions concerning the nature of the underlying dimension and of the associated assumptions concerning empirical quantification and scaling that have occupied much of the research activity of developmental psychologists during the last 15 years. In fact, the same set of assumptions has been used to demonstrate that variations in intelligence are determined not by the environment but by genetic factors (Jensen, 1969). Suffice it to say that if the approach embodied in Zajonc's assumptions has not been discarded altogether it has at least been seriously questioned (Hunt, 1961, 1967, 1969).

This issue has some serious implications for Zajonc's choice of a data base, that is, the Raven's Progressive Matrices. First, in spite of Zajonc's claim to the contrary there is little doubt that the Raven's is not a nonverbal test of intelligence (Jensen, 1968). It can also be regarded as a test of multiplicative relations from the point of view of Piagetian classification operations (Flavell, 1963). These intellectual skills presumably develop between the ages of 5 and 12 years, the so-called concrete operational period. It is highly questionable to base the kind of theory Zajonc develops on an intellectual skill which is known to mature prior to adolescence. There is little reason to assume that the intellectual products of cognitive operations at this period of development satisfy the characteristics of an interval or ratio scale. Similarly, the extent to which the intellectual operations involved in handling multiplicative relations are representative of intellectual skills in general during the preadolescent period is questionable. Furthermore, there is little reason to believe that these skills are at all representative of the intellectual abilities of mature adults. The general point is that the ontogenetic status of the particular intellectual skill under discussion (and/or observation) is relevant to the elaboration of individual differences within a social context, and should not be disregarded. Thus, Zajonc's concept of an "average intellectual environment" seems seriously flawed in three ways. There are serious reasons to doubt that his assumptions concerning the nature of the characteristics of the scale underlying the dimension of intelligence can be represented as an empirically quantifiable ratio scale. Second, even if his assumptions are acceptable in general, it is not clear that the data to which these assumptions are applied can be scaled in such a fashion. Finally, it is clear that the intellectual operations which characterize the Raven's test (multiplicative relations) emerge during the late preadolescent period. Yet Zajonc generalizes his discussion of intelligence to include simultaneous reference to the intelligence of newborns (near zero, presumably by definition) and to adults. If the generalization is not wrong, it is certainly questionable.

Concerning the second feature of this paradigm, the desirability of a large sample size, both Zajonc and Belmont and Morolla convey the very clear impression that large samples are good things for all the reasons that everybody knows. The sample size under discussion derives from the performance of nearly 400,000 19 year old males entering the army in the Netherlands between 1963 and 1966. Zajonc quotes another study by Breland (1974) using National Merit Scholarship participants with a sample size of 800,000. This is human science on a grand scale. Presumably, if one assumes that the dimension or quality under investigation (intelligence) varies continuously according to a normal distribution and is subject to ratio scaling procedures then he will want to have samples of this size to ensure generalizability and validity. Other strategies are available, however, and judging from the literature are just as acceptable in terms of both generalizability and validity. Much of the current research activity in developmental psychology derives from intensive observational studies of small numbers of infants or young children. For example, Piaget's (1952, 1954) longitudinal studies of the psychomotor development of his own children and Brown's longitudinal (Brown, Cazden, and Bellugi, 1968) studies of the speech utterances of a small number of young children must be regarded as seminal studies for the development of new research paradigms and priorities in developmental psychology during the last decade. From the slightly more distant past of developmental psychology in the area of learning theory, operant behavior modification has provided a seminal group of concepts sufficient to legitimize the intensive study of the individual organism. Presumably part of the impetus for the acceptance of these approaches is a growing awareness of the limitations of the traditional approach to the development of intelligence or adaptive functioning represented by the psychometric tradition. Zajonc's approach to this topic reintroduces most of the traditional difficulties simply by virtue of making the assumptions discussed above. Yet it is precisely these assumptions which are the subject of intensive scientific debate in developmental psychology. For example, the issue of whether cognitive intellectual development is continuous or discontinuous and the extent to which it can be accelerated or retarded through systematic or nonsystematic environmental intervention is by no means settled (Brainerd, 1973). Simply to assume, as Zajonc does, that intelligence is continuously variable and that its development can be explained entirely in terms of ". . . the mutual intellectual influences among children as they develop in the family context" disregards a number of central empirical and theoretical debates within developmental psychology during the last ten years. Minimally one would want some justification for these assumptions independent of the fact that they are required in order for the mathematical formalism to work.

Two virtues of a formalism are that it be powerful (as indicated previously, in terms of the scope and efficiency of the primitive assumptions necessary to make the formalism work) and that it be parsimonious (in the sense of making no more assumptions than are necessary to account for the data). Concerning the power of the primitive assumptions, the preceding discussion indicates that Zajonc's assertions concerning intelligence acquire scope and efficiency at the expense of ignoring other sets of assumptions, which at this point in time appear equally plausible. Zajonc's assumptions also achieve power at the expense of definitional clarity, and in some cases, at the expense of any definition at all. For example, in the classic style of the thematic physicalist, "intelligence" is defined operationally in terms of scores on the Raven's test. This type of move is no longer defensible without extensive discussion of whether it is a reasonable way to operationalize the concept of intelligence (note that the general requirement to operationalize theoretical constructs is not at issue here). Similarly, no independent definition (or even characterization) is given of another central construct in the theory, an "average intellectual environment." To define this construct in terms of the average of intelligence test scores of members of a family produces certain curious consequences. An "average intellectual environment" defined in terms of an average on test scores cannot be said to exert "intellectual influences" upon children, as Zajonc does. Furthermore an average of IQ scores cannot be taken as a valid reflector of process events occurring within the family. A great deal of energy has been expended in the area of early childhood education discovering that (changes in) IQ scores in almost no sense reflect process events between people (adults and children) in early childhood programs (Butterfield and Zigler, 1968; Soar and Soar, 1972; Ryan and Moffitt, 1974). There would appear to be equally little reason to assume that such scores are representative of anything occurring within a family context at the level of social interactions among participating members. Zajonc's notion of an average intellectual environment is uninteresting because it fails to characterize the concept of "intellectual environment" independently of its operationalization and because a large body of information suggests that it is not in fact a reasonable assumption. It also has the rather curious and implausible consequence of forcing Zajonc to attribute zero intelligence to the newborn child. This claim is either true by definition (and therefore, uninteresting) or it is silly, in the sense that the statement ignores a vast body of information on the study of infant development, which shows that the claim "infant intelligence = 0" is simply not true (see, for example, the relevant sections in Mussen, 1970). Similarly, it is worth noting in passing that the concept of "teaching," which is used to explain the relative intellectual deficit of first- and lastborn children, is simply undefined in the theory. Presumably an ordinary language interpretation of this term should suffice. Yet it is precisely this sense of the term "teaching" that is being called into question in experimental studies dealing with the training of cognitive concepts (Brainerd, 1973) and in the literature dealing with the effectiveness of the "teaching" of young children in early childhood programs such as Head Start and Follow Through (Gordon, 1972), or in the home situation in terms of the development of competence (White, 1971).

Zajonc's theory achieves parsimony in much the same way it buys power. To develop a formalism which will account for the Belmont and Morolla data with basically three concepts (the average intellectual environment, the temporal spacing between siblings, and the lack of teaching opportunity) achieves parsimony for the theory at the expense of the substantive credibility of the assumptions. Every assumption Zajonc's theory makes and every primitive concept he uses has been the subject of serious debate, criticism, and empirical investigation in developmental psychology during the last fifteen years. Furthermore, it is precisely the utility and plausibility of these assumptions that are now being questioned. As debates in other areas of developmental psychology have already indicated (Bever, Fodor, and Weksel, 1965a, 1965b; Braine, 1963, 1965), the rules for the application of Occam's razor (entities should not be multiplied beyond necessity) are not generally clear and cannot be satisfied simply by counting the number of concepts or operations required to account for a given domain by any particular theory. The fact that Zajonc's theory employs only three major constructs cannot be taken as evidence in favor of the theory. Indeed, such parsimony is sufficient to suggest the substantive implausibility of the theory.

Fruitfulness for future research and for social policy are primary criteria for the evaluation of the usefulness of any theory in social science. Zajonc claims that his theory is fruitful in both of these areas. Specific suggestions are made for the extension of the theory to the relation of birth order and personality development (status needs, dominance, dependency, affiliation), and also to ". . . temporary individual differences that characterize the individuals relation to a group . . ." (for example, group cohesiveness and differences in attraction). Closer examination, however, reveals a number of difficulties with these suggestions. Zajonc correctly notes that "to carry out this sort of analysis one requires a reliable measure of the individual quality under examination and a knowledge of the changes in this quality over time." But such information in the areas suggested as candidates for extension of the theory is simply not available. Zajonc, of course, is aware of this and quite correctly concludes that "... for some of these illustrations it is not possible at present to perform an analysis such as was done for intelligence. Large sample data, broken down for birth order, family size, and age gaps are not available, and there is no solid information about the rate of change of these behaviors during the course of the child's growth." The fruitfulness of Zajonc's model, then, is evidently fruitfulness in principle rather than in fact. By itself, such a consideration is not an argument against the model. Still, some doubts remain. What sort of empirical investigations would issue from an attempt to extend the range of the model? A massive effort would have to be mobilized simply to develop the instruments to quantify the particular quality under investigation, such as affiliation, dominance, or group cohesiveness. These instruments would then have to be applied to "... large sample data, broken down for birth order ... ," etc. The time scale and the financial expenditures required for these research projects to become even marginally feasible is simply staggering, to say nothing of the social context which this type of research requires in order to be carried out. Zajonc's proposals for extensions of the model are little more than a return to the type of empirical investigations that were popular during the psychometric test movement in a new dress. The reason that the empirical information necessary for the proposed extension of the model is not available is that a majority of the practicing researchers in developmental psychology stopped doing this kind of science a number of years ago precisely because the substantive returns on time and effort did not *generally* justify the large financial expenditures. It should also be obvious at this point in time that such large-scale testing, because it is used as a basis for social policy decisions (with or without validity), is socially offensive. To propose more of the same is to be blind to the social context of social science research. A further difficulty with the fruitfulness of Zajonc's model concerns treating intelligence, group cohesiveness, dominance, affiliation, etc., variously as "qualities," "traits," or "behaviors." It is sufficient to point out here that these are nonsynonymous terms and are not interchangeable without qualification. At issue here is the failure to specify the (theoretical) nature of the concept under investigation independently of the method of operationalizing the concept. Lacking such specification, one is free to multiply such "qualities" practically *ad infinitum*, limited only by imagination and the ontology implicit in ordinary language. The potential range of the model is thus absolutely vast, and is literally those qualities, traits, or behaviors for which we have names. One is entitled to a certain degree of skepticism concerning Zajonc's call for "top priority" being assigned to constructing a theory when the fruitfulness of his model depends *in principle* on the lack of theoretical specification of its major constructs.

Zajonc's model also demonstrates fruitfulness for social policy, specifically in terms of "optimizing" (maximizing or minimizing) the average intellectual environment. He does not suggest how this might be done in practice. However, in principle it would appear to be possible. Whether or not Zajonc would personally engage in producing such social policy recommendations is beside the point. Given the formalism he proposes and the availability of ". . . a reliable measure of the individual quality under examination . . ." (one might suggest Burros' *Handbook of mental measurement*), somebody will inevitably make such "optimizing" recommendations regardless of their validity. Furthermore, there is no reason to assume *a priori* that such recommendations will be in the form of maximizing the average intellectual environment. A Marxist might plausibly argue that a minimizing function (down to some level) would better suit the interests of corporate capitalism. In other words, it is in general no longer acceptable for a scientist (physical, biological, or social) to adopt a stance of value neutrality concerning the uses which can be made of his theories. Specifically, in Zajonc's case, it is not acceptable to make suggestions in principle concerning the optimizing of the average intellectual environment without at the same time discussing issues such as the validity and the limiting conditions of the theory, including range and applicability. As indicated at the beginning of this paper, much of the impetus for undertaking Project Head Start grew out of a theoretical framework concerned with the optimization of intellectual development (Hunt, 1961, 1967, 1969). Evaluations of the outcomes of early childhood intervention programs, however, have provided consistently contradictory or negative results (Westinghouse Learning Corporation, 1969; Gordon, 1972; Ryan, 1972). It is simply no longer acceptable for social or developmental psychologists to talk about the optimization of anything in the simplistic sense which Zajonc does when no *consistent* or *durable* gains in intellectual functioning can be produced either at the microlevel of individual programs or at the macrolevel of educational systems. It is abundantly clear that to deal with intellectual optimization or facilitation conditions of adequacy must be met on the nature of the intervention program, the nature of the evaluation procedures, and the underlying ontological assumptions of the theory that proposes optimization or facilitation as a corollary. The conceptual, methodological, and empirical difficulties in this area are almost hopelessly complex (Messick and Barrows, 1972). Furthermore, even if such optimization or facilitation is possible in principle, in practice it may be impossible to know whether the desired effects have been produced (Moffitt, 1974). Zajonc's suggestions concerning the optimization of the average intellectual environment are naive at best, and pernicious to the extent that they ignore nearly a decade of practical experience in this area by developmental psychologists.

The last feature of Zajonc's paradigm of scientific practice to be considered in this paper can be called "tone" or "clout." These terms refer to certain styles of expression that presumably are intended to produce in the reader a sense of the seriousness of the issues being considered. In view of the preceding considerations, this reader finds them both gratuitous and offensive. For example, in his discussion of the effects of temporal gapping between siblings (see Figures 5a and 5b in Zajonc's paper), reference is made to a child coming into a "severely impoverished intellectual environment" when the gaps between siblings are small, and into "a more favorable environment" when the gaps are larger. This point is pursued further in Table 1, in which the "intellectual environment at birth" ranges from 60.7 in a one-child family to 33.4 in a nine-child family with one-year gaps between siblings, and with two-year gaps from 66.7 to 56.6. Indeed, these figures suggest severe impoverishment. One could speculate that the emotional response of the readers of Zajonc's paper because they are professionals and therefore reasonably intelligent might range from relief at having none or only a few children (2.5?) to a deeper sense of the consolations of intellectual endeavor since this table "explains" why their life has been so difficult if they have made the mistake of having had a large number of children. One might wonder, however, whether the consolation amounts to much for the mother of nine faced with the fact of an average intellectual environment of either 33.4 or 56.6, depending on a one- or two-year gap between children. Zajonc's posturing, of course, is not to be taken seriously since it derives from the foolish maneuver of attributing zero intelligence to a newborn child. The objectionable tonal quality is continued in the conclusion of the paper. In discussing the intellectual interdependence of individuals in a family Zajonc suggests kindergarten teachers and parents of large families "suffer intellectual decrement" or "regress in their verbal habits" through prolonged interactions with intellectually immature individuals. In addition to being an offensive metaphor, it is factually incorrect. Observational studies of teacher–child interactions (Ryan and Moffitt, 1974) simply do not support a simple osmotic dilution model of social interaction. The metaphor is offensive because it assumes that the following dilemma covers the range of available choices: Do parents of large families become stupid because they have large families, or do they have large families because they are stupid? That Zajonc chooses the former alternative as his preferred explanatory model is of little consequence when the nature of the choices is considered. Furthermore, the implications of Zajonc's analysis are not politically neutral. Elsewhere in the discussion he suggests that large family size is "damaging to all," that is, intellectually damaging to all members of a family unit. Presumably it would be legitimate *ceteris paribus* to draw certain obvious inferences concerning birth control and population control, issues that are obviously political, social, and economic, as well as psychological in nature. The burden of the preceding analyses in this critique indicates that it would be illegitimate for Zajonc, or anyone else, to enter these debates with statements such as "Scientific studies of the effects of birth order and intelligence show . . . ," and proceed to draw inferences concerning the control of birth rate, family size, or population. Yet the superficial impression, the tone, is there suggesting that Zajonc's analysis had implications in these areas, if only covertly. These implications are unwarranted, as are the tonal qualities which suggest them. Yet it is in the conclusion of his paper that we find a discussion of the optimization of the temporal interval between siblings in order to optimize the average intellectual environment. How long it will take for someone to develop a "consulting service" using Zajonc's formulas and currently available IQ tests in order to "counsel" individual families or make recommendations concerning social policy is conjecture, but it probably will not be long. The ethics of such an enterprise, of course, would be questionable. Just as questionable, however, is the stance of value neutrality, which usually accompanies the way of doing science exemplified in Zajonc's paper. The point here is not that Zajonc must bear the ethical or moral responsibility of such extensions of his model. Rather, the point is that Zajonc's way of "doing science" represents a series of choices which are not only scientific but ethical and moral as well, and which have unacceptable ethical and moral consequences.

In conclusion, I would like to echo a theme from Zajonc's paper and return to smoking and praying. Like Zajonc, I have little wisdom to contribute about priorities and paradigms in social science, specifically in terms of recommending what we *should* do. Unlike Zajonc, however, I think as individuals we can make choices about the kind of science we can choose not to do. If Kuhn's (1970) book shows anything, it is that paradigms do not get disproved, they get discarded. This is another way of saying that science is a human activity encompassing a range of different alternatives, some of which are unacceptable for reasons that are extrinsic to the scientific questions involved. Thus, unlike Zajonc, I have a recommendation concerning a paradigm and its associated assumptions. "The paradigm" is Zajonc's way of doing science as exemplified in his paper, and the recommendation is this: Simply stop doing this kind of science. It is interesting, exciting, rewarding, and more-or-less legitimate, but if new paradigms and priorities are to develop individuals as individuals must choose to expend their energy, time, and creativity in developing new approaches, not in perpetuating older methods with known deficits. New paradigms and priorities require that we stop doing this type of science as a necessary if not a sufficient condition for their development.

References

Belmont, L., and Morolla, F. A. Birth order, family size, and intelligence . *Science*, 1973, 182, 1096–1101.

Bever, T. G., Fodor, J. A., and Weksel, W. Theoretical notes on the acquisition of syntax: A critique of "contextual generalization." *Psychological Review*, 1965, 72, 467–482. (a)

Bever, T. G., Fodor, J. A., and Weksel, W. Is linguistics empirical? *Psychological Review*, 1965, 72, 493–500. (b)

Braine, M. D. S. On learning the grammatical order of words. *Psychological Review*, 1963, 70, 323–348.

Braine, M. D. S. On the basis of phrase structure: a reply to Bever, Fodor and Weksel. *Psychological Review*, 1965, 72, 483–492.

Brainerd, C. Neo-piagetian training experiments revisited: Is there any support for the cognitive-developmental stage hypothesis? *Cognition*, 1973, 2, 349–370.

Breland, H. M. Birth order, family size and intelligence. *Science*, 1974, 184, 114.

Brown, R., Cazden, C., and Bellugi, U. The child's grammar from I to III, in Hill, J. P. (ed.), *The Minnesota symposium on child psychology*, pp. 28–73. Minneapolis: Univ. of Minnesota Press, 1968.

Butterfield, E., and Zigler, E. Motivational aspects of changes in IQ test performance of culturally disadvantaged nursery school children. *Child Development*, 1968, 39, 1–14.

Chomsky, N. A review of B. F. Skinner's "Verbal Behavior." *Language*, 1959, 35, 26–58.

Chomsky, N. Psychology and ideology. *Cognition*, 1972, 1, 11–46.

Flavell, J. *The developmental psychology of Jean Piaget*. New York: Van Nostrand, 1963.

Flavell, J., and Wohwill, J. Formal and functional aspects of cognitive development, in Elkind, D., and Flavell, J. (eds.), *Studies in cognitive development: Essays in honor of Jean Piaget*, pp. 67–120. New York: Oxford Univ. Press, 1969.

Gordon, I. (ed.). *Early childhood education* (the seventy-first yearbook of The National Society for the Study of Education). Chicago: Univ. of Chicago Press, 1972.

Guttentag, M. Models and methods in evaluation research. *Journal of the Theory of Social Behavior*, 1971, 1, 76–95.

Harvard Educational Review. *Environment, heredity and intelligence*. June 1969.

Hunt, J. McV. *Intelligence and experience*. New York: Ronald Press, 1961.

Hunt, J. McV. The psychological basis of using preschool enrichment as an antidote for cultural deprivation, in Passow, H., Goldberg, M., and Tannenbaum, A. (eds.), *Education for the disadvantaged child*, pp. 307–326. New York: Holt, Rinehart and Winston, 1967.

Hunt, J. McV. *The challenge of incompetence and poverty*. Urbana: Univ. of Illinois Press, 1969.

Jensen, A. R. Social class and verbal learning, in Deutsch, M., Katz, I., and Jensen A. (eds.), *Social class, race, and psychological development*, pp. 115–174. New York: Holt, Rinehart and Winston, 1968.

Jensen, A. R. How much can we boost IQ and scholastic achievement? *Harvard Educational Review*, 1969, 39, 1–123.

Kuhn, T. S. *The structure of scientific revolutions*, 2nd edition. Chicago: Univ. of Chicago Press, 1970.

Levine, M. Scientific method and the adversary model: Some preliminary thoughts. *American Psychologist*, September 1974, 661–677.

Messick, S., and Barrows, T. S. Strategies for research and evaluation in early childhood education, in Gordon, I. (ed.), *Early childhood education* (the seventy-first yearbook of The National Society for the Study of Education). Chicago: Univ. of Chicago Press, 1972.

Moffitt, A. R. Schools without curricula: Evaluation of some early childhood programs. Paper presented at the meetings of the Canadian Psychological Association, Windsor, Ontario, June 1974.

Mussen, P. (ed.). *Carmichael's manual of child psychology*, 3rd edition, Vols. 1 and 2. New York: Wiley, 1970.

Piaget, J. *The origins of intelligence in children*. New York: Int. Univ. Press, 1952.

Piaget, J. *The construction of reality in the child*. New York: Basic Books, 1954.

Postman, L., and Tolman, E. C. Brunswick's probabilistic functionalism, in Koch, S. (ed.), *Psychology: A study of a science*, Vol. 1, pp. 502–564. New York: McGraw-Hill, 1959.

Ryan, T. J. (ed.). *Poverty and the child: A Canadian study.* Toronto: McGraw-Hill Ryerson Ltd., 1972.

Ryan, T. J., and Moffitt, A. R. Evaluation of preschool programs. *The Canadian Psychologist*, 1974, **15**, 205–219.

Schooler, C. Birth order effects: Not here, not now! *Psychological Bulletin*, 1972, **78**, 161–175.

Soar, R. S., and Soar, R. M. An empirical analysis of selected Follow-Through programs, in Gordon, I. (ed.), *Early childhood education* (the seventy-first yearbook of The National Society for the Study of Education). Chicago: Univ. of Chicago Press, 1972.

Weimer, W. Psycholinguistics and Plato's paradoxes of the Meno. *American Psychologist*, 1973, **28**, 15–33.

Wheeler, H. (Ed.) *Beyond the punitive society.* San Francisco: W. H. Freeman & Co., 1973.

White, B. L., and Watts, J. C. *Experiences and environment:* Vol. I. Prentice Hall: Englewood Cliffs, N.J., 1973.

CRITIQUE
On Zajonc and Markus's
"Birth Order and Intellectual Development"

WOLFGANG STROEBE

Prior to my discussion of Dr. Zajonc's interpretation of the Belmont and Morolla (1973) data, I would like to make a few comments on that study. Their data are truly beautiful, and the birth order effect appears to be quite dramatic. However, with 386,114 subjects, even minor effects may show up very nicely. It would therefore be interesting to know in terms of raw scores what differences existed on average between adjoining sibling positions for a given family size. Unfortunately, the original study never uses raw scores, but what they call "class scores," that is, a classification applied to the raw scores by the Dutch military. It is therefore impossible to evaluate the seriousness of the disadvantage of children who have higher ordinal positions. It would appear to make a differ-ence, whether the disadvantage due to higher ordinal positions measures in terms of .10 or 10.0 IQ points.

This does not affect the value of the model. The real contribution of such a model is the specific assumptions on which it is based, which in themselves provide interesting hypotheses to be tested. The 1950 studies on physical and social deprivation suggested a strong relationship between environment and intelligence. But a further question is raised by Zajonc's assumptions that the average family intelligence constitutes the most important part of the environ-ment. How does this average family intelligence get transmitted to the child?

WOLFGANG STROEBE · Universität Marburg, Marburg, Germany.

What physical or social factors mediate this average intelligence? Knowledge of the particular nature of these mediating processes would provide an understanding of the different sized gaps at different age levels. It might also elucidate what exactly is derived by both older and younger siblings in the teacher–pupil relationship. Are the benefits purely intellectual, or are they motivational as well?

Dr. Zajonc's explanation of the Belmont and Morolla findings rests on the following assumptions:

(1) A child's intellectual development is affected by the average intellectual level existing in the family. The average intellectual level is not only affected by the number of children in a given family, but also by the "gaps" between the children, since the intellectual level increases as children grow up.

(2) A child serves as an intellectual resource for the next younger sibling and gains intellectually through his teaching.

These assumptions specify the variables assumed to mediate the relationship between birth order and intelligence. There are no data for any of these variables. There are no data showing the relationship between intellectual environment and intellectual development. There are no data regarding the gaps. In other words, Dr. Zajonc did not know what age intervals existed between the subjects of the study and he had to make assumptions. It is also merely an assumption that the assumed teacher–pupil relationship is typical for siblings of adjoining ages. Although Dr. Zajonc's assumptions seem to be quite reasonable, other assumptions might have been as reasonable. The fact, therefore, that his model accounts for 97% of the variance only demonstrates that the relationship between birth order and intellectual development *could have been* as Dr. Zajonc assumed. It *does not prove* at all the validity of his account of the Belmont and Marolla data.

However, Dr. Zajonc has developed an interesting and very unusual model with a wide variety of possible applications. His application to these intelligence data is to be considered just a description of the feasibilities of his model. It is actually my hunch that the confluence paradigm will be with us long after people have forgotten that it was initially applied to the question of birth order and intellectual development.

"The main feature of the paradigm," as Zajonc said, "is that the individual is *considered to be part of his own environment.* And this environment is conceived of not as a static, stable background condition, but as one that changes over time, and one that is dynamically interdependent with its components. The individual is continually influenced by his own environment, and being thus influenced and changed, himself brings about changes in his environment by virtue of his very own change" (pp. 173, emphasis added).

This, I think, is the kind of analysis social psychologists ought to be doing, instead of looking at the impact of the behavior of person A on person B, or the other way round. I can see this type of analysis applied to a wide variety of group problems, like group problem solving. One of the perfect examples of a "dilution pattern" seems to be the Jacobs and Campbell (1961) study, "Perpetuation of an arbitrary tradition through several generations of a laboratory microculture."

References

Belmont, L., and Marolla, F. A. Birth order, family size, and intelligence. *Science*, 1973, **182**, 1096–1101.

Jacobs, R. C., and Campbell, D. T., Perpetutation of an arbitrary tradition through several generations of laboratory microculture *Journal of Abnormal and Social Psychology*, 1961, **62**, 649–658.

ON THE ARCHITECTURE
OF INTERSUBJECTIVITY

RAGNAR ROMMETVEIT

1. Introduction

The Harvard–M.I.T. brand of psycholinguistics came into being as the love child of generative grammar and *individual* (as opposed to *social*) cognitive psychology. And transformational-generative linguistics, it was argued, represented a return to a prepositivistic view of science (Fodor and Garrett, 1966). Based on this philosophy, the idea of linguistic competence came to resemble the idea of ideal physical events (e.g., bodies falling freely through perfect vacua).

Fodor and Garrett's reference to perfect vacua is very deceptive, however. It is certainly true that Newton was concerned with ideal physical events, but his most impressive insight was that gravity is based on an attraction between bodies, that is, an *interaction*. A science of psycholinguistics based on the utterance *in vacuo* represents, therefore, actually a return to a prepositivistic, pre-Newtonian, and scholastic approach. Its obvious shortcomings cannot be remedied by additional scholastics, such as adding a set of increasingly complicated auxiliary hypotheses concerning contexts onto an explication of "deep structures" or "propositional form and content" of sentences *in vacuo* (see Chomsky, 1972; Fillmore, 1972; Lakoff, 1972).

The conceptual framework suggested in the present paper is based upon the assumption that language is a thoroughly and genuinely social phenomenon. The

RAGNAR ROMMETVEIT · University of Oslo, Oslo, Norway.

notion of an utterance deprived of its context of human interaction is as absurd as the notion of a fall deprived of the gravitational field within which it takes place. *What is made known* is an act of verbal communications can therefore be properly assessed only if we venture to explore the architecture of intersubjectivity within which it is embedded.

2. The Skeleton of Intersubjectivity

Communication aims at transcendence of the "private" worlds of the participants. It sets up what we might call "states of intersubjectivity." In order to explore such states, we need to start with a system of coordinates such as the one indicated in Figure 1. These coordinates may be defined in terms of three dimensions: the time at which the act of communication takes place, its location, and (in the case of spoken language) the identification of listener by speaker and vice versa. The I and YOU constitute the two poles of potential states of intersubjectivity, and they are immediately given in terms of an unequivocal *direction of communication.* Whatever is shared, presupposed, or assumed to be known already is hence shared, presupposed, or assumed by the I and the YOU within a temporarily shared HERE and NOW.

The intersubjectivity established HERE and NOW of a dialog will take on very different denotative extensions depending on what constitutes the topic of discourse. The spatial-temporal-social coordinates of states of intersubjectivity can therefore not be assessed independently of each other, nor—as we shall see—independently of *metacontracts* of communication endorsed by the participants in the communicative act.

3. On Complementarity of Intentions and Control of the Temporarily Shared Social World

In order to explore some of the basic prerequisites for intersubjectivity, let us now briefly examine what happens under certain conditions of serious communication disorders. Consider, for instance, the so-called *homonym symptom* of the schizophrenic. The patient may start out talking about a grand party, and he says:

(I) I too was invited, I went to the ball . . and it rolled and rolled away. . . .

His intention in this case is to make known something about a ball to which he was invited and what happened at that ball. We, the listeners, immediately comprehend what is said because we are spontaneously decoding it in accordance with the speaker's intention and *on his, the speaker's, premises.* At the moment of his pause, we thus very likely expect him to continue with "and

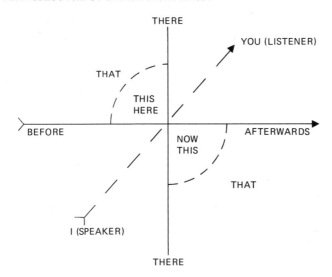

Figure 1. The spatial-temporal-interpersonal coordinates of the act of speech.

then . . ." or some such expression: We know he has been invited to that ball, he is going there, and we expect him to make known what happens next.

It is precisely at this moment, however, that our firmly rooted, though entirely intuitive and unreflective, assumption concerning complementarity between *the act of speaking and that of listening* is disconfirmed. Having uttered "*the ball* . . ." the schizophrenic seems to stumble, in a way. His act of speech is disrupted, his story does not continue in accordance with what he initially intended to make known. He pauses, apparently bewildered by what he himself has just uttered.

His answer represents a perfectly rational solution to this riddle, however, once we endorse *his* basic distrust in intersubjectivity and accept the riddle as such. The spoken form "ball" is, of course, also the word for a very familiar object: It refers to a toy having a spherical shape, which is used in play or athletic games. The word ball is in fact used more to refer to such objects than in the way the schizophrenic had intended to use it initially on this occasion. What he says after the pause about rolling is thus in some respect a "publicly" plausible completion of his act of speech. Instead of finishing what he intended to say, he tries to complete the sentence with a phrase that *may* have made something known to a listener who was not bound to his premises. His pause after having uttered "the ball" thus signals lack of control of the intersubjectively established HERE and NOW.

Such control is under normal conditions unequivocally linked to the *direction of communication*: The speaking "I" has the privilege of pointing out the objects, events, and states of affairs to enter the field of shared attention. Which of all possible entities of an experientially shared situation will be introduced and enter the slots of THIS, HERE and THAT, THERE of the formal skeleton of intersubjectivity is thus in principle determined by the speaker. The same holds true for any topic, whether introduced by deixis, by identifying descriptions, or by other means. The listener has to accept and engage in whatever social reality is introduced.

And this is exactly what *we* do when listening to (I). As the speaker is uttering "... it," we spontaneously make sense of what he is saying in terms of the ball to which he has been invited. The full-fledged act of verbal communication is thus, under normal conditions, based upon a reciprocally endorsed and spontaneously fulfilled contract of complementarity: *Encoding* is tacitly assumed to involve *anticipatory decoding.* It is taken for granted that speech is continuously *listener oriented.* The speaker therefore monitors his speech in accordance with his assumptions about the extent of social world and strategies of categorization which are shared by him and his listener. Conversely—and on precisely those premises—*decoding* is tacitly assumed to be *speaker oriented,* aiming at a reconstruction of what the speaker intends to make known.

Intersubjectivity has thus in some sense to be taken for granted in order to be achieved. It is based on mutual faith in a shared social world. Thus decentration in both interactants is a necessary basis for this reciprocally endorsed contract of complementarity. Wittgenstein's comment (1968, p. 108) that language is "habit and institution" certainly holds true for the fundamental complementarity inherent in acts of communication: What George Herbert Mead coined "taking the attitude of the other" (Mead, 1950) constitutes such a basic and pervading feature of normal social interaction that it remains entirely inaccessible to the reflective consciousness of the speaking I and the listening YOU.

4. On Metacontracts and Variant Premises for Intersubjectivity

In order to gain some more insight into the subtle interplay between *what is said* and *what is taken for granted* we are therefore forced to transcend the traditional paradigms of substitution within linguistics and literary text analysis. These paradigms are all intralinguistic, in that one segment of discourse is being replaced by another in order to examine similarities and differences between the two. Contractual and partly institutionalized aspects of intersubjectivity are, in such an analysis, of secondary concern if they are of any concern at all. In order to bring such aspects into focus, we have to engage in systematic substitutions of the I–YOU coordinate of the act of communication (see Figure 1).

Let us now transplant the incoherent segment of the schizophrenic's story about the party into an entirely different setting. This time, we are listening to a poet as he is reciting:

(I') I too was invited,
I went to the ball ...
and it rolled
and rolled away ...

Our immediate reactions on this occasion are entirely devoid of the kind of bewilderment we experienced when listening to the former incoherent story. When asked what is conveyed by (I) as part of a poem, some of us may perhaps answer that we honestly do not quite know. Others may express a feeling of having grasped its meaning intuitively and emotionally, without being able to put it into words. Still others may venture to verbalize the feeling that has been conveyed to them by the poet. They may maintain, for instance, that he has managed to portray conditions of human existence when our grip of "ordinary reality" is wavering because we discover that things are not what we firmly expected them to be.

Consider, next, what may happen when newspaper headlines about, for example, the war in Vietnam, the increase in sales of cosmetics, the famine in India, and the stabilization of the European stockmarket are brought together in a collage poem. Since firmly and unreflectively we assume that the poet wants to convey somethings over and beyond what is made known by professional news reporters, our habitual and desensitized orientation toward daily mass media novelties is immediately abolished. To the extent that the author indeed has constructed the collage on that assumption, our expectation is institutionally founded and essentially correct. It is, moreover, *eo ipso* self-fulfilling.

Spontaneous and contextually appropriate interpretations in such different settings testify to a capacity to adopt the attitude of different "others." The general paradigm of complementarity thus allows for variant premises for inter-subjectivity which can vary according to the institution and situation. Such premises have to do with what is unreflectively taken for granted, with the basic WHY of communication and what Ducrot (1972) has coined "les sous entendus" and "l'implicité d'enoncé." An utterance *in vacuo* can therefore only be examined with respect to its message *potential.* Its potential meaning must be considered by examining these *drafts of contracts concerning shared categorization and attribution,* which are conveyed in the speech act itself.

The significance of variant premises for intersubjectivity is more clearly illustrated if we transplant newspaper headlines into a book of poetry, segments of a patriotic speech into an academic lecture, excerpts from medical reports into a funeral sermon, and fragments of an informal conversation between two friends into an interpersonal setting characterized by an unequivocal master-to-servant relationship. The main lesson to be learned from such transplantations is very simple: What is made known is dependent on what kind of *metacontract* of communication has been tacitly and reciprocally endorsed in each particular case.

5. On Anticipatory Comprehension (Vorverständigung)

Hermeneutic philosophers of language (Apel, 1968) and scholars of literature (Wellek, 1966) argue that whatever is made known in acts of verbal communications has to be conceived of as expansions and/or modifications of a preestablished shared *Lebenswelt*. Let us now examine how their concept of *anticipatory comprehension* (Vorverständigung) may be explicated in terms of the logic of information theory.

The main features of the latter can be exhibited by means of a very simple question-and-answer task. An object is located in one of the cells of a square consisting of sixteen cells (see Figure 2). I know where it is, but you do not. Your task is then simply to find out in which of the 16 cells the object is located, and you are requested to do so by means of questions that can be answered by either yes or no. The dialogue may hence proceed as follows:

(1) "Is it in the right half?" "No."
(2) "Is it in the upper half of the left half?" "Yes."
(3) "Is it in the right half of the upper half?" "No."
(4) "Is it in the upper half of the left half?" "No."

What has been made known at this stage is that the object is located in cell X, and the entire dialogue can in this case be described as a sequentially arranged reduction of an initial state of uncertainty on your part. This initial state corresponds to the entire square in Figure 2: You know at the outset that the object is located in some as yet not identified cell of that square, that it may be located in any one of the sixteen cells. My first answer serves to eliminate one-half of that entire area, my second answer eliminates one-half of the remaining half of it, and so on. Let us deliberately ignore these purely quantitative aspects, however, and turn to the dialogue as such.

Notice, first of all, that the word "square" does not enter our dialogue at all, despite the fact that at every single stage the message transmission is based upon the assumption that the two of us have the same particular square in mind. We assume—correctly, and by a tacitly endorsed contract—that we are talking about the same square. This constitutes the *initially shared, unquestioned, or free information* onto which your very first question is nested or *bound*. Whether I have shown you a visual display of the square or carefully described it to you in advance is of no particular significance in the present context. It constitutes in either case an initially shared social reality and a *sine qua non* for further meaningful discourse on the location of the object.

This is not only true of the unmentioned square, however, but also of, for

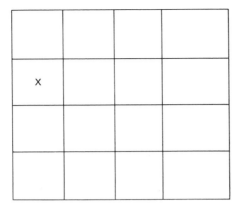

Figure 2. Square for the question-and-answer game.

example, *the right half of it* introduced in question (1)—or rather *the left half* implied by my answer—when it from stage (3) on is no longer mentioned. Notice, thus, how my answer at every successive stage is nested onto what at that particular stage has already been established as a shared social reality (or unquestioned, *free information*). Notice further how my answer at stage n is tacitly presupposed in your question at stage $n + 2$. Both of us know (and know that the other knows) after stage (1) that the object is located somewhere in the left half of the square in Figure 2. This shared knowledge is a prerequisite for what is made known at stage (3), even though at that stage it is tacitly taken for granted by both of us.

What is left of sequential structure in our dialogue, when we leave out quantification, is a particular pattern whereby novel information is nested onto what is already assumed to be the case. What is made known at any particular stage is thus not only made part of an expanded shared social reality, but serves at the same time as a prerequisite for making proper sense of what is said next. And this dual function is preserved also when my four successive answers are condensed into one single utterance such as:

(II) It is (in the square), in its left half, in the upper half of that left half, in the left half of that upper half, and in the lower half of that left half.

Analogous patterns of nesting are often encountered in narratives, for instance, when the identity of some person is taken for granted by the narrator—and *eo ipso* intersubjectively established—on the basis of inference from what has been made known at some earlier stage. We may, for example, hear about two persons, one old man and one young man. The latter is subsequently referred to as *the son*, although nothing has been *said* about kinship. Only two persons have so far been introduced into our temporarily shared social world. Therefore when "the son" (by virtue of the definite article) is assumed to be known already, he has to be the younger one of those two men and nobody else.

6. Message Structure: Nesting of Bound to Free Information

What appears from the general perspective of information theory as sequential constraints may, from the perspective of the architecture of intersubjectivity, be assessed as Vorverständigung based upon tacitly endorsed contracts concerning a temporarily shared social world. *Message structure* may accordingly be conceived of as a particular pattern of nesting, generated in an interplay of tacit and verbally induced presuppositions on the one hand and semantic potentialities on the other.

Consider, for instance, what may be made known by a sentence such as

(III) My spinster aunt is an infant.

The sentence is one of the many so-called *semantic* anomalies so eagerly documented by semanticists of the Harvard—M.I.T. school at an early stage: It has to be relegated to the abyss of unreason by scholars who believe in invariant semantic features rather than in semantic potentialities bound to variant premises for intersubjectivity (see Katz and Fodor, 1963, p. 200).

A great many things may be made known by such an utterance, however, depending on which metacontracts of communication have been endorsed and what is jointly and tacitly presupposed at the moment of speech. Its *message potential* may then, within each type of setting, be explored by examining possible questions to which (III) provides the answer. These may ask, for example, *how* the speaker's aunt is, *who* is an infant, *which of his aunts* is an infant.

Let us briefly consider two contextual variants. Consider, first, a conversation between two friends. The listener knows already the speaker's aunt by sight, and *an infant* is stressed in response to his question as to how that lady is. Message transmission must then be conceived of in terms of a pattern of nesting of information analogous to that of the question-and-answer game: What is made known by "an infant" is bound to "My spinster aunt," and the latter is in turn bound to an already intersubjectively identified entity within the temporarily shared social world at the moment of the act of speech. What is intended by the speaker and presupposed to be intended by him on the part of the listener is hence neither the early stage of life cycle nor the incapacity to speak, but rather only partially determined potentialities such as immaturity and dependency.

Let us next examine a case when (III) is uttered in response to *who* is an infant. The latter question may for instance be raised in an informal and noisy discussion about candidates for political offices, one of whom happens to be the spinster aunt. The conversation is in such a situation by a tacitly endorsed metacontract restricted to adult persons only. What is said about them, moreover, has to do with their potential capacities as politicians rather than as artists or athletes.

Even an overheard fragment of an utterance such as "... is an infant" is for that reason immediately understood in terms of the general abstract potentialities suggested above, but on this occasion constrained by *le sous entendu* that someone is claimed to be an infant when viewed as a politician. And (III) uttered in response to the question "Who is an infant?" is hence, by anticipatory comprehension, "perfectly understood": It makes known *whom* the speaker declares immature with respect to political insight and skill.

The meaning potentialities *intended* and *understood as intended* in the phrase "an infant" can thus only be revealed by assessing the message structure. We must therefore first examine how the phrase is bound to other segments of the utterance and to tacitly endorsed presuppositions. Its entire set of semantic potentialities must subsequently be matched against all presuppositions to which the phrase is bound. We must also examine *if* and eventually *how* what is already taken for granted overlaps with what otherwise (in other contexts) might be made known by the expression.

We find then that some potentialities have to be disregarded on the ground that what would be made known by them is already presupposed. Such potentialities are therefore redundant. This is the case with a semantic potentiality such as *animate* of the phrase "an infant" in the settings we have analyzed above. Certain other potentialities are overruled by what in that particular act of communication is taken for granted. This applies to age or stage of life cycle potentialities: Stage of life cycle is unequivocally conveyed by "spinster" and constitutes part of the unquestioned, free information to which "an infant" is bound. Such overruling is by no means an arbitrary or magic affair: The outcome is strictly determined by nesting of bound to free information. This precise phenomenon has for ages been explored in the literary analyses of metaphors.

An elimination of redundant and overruled semantic potentialities, however, yields only a partial determination of what is made known. We have thus so far only restricted what is made known in the expression "an infant" to a subset of its meaning potentialities defined by the elimination of animate and early stage of life cycle. What is left may therefore be described in terms of abstract, but largely open potentialities, such as dependency and immaturity. Such a description may in fact represent a very plausible account of what is conveyed by the expression in the conversation between the two friends: The listener may not be any more informed at all at that stage, and the innocent dependency and/or immaturity of that spinster aunt is possibly going to be a central theme as the conversation continues.

What is left open and largely undetermined after our procedure of elimination, however, may in other cases be further specified in view of additional presuppositions to which the expression is bound. This is clearly the case in the noisy and informal discussion of political candidates: Whatever is made known by "an infant" when said about some such candidate is by a tacit metacontract bound to refer to him in his capacity as a politican. This does not by any means imply that the expression has been fully and finally determined with respect to propositional content. On the contrary, the remark may very likely initiate a lengthy dialogue concerning what, more precisely, has been asserted by "an infant." What has been "perfectly understood," however, is that neither status as animate nor stage of life cycle nor immaturity in general has been asserted. Further clarification of the phrase may from now on be safely restricted to dealing with political immaturity and, possibly, of semantically mediated emotive and attitudinal contagion.

This is indeed a deplorably poor achievement when gauged against criteria developed within formal logic, yet not so poor when we keep in mind that it is achieved in and about a multifaceted, only partially shared, and only fragmentarily known world. Even such a partial determination of what is made known is in certain respects quite an impressive performance, definitely beyond the capacity of a person in a schizophrenic or autistic state of mind, and also, I believe, beyond what can be accounted for by the expanded versions of propositional analysis proposed by semanticists of the Harvard—M.I.T. school. It presupposes complementarity and reciprocal role taking. The speaker must monitor what he says on the premises of the listener, and the listener must listen on the premises of the speaker. Both of them, moreover, must continually relate what is said at any particular stage of their dialogue to whatever at that stage has been jointly presupposed.

7. On Commonality with Respect to Interpretation (Interpretationsgemeinschaft) and Shared Strategies of Attribution

Rossi (1973) maintains about Lévi-Strauss and the emphasis upon "l'inconscient" in structural analysis:

> The preoccupation with the unconcious is a preoccupation with discovering the basic structures which are common to the mental mold of the sender of the receiver of the message, and which enable a genuine intersection of two intentionalities. (p. 43)

Critics have accused Lévi-Strauss of having elevated the unconscious and irrational to a position of dominance and control in human and social life (see Corvez, 1969), but he may with equal right be praised for having brought to our attention basic taken-for-granted and not-reflected-upon cognitive preconditions for human interaction. Such preconditions, moreover, constitute a very intricate problem area in which a variety of philosophical, humanistic, and social scientific inquiries seem to converge. Wittgenstein (1962) claims that any scheme of interpretation ". . . will have a bottom level and there will be no such thing as an interpretation of that" (p. 739). Hermeneutic philosophers of language are concerned with such a bottom level in terms of an unreflectively taken-for-granted commonality with respect to interpretation, *eine Interpretationsgemeinschaft* (Apel, 1965, 1968). Merleau-Ponty (1962) conceives of situationally and interpersonally established premises for a given dialogue as "a certain kind of silence" (p. 184). And Lévi-Strauss' search for *l'inconscient* may indeed, as suggested by Rossi, be interpreted as an attempt to explicate a widely shared aspect of "silence," in other words, the common denominators of a whole range of situational variants.

Let us now ponder what, more specifically and from a social psychological point of view, is implied by such tacit preconditions for intersubjectivity. Imagine, for instance, a situation in which you are asked how a particular person is. And let us assume that you have never verbalized your impressions of that person until the very moment you are asked about it. Suppose, moreover, that your partner in the dialogue is considering the person he is inquiring about for a particular job. Being aware of that and knowing that the job is neither well paid nor particularly interesting, you may perhaps answer

(IV) He is easy to please.

Imagine, on the other hand, a situation in which you know that the person you are asked about has decided to start out on a long and solitary expedition that in all likelihood will be monotonous and devoid of exciting events. Assuming that your interrogator is worried about the person's capacity to endure months of solitary and uneventful traveling, you may very well answer

(V) Oh, he can gain pleasure from small things.

Making known your impression of a particular person in situations such as those described above is clearly something more than converting a readymade cartesian cognitive representation into a temporally extended sequence of speech sounds. It is a social activity in the sense that you spontaneously monitor what you say in accordance with tacit assumptions concerning what both of you already know and what more your listener wants to know. You may thus induce a shared perspective by which the person you are talking about is considered a potential manipulandum, or you may engage your listener in a verbally induced strategy of attributing talents to him.

What is made known by words such as "easy" in (IV) and "can" in (V), moreover, is clearly bound to a more comprehensive scheme for attribution (Heider, 1958). The latter is in some respects analogous to the square in Figure 1: It is taken for granted as a shared frame of reference for making sense of what is said. And this may hopefully be demonstrated in Figure 3 as we ponder what is made known by cryptic expressions such as

(VI) John is easy;
(VII) John can; and
(VIII) John is eager.

Some composite state of affairs of the general form [X(do)Y] is evidently taken for granted in all three expressions. The two poles of the composite state of affairs, moreover, make for a subdivisions analogous to that by which the square is divided into the right and the left half, since what is made known about John is dependent on which of two distinctively different capacities he is talked

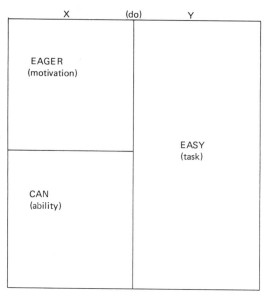

Figure 3. Tacit presuppositions inherent in EASY, EAGER, and CAN.

about in. The word "easy" in (VI) is thus comprehensible if and only if he is considered as part or aspect of some action or task [(do)Y]. What is conveyed by either "eager" or "can," on the other hand, can only be made known if John is attended to as a potential actor; as X is in [X(do)]. The word "eager," moreover, makes sense if and only if said about motivational aspects rather than his ability as a potential actor.

Heider's inquiries into attribution are investigations of behaviorally revealed inference rules rather than explications of interrelationships between words. They may hence, like the inquiries of Lévi-Strauss, be said to aim at discovery of "... basic structures which are common to the mental mold of the sender and the receiver of the message, and which enable a genuine intersection of the two intentionalities." Sharing rules of attribution is indeed a basis for enabling us to transcend our initial imprisonment in a private and egocentric world. These rules are, in fact, also prerequisites for obtaining consensus with respect to verification: What is made known by "John can" is proved true if he tries and succeeds.

The message potentials of expressions such as (VI), (VII), and (VIII) are thus bound to a particular commonality with respect to interpretation (*eine Interpretationsgemeinschaft*). None of them makes sense in acts of verbal communication unless some scheme for attribution such as the one suggested in Figure 3 is tacitly presupposed and mastered by both participants in the act. Each expression is of course incomplete when gauged against criteria for fully determined "propositional content," yet comprehensible and partially determined by aspects of the scheme about which nothing is said. Some task or intended action is thus always taken for granted, even though the particular nature of (do) in [X (do) Y] may remain unknown. A prerequisite for a temporarily shared social world in the case of (VI), moreover, is a capacity for decentered shifts of perspective on people such that a particular person can on one occasion be attended to as a source of action and on another occasion as (aspect of) a task. Figure 3 may thus be said to portray features of a culturally shared "kind of silence" out of which adult discourse about ease, eagerness, and ability is generated.

8. On Message Structure and Residuals in Acts of Verbal Communication

Irrational compartmentalization of knowledge is sustained by vicious circles. The *raison d'être* of an encapsulated expertise on *sous entendus* and literary exceptions must thus in part be sought in a general semantics concerned with "literal" readings and "propositional content." The hermeneutic scholar thus often deals with residuals from the general semanticist's analysis, and his own exegesis is addressed to us as insiders of a presumably universal, though entirely open and undefined *Interpretationsgemeinschaft*.

I have in the present paper examined basic premises for intersubjectivity such as complementarity of intentions, capacities for decentered categorization and attribution, and a capacity to adopt the perspective of different others. An analysis of message structure will thus—unlike assessment of propositional form and content—have to deal with residuals in terms of tacitly taken for granted shared social realities and/or presupposed commonality with respect to interpretation. Such residuals, however, are *not* to be conceived of as ad hoc manifestations of some undifferentiated and only intuitively revealed *Interpretationsgemeinschaft*, but must in each case be specified by a systematic analysis of nesting of *bound* to *free* information.

The residual may in some cases be conceived of as analogous to the axiomatic foundation for interpretation of particular scientific statements. What is made known by EASY, EAGER, and CAN in expressions such as (VI), (VII), and (VIII) thus appears to be bound to a tacitly and reciprocally taken for granted "space of action" in a fashion resembling that by which particular geometrically defined terms for distances, areas, and volumes are bound to axiomatically defined Euclidian space.

Partial determination implies on other occasions simply optional elaborations of some general draft of a contract. What is conveyed by the word INFANT in a particular situation may thus, by tacitly endorsed metacontracts, be intended and understood in terms of political immaturity, but such consensus may in turn serve as a point of departure for negotiations concerning specific criteria for verification. Moreover, what is made known by POOR may on two different occasions be unequivocally determined in a general fashion as the opposite of WEALTHY, yet in a conversation about inhabitants of the third world be specified as living conditions below the subsistence level and in a dialogue about neighbors as dependence upon public financial support. Full mastery of the general poverty–wealth potentiality of POOR is thus revealed in contextually appropriate optional elaborations–and so contingent upon the generalized capacity to adopt the perspective of different others.

Semantic competence can therefore only be appropriately understood as an integral component of *communicative competence.* Semantic potentialities inherent in ordinary language must be conceived of as drafts of contracts concerning categorization and attribution, bound to more comprehensive schemes, yet to a considerable degree negotiable and contingent upon metacontracts in the form of actively induced or preestablished *sous entendus.*

References

Apel, K. O. Die Entfaltung der "sprachanalytischen" Philosophie und das Problem der "Geisteswissenschaft." *Philosophisches, Jahrbuch*, 1965, 72, 239 289.

Apel, K. O. Szientifik, Hermeneutik, Ideologie-Kritik: Entwurf einer Wissenschaftslehre in erkenntnis-anthropologischen Sicht. *Man and the World*, 1968, I, 37–68.

Chomsky, N. *Studies on Semantics in Generative Grammar.* The Hague: Mouton, 1972.

Corvéz, M. *Les structuralistes.* Paris: Aubier-Montaigne, 1969.

Ducrot, O. *Dire et ne pas dire. Principes de semantique linguistique.* Paris: Hermann, 1972.

Fillmore, C. J. Subjects, speakers and roles, in D. Davidson and G. Harman (eds.), *Semantics of Natural Language*, pp. 1–24. Dordrecht: Reidal, 1972.

Fodor, J., and Garrett, M. Some reflections on competence and performance, in J. Lyons and R. J. Wales (eds.), *Psycholinguistic Papers*, pp. 133–154. Edinburgh: Edinburgh Univ. Press, 1966.

Heider, F. *The Psychology of Interpersonal Relations.* New York: Wiley, 1958.

Katz, J. J., and Fodor, J. A. The structure of a semantic theory. *Language*, 1963, 39, 170–210.

Lakoff, G. Linguistics and natural logic, in D. Davidson and G. Harman (eds.), *Semantics of Natural Language*, pp. 545–665, Dordrecht: Reidel, 1972.

Mead, G. H. *Mind, self, and society from the standpoint of a behaviorist.* Chicago: Univ. of Chicago Press, 1950.

Merleau-Ponty, M. *Phenomenology of perception.* London: Routledge & Kegan Paul, 1962.

Rommetveit, R. On message structure. *A conceptual framework for the study of language and communication.* London: Wiley, 1974.

Rossi, I. The unconcious in the anthropology of Claude Lévi-Strauss. *American Anthropologist*, 1973, 75, 20–48.

Wellek, R. From the point of view of literary criticism. Closing statement, in T. A. Sebeok (ed.), *Style in Language.* Cambridge, Mass.: M.I.T. Press, 1966.

Wittgenstein, L. The blue book, in W. Barret and H. D. Aiken (eds.), *Philosophy in the twentieth century*, Vol. 2, pp. 710–774. New York: Random House, 1962.

Wittgenstein, L. *Philosophische Untersuchungen* (Philosophical investigations) (G. E. Anscombe, ed.). Oxford: Blackwell.

CRITIQUE

On Rommetveit's
"On the Architecture of Intersubjectivity"

FRANCES E. ABOUD

The study of language and semantics has not often been considered a major area in social psychology. It has been left up to cognitive psychologists to formulate theories of meaning, while most social psychologists have kept on the fringes by looking at the norms of speech or the attitudes to social markers of speech. The conceptual framework developed by Rommetveit provides a theory of meaning which puts the unit of analysis of language at the social level rather than at the level of the words, the phrases, or the sentence. Thus his framework for the study of meaning has important implications for the direction of social psychological research.

The primary focus of Rommetveit's theory of language is directed toward answering the question: "What can social psychology do to aid in an understanding of the meaning conveyed by language?" Rommetveit is concerned here with an attempt to reduce language to social rather than linguistic units. Both units, of course, may be necessary for a full explanation of language, but until recently most language researchers have concentrated on the linguistic units. In one sense, Rommetveit has raised the issue of reductionism: How much should we reduce the unit of analysis in order to provide a good explanation of behavior? His theory reduces language to a form of social interaction, but this leaves the social psychologist with no clearer understanding of how to reduce social interaction.

FRANCES E. ABOUD · McGill University, Montreal, Canada.

The psychologist studying interpersonal attraction may ask "What does this theory tell me about why people like or dislike others?" But the issue of reductionism can never be satisfactorily resolved because the physiological psychologist wants to reduce social units to physiological units, chemists want to reduce physiological units to chemical units, and physicists want to reduce chemical units to physical molecules and atoms. Each level of analysis can be explained by yet smaller units, but this does not negate the validity or usefulness of any one of the levels. And many times we have missed the forest by concentrating on the trees—the whole may contain more than merely the sum of its parts. The evidence is clear that we may have missed the meaning of a sentence by analyzing only the words that comprise it.

By evaluating the usefulness of an explanation in terms of the extent to which the behaviors have been reduced to a smaller unit of analysis, it is implied that there is some hierarchy of explanatory units. In many cases this may be true, but in the case of Rommetveit's theory of langauge, this assumption is superficial. We have here not only a theory about the meaning of language but a theory about the meaning of any form of social interaction. A great deal of the dissatisfaction with social psychology as it has been studied in the past centers around its "meaninglessness." What does it mean when a person attributes consequences internally or when a Prisoner's Dilemma subject becomes competitive? Perhaps we have only been studying the "what is made known" part of the behavior, and not the assumptions or implicit contracts that underlie the objective behavior. A lower-class child may say that he aspires to occupational unemployment or welfare because he assumes that you know that he and everyone else in this society want money and power. He is simply telling you that he is aware of his social position and the low probability of getting such rewards.

The general feeling that we as investigators do not really trust self-report may be partly due to the fact that we do not understand the meaning of verbal statements, but this is equally true for our lack of understanding of any behavior. Like linguisits, we only look at the novel or "what is made known" part of a statement or behavior without analyzing the social contracts or assumptions in which the message is embedded. When an investigator does not share or will not consider these assumptions with his subjects, the message is likely to be misinterpreted.

Communication, as with all forms of social behavior, has meaning within its social context. This additional meaning has been thought to be derived from social relationships (Laing, 1972), expectations (Smith, 1971), pragmatics (Ervin-Tripp, 1964; Hymes, 1964), or contracts (Rommetveit's paper in this volume). Each theory attests to the depth of meaning that is embodied in these social bonds, meaning that we as social psychologists have done little to tap. The difficulty in tapping these meanings was demonstrated by Garfinkel (1972), who had students report on common conversations they had with friends or spouses.

On the left side of the page they were to write "what the parties had actually said" and on the right side "what they and their partners understood that they were talking about." This "understanding" took five times as many words as the speech itself to express. Garfinkel reported that he sent the students back again and again to elaborate more fully on their meaning since it was impossible for him to understand what was being conveyed. The students in turn found it increasingly difficult to do this task, essentially because they had no set of rules to go from what was actually said to precisely what was meant. These rules are exactly what social psychologists should be looking for in order to understand the meaning of social behavior. They are the shared knowledge or assumptions which underlie any act.

Although Rommetveit has taken it upon himself to explain how words convey meaning within a social contract, we may take this analysis one step further and suggest that often words are only secondary to the meaning of a communication. Other characteristics of the speech such as its length or inflection may convey the meaning that the speaker wishes to affirm or break the contract. For example, by simply asking a question regardless of what the question is, a listener can convey either doubt that the speaker is sincere about the contract or interest that the contract be maintained and the speaker continue. By simply repeating what the speaker has said, a listener may be conveying the meaning that he accepts what the speaker has said and wants to maintain the contract. The meaning here is derived not from the words themselves but from the reaffirmation of a contract that could otherwise have been stated as "I like you." Social psychologists have studied attraction in its many subtle forms, but it is conceivable that we use language in many indirect ways to convey the simple meaning that we like or dislike someone. By giving explicit street directions to an ethnic group member who has an accent, one is not only conveying the meaning of how to get to a certain location but also the idea that he perceives the member to be somewhat stupid or a foreigner. The study of attraction could therefore be broadened to explain how one can use language to set up or remove the feeling that he and his interactant share the same reality. By giving overly explicit instructions, I may be saying "You and I have nothing in common."

The controversy over linguistic competence versus communicative competence could also be instructive for social psychologists. The question here is: What do we value, correct grammatical and lexical structures or meaningful communication? Social psychology is not value free; we label internals as competent and externals as incompetent, nonconformists as competent and conformists as incompetent, independent children as competent and dependent children as incompetent. If we accept White's (1959) definition of competence as the ability to interact effectively with one's environment, then we must drop the notion of "ideal" competencies that exist *in vacuo* or in the middle-class environment of psychologists and start looking at social competencies or the ability to deal with one's own social environment. This means that we must get others in that social environment to evaluate the effectiveness of that behavior. It may be disastrous in a work situation to be internal, independent, and nonconforming. Bernstein (1972) has made this error when he described the elaborated codes of speech as allowing the speaker to make explicit his intentions. Restricted codes, he felt, did not convey intentions, but it is clear that these intentions need not be expressed in a close relationship since they are part of the shared knowledge. Spouses can express as much or more about their intentions and motives through a restricted code than they could using an elaborated code with a stranger. By ignoring this shared reality, he overlooked the richness in meaning that is conveyed in a seemingly sparse dialogue. Perhaps we should go even one step further and define competence in terms of the ability to deal effectively with one's own personal environment, one's needs and feelings. Personal satisfaction should be as much a criterion for competence as social harmony.

References

Bernstein, B. A sociolinguistic approach to socialization; with some references to educability, in J. J. Gumperz and D. Hymes (eds.), *Directions in sociolinguistics: The ethnography of communication.* Toronto: Holt, Rinehart & Winston, 1972.

Ervin-Tripp, S. M. An analysis of the interaction of language, topic and listener, in J. J. Gumperz and D. Hymes (eds.), The ethnography of communication. *American Anthropologist*, 1964, 66, 86–102.

Garfinkel, H. Remarks on ethnomethodology, in J. J. Gumperz and D. Hymes (eds.), *Directions in sociolinguistics: The ethnography of communication.* Toronto: Holt, Rinehart & Winston, 1972.

Hymes, D. Introduction: Toward ethnographies of communication, in J. J. Gumperz and D. Hymes (eds), The ethnography of communication. *American Anthropologist*, 1964, 66, 1–34.

Laing, R. D. *Self and others.* Baltimore: Penguin, 1972.

Smith, F. *Understanding reading: A psycholinguistic analysis of reading and learning.* Toronto: Holt, Rinehart & Winston, 1971.

White, R. W. Motivation reconsidered: The concept of competence. *Psychological Review*, 1959, 66, 297–333.

CRITIQUE

On Rommetveit's
"On the Architecture of Intersubjectivity"

PETER SCHÖNBACH

Ragnar Rommetveit has convincingly demonstrated how important the tacit presuppositions of speaker and listener are even in the most ordinary exchange of information, and he has directed our attention to various aspects of the explicit or implicit metacontracts that have to be established with respect to the overlap of these presuppositions in order to ensure the success of message transmissions.

Watzlawick, Beavin, and Jackson (1967) distinguished between the content aspects and the relational aspects of communications, and with respect to the latter they discussed the contractual features of dyadic communications. Rommetveit, one might say, emphasizes a perspective that implies the necessity of preestablished contracts for the realization of both the content- and the relation-oriented intentions of the communicators, and I agree with him in this respect. However, remembering the Watzlawick–Beavin–Jackson focus on the communication process has helped me to see and formulate a qualification I want to suggest concerning the temporal aspects of metacontracts and message transmission.

All the examples analyzed by Rommetveit and his references to presuppositions, *Vorverständigung*, or preestablished information imply that the metacontracts which regulate the specific interpretation of the semantic message potential always *precede* the message transmission. I would hold against this that quite often the information established by a metacontract and the information depen-

PETER SCHÖNBACH · Ruhr-Universität, Bochum, Germany.

dent on it and transmitted by a verbal message occur *simultaneously*, and I think that this fact is relevant for socio-psychological concerns with communication. Let me state this proposition a bit more precisely.

Obviously, no communication takes place in a vacuum but in a specific setting that exists before the verbal interaction starts. To the extent that this setting constrains the interpretation of the message potentials and thus forms part of the metacontract between speaker and listener, the contractual elements of the communication do, of course, precede the message component. However, I maintain that quite often the most important part of contract formation, its offer with or without agreement between the participants, takes place in the very act of the message transmission. An example may help to support this contention.

Suppose a prison psychologist known for his very active concern with the prisoners' fate has come under the suspicion of having granted illegal favors to the prison inmates. He is called to a hearing before a board, and he aggressively asks why he of all people has been accused of being part in the affair. One sympathetic board member takes it upon him to answer this question. One of the reasons for the suspicion has been the record of the psychologist's previous actions which sometimes had come very close to an infringement of the prison rules. This the sympathetic board member does not want to state openly; he rather chooses a euphemistic strategy and says: "One of the reasons is that you are known to be friendly towards the inmates." By answering in this way the board member simultaneously transmits a verbal message with its semantic potential and offers a metacontract with respect to both the information content of his message and its relational aspects. Concerning the content he tries to establish cognitive convergence on a rather peculiar meaning of the word "friendly." With respect to the relation he tries to establish the mutual understanding that he does not want to embarrass the psychologist in front of the board and possibly create biased opinions against him, and that he would like the psychologist to accept this sign of good will and abstain from further aggressions. The psychologist may well realize this contract and accept it. On the other hand, he may not do so either because he does not grasp the offer or because he chooses to ignore it, and in this case he may well retort in a sarcastic tone that being friendly and understanding he had always perceived to be the core of his role as a psychologist in a prison.

The point I want to make is that semantic contract formations are beset by hazards; especially so when contracts have to be reached at the very same time a message is transmitted whose information is to depend on the contractual information and when there is no time to check beforehand if the cognitive convergence intended by the contract has indeed been established. One important consequence of this quandary seems to be that contracts are not only quickly made but also easily broken when they turn out to be inconvenient. Just one more example.

Old people who are dependent on younger family members and thus in a weak social position frequently seem to choose indirect strategies of asserting themselves and defending their territories. An aged mother, visiting with her daughter's family, might, for instance, ask her daughter the seemingly innocuous question: "May I make myself another sandwich?" What she really intends by this message and what is also perfectly understood by her daughter is the needling insinuation that she feels so oppressed by the family that she does not dare to make a single move on her own. The communication may continue smoothly on the surface if the daughter manages to keep her temper under control. If, on the other hand, she blows her top and tells her mother that she feels insulted, the mother, realizing that for once she has gone too far, can easily break the tacit contract and protest that, not really thinking, she had asked a conventional but certainly harmless question; and she can now in turn take offense and nurse her feelings.

It seems that the architecture of intersubjectivity sometimes, and perhaps often, furnishes brittle constructions. Webster's New Collegiate Dictionary defines architecture as the "art or science of building." Rommetveit's analyses and my own afterthoughts lead me to view the architecture of intersubjectivity as an artistic phenomenon rather than a process guided by parascientific rules and thus easily accessible to scientific endeavors. What are the conclusions we should draw for our research?

It is, of course, always possible to attempt a summarizing approach that reduces within the confines of its categories the unmanageable variability of real interaction sequences. Thus one may look for dispositional and situational factors that influence in a general manner types and degrees of presuppositions made by various groups of communicators. Kähler (1974), one of my co-workers, has started to work along such lines with encoding tasks similar to the Krauss and Weinheimer (1966) type, as his dependent variables and his present interests concentrate on the density of the social networks of the encoders as a possible determinant of the implicit presuppositions on which the encodings are based.

However, with respect to the theoretical and empirical accessibility of the very essence of language behavior, the sequence of verbal interactions, it seems to me that Rommetveit's analyses do not offer much hope; they rather point to further obstacles in an already rather impassable domain. (I should be very happy if anyone could successfully disagree with this conclusion.)

References

Kahler, H. D. Dekodierungsleistungen in Abhängigkeit von Merkmalen der sozialen Herkunft und der Enkodierungen. Bochum: Studienverlag Brockmeyer, 1974.

Krauss, R. M., and Weinheimer, S. Concurrent feedback, confirmation, and the encoding of referents in verbal communication. *Journal of Personality and Social Psychology*, 1966, 4, 343–346.

Watzlawick, P., Beavin, J. H., and Jackson, D. D. *Pragmatics of human communication. A study of interactional patterns, pathologies, and paradoxes.* New York: Norton, 1967.

SOCIAL PSYCHOLOGY AND CULTURAL ANALYSIS

HARRY C. TRIANDIS

This is a particularly good time to reexamine research priorities and paradigms in social psychology. Much of social psychology today is like a torrent of water that has reached a mountain ridge and is unable to find an exit toward the sea. Most of it consists of going around in circles.

A distinguished experimental psychologist commented to me a few months ago that he sees social psychology in a state of stagnation. He continued:

> Research evolves in three main phases: the first is the hypothesis generating phase, in which a variety of elements is selected from a wide range of sources to suggest a particular pattern of analysis; the second is a phase of parametric studies. The second phase is not exciting, but essential for the third phase to become possible. The third phase is one where a theoretical model is developed that accounts for the myriads of observations that were generated in the previous two phases.

In his view, social psychology has been locked into the second phase. We do a lot of parametric studies, often on trivial variables, but seem unable to come up with any decent models. Furthermore, by being extremely attached to our parametric studies we do not do enough phase I studies that might lead to new insights, a completely different set of parametric studies, and eventually get us to the decent models.

HARRY C. TRIANDIS · University of Illinois, Champaign-Urbana, Illinois. I am most grateful to Drs. Strickland and Tajfel for the invitation to present a paper on cultural analysis and I am indebted to D. Carlston, M. Fishbein, P. Laughlin, J. McGrath, and R. Wyer for critical reviews of an earlier draft.

In order to be as relevant as possible to the central concern of the conference, this paper is organized as follows: First it gives my analysis of the nature of the crisis in social psychology, which involves an examination of both the types of theories and the types of methods that we have been using in social psychology. Then it shows how cross-cultural analyses can provide promising approaches toward different paradigms. Next it examines some studies that suggest what we might discover with such approaches. Finally, it contains a paradigm that is likely to emerge from such work, examines some of its likely features, and suggests the kind of methodology that might be used in conjunction with it.

The Crisis in Social Psychology

Some Deficiencies in Theoretical Approaches

The Variables of Our Theories Account for Too Little of the Variance of Behavior. In the early years of social psychology we had many grand theories. Disappointment with these theories has led to our present rejection of grand theories. We put all our efforts on minitheories, which are supposed to account for a particular, highly restricted phenomenon. Cook (1970) makes a good case, however, for the need to develop broader theories. I rather agree with him.

In the 1960s, very much effort was expended on consistency theories, particularly dissonance theory. In retrospect, I see a small accomplishment. One of the reasons is that dissonance phenomena account for very little of the variance of behavior or experience. They are real, all right, but to get such phenomena in the laboratory one needs to do all sorts of things "just right," for otherwise the phenomena are superseded by other phenomena.

Even more generally, I fear that much of what we publish is a reflection of demand characteristics and other artifacts because we manipulate such weak variables that the artifacts have a chance of interacting with our data.

I agree also with Pye's (1973) observation that most of the subjective events that psychologists are so fond of studying make very little difference for behavior. Let us face it: The human mind is capable of more discriminations than the human muscles. Note that our eye can discriminate 7,500,000 colors, but our behavior reflects awareness of two dozen colors only. Something similar is going on with respect to other subjective events and behavior. Most subjective events are too transitory, have too little social significance, and account for too little of the variance of behavior to be worth studying.

For this reason it is essential to have a model that relates the important subjective events to behavior. Such a model must have applicability in any culture. An attempt to develop such a model (Triandis, Vassiliou, Tanaka, and Shanmugem, 1972; Triandis, 1975) suggests that we already have enough evidence to know its major variables (behavioral intentions, norms, roles, expectations). These variables have been found to account for large amounts of the variance of behavior, but curiously they are not among the most popular variables in current social psychological theorizing. To compound this problem, in our experiments we often do trivial manipulations on pseudodimensions. We need to limit our investigations to those studies that are implied by broader theoretical considerations and eliminate the trivialities that we do so frequently. As Hebb (1973) said at the last APA meeting in Montreal, psychologists do methodologically impeccable research but "what is not worth doing is not worth doing well."

Our Theories Lead to Experiments of Limited Replicability and Generality. Related to the previous point, but also reflecting concern that the variables we select to study are of limited generality across cultures, is the present point. I believe that Moscovici (1972) correctly argued that much current American social psychology is culture bound. He called it the "psychology of nice people."

I once heard Siegfried Streufert make the facetious remark that those high in need achievement study need achievement, those concerned with logic and consistency study cognitive consistency, those who are complex study cognitive complexity, and so on. As usual, there is more truth than we want to admit in such humorous remarks.

Moscovici is probably right. A lot of the social psychology of nice people was developed by nice people (Heider, Hal Kelley, and the rest). The question is how general is it? Gergen (1973) has presented a somewhat exaggerated argument, but it makes essentially the same point. A substantial part of social psychology is transitory.

The problem, I believe, is that our theories utilize low levels of abstraction because they are designed to account for limited phenomena in a single culture. If they were designed to account for a wider range of phenomena, in many cultures, they would be more abstract.

Our theories are often reflections of current social concerns. The authoritarian personality was written about, by persons concerned with, Hitler and anti-Semitism. Consistency theories (Abelson *et al.*, 1968) have been advanced by people strongly influenced by Aristotelian logic. When we take our theories to non-Western cultures we find these models of lesser utility, although not entirely useless. In short, dissonance reduction seems more typical of Western man; tolerance for dissonance more typical of Eastern man. It is as though the variables that are important in our culture may be important in most other cultures, but they are not *as important* in those other cultures as they are in the West. We do not know yet what variables to include in a "universal social psychology."

Our Theories Do Not Account for the Complex Interactions of Types of People, Settings, and Behaviors. We treat individual differences as a nuisance in most of our theories. We design our experiments so that individual differences appear in the error terms. This is a very poor way to construct *social* psychology. We need theories that reflect differences in personality, ability, and cultural experience. Furthermore, social behavior is intimately dependent on setting. Barker and Wright (1955) have provided ample evidence that the behavior setting accounts for much of the variance of behavior. Yet none of the popular current theories have a place for the behavior setting. Finally, we often state our theories at such a level of generality that we seem to imply that they are good for *any* behavior. Yet, there are many kinds of social behavior and they may require different minitheories. I recognize that this is inconsistent with my earlier attack on minitheories, but what I am advocating are different mini-theories for different types of social behavior, and a single paradigm that will accommodate all minitheories as special cases. (For such an attempt, see Triandis, 1976.)

Our Theories Do Not Make Point Predictions. I think Meehl (1967) made a very important point when he remarked that psychologists design their experiments to determine differences, while physicists determine point values or shapes of functions. The weakness of theories that cannot predict values on a variable and designs that look for differences is that the more observations you make the more likely you are to find the differences you are looking for. Meehl has estimated that with our methodology the probability of finding support for theories that have no merit whatsoever is .5.

I will anticipate my later discussion and point out that in cross-cultural studies we should be primarily interested in similarities. Cultural differences should be embedded in similarities, for otherwise we cannot distinguish cultural differences from failures in communication with our subjects (Campbell, 1964). If our aim is to obtain mostly similarities, we can use the data of one culture as "a map" on which to place the data of another culture. Each data point should have a corresponding data point in the other culture. The *main* activity in the cross-cultural enterprise should be the establishment of similarities in psychological laws. When data contradict this expectation, it is desirable to find more general laws that hold universally, which permit particular parameters to vary and produce the cross-cultural differences.

Deficiencies in Methodology

Our Methodologies Often Reflect Much Method Variance. We often use experimental paradigms, such as Byrne's hypothetical stranger, which result in data that have paradigm-specific variance. Many of our findings with the Prisoner's Dilemma are suspect for similar reasons. The problem with the use of a single method of data collection is that it does not eliminate such undesirable variance; it also limits the generality of the results (Levinger & Snoek, 1972). Perhaps we must take the Campbell–Fiske multimethod approach much more seriously than we have so far.

We Do Not Dimensionalize. We do many 2^n experiments and too few 5^n experiments. In short, we typically do not have evidence about *true* dimensions, as one does with 3 to 5 points. Two points always define a pseudodimension, which may or may not be useful.

Summary of Deficiencies

The variables used in our theories account for too little variance. They have limited replicability and generality and do not account for the complex interactions between person, situation, and behavior characteristics. Our theories and designs are geared to determine the existence of differences; they reflect method variance and artifacts and often involve pseudodimensions.

As a kind of summary empirical point, recall that Vidmar and Hackman (1971) obtained different results, on otherwise identical experiments, between the laboratories at Yale and Illinois, and Kelley *et al.* (1970) also had differences among several American and among several European laboratories. If our theories and methodologies did not have the above-mentioned deficiencies, such instabilities in the findings would either have been predicted or not have occurred.

Advantages of Cross-Cultural Approaches

Cross-cultural studies have the potential of getting around several of these deficiencies. First, many variables have more variance when examined in cross-cultural perspective (Whiting, 1968) than in one culture, thus reducing restrictions of range in many investigations and permitting the discovery of curvilinear relationships. Second, the very fact that the researcher faces more explicitly a larger degree of complexity, has more variables to consider, forces him or her to concentrate on those variables that really make a difference. I have tried elsewhere (Triandis *et al.*, 1972) to examine what particular aspects of the tremendously rich subjective experience of humans appear to be worth studying. Cross-cultural studies force us to employ variables at higher levels of abstraction, which do not suffer from relevance only to a single culture.

Third, cross-cultural studies force us to examine a broad range of variables. When you go to the field for a limited period of time, knowing that you may never be able to come back, you tend to measure more things and examine the *context* of your measurements—or at least you should. This makes for less trivial investigations, since the neat and tried factorial design cannot be done, and having measurements on a lot of the context variables is often highly instructive.

Each of the points made in my analysis of some of the problems I see with current social psychology will now be discussed to show the utility of cross-cultural studies.

Variables That Account for Much Variance

Cross-cultural research often involves *new* variables, which often account for much variance. Consider a study by Feldman (1968) on helping behavior in three cities: Boston, Massachusetts, Paris, France, and Athens, Greece. Feldman constructed five situations such as asking a passer-by in a busy subway station to mail a letter. In this instance the criterion was whether the subject would agree to mail the letter. The differences, in one particular comparison, involved 51 versus 93% rates ($p < .001$). One does not need sophisticated statistics to analyze this kind of difference! Furthermore, the difference is directly predictable from other kinds of cultural analysis, such as Triandis, Vassiliou, and Nassiakou (1968).

Let me provide a little more detail. The experimenter in the particular situation was either a native, from the culture in which the study took place, or a foreigner. The rates of refusal to help were comparable for native and foreigner in all cultures but in Greece. In the latter culture refusals to help a foreigner were about the same as those observed in the U. S. or in France, but refusals to help a Greek were much greater than in the other cultures.

When Feldman did his study we had already completed a role differential study in Greece and Illinois. In that study we asked samples of university students to indicate, on nine-point scales, whether it was appropriate in their culture for a person in a particular role to behave in particular ways. We had some 100 roles and about 60 behaviors in each role. Comparison showed a particular clear pattern: The Greeks reacted to certain roles very differently from the way Americans reacted to the same roles. Specifically, roles which involved the family, friends, the person's physician, lawyer, and other people of that kind, were reacted to with greater degrees of association (help, support, work with) and intimacy (kiss, pet, discuss intimate thoughts with) in Greece than in America. The *remaining* roles, however, were reacted to with a lot *less* association and intimacy in Greece than in America. In short, there was a sharp discontinuity between what we finally called *in-group roles* and *out-group roles* in Greece, while such a sharp discontinuity did not appear in the American data. Note that the definition of the in-group is relatively narrow in Greece and excludes 99% of all Greeks. Further, and this is in retrospect most important, Greeks responded to the tourist—native roles and the host—guest roles about the same way as they responded to in-group roles. Putting these two empirical pieces of information together, one must expect Feldman's results on the help received by a foreigner or a Greek in an Athens subway.

As we looked at other analyses of the subjective culture of Greeks, using several other instruments, we found further support for the notion that Greeks make a major distinction between their in-group and out-group, one that can be used to predict a variety of other kinds of responses (Triandis and Vassiliou, 1972). In order to give some idea of the importance of this distinction in Greece, I believe that it is even more important than racial and religious differences, put together, in the United States.

Now this does not mean that differences in belief are not important in Greece. They are extremely important determinants of the variance of social behavior within the in-group, but not as important in relation to the out-group. Just to give some sense of this importance, there are several known historical examples of ideological differences such as communist versus capitalist which caused members of the in-group to refuse to speak to each other. Yet when a hostile behavior of an out-group member was involved, cooperation suddenly appeared, as in the case of members of the Communist Party who betrayed secrets of the party to save the lives of members of their in-group. For example, they would not let their disliked reactionary uncle be killed by unknown other members of the party (out-group) and they warned him and even arranged safe conduct through the communist army lines. To betray the in-group means that one is *aphilotimos*, which is the worse offense in the Greek value system (Vassiliou and Vassiliou, 1973).

To summarize then, here we have an example of a variable (in-group–out-group) that accounts for major amounts of the variance in social behavior. In all cultures this variable predicts behavior, but in some cultures much more than in others. Furthermore, these studies show the need to study the *definition* of who is the in-group in each culture. This is still another variable. These variables are reflected in a *variety* of paper and pencil and behavioral measures, which show much consistency and reliability and predict social behavior in a range of settings (Triandis and Vassiliou, 1972).

Replicability and Generality

The point was just made that the in-group–out-group variable leads to highly replicable results; but it is also useful to point out that each culture cuts the pie of experience differently. I think the extreme concern with interpersonal attraction in American social psychology reflects the importance of attraction as one of the bases of social organization in America. In other cultures it has a somewhat lower priority. One does not necessarily interact with those who are attractive, but rather with those who are powerful or members of one's caste, in-group, tribe, etc. In cultures where marriages are arranged there is less concern about romantic love. So Moscovici is correct, in my opinion, in his analysis of American social psychology.

Now if each culture has different priorities for the basis of social organization, it is obvious that when we put all our emphasis on research on the variables that are important in our culture, we will not develop a cross-culturally general social psychology. We need to discover higher order variables that will be systematically related to culture-specific variables. For example, all cultures have in-groups, but they define in-groups differently (e.g., same religion, race, or belief), and the consequences of in-group membership may be different.

Accounting for the Complex Interactions of Persons, Behaviors, and Situations

Consider as an example the Triandis and Davis (1965) study, which was recently replicated by Goldstein and Davis (1972). The data show that there are three sets of influences in the way the subjects respond: (a) the type of behavior (intimate behaviors are different from formal), (b) the type of person (one type emphasizes differences between himself and the stimulus persons in *race*, and the other in *beliefs*), and (c) the characteristics of the stimulus, which can be equated with the social setting for the purpose of this argument. The point is that one cannot make a general statement about these data without taking account of these three sets of influences. We need theories that will permit us to make statements that simultaneously account for these three sets of influences. To put it differently, information that the experimenter presents to a subject will have one effect on one type of subject and another effect on another, one effect for response type I and another effect for response type V, etc. We need to have theories that deal with the triple interaction.

Methodological Advantages

A major focus of cross-cultural studies in social psychology should be the discovery of culture-general phenomena. Only results placed in the framework of similarities across cultures can be used. For example, if we (Triandis et al., 1968) had not found similar dimensions of role perception, such as *association* and *intimacy,* we could not have been able to compare Greek and American role perceptions. There were culture-specific dimensions also, but these accounted for little variance and we were not sure they would replicate, so we have ignored them.

In short, the emphasis is on the discovery of similarities. When similarities are obtained, they are highly replicable because they occur in spite of the use of very different subjects, experimenters, social settings, and so on. Note also that similarities occur at high levels of abstraction leading to universal rather than culture-bound theory.

Perhaps I am stretching things a bit, but when looking for similarities the data from one culture can be used as "a map" that is to be matched by the data from the other culture. One no longer is looking for differences, but is making point predictions and predictions about the shape of functions. When there is a deviation from prediction one has the hard task of establishing the cause. Such work can only be considered as exploratory, hypothesis generating. I do believe, however, that such exploratory work is valuable, since it will lead to future parametric studies that may lead us to new and better models of social behavior.

I have emphasized the work of the social psychologist as one who looks for generalities, which is proper. Let the social anthropologist do the work that emphasizes differences. However, I must not give the impression that one cannot establish differences—the secret is a multimethod approach. If one uses several *different* methods and each suggests the same cultural difference, and there is a good deal of convergence in the results among them, he can assume that he has established a cultural difference. This is further confirmed if he can predict some phenomenon from hypotheses about these differences. It is very difficult work, but it is possible. This type of work has the additional advantage of not utilizing measurements with paradigm-specific variance.

To summarize thus far then, there are both theoretical and methodological reasons to engage in cross-cultural analyses.

What Have We Learned from Cross-Cultural Studies?

There are two major kinds of cross-cultural studies. One kind tries to establish that there are cultural differences involving some particular phenomenon and to indicate what causes these differences. An excellent example in this category is the Segall, Campbell, and Herskovits (1966) demonstration that cultural factors are implicated in perception. There have been a number of challenges to the thesis that carpentered environments make a person more susceptible to the Müller–Lyer illusion and so on, but my reading of this literature has convinced me that the Segall *et al.* position is reasonably secure.

The other kind of study is concerned with establishing generalities. Consider my work in this category: I am interested in showing that it is *possible* to provide equivalent measurements of various phenomena cross culturally, and the dimensions are the same across cultures. In short, my ambition is to determine the most desirable set of variables needed for a universal social psychology. This process is both inductive (e.g., via factor-analytic studies) and deductive.

Once a particular phenomenon is established cross culturally, one needs to do a lot more work. For example, why do the Greeks use the in-group in their particular way? Why do they have the values that they have? I believe that anthropologists are better equipped to answer such questions. The Human Relations Area Files can often provide data bearing on answers to such questions.

At some point we must place our social psychological theories within the framework of causal explanations that tie the nature of the physical environment to the nature of the social environment and hence to the particular social psychological phenomenon. As an example, consider Whiting's (1964) analysis of the determinants of initiation ceremonies. It is presented here not because I think it is correct, but because it illustrates the *kind* of analysis that I have in mind.

Whiting argues that climates favoring tropical rain forests make it difficult to produce milk because cattle are subject to disease and hence provide conditions of limited protein intake in children. This makes adaptive a long postpartum sex taboo, which permits mothers to breast feed their children for long periods of time. This increases the probability of polygamy, which increases the probability that the father will sleep in different places than where the baby and the mother sleep, so that boys sleep with their mothers and get very attached to them. Thus a severe initiation ceremony is required to introduce them to the male role. We have here an analysis in which climatic conditions are linked to the development of particular social norms, such as a sex taboo and polygamy, which caused particular behaviors, such as the father sleeping in different places, which caused particular types of interpersonal relationships, such as those between boys and their mothers, which require particular kinds of institutions and ceremonies. We can also guess that attitudes would generally be consistent with the social forms of institutions which develop according to the causal chain that was hypothesized by Whiting.

It seems to me that this is the direction in which social psychological studies should move. We should be able to tie physical conditions to the social environment, to specific behavioral patterns and consider experiences as phenomena that are both caused by and mediate the events in the physical environment.

An example of studies that relate features of the physical environment with variables of direct interest to the social psychologists is provided by Berry (1967). Berry predicted from the work of Barry, Child, and Bacon (1959) that in environments where there is little food accumulation there will be more independence in an Asch-type task, while in environments where there is much food accumulation there will be more conformity in the same task. The reasoning goes as follows: In the Arctic there is nothing growing; hence a person must depend on hunting. Such hunting is basically an individualized task. One does not depend much on the work of others. Parents in such societies train their children to be independent, to be able to work alone, which leads to a personality style that has been described by various anthropologists as reticent, involving "frozen affect," or reserved. The important value is independent self-reliance. By contrast, in the environment of the Temne of Africa, agricultural activities require much cooperation; a good deal of interdependence exists among individuals. Parents train their children to be cooperative and to conform. Berry's data showed large differences in the conformity scores of samples of Eskimo and Temne, in the predicted direction. An interesting additional finding is that "transitional" Temne and Eskimo, with considerable Western exposure, have scores that were not significantly different from those obtained by members of their cultures without such exposure. In short, once the tendency to be independent or to conform is learned it persists even when the conditions which caused it no longer exist.

I could go on summarizing interesting studies, but there is a rich literature which has already been summarized elsewhere (Tajfel, 1969; Triandis *et al.*,

1972, 1973). Some of it establishes the generality of certain phenomena; some of it (e.g., Meade, 1967, 1970) shows that classic social psychological studies do not replicate in other cultures. Instead of reviewing this literature, I will try to tackle a much more difficult problem, namely, what is the promising approach or paradigm that is likely to emerge from such work? This is, in a sense, our charge, as I understand the topic of this conference. Thus, it is my obligation to *try* to give an answer to this question.

Toward a New Paradigm

One of the more important books on our subject is Harré and Secord's (1972) analysis of social behavior. Human beings are conceived as rule-following agents:

> A social individual is made up of a fairly consistent set of inner and outer responses to his fellows and to the social situation and is backed up by accounts for his actions in terms of a unified set of rules and plans and a coherent system of meanings. (p. 7)

The authors invite us, among other things, to take seriously the explanations that people give concerning their own behavior: "To achieve full scientific status, then, social psychology must make room for attempts to unravel the models of generation of social behavior within the person" (p. 133).

This way of thinking agrees very closely with my analysis of subjective culture (Triandis *et al.*, 1972). In that analysis I took the position that we must study how humans process information. The environment is extremely complex. To respond with any degree of economy, humans treat vast arrays of actually different stimulus entities as though they are identical. This is what we call categorization. Categories are culturally determined. They are conventions for responding to the environment. The well-known multiplicity of names for snow among the Eskimo and for camels among the Arabs is a clue to the way we humans cut the pie of experience. When our interactions with the environment are very frequent in a particular domain, we differentiate that domain and develop numerous categories.

LeVine's (1973) analysis of personality development in different cultures is a neo-Darwinian argument concerning survival of the fittest *behavioral patterns*. One can extend this argument to both sides of the information-processing mechanism: At the input side we have stimuli, which are connected with cognitive schemata, which have been generated through experience because they led, in the past, to behaviors that were rewarded. The inputs and outputs are held together by information-processing strategies. These are what Harré and Secord called "models of generation of social behavior." These information-processing strategies account for (a) what attributes are responded to by a person, (b) how the attributes are organized into schemata, (c) how the schemata are connected to each other and to responses.

As far as we can tell, there are no cultural differences in information processing (Triandis, 1968). Specifically, at a level of analysis in which we present to a subject a list of characteristics of another person, such as the other person's age, sex, wealth, religion, race, nationality, etc., and ask for a response, such as a behavioral intention, the degree of liking, or a reaction to the stimulus on a semantic differential, information integration follows similar laws. Humans use the same dimensions to make their responses (e.g., in semantic differential studies *evaluation, potency, activity*; in behavioral differential studies: *respect, friendship, intimacy, hostility, subordination*) and combine the information we give them in more or less the same manner. In short, the within-culture variance is larger than the between-cultures variance.

Where the difference occurs is in the *weights* they give to the information. Some pieces of information are given a large weight in one culture and a zero weight in another. For example, a Greek will typically give more weight to the information that the other person "is a friend of a friend" than will an American (Triandis and Vassiliou, 1972). In the United States the attribute "black" has implications for the response "exclude from the neighborhood"; in Japan such a cognitive schema does not exist.

We have at our disposal very good methodologies for the study of the way people weigh different pieces of information. There are several varieties of multidimensional scaling. For example, by presenting to a person triads of stimuli, consisting of three real persons or three experimentally created persons, and asking the subject to judge which one is most different from the other two, we can obtain "pictures" of the way such stimulus persons are ordered in a perceptual space. I have described elsewhere (Triandis *et al.*, 1972, pp. 48–68) how factor analysis can be used to extract attributes, how facet and feature analysis can be used to test hypotheses about the existence of an important attribute, and how analysis of variance can be used to determine the relative importance of each attribute. The recent work of Anderson (1972) on functional and Krantz and Tversky (1971) on conjoint measurement is particularly useful in this enterprise.

What we need to uncover is a variety of cognitive schemata linking particular persons, and social situations on the one hand and particular social responses on the other. At a high level of abstraction, such cognitive schemata are probably universal. They are the culture-general laws of social behavior. Where cultural differences become important is in the *weights* that we assign to the components of these cognitive schemata.

For example, in all cultures norms of behavior will have some relevance in determining social behavior, but in some the relevance will be large and in others it will be small. Pelto (1968) provided a typology of cultures, from loose to tight. Tight cultures specify behavior in many social situations and rigidly enforce it. A theocracy is a good example. Loose cultures do not specify or do not enforce the norms. In all cultures some people are allowed to do what they like. But again in some cultures one is allowed to do what he likes more often than in others. To some extent doing what is specified by norms restricts doing what is enjoyable, although there are many norm-specified behaviors that are enjoyable. Conversely, doing what is enjoyable may conflict with norms, although norms do not exist or are not enforced, concerning many enjoyable social behaviors. This suggests that in deciding how to behave an individual will have to pit norms against the liking he associates with the behavior, in some cases. The question then becomes one of assessing the relative weight of norms and affect (Fishbein, 1967; Ajzen and Fishbein, 1973).

If the paradigm that is to emerge from cross-cultural studies is to reflect the major kind of cultural difference identified above, it should be capable of reflecting different *weights*. We must pay much more attention to the whole matter of how information about another person is integrated. Anderson (1970) has shown that a weighted average model does an adequate job. It remains to be seen if it can be used cross culturally with similar success.

Cultural groups differ in the weights they use (Triandis, 1967). The question becomes, then, Why do some cultural groups give so much weight to one piece of information and other cultural groups give so much weight to another? I suspect that the physical environment, historical and economic determinants will have to be used to explain that. Recall that some suggestions were provided of how such factors might be analyzed, in the summary of one of Whiting's studies.

Now if the needed paradigm is to reflect such differences in weights, what would it look like?

I have presented elsewhere (Triandis, 1975, 1976) a model for the prediction of social behavior that utilizes social determinants, such as norms, the affect toward the behavior, and the perceived consequences of the behavior. I have summarized numerous studies that have reported data consistent with this model. Limitations of space prevent me from presenting the model here, but I want to make two points: (a) each of the variables of the model has a weight and each weight can be determined through regression analysis or functional or conjoint measurement. (b) These weights differ depending on three parameters: (i) the type of behavior, (ii) the type of person, and (iii) the type of social situation.

In Table 1 there is a typology of social behavior that appears to emerge in several cultures. So far, in our studies, we have not found any cultures in which any one of the four facets of this typology is unimportant. Different cultures utilize additional distinctions, which are unique to them. I am here only describing universals of culture. Corresponding to this typology of behaviors is a typology of social situations generated by a facet design having the following facets:

(i) promotive versus contrient interdependence between two persons—as discussed by Deutsch (1949),

Table 1. A Typology of Social Behaviors

	Dissociative		Associative		
Superordinate	Scold Castigate Denounce	Reject Dislike Feel in- dignant toward	Pet Advise Appoint	Feel nur- turant Like Support	Intimate Informal Formal
Coordinate	Quarrel with Dispute Fight	Hate Not trust Be enemy of	Marry Gossip with Discuss with	Love Enjoy Not insult	Intimate Informal Formal
Subordinate	Hide from Avoid Be black- mailed	Envy Feel disgust Fear	Fall in love Ask help Obey	Idolize Admire Respect	Intimate Informal Formal
	Overt action	Feeling	Overt action	Feeling	

(ii) one person having greater-equal-smaller access to significant resources than the other person,

(iii) the age of the social relationship (e.g., old versus just met).

I do not have good data on the next point, but I suspect that in all cultures, these three factors make a difference.

Note the correspondence between the dimensions of the social situations and the typology of social behavior. Different people will give different responses, in different cultures, to a person in different social situations. Let us be more specific. Take a behavior such as *to pet*. It is obvious, from your experience, that not all members of your culture are equally likely to do this, in all social situations, with respect to all persons. In some cultures touching and caressing is much more acceptable than in others; persons who are younger and of the opposite sex may be targets in one culture; in another the critical determinant may be in-group membership. Petting is taboo in some social situations (e.g., in church) but it is permissible in other social situations.

In my model the question is raised, What determines variations in the weights?

It is possible to show that the weights are systematically related to personality characteristics (e.g., *F*-scale measures), social setting (e.g., formal versus informal), and culture (e.g., the Greeks giving a large weight to the in-group–out-group characteristic of the other). Thus, we have a model that explicitly takes into account variations in persons, settings, and behaviors. The task of social psychology *becomes* first the development of some typologies of persons, settings, behaviors, and cultures, and second the development of higher order generalizations that will relate these typologies to each other. The typologies should *dimensionalize* persons, settings, and behaviors. There is much more work to be done here than has been done so far, but the point is that it appears to be on the right track and it may be able to meet some of the challenges facing social psychology head on. Since this discussion may be too abstract and some practical suggestions are needed, I conclude with one more comment about methodology.

An Example of the Methodology of the First Step

The methodology that is suggested by the paradigm sketched above has many facets, only one of which will be described: the "social problems approach." One presents to a subject a social problem, much like a mathematician presents a problem. The subject is given different kinds of information and he is asked to make judgments. For example,

Two 20 year old, male students, at an American university, room together. Student O asks student P to help him solve a mathematical problem. P is busy writing an essay for his literature class. What is the likelihood that P will help O?

0	1	2	3	4	5	6	7	8	9
	Impossibility				Maybe			Certainty	

Before making a judgment, the subject is supplied with background information, such as:

A. P and O take the same course in math which is graded on a curve.
   versus
   P and O are not taking the same course in mathematics (i.e., if P does well it will not affect O's grade).
B. P and O have been friends for ten years.
   versus
   P and O have become roommates just a few days ago and did not know each other before.
C. O is generally very good at math, but P is not.
   versus
   P is generally very good at math, but O is not.
D. P has helped students like O, three times in recent days, with math problems of a similar kind and has found the experience disagreeable (versus agreeable).
E. P likes (versus dislikes) helping with math problems.

F. P perceives helping O likely to lead to O saying "thank you," and not much more. He is rather indifferent to O's thanks.
    versus
    P perceives helping O likely to lead to O inviting him to dinner at a fancy restaurant, which he would dearly love.
G. P comes from a family where people are expected to help when they are asked to help. Helping is typically rewarded in his family.
    versus
    P's family does not expect him to help when asked to help.

It should be clear from this example that some elements of the situation were kept constant and others were varied. Specifically, the age, sex, occupation, and setting were constant, while we indicated potential manipulations of (a) the type of interdependence, (b) age of the relationship, (c) resources of each, (d) habits of P and outcome from previous similar behavior, (e) P's liking for the behavior, (f) P's perceived consequences of the behavior, and (g) norms about the behavior.

To do a cross-cultural study with such materials one would need to develop *several* items that tap each of these contrasts. The items should be appropriate for each culture. This requires collaboration with psychologists in the other cultures. For example, the idea of promotive versus contrient interdependence may be culture bound. I rather doubt this, but at any rate one needs to check. Second, the items that tap the contrast must make sense in the particular culture and provide the same degree of contrast (each have the same distance from the neutral point) in each culture. This requires much pretesting, but it can be done (Triandis and Triandis, 1962).

To make this point clearer we need to consider the distinction between *emic* and *etic* constructs that anthropologists and linguists have adopted. Emic constructs are defined by members of a culture in their own terms, etic constructs have cross-cultural generality. In the proverbial comparison of apples and oranges, size, price, etc., are etic dimensions, while orange flavor and apple flavor are emic. It is obvious that comparisons can be made only on etic dimensions.

We illustrate this point with some of my work on social distance. Before starting such studies I discussed the idea of "social distance" with colleagues in different countries (Triandis and Triandis, 1962; Triandis *et al.,* 1965). They assured me that the concept made sense in their own cultures; in other words it is *etic*; but they indicated that the way the variable can be indexed requires very different items. Of course, the classical Borgardus scale included items such as "I would marry" and "I would exclude from my country." Some of these items are relevant in other cultures, but have different meaning in terms of the amount of social distance implied when endorsing a particular item, as determined by Thurstone successive-interval procedures. Other items make no sense; for example, the item "to exclude somebody from the neighborhood" is inappropriate in Japan. As my Japanese colleague put it, "No matter how much we dislike a person, if he becomes our neighbor we do invite him to tea and while saying to ourselves what a terrible fate has struck us in having this terrible person as one of our neighbors, we do behave politely."

In our studies we used emic social distance items and *standardized them independently* in each culture. Since the Thurstone successive-intervals technique results in equal-interval scales, we employed it *independently* in each culture, referring the judges of the *emic* items to the *etic* concept of social distance. The zero point was equated with marriage in all cultures. Thus we were able to get different scales that had comparable psychometric characteristics. Another way to accomplish this is to obtain ratio judgments (e.g., A is twice as distant as B) (Jones and Thurstone, 1955).

When the work is done independently in each culture, essentially one has as many independent replications as they are cultures. When *most* of the results are similar, one can make some sense of the obtained differences.

To return to the model, we need to check if the variables of the model are etic. My conversations with colleagues from all continents so far suggest that they think the variables selected are etic. We are beginning cross-cultural tests. However, while the variables of the model are etic, we must index them with emic items. This requires much pretesting and is time consuming. In short, the approach I advocate is not easy but seems more promising than other approaches we have tried so far.

Summary

We hope this paper has suggested some of the theoretical and methodological features of promising paradigms. They must include etic variables and allow for differences in the weights of these variables across (a) cultures, (b) social situations, and (c) individuals. They must bring together the more sophisticated approaches of mathematical psychologists and the data of cultural anthropologists, while using multimethod designs.

References

Abelson, R. P., Aronson, E., McGuire, W. J., Newcomb, T. M., Rosenberg, M. J., and Tannenbaum, P. H. *Theories of cognitive consistency: A sourcebook.* Chicago: Rand McNally, 1968.

Ajzen, I., and Fishbein, M. Attitudinal and normative variables as predictors of specific behaviors. *Journal of Personality and Social Psychology*, 1973, 27, 41–57.

Anderson, N. H. Functional measurement and psychological judgment. *Psychological Review*, 1970, 77, 153–170.

Anderson, N. H. *Information integration theory: A brief survey.* La Jolla, California: Center for Information Processing, 1972.

Barker, R. G., and Wright, H. F. *Midwest and children.* New York: Harper, 1955.

Barry, H., Child, I., and Bacon, M. Relation of child training to subsistence economy. *American Anthropologist*, 1959, 61, 51–63.

Berry, J. W. Independence and conformity in subsistence level societies. *Journal of Personality and Social Psychology*, 1967, 7, 415–418.

Campbell, D. T. Distinguishing differences of perception from failures of communication in cross-cultural studies, in F. S. C. Northrop and H. H. Livingston (eds.), *Cross-cultural understanding: Epistemology in anthropology.* New York: Harper & Row, 1964.

Cook, S. Motive in a conceptual analysis of attitude-related behavior. In *Nebraska Symposium of Motivation*, 1969. Lincoln: Univ. of Nebraska Press, 1970.

Deutsch, M. A theory of cooperation and competition. *Human Relations*, 1949, 2, 129–152.

Feldman, R. E. Response to compatriot and foreigner who seek assistance. *Journal of Personality and Social Psychology*, 1968, 10, 202–214.

Fishbein, M. A behavior theory approach to the relations between beliefs about an object and the attitude toward the object, in M. Fishbein (ed.), *Readings in attitude theory and measurement*, pp. 389–400. New York: Wiley, 1967.

Gergen, K. J. Social psychology as history. *Journal of Social Psychology*, 1973, 26, 309–320.

Goldstein, M., and Davis, E. E. Race and belief: A further analysis of the social determinants of behavioral intentions. *Journal of Personality and Social Psychology*, 1972, 22, 346–355.

Harré, R., and Secord, P. F. *The explanation of social behavior.* Totawa, New Jersey: Rowman and Littlefield, 1972.

Hebb, D. O. What psychology is about. *American Psychologist*, 1974, 29, 71–79.

Jones, L. V., and Thurstone, L. L. The psychophysics of semantics: An experimental investigation. *Journal of Applied Psychology*, 1955, 39, 31–36.

Kelly, H. H., *et al.* A comparative experimental study of negotiation behavior. *Journal of Personality and Social Psychology*, 1970, 16, 411–438.

Krantz, D. H., and Tversky, A. Conjoint measurement analysis of composition rules in psychology. *Psychological Review*, 1971, 78, 151–169.

LeVine, R. A. *Culture, behavior and personality.* Chicago: Aldine, 1973.

Levinger, G., and Snoek, J. D. *Attraction in relationship: A new look at interpersonal attraction.* Morristown, New York: General Learning Press, 1972.

McGuire, W. J. The yin and yang of progress in social psychology. *Journal of Personality and Social Psychology*, 1973, 26, 446–456.

Meade, R. D. An experimental study of leadership in India. *Journal of Social Psychology*, 1967, 72, 35–43.

Meehl, P. E. Theory testing in psychology and physics: A methodological paradox. *Philosophy of Science*, 1967, 34, 103–115.

Moscovici, S. Society and theory in social psychology, in J. Israel and H. Tajfel (eds.), *The context of social psychology: A critical assessment.* New York: Academic Press, 1972.

Pelto, P. J. The differences between "tight" and "loose" societies. *Transaction*, April 1968, 37–40.

Pye, L. Culture and political science: Problems in the evaluation of the concept of political culture, in L. Schneider and C. M. Bonjean (eds.), *The idea of culture in the social science.* Cambridge: Cambridge Univ. Press, 1973.

Segall, M. H., Campbell, D. T., and Herskovits, M. J. *The influence of culture on visual perception.* Indianapolis: Bobbs-Merrill, 1966.

Tajfel, H. Social and cultural factors in perception, in G. Lindzey and E. Aronson (eds.), *Handbook of social psychology*, pp. 315–394. Reading, Mass.: Addison-Wesley, 1969.

Triandis, H. C. Towards an analysis of the components of interpersonal attitudes, in C. and M. Sherif (eds.), *Attitudes, ego involvement and change*, pp. 227–270. New York: Wiley, 1967.

Triandis, H. C. Some cross-cultural studies of cognitive consistency, in R. P. Abelson, E. Aronson, W. J. McGuire, T. M. Newcomb, M. J. Rosenberg, and P. H. Tannenbaum (eds.), *Theories of cognitive consistency: A sourcebook*, pp. 723–730. Chicago: Rand McNally, 1968.

Triandis, H. C. Culture training, cognitive complexity, and interpersonal attitudes, in R. Brislin, S. Bochner, and W. Lonner (eds.), *Cross-cultural perspectives on learning*, pp. 39–77. New York: Sage & Wiley/Halsted, 1975.

Triandis, H. C. *Interpersonal behavior*. Monterey: Brooks/Cole, 1976.

Triandis, H. C., and Davis, E. E. Race and belief as determinants of behavioral intentions. *Journal of Personality and Social Psychology*, 1965, 2, 715–725.

Triandis, H. C., Davis, E. E., and Takezawa, S. I. Some determinants of social distance among American, German and Japanese students. *Journal of Personality and Social Psychology*, 1965, 2, 540–551.

Triandis, H. C., Malpass, R. S., and Davidson, A. Cross-cultural psychology. *The Biennial Review of Anthropology*, 1972, 1–84.

Triandis, H. C., Malpass, R. S., and Davidson, A. Cross-cultural psychology. *The Annual Review of Psychology*, 1973, 24, 355–378.

Triandis, H. C., and Triandis, L. M. A cross-cultural study of social distance. *Psychological Monograph*, 1962, 76, No. 21 (whole No. 540).

Triandis, H. C., and Vassiliou, V. Interpersonal influence and employee selection in two cultures. *Journal of Applied Psychology*, 1972, 56, 140–145.

Triandis, H. C., Vassiliou, V., and Nassiakou, M. Three cross-cultural studies of subjective culture. *Journal of Personality and Social Psychology Monograph Supplement*, 1968, 8, No. 4, 1–42.

Triandis, H. C., Vassiliou, V., Vassiliou, G., Tanaka, Y., and Shanmugam, A. *The analysis of subjective culture*. New York: Wiley, 1972.

Vassiliou, V., and Vassiliou, G. The implicative meaning of the Greek concept of *Philotimo*. *Journal of Cross-Cultural Psychology*, 1973, 4, 326–341.

Vidmar, N., and Hackman, R. Interlaboratory generalizability of small group research: An experimental study. *Journal of Social Psychology*, 1971, 83, 129–139.

Whiting, J. W. M. Effects of climate on certain cultural practices, in W. H. Goodenough (ed.), *Explorations in cultural anthropology*, pp. 496–544. New York: McGraw-Hill 1964.

Whiting, J. W. M. Methods and problems in cross-cultural research, in G. Lindzey and E. Aronson (eds.), *Handbook of social psychology*, Vol. 2, pp. 693–728. Reading, Mass.: Addison-Wesley, 1968.

CRITIQUE

On Triandis's
"Social Psychology and Cultural Analysis"

J. W. BERRY

There are essentially two questions I want to raise, both stemming directly from the title of Triandis's paper, "Social Psychology and Cultural Analysis." The first is: What can cultural analysis (or the use of the cross-cultural method) do for social psychology, how can we improve the social psychology that we do, how can we extend it by taking heed of the activities of anthropologists and psychologists who have been working cross culturally? The second question is: What can social psychology do for cross-cultural psychology; what can social psychology do for the understanding of behavior in a variety of cultural contexts?

In the first question, we need to remind ourselves of the *emic–etic* distinction Triandis has mentioned. The *etic* approach is to search for generality in descriptions of human behavior, while the *emic* approach is to search for specific, local, meaningful characteristics in behavior (see, for example, Berry, 1969). This distinction, when crossed with the two questions I raised earlier, produces a chart that will help the coming remarks:

Two basic questions	*Emic–etic distinction*	
	Etic	*Emic*
(1) What can the cross-cultural approach do for social psychology?		
(a) What should we study? (b) How should we study it?		
(2) What can social psychology do for cross-cultural psychology?		

J. W. BERRY · Queen's University, Kingston, Ontario, Canada.

Within our first question, we can pose two separate questions to which the cross-cultural method has made us sensitive: What kinds of behavior should we be looking at? How should we be looking at it? In the etic column, the "What do we look at" question is answered simply by saying that we examine those behaviors which we are already looking at; as social psychologists, we transport the behavioral observations, the data, and the systems that we have generated to see how universal they are in other sociocultural settings. To a certain extent this has been done; the examples Triandis mentioned are good illustrations of checking on the generality of a social phenomenon.

However, the question "How do we look at it?" in the etic column has not been sufficiently attended to, and raises the very important question: How generally applicable are the theories that guide our own research in our own Western sociocultural tradition, and how generally applicable are the models that we typically use to bring together the varied observations we have been making? This latter question has been very much underexamined in the attempts of social psychologists to seek out the help of the cross-cultural method.

In the emic column (where we look for unique and locally relevant phenomena), what we usually look at is to a large extent informed by the etic assumptions we carry with us into the field; I have termed this an *imposed etic* (Berry, 1969) and Triandis a *pseudoetic* (1972). Thus it is very important, as he has pointed out, to seek out local colleagues or associates so that we attain some understanding of how local people conceive of what they do in their own particular culture, and to obtain information about problems or phenomena that are unique or specially relevant in that situation. I have previously raised this point (Berry, 1974) with respect to Canadian social behavior: What are the unique phenomena of social behavior and its analyses in Canada, how do they differ from those in other parts of the world, and where should we be directing our attention? More generally, what is so specially characteristic of behavior in different sociocultural systems that require special cultural (that is, emic) understanding? This question, too, has been very much underexamined.

However, even more important in the emic column than "what to study" is "how to study." Moscovici, of course, has raised this question in the European context, and others in Canada have also considered it. At issue is the set of sociocultural assumptions underlying social–behavioral research systems. They have been generated largely in one sociocultural system (the United States), and they carry with them their own assumptions, which may or may not be applicable in other sociocultural settings. For example, I have been concerned with the applicability of the concept of *ethnocentrism* in Canadian life. We have formal Federal Government policies that encourage the high valuation of one's own ethnic identity, on the assumption that this will lead to a high level of tolerance of other people's ethnicity. This combination of high valuation of one's own ethnicity and high acceptance of others is, of course, the reverse of the assumptions that underlie the concept of *ethnocentrism* (where those who value their ethnicity are thought to disparage the ethnicity of others). Another concept that has been widely used is that of *cultural deprivation*; this notion, of course, must have limited applicability in sociocultural systems where there are plural sets of norms. If there are many cultural standards within a society, who is deprived in relation to whom? In particular, I am thinking of native peoples in this country, who are being encouraged to retain or seek their own lifestyle. The question then is an important one: How does a social psychologist assess performance or compare behavior against norms that are plural, rather than singular? This is the crucial difference for psychologists working in a pluralist, as opposed to an assimilationist, society.

Finally on our first question, I see a strong resemblance between these issues and the ethnoscience approach in anthropology (which is to seek out the understanding that a people have of the world around them). Within this approach, there is an ethnobotany, ethnogeology, and so on; an ethnopsychology in these terms would be precisely what Harré and Secord are arguing for at an individual level. The major question, however, for work in other cultures, is: How can we get social psychologists, who are in a sense unacculturated, to come forward with unacculturated theories about human behavior? For example, how can we encourage Indian, Japanese, Chinese, African, and Amerindian peoples to come forward with points of view on behavior that are derived from their own sociocultural systems, so that we can be informed by them, and perhaps achieve a true etic (termed a *derived etic* by Berry, 1969) understanding of behavior? The final session at IUPS in Tokyo was devoted to this question, trying to get Asian psychologists to come out and state their own assumptions, theories, and philosophical traditions, to expand the theoretical base of psychology.

The second basic question I raised was: How can social psychology help the cross-cultural enterprise? Many of us have come to realize that a lot of work has been done in cross-cultural psychology recently. Most of it has been in perception and cognition, and almost none of it on social behavior. Triandis and three or four others have done some systematic work, but I would guess that no more than 5–10% of the bulk of the literature in cross-cultural psychology has really been concerned with varieties of social behavior in other cultural systems. This is particularly strange, because the study of social behavior has some very useful cultural universals or etic dimensions from which to start. Aberle (1950) lists a number of things that all social systems must accomplish in order to hang together, and these are tailormade etics or universal bases upon which to establish the examination of social behavior in other cultures. But for some reason, social psychologists have not taken up the challenge in the same way other psychologists have, in seeking out the variations of behavior that can be found in other cultural systems. Now the answer to the question, "Why so little?" may be found in some of the points that Triandis raised at the beginning of his paper (the nature of the crises, the level of our gaze, the small scope of our interests); but the result is that we have not been looking for the generalizations that could emerge in the cross-cultural arena, and that could provide us with the basis for a truly universal statement about human social behavior.

Finally, since Gustav has mentioned ecological functionalism, let me say that I concur. The work I have been pursuing cross culturally [e.g., the study Triandis referred to in his paper (Berry, 1967)] has been largely within the ecological framework (e.g., Berry, 1975). If we are going to attempt to generate the larger, more comprehensive models that Triandis has urged, this framework may be a good place to begin. What is needed immediately is to carry out what I call "behavioral mapping"—finding out who does what, where, in relation to what variables, all at a global level. Eventually the task will be to hone in on precise relationships, but the central task before us is to comprehend the varieties of behavior (including social behavior) that will develop as a function of ecological and cultural factors.

References

Aberle, D. F. *et al.* The functional prerequisites of society. *Ethics,* 1950, **60,** 110–111.

Berry, J. W. Independence and conformity in subsistence-level societies. *Journal of Personality and Social Psychology,* 1967, 7, 415–418.

Berry, J. W. On cross-cultural comparability. *International Journal of Psychology,* 1969, 4, 119–128.

Berry, J. W. Canadian psychology: some social and applied emphases. *Canadian Psychologist,* 1974, **15,** 132–139.

Berry, J. W. An ecological approach to cross-cultural psychology. *Nederlands Tijdschrift voor de Psychologie,* 1975, **30,** 51–84.

Triandis, H. C. *et al.* Cross-cultural psychology. *Biennial Review of Anthropology,* 1972, 1–84.

CRITIQUE
On Triandis's
"Social Psychology and Cultural Analysis"

GUSTAV JAHODA

Triandis attacks the problem with his customary zest and vigor, suggesting where we should blast an outlet through the rocks confining social psychology. Actually the image is perhaps not altogether reassuring; for if there is such a breakthrough social psychology, while ceasing to go around in circles, will find itself all at sea. This would mean being utterly diluted and lacking any clear identity. This is a fairly serious joke, because while I certainly agree with the general direction toward more cross-cultural work, the particular proposals put forward appear to have some dangers, or at least considerable disadvantages. This being a discussion paper, it is inevitable that the burden of it will be concerned with aspects on which I disagree. Hence I would like to record at the outset my appreciation of the breadth and depth of Triandis's ideas, and the skill with which he has presented them.

The way I intend to tackle my task is to look at his diagnosis of social-psychological ills and consider how far the particular remedies he suggests are likely to prove useful and what their side effects might be. The diagnosis of the crisis is in terms of deficiencies of theories and methods (and I agree with what is said about methods). However, it is noteworthy that there is no specific discussion of objectives, i.e., what social psychological theories can or could or should explain; this issue is approached indirectly, involving certain assumptions

---

GUSTAV JAHODA · University of Strathclyde, Glasgow, Scotland.

that will have to be examined in due course. It seems to me that this lack of clarification of objectives leads to statements which have a distinctly utopian flavor. For instance, we are told that we need theories which will "account for the complex interactions of types of people, settings, and behavior." These should reflect differences in personality, ability, and cultural experience and incorporate the influence of behavior settings. Moreover, these theories should not be transitory and at such a level of abstraction as to be applicable universally in all cultures. Put baldly in this way, it becomes evident that Triandis is offering directional ideals as a means of highlighting what he sees as the major current deficiencies; and in examining his proposals one will ask the question how far they appear to take us in these desirable directions.

So far I have not mentioned the critique that "the variables of our theories account for too little of the variance of behavior." The point is of course well taken, but it does perhaps need some qualification or expansion since it is not entirely meaningful as it stands. First of all, the ability of a variable to account for a large part of the variance of a particular kind of behavior is not necessarily a virtue, *because such variables tend to be obvious and therefore uninteresting.* For example, if we are concerned with the nature and size of vocabulary from infancy to late childhood, then age, social class, and nationality are likely to account for a major part of the variance. Yet I shall not earn any great praise for this piece of theoretical insight, and rightly so. On the other hand, if all these factors were kept constant, substantial unaccounted variance will remain. If I produced a theory which succeeds in consistently accounting for even a modest part of this variance, it would probably be recognized that I have achieved something. It seems to me that this relativity must be kept in mind when evaluating theories.

In connection with this issue, Triandis refers to the need to select appropriate "subjective events" that make a difference to behavior; and he indicates that psychologists too often pick the wrong ones. He maintains that we must have a universally applicable model relating *important* subjective events to behavior. Elsewhere (p. 227) he declares one of the advantages of the cross-cultural approach to be that it forces us "to concentrate on those variables that really make a difference." My difficulty here is that the statement appears to be too general, and I can envisage two quite distinct possibilities. First, it may be that the phenomena to be studied are already well understood, and therefore one would know in advance what is or is not "important"; in that case, however, the main object of the study would be a comparative assessment of the kind described by Triandis in terms of relative "weights." Second, the phenomena may be little understood, and then it would be hard, if not impossible, to specify in advance what the "important" variables are; for if one knew this the problem would already be solved.

I suspect that some of the points made so far arise mainly from misunderstandings on my part, possibly because as Triandis himself explained his presentation had to be highly condensed. Yet some of them are probably substantive, since they are confirmed by the further elaboration in the main part of the paper, to which I now turn.

First of all, Triandis promises *new* variables in cross-cultural research that account for much variance. It turns out that these are variables like norms, roles, behavioral intentions, and expectations. Let us note here that these refer to the actor's perception of social behavior. One example of such a variable is the in-group versus out-group distinction, as well as the definition of who belongs to these in a particular culture, which becomes another variable. I find this confusing in the context of the emphasis on general laws rather than differences being the proper object of study for social psychologists. In practice it seems to me that Triandis is rightly concerned with both similarities and differences. In fact, he notes that in America, unlike other cultures, "attraction is one of the bases of social organization." While I am not sure whether there is evidence to warrant such a statement, it is obviously concerned with differences. Hence I must confess that the subsequent discussion about looking for similarities and no longer differences, and making point predictions and predictions about the shape of functions has me lost; but this may well be a reflection of my own shortcomings in technical competence. On the other hand I very much agree with the remarks made about the desirability of the multimethod approach.

In outlining his proposed paradigm, Triandis refers to the work of Harré and Secord and of Le Vine, giving them a new twist in a tantalizingly brief paragraph. This relates to the formation of cognitive schemata and the function of information-processing strategies in ordering social behavior. I found this the most exciting idea in the whole paper, and wish it had been further developed. Unfortunately Triandis went on to assume both that we know enough about such processes and that they are pancultural to save us bothering much further about this aspect. I am not sure that there is sufficient evidence about this, especially as most of the work has been done with paper-and-pencil measures in literate cultures. Because of this (in my view) questionable assumption, Triandis goes on to argue that our task is essentially that of determining the *weights* assigned in different cultures to components of cognitive schemata. He describes an elaborate and ingenious typology as well as methological strategies for the analysis of the interrelationships between persons, settings, and behaviors.

When it comes to the example illustrating the first step in the methodology, I experienced some disappointment. One comparatively minor reason is that the task is so narrowly confined to subjects with a considerable amount of formal education. What worries me far more is the fact that this kind of task appears analogous to a chemist taking various substances and mixing them, heating them, putting them into acid, and recording what happens each time. No doubt he could produce some kind of a typology of substances in the end, but he is unlikely to arrive at any chemical laws in this manner. There is also the practical question of when you stop, and why. As one of the people with much scarcer resources than those Triandis can command, I am forced to look more apprehensively at the likely payoff; and even supposing that the method could achieve its declared aim, it is probably too costly as a strategy for most social psychologists.

Quite apart from this practical issue, however, I feel that the ultimate outcome of such an effort would necessarily remain descriptive. Let me say that this is not intended as a critique of description as such, which is no doubt an essential preliminary step. Moreover, the description will no doubt be highly sophisticated in Triandis's hands, and as such be most valuable. What I do not believe is that this could be a way of establishing any general psychological "laws" of cross-cultural generality. The approach advocated is a kind of psychological ethnography rather than social anthropology.

I take this opportunity to make some observations on the way Triandis conceives of the work of anthropologists. Thus he says (p. 231), "let them do work that emphasizes differences," implying that they have a uniform approach. In fact, there is a continuing debate in anthropology as well as in psychology about the possibility of universal cross-cultural "laws." Thus Murdock stated that the elements of social organization "conform to natural laws of their own," while Evans-Pritchard took the view that social facts are totally different from those of even the biological sciences so that "neither the comparative method nor any other is likely to lead to the formulation of generalizations comparable to the laws of those sciences." Now we have to remember that our raw material, i.e., that of social psychologists, is really not very different from that of social anthropologists. In fact, some social anthropologists such as Goodenough have employed scaling devices for the analysis of informant's perceptions of role and status that appear to me in principle similar to the methods used by Triandis: moreover, Goodenough also had as one of his objectives the exploration of cross-cultural differences.

There is, however, an important divergence between social psychologists and anthropologists in what they are ultimately aiming at. Anthropologists are quite clear about this and hold to a fundamental tenet irrespective of theoretical stance or school. "This [to quote Kuper] is to begin by assuming that the actors' models are part of the data, not useful analyses of the systems being studied." In other words, a set of *secondary* explanatory concepts is needed for making sense of the data, and these concepts relate to the nature of the social system to which the actors belong. Thus anthropologists move from individual social behavior and perceptions of such behavior to an analytical account of the social system.

Unfortunately social psychologists lack such a neat conceptual framework, and I doubt if there would be much consensus about where we are moving from the primary data. Probably there would be agreement that we do not move up toward the social system, but either remain at the same level or move down. In both cases social psychologists presumably aim at the uncovering of behavioral regularities (to avoid the slightly pretentious term "laws") that hold beyond the boundaries of any single culture or society and if possible are universal.

The second course, i.e., moving down to the individual level, is perhaps slightly less contentious. Here one is concerned with universal features of individual social behavior, and the approaches of developmental psychology and ethology must supplement social psychology for this purpose. Studies like those of Ekman on the universality of emotional expressions are also relevant at this level, as is the issue raised by Triandis about the modes of processing social information.

There is an intermediate category represented by the work of Exline, Argyle, von Cranach, and others on social interaction. Since most of these investigations have been conducted in Western cultural settings one cannot be sure about the generality of their findings. It seems to me likely that a good deal of it will turn out to be culture specific; thus I suspect that if their studies on gaze direction had been conducted with demure Victorian maidens instead of modern emancipated female undergraduates the outcomes would have been very different. Yet there may well be certain features of relatively complex social behavior (e.g., an informal conversation among same-sex peers) that are cross-culturally invariant. There is of course no real discontinuity between such elements as facial expressions, paralinguistic communication of other kinds, greeting and other bond-forming rituals, and common forms of social interaction like conversation; hence they may eventually be understood in terms of a single theoretical framework.

Finally, there is the strategy of those who remain at the actors' normal operating level and are concerned with their norms, roles, behavioral intentions, and expectations; and this is the strategy advocated by Triandis. Now we have already seen that anthropologists reject this, and I have said previously that its outcome would be primarily descriptive rather than theoretical/explanatory. It therefore only remains to point out the main reason for this limitation: namely, such data are probably more closely related to the particular sociocultural system within which they are collected than to any cross-culturally general characteristics of the populations concerned. If one were to go beyond such descriptions of "the way subjects in different cultures think about social behavior," and to make attempts to relate the modes of thinking to certain key features of sociocultural systems, then one might arrive at higher-order generalizations of potentially universal range. There is no indication that this is what Triandis had in mind, and he makes scant reference to social system variables. It may, of course, be a feature of the promised model, which I look forward to reading.

Before concluding, I would like to emphasize again that my critical observations were not directed at the extremely interesting and important work done by Triandis. They are directed only at his suggestion that this work is a kind of rescue boat for those of us adrift at sea, so we could all climb on board and sail happily toward the distant shores of cross-cultural laws of social psychology. In my view the boat is not equipped for such a journey, and I am not even confident that there are such shores to be reached.

BEYOND ATTRIBUTION THEORY

The Human Conception of Motivation and Causality

RICHARD DECHARMS AND DENNIS J. SHEA

Introduction

Attribution theory concerns the processes that the average individual uses in attempting to infer the causes of observed behavior. The data generated by the theory are beginning to give important insights into these processes. Attribution theory assumes a conception of causality, yet philosophy should warn us that the concept of causality is a cornerstone set in quicksand. Our major thesis is that to use the concept of physical causation as a cornerstone on which to build an understanding of human behavior is to use what is "out there" to understand what is "in here." Our only possible understanding of what is out there (physical causation) is in terms of what is in here (our feelings of personal causation). Therefore, attribution of causality must start in here and the study of it should start by more carefully analyzing the aspects of phenomenal causality. Such an analysis of the conceptual framework that we bring to the study of persons in action suggests (a) that some of our research efforts are attempts to demonstrate nonempirical propositions, i.e., relationships that are logically implied in our premises, and (b) that a step beyond present-day attribution theory to the question "what is entailed by a concept of man as a personal cause?" may point the way to more cumulative and practically useful empirical research.

RICHARD DECHARMS AND DENNIS J. SHEA · Washington University, St. Louis, Missouri. The preparation of this paper was facilitated by an NIMH grant (MH 22127-02). The research reported was supported by a grant from the Carnegie Corporation of New York.

In sketching such an approach we shall be first concerned briefly with the historical development of attribution theory out of object perception and person perception. This history will be compared with the history of the concept of physical causation and the position will be taken that to understand the human conception of physical causation one must have a prior knowledge of human motivation. The attempt to base an understanding of personal causation on knowledge of physical causation has blurred the distinctions between impersonal and personal causation on the one hand, and the self versus other causation on the other. Further, a distinction must be made between intentional causation and imposed causation both of the personal kind.

Orthodox attribution theory stemming from the writings of Heider has usually confined itself to the study of one person observing another's behavior. Personal states such as intentionality are often central (as in Heider's discussion) to these analyses, yet the origin of knowledge of intentionality is left open. We suggest that the distinction between internally caused actions and externally imposed behavior is based in part on personal knowledge and cannot be derived from observation only. Within this context we will ask: How does anyone (the average individual or the psychologist) distinguish between the locus of causality for behavior as internal or external? What difference does such a distinction make for understanding the person being observed? Finally (a question of some practical importance), can a person be helped to initiate more of his own intended behavior? Some suggestions will be made concerning empirical means of addressing these questions.

The Antecedents of Attribution Theory

The specific origin of the concept of attribution of causality is easily traced to Heider (1944, 1958). The context within which it developed was originally known as the study of person perception, specifically impression formation. Classically the study of perception in psychology was the study of object perception; a physical *object* was a stimulus the perception of which was studied. Asch's (1946) classic studies of impression formation moved beyond the perception of a person as *object*, yet the influence of object perception studies lingered in person perception. Heider's notion of attribution broke away from the perception label but stayed with the perception procedure of observing another's behavior. Attribution was the result of an inference from observed behavior. People were assumed to attribute nonobjective internal states to persons under observation. Finally, it was suggested that we might infer our own internal states by an identical process of observing our own behavior (Nisbett and Valins, 1971; Bem, 1967).

The point of this brief sketch is that starting with object perception under the influence of scientific objectivism, psychology has slowly worked its way back to the subject as a person. Yet, paradoxically, it was the radical behaviorist approach (Bem, 1967) that finally confronted self-perception and self-attribution.[1] Epistemologically, radical behaviorism is unable to cope with a subject as person or with the problem of intentionality posed by Heider.

The Concept of Causality

Many philosophers have for years been trying to convince themselves and the physical and the social scientists that the concept of causation is "a relic of a bygone age" (Russell, 1918). Despite Bunge's (1959) attempt to give it a small place under the universal principle of determinacy, the predominant view follows empiricist tradition of Bacon, Locke, Hume, and Mill and rests on the assumption that there is no empirically demonstrable evidence for a necessary causal connection between two events in the physical world. The history of philosophical debate has centered around trying to find a concept of *physical causality* that was adequate for the physical sciences. Hume insisted that the origin of causation could not be found empirically, i.e., in external impressions of the physical world. In this tradition, Michotte (1963) demonstrated that certain stimulus properties in the physical world lead more probably than others to the causal inference, but these stimulus properties certainly do not give a direct access to necessary connection. Again, as in the case of perception in psychology, the study of causation has started with the objects in the physical world and tried to maintain an objective empiricism.

We have obviously oversimplified our sketch by confining it exclusively to the empiricist tradition, which rejects the concept of causation; and that is the point, namely, that within that tradition it is impossible to confront problems posed by attribution theory, which assumes a concept of causality. Attribution theory stands uncomfortably at the confluence of objective psychology (with its Humean rejection of causality and behaviorist rejection of internal states) and the "naive analysis of action" (with stress on personal causality and intentionality).

In contrast to the empiricists, Kant saw causation not as something that inheres in the physical world but as a construction or framework that the mind imposes on the data from the world. The Gestalt psychologists were closer in their theorizing to this idealist tradition than to the empiricist. Thus, for instance, Köhler took the Kantian notion of mental organization imposed on the

---

[1] The paradox of the more rationalist Heider, stressing the observation of the other, while the radical behaviorist (empiricist) Bem moves to using the concept of self, smacks of a twist on the classic idealist versus realist debate in philosophy. Fascinating and relevant as this problem is in light of data such as those presented, for instance, by Jones and Nesbitt (1971) and Storms (1973), it is beyond the scope of the present paper.

data from the physical world and tried to show a naturalistic basis in brain physiology for the organization of thought. He speculated that the way our brain works physiologically "required" us to perceive and think within certain constraints in such diverse areas as object perception and the realm of ethics (Köhler, 1938). He saw causation as a basic category of human thought that was fundamental to the perception of meaningful relationships in the world. Insight for Köhler was perceived causation but he was not content, as was Kant, to leave the basic categories of thought in the mystical realm of innate ideas. His major goal was to demonstrate that the laws of perceptual organization were determined by purely naturalistic processes of brain functioning.

If we look back at the seminal articles that form the point of departure for most studies in attribution theory, we find that Heider (1944) presents the thesis that the Gestalt principles of perceptual organization "can be profitably applied to the perception of other persons and their behavior" (p. 358). In this early paper Heider seemed to take the epistemological stand that there are universal properties in the perception of others that derive from the basic unit formation between an actor and his act. The basic assumption is that of a perceived causal relationship. It seems then that attribution theory stands on the assumption that men have (either innately or acquired from somewhere) the ability to construe the world of personal interaction in terms of causal relationships. Our concern here is to ask where such a universal ability comes from and we, like Köhler, are hesitant to be satisfied with relegating it to the realm of an innate idea.

Personal Causality as a Universal Human Conceptual Framework

The history of philosophical debate has centered around trying to find a concept of physical causality that was adequate for the physical sciences. This is what Heider and the attribution theorists would call *impersonal causation.* If the distinction between personal and impersonal causality is invoked one may ask whether the philosophical debate is relevant to personal causation. If personal causation is taken to mean only the observation of an act of another person and its effect in the environment with the emergent inference that the person caused the effect, the perceptual events may have some of the characteristics of the time-honored billiard ball example of physical causation. However, personal causation always and invariably raises the problem of *intention* and in many respects seems quite different from physical causation.

In the history of the concept of causation one frequently finds references to human and animal actions that have a causal flavor but seem almost to be mentioned in passing and rejected as a kind of magical thinking. As examples we may mention Piaget and Michotte. Piaget discusses efficacy—("the dim sense that the inchoate feelings of effort . . . are somehow responsible for external happenings" (Flavell, 1963, p. 142)—as a precurser of causality in the child but rejects it as a real basis for physical causality. Michotte discovered conditions that lead to what he called the "perception of qualitative causality." He presented subjects with a physical display that resembled a moving "caterpillar" and it was described as "moving itself" a type of *immanent* causality. Again the lead was not followed (Michotte, 1963, p. 185).

It is apparently always assumed that the concept of physical causality is primary and that personal causation is some little understood derivative. Even Heider was implicitly trying to understand the notion of personal causation by means of prior analysis of perceptual organizational properties that lead to the causal inference from observation of physical events.

The major thesis of this paper is that personal causation is the primary human experience and physical causation is secondary. This idea is not new, as we shall see, but it has been consistently rejected because it seems to be an inadequate basis for the understanding of physical causation. We have failed to look closely at the experience of personal causation, one of the most ubiquitous phenomena of human actions, because of the assumption that it was not an adequate base upon which to built an explanation of physical movement. In attempting to follow the dictates of physical science we have overlooked a basic phenomenon unique to our area of inquiry. It is analogous to our extreme attempts to avoid anthropomorphism in studying human beings (Harré and Secord, 1973).

Confining ourselves for the moment to personal causation in attribution theory (and making no claims for physical causation), there is no reason to reject the concept just because it may not be an adequate basis for understanding physical causation.

Reconceptualizing personal causation as primary human experience suggests that it is important to distinguish between personal and impersonal (or physical) causation, and it is clearly a mistake to attempt to understand personal causation from a prior investigation of impersonal or physical causation.

Maine deBiran

The proposal that personal causation is primary and prior to physical causation was put forth a century and a half ago by Maine deBiran. This French philosopher—psychologist of the Napoleonic era was essentially "an empiricist, the intellectual descendant of Locke and Condillac, and like his predecessors is primarily an epistemologist" (Truman, 1904, p. 39). For him the primary reality was experience, that is, raw impressions. What we experience in here is what is *real* not the apparent world out there. Thus the idea of causation must be found in the "original sentiment" or impression in experience. Original impressions were for Maine deBiran, as for Hume, more distinct and clearer than ideas. Hence causation as an innate idea was rejected. Biran insisted that the origin of causation could not be found in external impression of the physical world and credited Hume with demonstrating this fact. Where he departed from the Humean analysis, however, was when Hume insisted that the origin of the impression of causation could only be traced to the experience of expectation, the famous learning or habit explanation as applied to successions of physical events. Maine deBiran felt that there was a clear difference between our impressions after observing repeatedly successive external events and our immediate impressions of self as a cause. The feeling of the verity of causation comes from

> our constant experience of our own voluntary creation of bodily movement, which is quite different from an expectation of a succession of external impressions. This experience 'presents itself . . . obstinately to our minds, and subsists . . . despite us, in the intimate regions of our consciousness' . . . But for several reasons many men do not explicitly acknowledge this experience of an efficacious cause, except indirectly by imagining it to reside *outside* themselves hidden in the 'ultimate springs' of nature. (Hallie, 1959, p. 87)

Earlier in this paper we suggested the distinction between observed *impersonal causation* and experienced *personal causation* and implied that trying to find a route to personal causation through physical causation was an example of aping the physical scientists and missing the unique contribution of our own science. Now we find Biran arriving at a similar conclusion a century and a half ago. Causality plays a different role in psychology than it does in the nautral sciences. Biran speaks of

> two orders of phenomena, distinct and even opposed, and consequently two sorts of observation which have nothing in common in their means, their object, and their aim—and even seem generally to be at odds with each other. . .
> It is no doubt with this divergence in the means and the direction of the two sciences in mind that Newton, touching on the question that concerns us, cried, 'Physics, preserve yourself from metaphysics.'
> We also, having in mind the observation, necessarily two-fold, of two classes of phenomena of which the mixture and confusion offer so many errors, illusions and miscalculations, may cry out in our turn 'Psychology, preserve yourself from physics.' (Biran, quoted in Moore, 1970, p. 45).

Objectivism versus Subjectivism

In the years that have intervened since the writing of those words we have witnessed the radical division between objective approaches to science and subjective approaches that are rejected by science. In our own day we have objective radical behaviorism trying to conform to the tenets of logical positivism and we have phenomenology.

The radical dualism (either mind or matter is real) foisted on us by Descartes has, in the midtwentieth century, begun to yield to a more unified concept of man (Ryle, 1949; Polanyi, 1958). The trouble with starting "out there" is that we are left as outside observers and not as persons in the world. The trouble with starting "in here" is that it leads to a contentless introspectionism or worse to solipsism. What is needed is a concept of the *personal* to mediate between objective things "out there" and one's private sensations "in here."

Persons and the Philosophy of Action

The new approach is based on the concept of a *person* as an *agent* in the world. (Not the Cartesian "I think, therefore I am" but "I exist only in so far as I do," i.e., in so far as I am an agent.) As an agent the person engages in *action*. The distinguishing characteristic of an action is that it is done *by a person* who has an *intention*. An action does not occur of itself, a person does it; therefore, action cannot be separated from the person who does it. [The interested reader can follow up this brief sketch by referring to Schutz (1970), White (1968), Mischel (1969), Macmurray (1957), Ossorio (1966, 1968). To present this position in detail is beyond the scope of this paper.]

For our purposes it is sufficient to point out that neither personal causation in here nor impersonal causation out there is adequate for the understanding of human actions. We must start with the concept of "person" and his "intentional acts."

Persons, Intentions, and Attribution Theory

Ossorio has suggested that in descriptive terms attributing an intentional action to a person logically entails that the person (a) wants something, (b) knows something, (c) knows how to do something, and (d) tries to do something. These aspects are all necessary to the complete description of our concept of intentional action by a person. They are, in fact, the way we distinguish a person from an animal or an object. On this view Heider's (1958) concepts of "can" (know how) and "try" are intrinsic to our concept of person. So are Weiner's (1972) concepts of ability and effort (but not luck and task difficulty).

Ossorio and Davis (1968) have pointed to the necessity to distinguish between empirical and nonempirical questions. They suggest that "a substantial portion of research in social psychology has been presented as a matter of establishing empirically the very relationships which are non-empirical and *could not* be established empirically (like announcing the 'experimental finding' that six and four are ten or that bachelors are not married)" (p. 355). One might conclude that attribution theory is guilty of a similar flaw in attempting to demonstrate the proposition, e.g., that persons (the definition of which entails intentional actions) engage in intentional actions.

The situation is, however, more subtle than that in most cases. In a typical study, person A (the experimenter) attributes to person B (the subject) the ability to distinguish between, e.g., personal and impersonal causality in person C (the stimulus person). The data from many subjects (persons B) confirm that persons do this and it is concluded that persons in general do, in fact, make these distinctions. The problem is that the experimenter carefully contrived the stimulus situation to conform to his notion of personal versus impersonal causality and carefully contrived the questionnaire to reveal that the subjects could see the same distinction that he did. The result shows that subjects can make the same distinctions that the experimenter does (as would be expected if their conception of a person is similar to that of the experimenter). What the data *do not* show is that subjects do in practice make the distinction. More important, they do not tell us anything about the effect of making the distinction on the actions of the observer (person B). The first problem may be merely a measurement problem. Alternatives on questionnaires could be increased or more free response-type measures could be used. The question raised by the second problem (the effects of different attributions on behavior) is the fundamental question of attribution theory and demands more careful analysis of phenomenal causality.

The reason that attribution theory studies have concentrated on demonstrating the use of attribution and slighted the study of its effects on behavior is because of the consistent approach from "outside in" and the predominant study of observers rather than actors. This allows the experimenter to present to the observer a bit of behavior that is "identical" under two different situations, which he (the experimenter) assumes the subject will see as different.

A more careful analysis from the point of view adopted here of conceiving of persons in action suggests that at least two more analytic distinctions must be made before we can proceed. The first is the distinction between "action" and "behavior" and the second (a derivative of the first) is the distinction between an intentional action performed by a person, which has intrinsic relevance to his own wants, versus an imposed behavior performed at the behest of someone else, which has no intrinsic relevance to the actor's own wants.

Action versus Behavior

A distinction advanced recently by Mischel (1969) and others pits the word "action" against the word "behavior" and suggests that in sorting out questions in psychology we should distinguish between questions about human *behavior* and questions about human *action*; and, correspondingly, between two different activities of inquiry and two different kinds of explanation (Braybrooke, 1965, p. 1). In this distinction behavior is reserved for the description of movements, either human or animal, in the context of objective analysis and laws of natural phenomena. Human action is proposed as a unit of analysis in the explanation of the meaning of human activities from the unique point of view of one human being "knowing" what another human being is doing. The type of knowing that is involved in the prediction and control of behavior is fairly well established, but the type of knowing that is involved in the explanations of the meaning of human action is fraught with epistemological difficulties.

In attribution studies we talk about presenting our subjects with "behavior" to observe but we accept their response, which imposes meaning and thereby construes the observed vignette as "action."

Again we are being influenced by our "outside" behavioristic training. As Alfred Schutz has pointed out, it is in vain that we look to behaviorism for distinctions in the "experience" of action (phenomenology of personal causation): "At its best, behaviorism is a scheme of reference useful to the observer of other people's behavior . . . What appears to the observer to be objectively the same behavior may have for the behaving subject very different meanings or no meanings at all" (Schutz, 1968, p. 62).[2]

We turn then to the relevance (or meaning) of the action to the actor and to a distinction between intrinsic relevance and imposed relevance.

Intrinsic versus Imposed Relevance of Action

> The intrinsic relevances are the outcomes of our chosen interests, established by our spontaneous decision to solve a problem by our thinking, to attain a goal by our action, to bring forth a projected state of affairs . . .
>
> We are, however, not only centers of spontaneity, gearing into the world of creating changes within it, but also the mere passive recipients of events beyond our control which occur without our interference. Imposed upon us as relevant are situations and events which are not connected with interests chosen by us, which do not originate in acts of our discretion, and which we have to take just as they are, without any power to modify them by our spontaneous activities except by transforming the relevances thus imposed into intrinsic relevances. (Schutz, 1970, p. 114)

Schutz' distinction between imposed and intrinsic relevance underlies the distinction in the literature between internal and external locus of causality for behavior (Thibaut and Riecken, 1955) and recent work on intrinsic motivation (Deci, 1975, and Lepper, Greene, and Nisbett, 1973). It is clear that two identical looking "behaviors" from the observer's point of view may be entirely different "actions" from the point of view of the actor. If the action is

---

[2] This distinction is at the root of Jones and Nisbett's (1971) discussion of divergent perceptions of the actor versus the observer and Nisbett and Valin's (1971) "perceiving the causes of one's own behavior." Again, however, they are attempting to see the actor as an *observer* of his own behavior as he reflects back on it. This is only one aspect, as Malcolm (1964) has pointed out, and is quite different from the actual experience of ongoing action. Important as this distinction between reflective recall of an experience and the immediate experience is, it can only be noted here. It is clear, however, that the former is what is tapped by most measurement techniques.

embedded in the complete stream of intentional action including wanting, knowing, and knowing how, as well as the action that comprises the trying, then the action will have intrinsic relevance and the locus of causality can be said to be internal. If the action results from imposed relevance, the actor does not experience it as embedded in the stream of intentional action, a situation where the external locus of causality is applicable. It should be noted that, although the notions of imposed and intrinsic relevance shed light on the concept of internal and external locus of causality, Schutz' distinction makes it clear that the term "locus of causality" suffers from the "outside in" problem in attempting to characterize a personal phenomenon purely in terms of an observer.

We are now in a position to summarize some of the rough distinctions that seem prerequisite to the empirical study of some of the phenomena under investigation by attribution theorists. We make no claim for a complete analysis but we do suggest that the two major distinctions are *necessary* in the logical sense if we are to proceed to investigate the "personal" aspects without succumbing to the pitfalls of either objectivism or subjectivism.

The first and most important distinction then is between personal and impersonal causation. If impersonal causation is taken to be physical causation, then personal causation is seen to be radically different from it. Personal causation is the locution we use to discuss intentional actions of persons and entails our concept of persons. Persons, as distinct from all other "things" in the world, engage in the full complex entailed by intentional action.

In the attribution theory literature, Kelley (1971) has lumped personal and impersonal causation together, although he suggests that there may be a need to treat them differently (p. 173). As Ossorio (1966) has pointed out, a degenerate form of a complex concept, such as intentional action, may exist that does not partake of the full complex. Our second distinction between intentional actions and imposed behavior (based on the distinction between action and behavior) may be seen as singling out an important degenerate form for human beings, namely, imposed behavior, which does not partake of the full complex of intentional action in that the "want" and the "know" and even the "know how" are not present within the person but imposed upon him from without.

We have not attempted to give formal definitions of the concepts but rather tried simply to point to some distinctions that we find necessary to guide empirical investigations of persons in action. We are attempting to gain some conceptual clarification to guide research in the spirit of Heider's (1958) book, where his purpose was "to present some considerations that may be helpful in building a conceptual framework suitable to some of the problems in this field" (p. 4). We side with Heider and "with those who think that we shall not attain a conceptual framework by collecting more experimental results. Rather, conceptual clarification is a prerequisite for efficient experimentation" (p. 4).

A word is in order about conceptual frameworks in general. First, clearly the one suggested here is a very rough unfinished scaffolding but it is enough on which to build some empirical research, as we shall see. Second, it should be noted that what we have tried to do is to bring to light at a much more global level what Rommetveit, elsewhere in this volume, has called the architecture of intersubjectivity. Rommetveit explicitly starts with the analysis of language and suggests that any verbal utterance is embedded in tacit preconditions and premises that affect the meaning of the utterance. Similarly, we are saying that attribution theorists' tacit concept of persons and intentional actions affect their research.[3]

Implications for Research

The philosophy of action (White, 1968) and the concept of the personal (Polanyi, 1958; Macmurray, 1957) imply much more than mere rational analysis. They imply that even the social psychologist must conceive of himself as an agent, that he must go into action to learn about other human beings. For our part we have tried to study the "personal" more directly than through the observation of subjects observing others. We have tried to study subjects in action themselves under imposed or intrinsically relevant conditions. We have even tried to get into the action ourselves by intentionally trying to help teachers and school children transform some of the relevances imposed upon them in the school situation into more intrinsic relevances, to use Schutz' terminology.

This is no place to enter into a long description of an intricate research program. Rather, let me illustrate with a brief description of two studies, one in the laboratory and one field experiment.

Imposed (Pawn) versus Intrinsic (Origin) Relevance in the Laboratory

In observations preliminary to his dissertation Kuperman (1967) spent hours behind the one-way screen observing students building tinker-toy models. The basic problem was to determine whether there were measurable differences between what students did when they engaged in an imposed task [or in other terminology (deCharms, 1968) when they acted as pawns] and when there was

---

[3] The reader may note that both Rommetveit and many of the other authors cited here in the discussions of actions and persons take their departure from the analysis of language in the tradition of the ordinary language philosophers. It is assumed that the distinctions needed in discussing action are contained already in our ordinary language (White, 1968, p. 2; Austin, 1956–1957, p. 5). Further language is our bridge between thinking and acting if it is conceived as verbal utterances, i.e., something people do, rather than an inelegant reflexion of "pure thought."

more intrinsic relevance to their actions (when they acted as origins) because they originated their own behavior. Although he looked for any possible indications such as smiling or whistling while they worked, Kuperman ultimately found himself in the trap of our measurement techniques based on self-report questionnaires. He did find large differences in reported liking for the origin models compared to pawn models and the expected feeling of freedom and self-directedness. But it remained a question (similar to that discussed by Daveney, 1974) whether objective observations could distinguish between the two situations.

In a follow-up study, deCharms, Dougherty, and Wurtz (reported in deCharms, 1968) using the Kuperman origin and pawn situation manipulation did obtain behavioral measures of differential task accomplishment and recall of the project. The origin—pawn manipulations (which were both administered to every subject) strongly affected choice to complete the origin model more elegantly and recall of names associated with the origin model, as well as liking and feelings of freedom in the self-reports.

A Field Experiment to Help Convert Imposed to Intrinsic Relevance

In 1967 we moved from the laboratory to the complex world of the elementary school and started a longitudinal study in which we attempted to help Black inner-city children to feel more personal causation in the school situation (deCharms, 1976). Briefly we gave personal causation training to teachers and with them developed techniques for training their pupils. We started in the fifth grade and followed the children through eighth grade, training new teachers each year and comparing trained teachers and their pupils with untrained teachers and their pupils. The training succeeded in changing many aspects of the behavior of the experimental pupils. For instance, a measure that we developed of the origin—pawn variable increased as a function of training each year but did not increase when training did not intervene. Both the pupils attendance at school and their academic achievement were positively affected by the training.

These studies represent a beginning in answering the questions raised in the introduction of this paper. The most difficult question is the first, viz., how does anyone (psychologist, or observer) verify that a person sees intrinsic relevance in what he is doing or that the relevance is imposed on him (distinguish between an internal versus external locus of causality). The actor has private access to this knowledge and it may be that the only possible recourse is to ask him (Harre and Secord, 1973). Kuperman's data on self-report show that this can be done.

To distinguish between intrinsic and imposed relevance is to distinguish between intentional action and something less central to the person (nonintentional movement at the extreme). Daveney (1974) has claimed "if the intention the agent has in mind is indispensible to the way in which the action is described, . . . verification by external observation alone is impossible" (p. 111); but people do identify intentional actions; therefore, "we do have more to go on than the material movements" (p. 120). Daveney seems to admit only "the evidence of what other people tell us about their intentions [but] the fact that such reports are available accounts for our knowledge of the external signs of intentional behavior" (p. 120).

We could then parsimoniously say that we are able to distinguish, as in the deCharms, Dougherty, and Wurtz study (deCharms, 1968), between intentionally relevant actions and imposed behavior through a combination of external signs and knowledge gleaned earlier from self-reports. This explanation has the merit of parsimony only if we can solve the problem of how the earlier reports were verified. We are caught in the trap of using two "outside" signs. The solution may be that verbal utterances are not mere movements but partake of the "personal." Based on our concept of personal causation (from Biran) and Polanyi's (1958) personal knowledge, it seems inevitable, however, that the ultimate trust in self-reports comes from the personal knowledge of the observer, to which only he is privy.

However this controversy should come out, it does seem clear that we can have some reliable knowledge of a person's intentions but only when one person observes the other's movements and either (a) has a stock of prior knowledge about self-reports, or (b) has personal knowledge about his own intentions in similar situations, or (c) both. Our position is that *both* are necessary.[4]

Having made some progress in the laboratory in distinguishing between intrinsically relevant actions and imposed behaviors, we attacked the question "what difference does it make?" in a real-life setting, hoping to have a real impact. First, we developed a free-response thought sample measure (the origin–pawn measure, Plimpton, 1970) and content-analyzed school children's stories for intrinsically relevant actions (origin) versus imposed (pawn) behavior. Note that we have measured whether the children *do* make the distinction not whether they can when it is pointed out in a questionnaire. We found low but significant correlations between this measure and academic achievement, showing that some do make the distinction and to the extent that they do they have higher achievement.

Then we attacked the question "can school children be helped to distinguish more and to initiate more intentional action?" Using our origin–pawn measure

[4] Strawson (1958), for instance, postulates the need to conceive of ascriptions to humans that can be both self- and other-ascribable. He calls them P-predicates: ". . . It is essential to the character of these predicates that they have both first- and third-person ascriptive uses, that they are both self-ascribable otherwise than on the basis of observation of the behavior of the subject of them, and other-ascribable on the basis of behavior criteria. To learn their use is to learn both aspects of their use." (p. 346). Strawson invokes these predicates precisely in discussing "actions" that "clearly imply intention."

we showed that (a) we could increase the number of intrinsically relevant (origin) themes in a trained group compared to an untrained group, (b) the trained group increased in academic achievement (and other measures), and most strongly, (c) those who showed the greatest increase in number of intrinsically relevant themes showed the greatest increase in academic achievement.

Conclusion

We have concentrated our major effort in this paper in showing the potential impact of a very broad conceptual framework involving conceptualizations of "persons" and "intentional action" on research in what is now called attribution theory. The person as agent is our central theme and necessitates an acceptance of evidence of self as a cause and the distinctions between personal and impersonal causation as well as between intentional action and imposed behavior. The small space devoted to empirical research does not reflect our opinion of its importance. We have just begun to scratch the surface in finding techniques to study intentional behavior.

References

Asch, S. E. Forming impressions of personality. *Journal of Abnormal & Social Psychology*, 1946, 41, 258–290.

Austin, J. L. A plea for excuses. *Proceedings of the Aristotelean Society*, 1956–1957, 57, 1–30.

Bem, D. J. Self perception: An alternative interpretation of cognitive dissonance phenomena. *Psychological Review*, 1967, 74, 183–200.

Braybrooke, D. (ed.). *Philosophical problems of the social sciences.* New York: MacMillan, 1965.

Bunge, M. *Causality.* Cambridge, Mass.: Harvard Univ. Press, 1959.

Daveney, T. K. Intentional behavior. *Journal of the Theory of Social Behavior*, 1974, 4, 111–129.

DeCharms, R. *Personal causation.* New York: Academic Press, 1968.

DeCharms, R. *Enhancing motivation: Change in the classroom.* New York: Irvington Publishers, 1976.

Deci, E. L. *Intrinsic motivation.* Plenum Press, 1975.

Flavell, J. H. *The developmental psychology of Jean Piaget.* Princeton, New Jersey: Van Nostrand, 1963.

Hallie, P. P. *Maine deBiran: Reformer of empiricism, 1766–1824.* Cambridge, Mass.: Harvard Univ. Press, 1959.

Harré, R., and Secord, P. F. *The explanation of social behavior.* Totowa, New Jersey: Rowman & Littlefield, 1972.

Heider, F. Social perception and phenomenal causality. *Psychological Review*, 1944, 51, 358–374.

Heider, F. *The psychology of interpersonal relations.* New York: Wiley, 1958.

Jones, E. E., and Nisbett, R. E. The actor and the observer: Divergent perceptions of the causes of behavior, in E. E. Jones, D. E. Kanouse, H. H. Kelley, R. E. Nisbett, S. Valins, and B. Weiner (eds.), *Attribution: Perceiving the causes of behavior.* Morristown, New Jersey: General Learning Press, 1971.

Kelley, H. H. Causal schemata and the attribution process, in E. E. Jones, D. E. Kanouse, H. H. Kelley, R. E. Nisbett, S. Valins, and B. Weiner (eds.), *Attribution: Perceiving the causes of behavior.* Morristown, New Jersey: General Learning Press, 1971.

Köhler, W. *The place of value in a world of facts.* New York: Liveright, 1938.

Kuperman, A. *Relations between differential constraints, affect, and the origin–pawn variable.* Unpublished doctoral dissertation, Washington Univ., St. Louis, Missouri, 1967.

Lepper, M. R., Greene, D., and Nisbett, R. E. Undermining children's intrinsic interest with extrinsic rewards: A test of the "over justification" hypothesis. *Journal of Personality and Social Psychology*, 1973, **28**, 129–137.

Macmurray, J. *The self as agent.* New York: Harper, 1957.

Malcolm, N. Behaviorism as a philosophy of psychology, in T. W. Wann (ed.), *Behaviorism and phenomenology*, pp. 141–155. Chicago: Univ. of Chicago Press, 1964.

Michotte, A. *The perception of causality.* New York: Basic Books, 1963.

Mischel, T. (ed.). *Human action.* New York: Academic Press, 1969.

Moore, F. C. T. *The psychology of Maine deBiran.* Oxford: Clarendon Press, 1970.

Nisbett, R. E., and Valins, S. Perceiving the causes of one's own behavior, in E. E. Jones, D. E. Kanouse, H. H. Kelley, R. E. Nisbett, S. Valins, and B. Weiner (eds.), *Attribution: perceiving the causes of behavior.* Morristown, New Jersey: General Learning Press, 1971.

Ossorio, P. G. *Persons.* Boulder Colorado: Linguistic Research Institute, Report #3, 1966.

Ossorio, P. G. *Syllabus* # 2. Unpublished manuscript, Boulder, Colorado, 1969.

Ossorio, P., and Davis, K. E. The self, intentionality, and reactions to evaluations of the self, in C. Gordon and K. J. Gergen (eds.), *The self in social interaction*, pp. 355–369. New York: Wiley, 1968.

Plimpton, F. H. *The effects of motivation training upon the origin syndrome.* Unpublished doctoral dissertation, Washington Univ., St. Louis, Missouri, 1970.

Polanyi, M. *Personal knowledge.* Chicago: Univ. of Chicago Press, 1958.

Russell, B. (1918). *Mysticism and logic.* London: Penguin, 1953.

Ryle, G. *The concept of mind.* New York: Barnes & Noble, 1949.

Schutz, A. On multiple realities, in C. Gordon and K. J. Gergen (eds.), *The self in social interaction*, pp. 61–70. New York: Wiley, 1968.

Schutz, A. On phenomenology & social relations, in H. R. Wagner, (ed.). Chicago: Univ. of Chicago Press, 1970.

Strawson, P. F. Persons. In *Minnesota studies in the philosophy of science*, 1958, Vol. II, pp. 330–353.

Thibaut, J. W., and Riecken, H. W. Some determinants and consequences of the perception of social causality. *Journal of Personality*, 1955, **24**, 113–133.

Truman, N. E. *Maine deBiran's philosophy of will.* New York: Macmillan, 1904.

Weiner, B. *Theories of motivation.* Chicago: Markham, 1972.

White, A. R. (Ed.). *The philosophy of action.* New York: Oxford Univ. Press, 1968.

CRITIQUE

The Interdependent Mode of Personal Causality

JOHN T. PARTINGTON

This discussion of deCharms and Shea's article will focus on their field research. First, however, I would like to support the authors' judgment in selecting the human conception of causality as an area of concern. The concept of causality has been the cornerstone in the history of scientific thought. Moreover, within individual human experience the illusion of personal causality has been referred to as "the bedrock on which life flourishes" (Lefcourt, 1973); and its counterpart, the experience of helplessness, may be the key for understanding heretofore inexplicable untimely deaths in all manner of species (Seligman, 1974). It may be inferred from the paper that the topic of personal causality has everything to challenge the scholar—a rich history, theoretical relevance, methodological issues and problems, practical significance, and opportunities for cross-cultural and interdisciplinary research. In addition to these plums, I believe that the topic is particularly rich and timely for North American scholars since it seems to express a central component of our contemporary zeitgeist, which is characterized by concern for the issue of free will and determinism. Our concern about deterministic forces is escalated daily by media reports of gross invasions of privacy not only by psychologists but by corporations and, yes, even governments. Within psychology Skinner's musings (Skinner, 1971) have done little to dispel our concern. As is well known, McClelland (1971) has conceptualized our pervasive concern for control as a social motive labeled "need-power." His content coding of popular literature in the 1950s to 1960s suggested that the

JOHN T. PARTINGTON · Carleton University, Ottawa, Ontario, Canada.

United States has been moving into an unprecedented era of high need-power. Probably associated with or in reaction against the control-power dogma we are now witness to a massive expression of interest in personal freedom manifest in the encounter movement, the chemical revolution, and most recently in the enthusiasm for eastern philosophies. In sum, the authors are to be commended for identifying and clarifying the epistemological bases for this very important problem area and for opening the topic for our further consideration.

The next section of this discussion examines broad implications of the authors' longitudinal field study in which they attempted to help black inner-city children to feel more personal causation in the school situation. Axiomatic to my discussion is the position that as scholars we cannot help but serve knowingly—willingly or otherwise—as agents of social change. We psychologists serve as models when we choose to study something. Through our research priorities and decisions we reinforce the significance of phenomena for others— our subjects, students, peers, and the general public. The phenomena reinforced by Shea and de Charms is "origin-mode" personal causality. What are the consequences of such a decision? Consider the possibility that the belief that one is the locus of control in his own life may be a myth or illusion created and maintained by our particular world view. How should we proceed if that illusion creates difficulties for us as scientists and for human adjustment in general? Do we pursue "origin-mode" causality, recognizing that our privileged position as scholars may reinforce the harmful myth? Some would argue that an empirical assault to get at the facts might more quickly dispel the myth. Others would feel that myth or not it is important for our discipline to understand the processes involved regardless of the consequences. However, I have become both cynical about the power of facts, and existentially concerned about the role of psychology in the world. My own preference in this hypothetical dilemma is to attempt to identify conceptually a style of causal attribution that might reveal itself among people if their cognitive development could proceed unhindered by cultural myths—a style of causal attribution that seems most consistent with our most valid estimate of human nature and of physical and social realities. Research guided by that new perspective of causality would be less likely to contribute to the maintenance of our myth about origin mode causality and might contribute to the development of better adjustment among all who come in contact with the new conception—scholars, subjects, and people in general.

But is the origin-mode of personal causality a harmful illusion? There are millions in India and growing waves of converts in other parts of the world who feel that it is an illusion. These people subscribe to the Hindu belief in a nondialectic conception of the universe, a conception that holds that if people can overcome ignorance, they will discover the artificiality of concepts such as time, space, and causality and experience everything as one reality. But perhaps that is just another myth supported by a different paradigm. Of more relevance to us here is the answer to this issue that one might extrapolate from the prevailing dogma of those immersed in the accepted physical science paradigm in psychology. We will use Skinner's position since he has become idol to some, straw man and scapegoat to others, but central to all. As we learn from *Beyond Freedom and Dignity* (Skinner, 1971) Skinner feels that personal freedom is an illusion and our destinies are controlled by reinforcement contingencies. This model clearly denies the validity of the myth of origin-mode personal causality while assuming the validity of physical causality. Skinner's position derives from a mechanical model of the universe. Paradoxically, faith in such absolute determinism was shattered years ago by developments in quantum physics. The hardest-nosed physical scientists have for the past forty or fifty years been questioning the certainty of physical causality and many have been turning toward religion in their private lives. Because of space limitations, I will state arbitrarily from the above that there is reason to feel that origin-mode causality may be illusory. Such a position is consistent with that of some scholars actually working in the area of personal control (e.g., Lefcourt, 1973; Seligman, 1974) who view freedom as a personal construction or illusion, though very significant notwithstanding.

My conceptual analysis will now consider any possible negative consequences of the belief in personal control. This may be difficult since the acceptable literature as usual is beginning to be padded by positive results. The two articles from which I will extrapolate appear in my favorite journal, *Psychology Today*. In *The Myth of the isolated artist* (Oates, 1973) it is argued that the very high rates of suicide and mental breakdown among gifted people may be due to the illusion created by readers and critics that the artist is the sole source of his productions. It is further suggested that artists might be better adjusted if we, as public, allowed them to recognize their interdependence with others for their productions. The point is that too great an emphasis on personal causality may get the artist into trouble. I shall generalize this position now with reference to a more recent article entitled *Submissive death* (Seligman, 1974). This article concludes from a survey of human and animal research that in marginal situations organisms that experience helplessness become more vulnerable to a wide variety of disorders, including death. My thesis is that the panic engendered by helplessness, in fact, the very conception of helplessness, might be a function of a misconception concerning the scope of one's personal control. In personality jargon, too great a belief in one's autonomy may be a bad thing. Turning this line of reasoning toward our own discipline I would suggest that the arrogance, competitiveness, and frivolity identified among many social psychologists in the 1960s (Ring, 1967) may have stemmed from a misconception of their locus of control. Fortunately, we have experienced a reformation known as the "social psychology of the psychological experiment," which has revealed the obvious— that we cannot isolate ourselves, that our destinies and those of our subjects and of our public are inextricably linked. This reformation has given birth to different methodologies including a renewed interest in the human subject as an active agent working in collaboration with the scientist (Mixon, 1972), an interesting diffusion of control within our discipline.

The analysis to this point has suggested that origin-type personal causality may be an illusion created by our particular world view, an illustion, moreover, with possible negative consequences. Accordingly, it is suggested that an alternative conception of causality be identified as our target for future research. This is because people may be influenced by what we choose to study even though we do not intend this to happen. Thus, we had better select carefully among our alternative targets of research.

What alternative conceptions of causality are there? Heider's (1958) original attribution model suggested that with individual cognitive organization there exist two mutually exclusive polarities, environmental forces (the "pawn" orientation), and personal forces (the "origin" orientation). However, our great mentor Kurt Lewin proposed that these forces might profitably be viewed as interacting. This integrated perspective makes a great deal of sense with reference to my sketchy understanding of cognition. To explain I will use Piaget's (1968) equilibration model of cognitive development. Recall that Piaget assumes that we organize our world in accordance with certain structural givens, which interact with the environment to produce more complex schemata, and that these in turn provide a better fit to the world. To illustrate, consider the child playing with modeling clay. Initially, he employs his simple schemas of length and circumference independently when he estimates the size of the piece. This means that at times he may think he has more clay because the piece becomes longer as he rolls it. His estimate of size is distorted because he focuses on only one dimension of the piece—length. Later, however, the child's length– circumference schemas will become integrated through the advanced cognitive operation and he will be less likely to be fooled in his size and shape estimates by changes in shape. This cognitive development involves a decentering from each of the simple schemas in order that they might be simultaneously coordinated into a new schemata. Although such developments progress according to stages, their emergence may be facilitated or impaired by experience (Winokur, 1972). Thus a child who has the opportunity to play with changeable substances like clay is more likely to discover contradictions between his length and circumference schemas when they are used independently to estimate quantity. He will therefore be more likely to decenter from them and coordinate them into a better fitting schemata. I have chosen this model as a guide for discussing modes of causal attribution since it has already been applied to social problems (e.g., Kohlberg, 1964; Feffer, 1959). In each extension of the model, better social adjustment was seen to be associated with the development of higher order schemata formed by coordinating previously isolated schemas.

It may be inferred from this that in terms of the equilibration model both origin and pawn modes of personal attribution of causality reflect relatively primitive levels of social cognition since each employs a unidimensional schema.

In contrast, Lewin's interaction model may be interpreted to evidence advanced social cognition. I will label this latter alternative the "interdependent mode" of personal causality. Perhaps some illustrations may be useful as conceptual pegs. I believe that the interdependent mode is reflected in the causal attributions of many artists such as Michelangelo, who apparently felt that he was merely cooperating with the marble to release the finished figure. I also feel that the interdependent mode is evident in the TV interviews of many great team-playing athletes. Finally, another way to grasp this new conception for those familiar with the attribution literature is to imagine a coordination between the actor and observer perspectives (Jones and Nisbett, 1971). The interdependent mode is an organic construction of causality. Those who use it view results of their actions as a joint function of their own specific behaviors together with all the probabilistically charged events at work in the world. I believe that such an attribution mode could influence dramatically our most basic attitudes and values concerning life and death. As social psychologists armed with this mode we might *not* have become entrapped by behaviorism and all the unreal experimenter–subject interactions associated with that movement.

I will conclude the discussion by asking why interdependent causal schemata have not been widely identified by investigators in the attribution camp. Several reasons come to mind: Perhaps the polarized person–environment model proposed by Heider guided research design and questionnaire construction in such a way as to obviate the possibility that subjects might manifest this particular mode of response; or perhaps the achievement and power orientations in the prevailing Western culture have been so well built into socialization practices that all those who are part of the culture by fiat employ the origin mode. Others, the marginal, alienated, anomic, and disadvantaged groups by dint of the almost insurmountable repressive social and economic forces that they usually encounter from the environment may naturally have developed the pawn orientation. Thus, only origin or pawn styles of personal causality may in fact be encountered in our investigations. Finally, perhaps our practice of advancing students at around 12 years of age from grades 7 or 8 where they have begun to feel "on top," to high school where they are "at the bottom of the heap," may be unfortunately timed. It is possible that this role change occurs precisely at the critical period in the development of personal causal schemata and therefore aborts what would have been a normally expected coordination of origin–pawn perspectives. Whatever the reasons for the relative absence of concern about interdependent causal schemata, it is hoped that deCharms and Shea will reexamine the focus of their field research in light of these remarks.

I close with a comment on freedom especially in view of one of Zajonc's responses at the conference to some of Moffitt's points. Recall that Moffitt was questioning the appropriateness of Zajonc's formalism as applied to an understanding of intellectual development. Among other things Zajonc replied that we should all be free to take whatever approach makes us feel most comfortable. I agree, but I would also like to note that those who have chosen a conceptual approach, especially young scholars, have not really been free in the past. When the power structure in the politics of psychology—the senior professors on tenure and promotion committees, journal editors, and reviewers of grant applications—when most of these people subscribed to the achievement, origin mode, which favoured action over reflection, the scholar who chose to think about the broader context of his research, to question paradigms and so on, was in trouble. Why? Because from the "origin" perspective, in a production-conscious technological culture, reflection and discourse look like doing nothing. It was far safer to launch several badly conceived studies than to think. After all, one could lump them all together in the form of a paper to get publication "credit." I feel that those who engaged in empirical productivity no matter how poorly conceptualized have been freer in the past than those who chose to conceptualize—for many of the latter did not earn tenure due to their weak publication records. It is my sincere hope that this conference has assisted in establishing a more balanced perspective among our power elite in order that scholars with different search preferences will be equally free.

References

Feffer, M. The cognitive implications of role-taking behavior. *Journal of Personality*, 1959, 27, 152–168.

Heider, F. *The psychology of interpersonal relations*. New York: Wiley, 1958.

Jones, E. E. and Nisbett, R. E. *The actor and the observer: Divergent perceptions of the causes of behaviour*. New York: General Learning Press, 1971.

Kohlberg, L. Development of moral character and moral ideology, in M. L. Hoffman and L. W. Hoffman (eds.), *Review of child development research*, Vol. 1. New York: Russell Sage Foundation, 1964.

Lefcourt, H. M. The function of the illusions of control and freedom. *American Psychologist*, May 1973, 417–425.

McClelland, D. C. *Motivational trends in society*. New York: General Learning Press, 1971.

Mixon, D. Instead of deception. *Journal of Theory of Social Behavior*, 1972, 2, 145–177.

Oates, J. C. The myth of the isolated artist. *Psychology Today*, May 1973.

Piaget, J. *Six psychological studies*. New York: Vintage Books, 1968.

Ring, K. Experimental Social Psychology: Some sober questions about some frivolous values. *Journal of Experimental Social Psychology*, 1967, 3, 113–123.

Seligman, M. E. Q. Submissive death: Giving up on life. *Psychology Today*, May 1974.

Skinner, B. F. *Beyond freedom and dignity*. New York: Knopf, 1971.

Winokur, M. The effect of external evaluation on subject–object interaction. Unpublished doctoral dissertation, Yeshiva University, New York, 1972.

CRITIQUE

On deCharms and Shea's "Beyond Attribution Theory"

CARYLL STEFFENS

DeCharms and Shea seem to be suggesting that:

(1) Behaviorism is an inadequate paradigm for understanding human behavior. Its attempt to reduce all behavior to the level of objectively observable physical movements has been heuristic but there is a need for an additional paradigm.

(2) This new paradigm would include the study of a uniquely human, nonphysical phenomenon. This phenomenon is, I think, what Weber calls "verstehen," intuitive understanding. This new paradigm is necessary because human behavior is not objectively meaningful and the same behavior may mean different things to different people or under different circumstances.

(3) Attribution theory should address itself to the task of providing this new paradigm. Attribution theorists study paradigms used by people. In addition they should develop a paradigm for the study of paradigms. How should they do this? By trying to identify the implicit paradigm they are using. Heider began this task by identifying causality as a central issue in understanding attribution but he limited himself to consideration of how an observer identifies causes. He did not discuss the actor's experience of being a cause. DeCharms and Shea argue that this existential experience of being a cause is the source of attribution of personal causation. They say that their main thesis is that personal causation is a primary human experience. Perception of physical causation is secondary. They, therefore, are stressing the importance of an unobservable existential state as a

CARYLL STEFFENS · Carleton University, Ottawa, Ontario, Canada.

major "independent" variable. This, I feel, is the source of their claim to be developing a nonbehavioristic paradigm. I take it then that they are suggesting in general that verstehen is the source of attributions. People attribute motives and other internal states because they experience these phenomena. Attribution theorists, therefore, should study these experiences.

Shea and deCharms then discuss the research they feel was an outcome of this conception. They discuss studies in which they demonstrate that a conceptual scheme of origins and pawns was useful in self-descriptions and in the descriptions of others. They discuss ways of generating a feeling of being an origin and show some of the consequences of this feeling.

I shall address my discussion to three major issues: (1) Is there a need for a nonbehaviorist paradigm? (2) If so, where does attribution "theory" fit in? (3) The research discussed by deCharms and Shea.

Is There a Need for a Nonbehaviorist Paradigm?

Clearly many people are now saying that there is. In psychology, the phenomenologists are making the loudest demands. They argue that individuals do not have privileged access cognitively to their own minds. In sociology, ethnomethodologists argue that we have collectively a privileged access to the understanding of social life. They suggest that sociologists should study human methods for dealing with everyday life and that this should include looking at the projects, plans, and intentions of ordinary man. "Idealists" like Peter Winch share this view, arguing that social phenomena only exist insofar as they have meaning for those who engage in social conduct. The explanation of social conduct thus consists in the elucidation of motive and meaning. Phenomenologists, ethnomethodologists, and idealists seem to share at least two concerns:

(1) The insistence that human behavior is not the same as the behavior of nonliving phenomena (they are usually rather silent about nonhuman living organisms unless they are attacking the behaviorists for generalizing from animal studies). The unique characteristic of human behavior is "verstehen" and should be studied by social scientists;

(2) A total rejection of behaviorism—particularly the behaviorist's assumptions that (a) theories need not include references to internal states, (b) behavior is determined (by external forces), i.e., the denial of free will, and (c) psychology is explicable in principle by the theories of physiology, biochemistry, and (ultimately) physics.

DeCharms and Shea share the first concern and the first objection to behaviorism while not explicitly (nor do I think implicitly) denying either that determinism is possible, or the possible unity of science.

I am not sure that there are uniquely human behaviors. A table may will itself to stand still because it defined this situation as being one in which that behavior is appropriate. If consciousness is not material, I do not know how to reject this hypothesis. But pragmatically it does seem to be true that I do not really need to take a table's intentions into account. I do (to show a bit of my "verstehen") take other people's intentions into account. I agree that this statement and the statements of other people about subjective states should be taken into account in some way by social scientists. I think that self-reports and ontological assumptions are relevant data in the study of human beings. However, it is surely obvious that people sometimes lie and are sometimes wrong. Human beings simply cannot be counted on to tell the truth or to perceive objectively. That is why the species invented scientific methods (some ways of testing our statements) and obviously even these techniques have their drawbacks—as social psychologists like Rosenthal and Orne and philosophers like Popper have pointed out. Popper believes that scientific objectivity is only a function of the intersubjectivity of the scientific method. He argues that free criticism and the attempt to speak the same language so as to guarantee replicability will result in objectivity. If people with alternative hypotheses are free to test them, ultimately we will have objective knowledge. This is fine so long as people within a society have different biases so that someone will recognize biased observations. Unfortunately if all people misperceive in a society, biases cannot readily be corrected. The only hope under these circumstances is that people from other societies or people at another time will identify biased information. There is, however, no guarantee that this will happen. There is, therefore, no guarantee that any observations—even our scientific ones—are unbiased.

I do not, however, believe that this critique of our traditional methods justifies throwing them out. At the same time I cannot justify throwing out data simply on the grounds that they are not objective. There should be room in the social sciences for Goffman, for Laing, for Castenedes—for people who are very explicitly using nonbehaviorist paradigms. I agree with deCharms and Shea that descriptions of ontological experience are legitimate data. I do not think that this belief negates the possibility that there is unity in science—that the manipulation of atoms may affect verstehen; there may even be a perfect correspondance between the two. One of the strengths of the deCharms and Shea's position is that they speak of complementary paradigms, not alternative paradigms. I believe that it is far too soon for us to accept completely the assumptions of determinism and unity of science, but it is also too soon for us to reject them. If these assumptions are accurate the data provided by the nonbehaviorists should ultimately be explicable in behaviorist terms, which leads to my second point.

Where Does Attribution Theory Fit In?

I disagree with deCharms and Shea that attribution theory is outside the behaviorists' tradition—nor do I think it should be (except in the sense that it treats references to internal states as observable data). I believe that the de-

Charms and Shea discussion of ontological sources of attributions is a discussion of verstehen. It is probably untestable (unless we perfect our esp skills) and is in the Goffman *et al.* tradition. It is then implied that this verstehen is the source of the research reported. The generation of hypotheses is clearly one recognized function of verstehen. There does not, however, seem to be any logical connection between their verstehen and their research. I think that an attribution theorist would wonder why the particular verstehen described by deCharms and Shea would lead to their hypotheses. He or she would want some assurance (besides self-report) that the two were connected. Theorists would probably believe that they had a type of understanding of this phenomenon if they could get other subjects to behave in the same way that deCharms and Shea behaved by manipulating relevant independent variables. They would not be surprised if ultimately a physicist could manipulate atoms and produce the same changes that the social psychologist produced. Attribution theorists would not be surprised if a Skinnerian translated their variables into behaviorist terms—although they would deny that this negated the value of their own terms.

I would probably define deCharms and Shea's discussion of their *verstehen* as phenomenology, ethnomethodology, or idealism. I would define their hypotheses and related data as attribution theory. I do this not because I like making arbitrary divisions but because I think that it is functional to think in terms of private experience, communication about private experience, and research about communication about private experience. I think the phenomenologists are urging us to talk about private experience and the attribution theorists are urging us to study this talk.

The Research Discussed by deCharms and Shea

The third topic is the research reported by deCharms and Shea. I found it strange that, in a paper emphasizing the importance of conceptual frameworks, the framework used should be so simplistic. Following their advice, I asked myself, "What am I—an origin or a pawn?" I could not answer the question. Emotionally, I probably accept a soft determinist position. External and material factors determine the ontological self that makes my choices. I am, therefore, both an origin and a pawn. I then asked myself how this approach to causality affected my behavior. I do not think it does at all (although I could be lying and I may be wrong). I do, however, think that my perception of the probability of success of a given behavior (combined with the strength of my motivation and the attractiveness of incentives) does affect my behavior. I strongly suspect that deCharms and Shea's measures may be tapping that variable and behavioral changes which they observe are a function of changes in perceived probabilities of success.

Ideologically I am very suspicious of any program that seems to be trying to eradicate poverty by changing the poor. I do not myself feel that anyone can get anywhere in the social system if he tries. Sometimes there is a low probability of a group of people being successful at particular types of activities—unless something is done about reward structures controlled by other members of the society. Sometimes people are powerless—although I will freely grant that individuals and groups may have more power than they think they have. But the point I want to make is that I think power and perceived probability of success are better variables for analyzing the inner-city field experiment than is "source of causality." At the very minimum I suspect that the confounding of these variables makes deCharms and Shea's empirical conclusions questionable. I think that most of the ancient kings and surely some of the popes felt that they were simply God's pawns, but I suspect that their behavior was vastly different from the black kid with the alcoholic mother, no father, and nine brothers and sisters who says "I don't feel like the causal locus of my behavior."

EXIT, VOICE, AND
INTERGROUP RELATIONS

HENRI TAJFEL

If you customarily buy a certain brand of toothpaste, and its price goes up or its quality deteriorates, you will change—without much difficulty or conflict—to another brand. If you discover that the car you have just bought has certain features you dislike, you may decide to sell it and buy one of another manufacture; but if you cannot very well afford the new transaction you may decide to write to the manufacturer pointing out the defects and demanding improvements. If your child goes to a state school that dissatisfies you for various reasons, you may decide to change to a private school. But changing schools may be a traumatic experience for the child; or you may not be able to afford a private school; or there may be no private schools easily available; or they may not be available at all. Whenever any combination of these circumstances arises, the more strongly you feel about the quality of your child's education, the more you are likely to try to do something about the quality of his or her present school, and to find allies among other parents who feel the way you do. If you have been active for many years in a political party, and you are increasingly dissatisfied with some of its policies, you will not just leave and join another party; before you decide to do so, you will try again and again to change the

HENRI TAJFEL · University of Bristol, England. This paper is an extensively modified version of a contribution to a collection of articles on the "exit-voice" theme (Tajfel, 1975), which appeared in *Social Science Information* (Paris) in 1974 and 1975. Reprinted by permission.

present policies in a direction which suits you better, and the stronger has been your past affiliation, the more difficult you will find it to leave, and the more you will try all possible means to modify the situation from the inside. If you are miserable in your own country, you might try to emigrate. But emigration is a harsh decision to take, and sometimes it may not be possible at all. The harsher or the more nearly impossible it is, the more likely you are to join the ranks of those who try to change things from inside, even by revolutionary means.

There is nothing very startling about this list of examples. In the language used by the economist Hirschman (1970)[1] they can be arranged, from those mentioned earlier above to those mentioned later, on a dimension that moves from the likelihood of the use of "exit" to the likelihood of the use of "voice" as an individual's way of dealing with the problems he confronts. Or, in Hirschman's terms: "Some customers stop buying the firm's products or some members leave the organization: this is the *exit option*" (p. 4). And: "The firm's customers or the organization's members express their dissatisfaction directly to the management or to some other authority to which management is subordinate or through general protest addressed to anyone who cares to listen: this is the *voice option*" (p. 4). Very soon we learn that "voice is political action by excellence" (p. 16).

Hirschman's influential book *Exit, voice and loyalty* (1970) was concerned, as its subtitle (*Responses to decline in firms, organizations and states*) indicates, with the relative efficiency of the options of exit and voice, and of their various combinations ("the elusive optimal mix of exit and voice"), in preventing a decline in the functioning of various kinds of social institutions, public or private. His analysis, grounded in economics, reached further to consider conditions for various modes of effective political action. It is not my purpose here to comment in any detail upon this analysis or to redescribe it. But the complex relationships described by Hirschman between the availability of exit to an individual and his use of voice, as they apply to his "responses to decline" of a social institution, have a number of far-reaching implications for the social psychology of intergroup relations. These implications concern (i) a transposition of the exit–voice relationship from individual behavior to the behavior of a social group, and (ii) the theoretical possibility that the use of voice in an intergroup context may become a powerful force toward the maintenance of status quo rather than helping to prevent the decline in the functioning of an organization.

The language of exit and voice converges closely with the language of "social mobility" and of "social change," which I adopted in a recent paper (Tajfel, 1974a).[2] The two equivalent descriptions are as follows:

---

[1] All quotations from *Exit, voice and loyalty* used in the present text are taken from the second edition (1972); so are the page numbers of the quotations.

[2] The Katz–Newcomb Lectures for 1974 delivered at the University of Michigan. These lectures will be published in a modified form: copies of the present text are available on request. A preliminary version of one part of the lectures appeared in *Social Science Information* (Tajfel, 1974b).

What I mean by social mobility is an individual's perception that he can improve his position in a social situation, or more generally, move from one position to another, *as an individual.* The first direct implication of this definition is that the individual's system of beliefs about the society in which he lives contains the expectation that, in principle, he is able to leave his present social group or groups and move to other groups which suit him better. Social mobility in this sense consists therefore of a subjective structuring of a social system (however small or large the system may be) in which the basic assumption is that the system is flexible and permeable, that it permits a fairly free movement of the individual particles of which it consists. At this point of the argument, it does not matter very much whether the causation of free individual movement is perceived as being due to luck, merit, hard work, talent or other attributes of individuals.

The concept of social change, as I would like to use it in a social psychological sense, is at the other extreme of the subjective modes of structuring the social system in which an individual lives. It refers basically to his belief that he is enclosed within the walls of the social group of which he is a member; that he cannot move out on his own into another group in order to improve or change his position or his conditions of life; and that therefore the only way for him to change these conditions (or for that matter, to resist the change of these conditions, if he happens to be satisfied with them) is together with his group as a whole, as a member of it rather than as someone who leaves it. In other words, in the old American usage of "passing" and "not passing" this is in some ways similar to the "not passing" extreme. (pp. 5–6)

Here, however, the aims of the two discussions diverge. As just stated, Hirschman's analysis of the "responses to decline" is largely concerned with the relative efficiency of the exercise of the two options, or their various combinations, in preventing the decline in the functioning of various kinds of social institutions, public or private. The distinction between "social mobility" and "social change" attempts to define two (theoretical) extremes in a continuum of individuals' beliefs about the relationship between the social group or groups to which they belong and other groups. The "behavioral" translation of this continuum of beliefs relates it to three other pairs of extremes that are associated with it:

The relationship I outlined earlier between intergroup behaviour and social change must be supplemented by another theoretical continuum in addition to the one moving from the belief structure of social mobility to the belief structure of social change. This is a continuum which, when it is related to the previous one, provides a bridge between a system of social beliefs and a system of social behaviour. This second continuum can be applied to many interactions between two or more people. One extreme of it would be represented by an individual interacting with others in terms of self; the other extreme—by an individual interacting with others entirely in terms of his and their group membership. Neither of these extremes can probably be found in "real life"; but there is no doubt that approaching the one or the other is crucial to the form that one's social behaviour will take.

There are three important points concerning this behavioural progression. The first concerns the relationship between the social change–social mobility continuum of structure of beliefs and the self-group continuum of the structure of social interaction. On the basis of my argument so far, a prediction can be made that, in any situation perceived as relevant to relations with another group, the nearer an individual is to the social change extreme on the belief continuum, the nearer he will be to the group extreme of the behavioural one. The second point concerns a prediction about individual differences: the nearer a collection of individuals is to the social change end of the belief continuum, the more uniformity they will display in their behaviour towards the relevant outgroup. This prediction must be backed up by considerations about the nature of certain social communication processes to which I shall return later. The third prediction is closely related to the second, as it follows logically from it; the nearer a collection of individuals is to the social change extreme of the belief continuum, the less they will take into account in their intergroup behaviour the individual differences between members of the outgroup, and the more they will react to them *en masse*, treating them as undifferentiated items in a unified social category." (Tajfel, 1974a, pp. 8–9)

The main purpose of this continuum-splitting exercise was to contribute to a social psychological theory of intergroup relations from which predictions could be made about certain uniformities in the behavior and attitudes of members of some social groups (or categories) toward members of other social groups (or categories) (Descriptions of other theoretical assumptions and of various predictions from them can be found in Tajfel, 1974a, 1974b). The convergences with Hirschman's exit–voice pair (I shall discuss loyalty later) are of two kinds: (i) the nature of the concepts used and of some consequences following from them, and (ii) the relationship of the general approach to certain strands of an intellectual tradition.

One of the phases of Hirschman's discussion uses a continuum in which the transition from a fully free (or costless) exit to its virtual impossibility interacts with the appearance of voice and with conditions for its effectiveness. We move here from the free and easy change of a brand of toothpaste to an enormous variety of social situations in which the cost of exit is, subjectively or objectively, so high as to make it impossible or unbearable, such as may be the case with family, national, or political affiliations. Between these extremes, the various degrees of access to exit *may* determine the strength of voice, or of attempts to change from within a deteriorating situation. This is well summed up in the quotation by Hirschman of Erikson's (1964) dictum: "You can actively flee, then, and you can actively stay put."

Sometimes, of course, you cannot actively flee and you must stay put, actively or not; or, having unsuccessfully tried to flee, or seen other people try, you may come to believe that escape is impossible and that you must take the consequences of staying put. These consequences include those to which Hirschman referred in describing voice as "political action by excellence." For a social psychologist, they would imply the numerous behavioral and attitudinal effects on intergroup relations of the belief system previously described as "social change"; particularly so when the effective diffusion of the idea that "passing" individually from one's own group to another is impossible or extremely difficult causes more and more people from that group to feel and act in unison.

This form of voice in intergroup attitudes and behavior need not only apply to those groups who wish (or need) to modify the nature of their relationships to other groups. It may also appear in groups who aim at preserving or strengthening the status quo. I shall return to this issue later.

The second point of convergence relates more directly to exit and "social mobility." In his discussion of the cultural and historical background of exit and voice in the United States, Hirschman (1972, Chapter 8) refers to the "extraordinarily privileged position" that has been accorded to exit in the American tradition:

> The traditional American idea of success confirms the hold which exit has had on the national imagination. Success—or, what amounts to the same thing, upward social mobility—has long been conceived in terms of evolutionary individualism. The successful individual who starts out at a low rung of the social ladder, necessarily leaves his own group as he rises; he "passes" into, or is "accepted" by, the next higher group. He takes his immediate family along, but hardly anyone else. (pp. 108–109)

In contrast, "the black power doctrine represents a totally new approach to upward mobility because of its open advocacy of the group process. It had immense shock value because it spurned and castigated a supreme value of the American society—success via exit from one's group" (p. 112). This "supreme value" seems to have been reflected in some of the intellectual traditions of social psychology. A distinction can be made

> between two possible kinds of theories of intergroup behaviour ... [those] concerned with the interindividual psychology of intergroup behaviour and those concerned with the social psychology of intergroup behaviour. It is theories of the first kind, the interindividual ones, which have been predominant. Their general implication is that the study of processes responsible for various forms of interaction between individuals *as* individuals will tell us all—or most—that we need to know about forms of interaction between individuals as members of separate groups which stand in various kinds of social relations to one another. (Tajfel, 1974a, pp. 3–4)

Consequently,

> most of our social psychology of intergroup behaviour derives from the belief structure of social mobility, and very little of it from the belief structure of social change. In parallel, and as might be expected, most of our social psychology of intergroup behaviour applies to the behaviour of individuals who are assumed to have the belief structure of social mobility and very little of it to the behaviour of individuals who are assumed to have the belief structure of social change. (pp. 6–7)

The differences between the "social mobility" and the "social change" approaches to the social psychology of intergroup relations must be clarified in more detail before we can go further. National, racial, ethnic, or social class relations may be considered as amounting together to what is the substance of social conflict, since conflict becomes "social" when it involves relations between large-scale social groups or "categories" rather than between small groups or between individuals. In social psychology, much of the work relevant to various aspects of social conflict proceeded to extend to it the implications of the theory and research about individual and interindividual functioning. Thus, we have been much concerned with the development of prejudiced attitudes and discriminatory behavior in individuals—and we drew upon general theories of individual motivation and cognition or upon the etiology and the symptomatology of personality development in order to account for various forms of hostility against out-groups. The study of interindividual behavior provided us with theories of competition and cooperation, and more generally, of the interindividual adjustment of goals and strategies that, as it was hoped implicitly or sometimes stated explicitly, could contribute to our understanding of the psychology of the wider forms of conflict. No doubt a great deal has been achieved, and still more can probably be done. There is also no doubt that an understanding of these individual and interindividual processes may be *necessary* for the analysis of some aspects of the psychology of social conflict. The difficulties arise with regard to the question whether it is also *sufficient*.

These difficulties concerning sufficiency become clearer when we consider the psychological aspects of social conflict (as previously defined) in the perspective of a phenomenon which is inseparable from it, namely, social movements. In the context of intergroup relations, social movements can be roughly described as presenting three inherent and defining characteristics: a certain duration; the participation of a significant number of people from one or more social groups; and a shared system of beliefs. The former two characteristics are explicitly quantifiable, but—to put it bluntly—it would be no less than foolish to attempt specifying the limits of minimal and maximal duration, or the minimum and maximum numbers of people that would clearly distinguish between what is and what is not a social movement. It seems more useful to attempt a list of negative examples of social phenomena that are not social movements. Such a list of examples would include an isolated and haphazard riot; a series of individual crimes of various kinds, however much on the increase; a palace conspiracy; a Watergate; vegetarian restaurants; a chamber music society, etc. These negative examples make sense when one remembers that a shared system of beliefs defining a social movement *in the context of intergroup relations* must include a set of aims relating to out-groups. In the most general way, these aims must include either changing the nature of the intergroup situation in conflict with groups wishing to maintain the status quo, or maintaining the intergroup status quo in conflict with groups wishing to change it. All the previous negative examples do not qualify either because they lack the intergroup conflictual system of beliefs; or because these beliefs are not significantly shared within a social group; or because of the ephemeral character of the social actions involved; i.e., they do not meet one or more of the relevant criteria.

The assumed "sufficiency" of the individual or interindividual theoretical approaches to the explanation of social movements in an intergroup context is based, to a large extent, on two conceptual transpositions, which both seem, on the face of it, highly plausible. Let us consider as an example the experiments on interindividual games (of whatever kind) in comparison with some of the experiments introducing explicitly in their designs the notions of in-group and out-group, such as the studies by Sherif (e.g., 1966) and the initial Bristol experiments (Tajfel, 1970; Tajfel *et al.*, 1971) together with studies following from them (e.g., Billig and Tajfel, 1973; Branthwaite & Jones, 1975; Caddick, 1974; Dann & Doise, 1973; Doise *et al.*, 1972; Doise & Sinclair, 1973; Tajfel & Billig, 1974; Turner, 1975b).

The crucial difference between Sherif's field experiments and the experimental interindividual games of all kinds is in the nature of the extrapolations from individual to group behavior. In the case of competitive, cooperative, "trusting," or "threatening" behavior found in the various conditions in which these games are played by individual subjects, the extrapolations are based on the finding that the social behavior of the subjects reached an acceptable level of uniformity as a function of the independent variables. The extrapolation then bridges the gap between the interindividual and the intergroup social behavior; the fact that a number of individuals behaved in a similar manner under similar conditions leads to the conclusion that the same individuals would behave in a similar manner if they were in a group for which would pertain conditions of competition, conflict, or cooperation with another group, similar to these conditions in the games played with, or against, other individuals. The inescapable conclusions are (i) the fact that a *collection* of individuals has become a *group* composed of the same individuals makes no difference to their behavior, since the same "kind" of individuals are still involved; and therefore (ii) the fact of those same individuals being constituted as a group in relation to another group (or groups) does not constitute a set of new independent variables, since conditions of competition, conflict, or cooperation are outwardly similar to those involved in the interindividual situations.

In sharp distinction, Sherif's conclusions were not *only* based on a number of individuals behaving in the same way; they were based on those individuals behaving in the same way *together* and as a group, i.e., being aware that they were a group. It does not require much methodological sophistication to conclude that, since new independent variables *may* well be involved, they need to be considered theoretically before conclusions from studies of interindividual conflict are applied to situations of intergroup conflict. It should be made clear at this point that I am not concerned here with the behavior of "leaders" or others meeting face to face to represent their groups in situations of diplomatic, international, industrial, or any other intergroup negotiations. Although there is some evidence that being a group representative, as distinct from representing nobody but oneself, does make a difference in the social behavior involved (e.g., Hermann & Kogan, 1968; Lamm & Kogan, 1970; Sawyer & Guetzkow, 1965),

the concern of this argument is, as mentioned earlier, with the "social movement" aspects of intergroup behavior in which interindividual face to face
relationships are not necessarily of crucial importance.

In the experiments of Tajfel *et al.* (1971) and others using a similar design,
the inference from interindividual to intergroup group behavior is methodologically nearer to the interindividual game studies than to those of Sherif. Each
subject worked separately, in complete ignorance of what the others, both from
the in-group and the out-group, were doing; and therefore it cannot be said that,
as in Sherif's case, the subjects acted together as a group. The inferences to
intergroup behavior were therefore made, like in the game experiments, from the
relative uniformity of a collection of individual responses. There is, however, a
crucial difference between the two types of study; in the social categorization
experiments the subjects, dividing rewards between two anonymous *others*, one
from the in-group and one from the out-group, acted in terms of their group (or
rather, social category) membership. There was no way to engage in this
situation in any form of an interindividual game, although responses other than
those showing intergroup discrimination were fully possible and extensively used
by the subjects. The crucial importance of this explicit importation of the
intergroup context into the subjects' perspective on the situation was clearly
shown in a recent study by Turner (1975a, 1975b), who introduced within the
same kind of experimental design the possibility of acting in terms of self. After
the preliminary induction of social categorization through esthetic preferences,
as in some of the previous experiments, in one of the experimental conditions
the subjects *first* decided on a division of money between self and an alter who
was either in their own group or in the out-group; then they went on to deciding
on awards between two others, one from the in-group and one from the
out-group, as in the original experiments. Subjects in another condition had this
sequence reversed: first, they worked on decisions between two others, and then
went on to decisions between self and an alter who was either in the in-group or
in the out-group. In other conditions subjects underwent identical procedures
with the only difference that their decisions did not relate to amounts of money
but to unspecified "points" that had no explicit value of any kind. Out of a
complex set of results, the following are the most relevant here:

(i) In all the "other—other" conditions, out-group discrimination was shown.

(ii) There was no out-group discrimination (but only discrimination in favor of
self) when the choice between self and an in-group or out-group alter came *first*
in the sequence of decisions; when the choice between self and an in-group or
out-group alter came *second* in the sequence of decisions (i.e., after a set of
alter-alter decisions) the subjects, in addition to discriminating in favor of self,
also allotted less to members of the out-group than to those of the in-group.
There is little doubt that the relative salience of the intergroup perspectives,
manipulated in Turner's experiment through their relative priority in the order

of tasks, was responsible for the important differences in social behavior shown in the differing experimental situations.

The interindividual games were compared above with studies using directly the intergroup context and/or subjects acting *as* members of their group in order to argue the case that the emergence of one or both of these additional variables throws doubt on the validity of direct extrapolations from one kind of setting to the other. But the interindividual games and strategies are no more than one example among many. I referred above to direct inferences to intergroup behavior from studies of the "development of prejudiced attitudes and discriminatory behavior in individuals (which) drew upon general theories of individual motivation and cognition, or upon the etiology and symptomatology of personality development." These inferences present exactly the same logical and methodological gaps as is the case for interindividual games if conclusions are applied *directly* to intergroup behavior. But it is not enough to assert that there is a gap. The need for a new social psychological analysis of social conflict must be shown to exist; such an analysis must, in order to remain valid, take for granted the achievements of the "individual" theories, but it must also attempt to specify the nature of the new and emergent intergroup variables.

It is here that a combination of the exit–voice perspective of Hirschman (1972), with its background in economics, with the social mobility–social change perspective (Tajfel, 1974a), with its anchorage in social psychology, seems to prove fruitful. As was pointed out earlier, social mobility corresponds to the *belief* in an easy and costless "exit" from one's social group; social change is the corresponding no-exit situation, which may determine the use of "voice" in the attempts to change the existing unsatisfactory situation. In other words, the "objective" absence of access to exit, and/or the belief that this access does not exist, may lead to a certain kind of social behavior ("political action by excellence") for which Hirschman uses the shorthand expression "voice." His preoccupation is essentially pragmatic: he asks questions about the utility of the two options, and of their combinations, as a recuperation mechanism for ailing social organizations. But other questions concerning intergroup behavior can also be asked in the context of the two theoretical pairs of exit–voice and social mobility–social change. Some of these questions will be considered in the next two sections of this paper. For the present, our concern is with the emergent intergroup variables, as seen from this particular theoretical vantage.

We noted earlier, in a quotation from Tajfel (1974a), that the social mobility–social change continuum was directly and logically related to three other continua: the self-group continuum of social behavior, the variability–uniformity continuum of behavior of members of the in-group toward the out-group, and the variability–uniformity continuum in the extent of differentiation between individual members of the out-group (e.g., from minimum to maximum stereotypy). If exit in Hirschman's sense means not "exit" from buying a product but exit from a group in order to enter another group, i.e., exit in its narrower sense of social mobility, then any number of "individual" theories of social behavior can be successfully used to describe the motivational and cognitive aspects of the situation. The limitations here, to be discussed later, will appear when we move from an individual's exit from his group to a group's exit from a multigroup structure. However, as long as we deal with individual exit from a group, or even a collection of individual exits, we are still within the confines of, for example, the interindividual games and strategies, with the only difference that the individual adjusts his or her strategies to the requirements of a complex social environment rather than just to the strategies of another individual. The individual calculations predicted by, for example, the various versions of the exchange theory will yield their outcomes (usually *post hoc*) and no other *kind* of theoretical framework seems to be required.

The situation changes dramatically, however, when the pair voice–social change is considered in its intergroup framework. Here, the individual has come to the conclusion that he can change his unsatisfactory situation or prevent the change in his satisfactory situation only as a member of his group, only acting as a part and parcel of it, together with other members. His social environment is even more complex than is the case in the social mobility situation. There is the "inside" of his own group, with all the usual individual, interindividual, and structural conflicts, difficulties, and problems. There is the "outside" environment consisting of other groups, which either oppose a change that he wants or want a change that he opposes. The processes of social comparison will apply, in all the relevant social situations, *directly* to these groups, however similar or dissimilar they may be to his own (cf. Tajfel, 1974b, for a more detailed discussion). These same processes of social comparison compounded with the growth of a group (or social) identity will brew a powerful combination of motives, cognitions, and social actions in which the more obvious individually considered reinforcements and the simple calculations of individual utility will go by the board as often as not.

The point of discussing social movements earlier was that the individual frustrations, individual reinforcements, and individual personality patterns cannot account for uniformities of social action and social attitudes toward other groups shared—as they often are—for long periods of time by large masses of people. It is always possible to balance respectably the total theoretical account by throwing in notions such as conformity, common features of socialization, or reward structures of social learning. But these are blunt and *post hoc* tools; blunt, because they are not capable of distinguishing theoretically between the diverse structures of various intergroup situations; *post hoc* because no one has ever been able to predict (and even less to understand) the social psychology of a social movement, be it a surge of conservative reaction or a revolution, by invoking conformity or schedules of individual reinforcements. What is more, social movements are often started by counterconforming minorities and joining them often involves the sort of individual calculation of self-interest that would drive to despair any sensible bank manager approached about a loan or an overdraft. It is the contention of the present argument that the consideration of a "social change" structure of beliefs provides an adequate theoretical basis from which to understand these phenomena, and that its integration with other *socially shared* processes of group identity, of social comparison, and of social diffusion of ideas and beliefs (such as shared evaluations and shared social expectations) provides the possibility of making differential predictions about intergroup behavior *en masse*. The details of these various predictions can be found elsewhere (cf. Tajfel 1974a, 1974b; Turner, 1975a).

Two general additional comments need to be made to conclude this introductory discussion. The first relates to the fact that, as it will be clear from the preceding paragraphs, it would be grossly simplistic to attribute the interindividual tradition of "social mobility" in the social psychology of intergroup relations to nothing but the overwhelming predominance, mentioned earlier, of the "exit option" in American social history. Much of it goes back to the background of the social psychologists' theoretical concern with individual or interindividual problems. The second point is that if Hirschman, Hofstadter (1945), and others are correct about "the hold which exit has had on the national imagination" and about success having "long been conceived in terms of evolutionary individualism," then it follows that "most of our social psychology of intergroup behavior" *should* apply "to the behavior of individuals who are assumed to have the belief structure of social mobility." Undoubtedly, this is why good progress has been made in our understanding of the individual patterns of prejudice, discrimination, and hostility. However, the intention of the present argument is not to question the validity of much of this work; the concern is not with its achievements but with its limitations.

The American tradition of exit developed against a background of belief in individual mobility which, although by no means exclusively American, has probably been more salient in the social history of the United States than almost anywhere else. This tradition has been weaker elsewhere and almost nonexistent in some cultures (including many ex-"primitive" ones). This being the case, the question arises whether findings derived from a social context overwhelmingly dominated by the exit (or social mobility) option can be said to have a wider general validity. Moreover, an explicit social psychology of voice or "social change" in intergroup relations is as necessary in the United States as it is anywhere else. The example of black power is one case in point, and many other similar social and national movements are not far behind—in America and elsewhere.

There is, however, one further point which is equally important. It is banal to say that in the social past (or present) of the United States, as in so many other countries, the belief in, or the myth of, individual mobility was (and is) conceived by many not to apply with indiscriminately equal generosity, liberality, and force to everybody. This denial of equal opportunity (or sometimes "ability") to scramble up the social ladder to members of some social groups is one of the psychological effects of the "objective" intergroup conflicts of interest; but it also finds its roots in some fundamental aspects of the social comparison processes. To put it crudely, very often we are what we are because "they" are not what we are. The psychological and "superior" distinctiveness of a social group, sometimes achieved at the cost of strenuous efforts, must be maintained and preserved if the group is to conserve some kind of a common and valued identity. It is at this point that voice will be used, sometimes in remarkable unison, by members of the "superior" groups, particularly since exit is very often unthinkable for them. At this point of the argument, this function of voice is stressed because it points to an additional and important limitation of the "social mobility" approach to the psychology of intergroup relations, even against the background of the American tradition of exit. I shall return to it in more detail later in the discussion of the contribution of voice to the preservation of status quo in intergroup relations and behavior.

Individual Exit, Group Exit, and Group Chorus

We must now return to the economics of expendable products as it relates to the social psychology of intergroup relations. The change of a brand of toothpaste is the simplest paradigm of a costless exit. It is basically and inherently an individual reaction. If we can imagine a brand of toothpaste that suddenly becomes twice as expensive as all the others without any corresponding softsell about its unique and outstanding qualities, or that—from one day to the next without warning—begins leaving in one's mouth a powerful taste of rotten fish for three hours after use, we can easily predict a massive escape of the customers to other brands. (For theoretical purposes, we can ignore the small minority who would enjoy the lingering taste.) But even this massive escape could not be treated as a social movement inserted in a context of intergroup relations. It would be a collection of individual exits. The criteria distinguishing the collection of exits from a social movement in an intergroup social change situation are simple: even if the manufacturers of the expensive or the smelling toothpaste were considered to be an "out-group", the simplest solution for the members of the customers' "in-group" is still to go away and forget all about it. Presumably, in doing so, they would form some unflattering "stereotypes" about the manufacturers, but it is unlikely that these would be related to any form of durable, commonly shared, and large-scale social action, outside of leaving in very large numbers. For the same reasons, it is just as unlikely that the abused customers would amount together to an effective social group or social category. This is so despite the fact that they would share the two most important *a priori* defining characteristics of a social group: a certain similarity between the members (they all dislike the toothpaste); and a certain equivalence of "fate" (they all wish to change, or have to change, to another brand). The point is that they do not have to change, or wish to change, as a group; everyone can do it individually, whatever the others do or do not do.

This extreme social mobility paradigm (changing from the group of brand X users to the group of brand Y users) is unlikely to find its equivalent in most social structures in which the move from one group to another involves effort, hard work, luck, heartbreak, etc. As exit becomes more costly or more painful, Hirschman's analysis of its interaction with voice becomes increasingly pertinent in relation to the effectiveness of this interaction as a recuperation mechanism for declining organizations. It is interesting to see, however, that with the increase in the difficulty of exit and the corresponding increase in the attempts to change the situation from the inside, one important aspect of the initial simple paradigm of toothpaste exit does tend to remain a constant in Hirschman's exit–voice analysis. Exit, or the threat of it, or the use of voice, remain theoretically an individual action or a collection of individual actions. At best, this collection of individual actions becomes an organized activity (this is why voice is "political action by excellence") aiming to change the mode of functioning of the group to which the activists belong; in other words, the implicit theoretical presupposition is that of an intragroup activity. That this is so becomes quite clear in Coleman's (1974) contribution to a recently published collection of articles on the exit and voice theme:

> Intrinsic to the paradigm of exit and voice which Hirschman (1970) has set forth is the recognition that social structure is composed of two kinds of actors: *persons* and corporate actors. For it is these persons for whom the problem of implementing their will reduces to the dilemma of exit, that is, withdrawal of resources from the corporate actor, or voice, which attempts to control the direction of action of the corporate actor. (p. 7) (my italics)

A little further in the same paper, Coleman adds: "Hirschman was largely concerned with the maintenance of the efficiency of corporate actors and with the processes through which *persons* contribute to that maintenance (p. 7) (my italics).

Before we proceed, one further conceptual distinction must be made. There is hardly anything new in asserting that members of a group will act together as a group when their individual goals converge and can only be achieved through common action as a group. It is trivially true that this is often the prime condition for the formation of a group which is likely to remain "cohesive" for as long as the goals remain common. In this sense, it may well be that the moderating effects on intergroup hostility of Sherif's (1966) superordinate goals cannot be generalized too far, since the stringent requirements of common action in the hour of common need must have gone quite a long way toward replacing the previously separate identities of the two groups by a larger and common identity of one group confronting a hostile environment. In this final phase of one of Sherif's studies, there were no remaining divergent "objective" interests that would have helped the groups to maintain their separate identities. Therefore, it may well be that the effectiveness of the superordinate goals was due, in part at least, to the beginning of a process of dissolution of the two separate groups toward the formation of a single group confronting "nature." It is difficult to know whether a similar reduction of hostility would have occurred had the initial groups been in the position of preserving clear-cut separate goals, interests, and other features of their previous distinctiveness in addition to the new and powerful requirements of their common welfare. This is undoubtedly an intergroup problem which stands in urgent need of further research.

The point of this brief diversion about Sherif's superordinate goals is that it helps to illustrate the conceptual distinction that needs to be made between the notion of group cohesion, which is generally due to common goals, and the notion of common goals in a situation of social change as defined above, i.e., a situation in which the achievement of these goals is only possible through a change in the structure of the existing intergroup relations, or conversely through opposing such change when it is attempted or initiated by an out-group. The difference between the two situations is quite fundamental: it is in the nature of the hostile environment confronting the in-group. Sherif's final superordinate goals did not involve a confrontation of the total boys' camp with any other group (apart from the hidden group of the manipulating experimenters of whose dark designs the subjects were presumably unaware; cf. Billig, 1976, for a discussion of the relevance of this situation to the issue of "false consciousness"). Although the details of the attitudinal and behavioral structures resulting from an intergroup social change situation cannot be discussed here (cf. Tajfel, 1974a), a brief list of the emergent variables, distinguishing this situation from one in which only nonsocial "nature" is confronted (or perceived as confronted), will be sufficient to characterize its specificity. These interacting variables would include causal attributions of responsibility, processes of intergroup social comparison together with the consequent formation of a *relational* group (or social) identity, assessment of the legitimacy of the perceived intergroup situation, the relationship of this assessment to the "objective" intergroup differences and to the consensual status differentials between the groups, and the attempts to create or maintain a positively valued distinctiveness of the in-group from the out-group as a major dependent variable.

So far, an attempt has been made in this paper to argue for a theoretical specificity of a certain category of intergroup relations which would distinguish it both from problems inherent in interindividual relations and from those encountered by a group confronting a problem common to all of its members and presented to it by a nonsocial or nonhuman "nature." It is to the former of these distinctions, in its variant of intragroup versus intergroup considerations, to which we must now return in pursuing the implications of the paradigm of exit and voice for the social mobility–social change paradigm. The asymmetry of the respective intragroup and intergroup points of departure has already been noted.

Social mobility is exit of an individual from his group. Social change is the situation in which the extreme difficulty or impossibility of individual exit leads at least some of the people concerned to develop, or try to develop, an effective common voice for their group. The various modes of this voice or the conditions under which these modes may develop are not of direct concern at this point of the argument (cf. Tajfel, 1974a, 1974b). The asymmetry between voice and "social change" resides in the comparison of the relation, described by Coleman (1974), of persons to corporate actors with the relations of members of one group to other groups. In both cases voice will be used in its various forms. But in the case of a group, the persons composing it may be concerned with the prevention of decline in the "efficiency" (i.e., conditions of life, status, opportunities, etc.) of the corporate actor, which in this instance is their own group. Therefore, in an organization consisting of many groups, their voice may have to be directed toward a change in the nature of the relations between their own and other groups, i.e., other corporate actors. In this process voice may become a chorus.

An example of similar asymmetry is provided by the notion of relative deprivation, as it has sometimes been used (explicitly or implicitly) in social psychology. The focus of the theories has been on individuals comparing themselves with other individuals (e.g., Festinger, 1954, on social comparison). This is entirely adequate as long as conclusions are drawn about the effects of these comparisons on interindividual attitudes and behavior—which is what Festinger (1954) has been aiming to do. As a matter of fact, he explictly denied the possibility of operation of social comparisons so understood in the context of intergroup relations: "Comparisons with members of a different status group, either higher or lower, may sometimes be made on a phantasy level, but very rarely in reality" (p. 136). Festinger's interindividual emphasis is closely related to the economic version of relative deprivation, the "relative income hypothesis," which Hirschman (1973)—after Duesenberry—described as follows: "The welfare of an individual varies inversely with the income or the consumption of those persons with whom he associates" (p. 546).

Difficulties begin when these interindividual comparisons are transposed to intergroup situations. One of them concerns a basic canon of the social comparison theory in social psychology and of the relative income hypothesis in economics: people who provide the basis for comparisons must not be too different from those who are doing the comparing. I have argued elsewhere (Tajfel, 1974a) that this limitation does not hold in the case of intergroup comparisons in which the requirement of a certain degree of similarity between the comparer and the compared is replaced by the perceived legitimacy of the perceived relationship between the groups. If perception of illegitimacy enters the comparison, then we are soon very far indeed from Festinger's assertion that comparisons with members of groups of different status happen "very rarely in reality" and perhaps even further from his "phantasy levels" (cf. Danziger, 1963; Geber, 1972). The difference between the two kinds of comparisons is simply described: in the case of interindividual comparisons, a person relates his position to that of other persons; in the case of intergroup comparisons, an individual compares himself *as a member of his own group* with other individuals as members of their groups, or with out-groups conceptualized as an entity. The questions are: Under what conditions do these intergroup comparisons become widely diffused within a group, and what then are their social, political and psychological consequences? But these are large issues outside the scope of this paper.

Let us return to the asymmetry of voice and chorus. In the case of social comparison theory a collection of interindividual comparisons is sometimes endowed with the capacity to contribute to long-term uniformities of behavior in large masses of people (e.g., Berkowitz, 1972), although how this is supposed to happen remains a little obscure. In Hirschman's exit–voice analysis, transpositions of this kind are not made. Also in his discussion of "changing tolerance for income inequality in the course of economic development" (Hirschman, 1973) there is a clear awareness of the psychological differences between groups that can afford to wait for a time to catch up with others and those which feel they cannot: "the group that does not advance must be able to empathise, at least for a time, with the group that does. In other words, the two groups must not be divided by barriers that are or are felt as impassable" (p. 553). He returns to the theme in suggesting that the temporary, patient waiting by some while others advance "need not happen if each class is composed of ethnic or religious groups that are differentially involved in the growth process. Hence, the contrast between fairly unitary and highly segmented society is particularly relevant for our topic" (pp. 553–4).

In Hirschman's analysis voice comes from a collection of individuals (sometimes organized into a group) who wish to change the institution or the organization of which they feel themselves to be an inherent part. In one fundamental sense, this may also be true of a social group which attempts to change its relationship to other groups within a larger social structure common to all of them. But the question immediately arises of how, if at all, is this chorus form of voice related to the potentiality or the actuality of *group* exit.

There are two kinds of group exit discussed by Hirschman from his perspective that are of interest here. The first of these is opting out, or the " 'cop-out' movement of groups like the hippies," which is "flight rather than fight" (1972, p. 108), i.e., exit without voice. This exit is no more than temporary for some of the people involved; but their choice to come back (or not to come back, in the case of permanent or long-term opters-out) is not dependent on the past instrumentalities of their use of voice. If they come back, it is because they have changed, or society has changed, or they think society has changed. In addition, they often become a group with well-defined common interests and a common identity only after they have opted out (e.g., in communes) rather than before; so that just as in the case of voice we are dealing, in Coleman's (1974) words, with "the processes through which persons contribute to (the) maintenance" of a corporate actor; here we are dealing with persons who wish to get as far away as they can from a vast collection of corporate actors. In this sense, therefore, their exit cannot be considered as relevant in the context of the group exit–group voice relationship.

The other kind of group exit is boycott (Hirschman, 1972, p. 86). It is a "phenomenon on the borderline between voice and exit," since this action "is undertaken for the specific and explicit purpose of achieving a change of policy on the part of the boycotted organization" (p. 86) and is accompanied by "a promise of re-entry" should the desired changes take place. To be effective, boycott (like a strike) cannot, of course, be an action by isolated individuals.

This "true hybrid of the two mechanisms" (p. 86) raises a number of interesting psychological questions about the relationship between a dissatisfied group and the organizational or institutional structure defining the position of that group vis-a-vis other groups within the same structure. For example, an underprivileged group in a strongly stratified social system (i.e., a system preventing social mobility and/or a belief in this option) cannot really exit; there is nowhere to go, unless all of its members chose to emigrate, or—as in the case of ethnic or national groups—the exit option is fought for in the form of a separatist movement. The possibility of an exit that is neither emigration nor separation must be sought elsewhere, and like Hirschman's boycott, it is bound to be a "hybrid of the two mechanisms" of exit and voice. But in the case of social groups which are strongly disaffected and see their only hope in a fundamental change of the system, it is also a hybrid from another point of view. The individuals involved are strongly identified with one of the corporate actors (their own group); but the efficiency of functioning of that corporate actor is part and parcel of the functioning of a wider system consisting of their own and other groups. Therefore, the prevention of a continuing decline in the functioning of the corporate actor (the in-group) may be perceived as possible only through a change (more or less fundamental) in the functioning of the wider multigroup system.

In such cases, one of the solutions which may be adopted is as much of a hybrid of exit and voice as is boycott. It is obviously voice since it is a form of political or social action from within; it is also exit or threatened exit to the extent that it consists of a refusal to accept the rules by which the present relationships between the groups are regulated, and contains a "promise of re-entry" when these rules are changed. Once again, we have a continuum here which moves from total acceptance of the rules to partial acceptance to total rejection.

This continuum closely reflects a progressive transition from group voice to group exit. The relationship in this transition between the psychological and the "objective" determinants of group exit can be considered, once again, in terms of legitimacy. But here an interaction between three forms of it would have to be taken into account: the legitimacy of the intergroup relationship as it is perceived by the disaffected group, the legitimacy of this relationship as it is perceived by the other groups involved, and an "objective" definition (i.e., a set of rules and regulations) of legitimacy, whenever such a thing is possible.

In considering these three kinds of legitimacy, it can be assumed that group exit (or the threat of it) will be, on many occasions, the more likely the greater is the discrepancy between the first two kinds of legitimacy, and the narrower are the confines of action from within (voice) encompassed by the third. On the face of it, the second part of this statement seems to contradict Hirschman's (1972) view that "if exit is followed by severe sanctions the very idea of exit is going to be repressed and the threat (of it) will not be uttered for fear that the sanctions will apply to the threat as well as to the act itself" (pp. 96–97). There is no doubt that this proposition holds in a vast number of cases for individual exit or a collection of individual exits. But it would be useful to consider the many important exceptions to it that may occur in the relations between separate groups within a system rather than in the relations between persons and corporate actors. It seems not unreasonable to assume that in many multigroup systems these important exceptions are likely to occur when the contribution from the disaffected group is essential to the continuing efficient functioning of the system as a whole.

Some of the social psychological consequences of this kind of actual or threatened group exit can be discussed in terms of its relationship to the impossibility or difficulty of individual exit from the in-group. The tendency to try for this kind of individual exit, or even to conceive it as a possibility, may be in this case inversely related to the reality or the perceived potentiality of group exit. This relationship can become a powerful ingredient of in-group loyalty. The second social psychological consequence is the increasing uniformity within the group of the relevant in-group and out-group attitudes and behavior—a phenomenon mentioned earlier in this paper in relation to the three theoretical continua associated with the trasition from social mobility to social change. In this case a social psychological analysis of the situation must take explicitly into account the increased sharing by many individuals of their "expectations about, and evaluations of, other people's behavior" (Tajfel, 1972).

In turn, the positive feedback triggered into action by this sharing of social expectations and evaluations provides a parallel to the "joys of participation" which find their place amongst Hirschman's (1974) "new economic arguments in favour of voice" (p. 7). "The activities connected with voice can on occasion become a highly desired end in itself" (p. 8) and thus they decrease the cost of voice and may even turn it into a benefit. But in the case of group exit it is the cost of this exit rather than of voice that is psychologically decreased in this way. This cost can sometimes be enormous for the individual concerned. Its acceptance by many would be incomprehensible without the existence of a compensating mechanism of increasing loyalty to the in-group as the dangers of group exit loom larger and the deviant status of its members in the outside world becomes sharper and clearer.

Voice, Status Quo, and Social Comparison in Intergroup Relations

In the previous section of this paper group exit and some forms of its interaction with group voice were discussed as a recuperation mechanism for groups which perceive their position in a multigroup system as being less than satisfactory. One of the conditions in which, as Hirschman (1972) wrote, "a no-exit situation will be superior to a situation with some limited exit [is] if exit is ineffective as a recuperation mechanism, but does succeed in draining from the firm or organization its more quality conscious, alert, and potentially activist customers or members" (p. 55). It is likely, of course, that customers or members who display the qualities just mentioned are often nearer to the top of the social heap than are the more passive ones.

In the case of individual members of an organization, the greater involvement in it of those who are nearer to the top makes exit for them more costly or difficult than for others, and at the same time their voice is likely to be louder, more enthusiastic, and more effective. As individuals, they may be simultaneously concerned with preventing the decline of the organization and preventing the decline of their relative position in it. The same will be true of the higher status groups when the organization consists of groups that are clearly separate from one another.

We have here a situation which is parallel to that discussed in relation to the exit of disaffected groups in the previous section of this paper. The position of an individual belonging to a higher status group needs to be considered in relation to his group at the same time as the position of his group in relation to other groups in the organization. This can be done with regard to the possibilities of an individual's exit from his group, his group's exit from the organization, and the corresponding functions and directions of voice.

The membership of a high-status group is often satisfying in a variety of ways. Exit from it is therefore, on the whole, unlikely. But the point is that whether *some* individuals do or do not leave the group (and they may leave for a number of reasons, including a conflict of values that the "superior" position of their group sometimes entails) the intergroup situation within the organization remains the same. The high-status group as a whole cannot exit unless it is intent upon collective self-destruction, actual or symbolic. As distinct from the disaffected group, its members have a great deal to lose and very often nothing to gain from any form of exit—be it emigration, separation, or refusal to play by the rules. From their point of view, the decline in the efficiency of the organization can take one of two forms: a decline in the overall functioning of the system, or a decline in the relative position of their group within the system. The former without the latter would lead to the use of voice, individually or collectively, in the ways described by Hirschman. The decline in the relative position of the group, or the threat of such a decline, has certain psychological consequences relevant to the use of group voice, which may be considered by returning briefly to some aspects of the theory of social comparison.

In a letter to *The Times* (October 29, 1974) concerned with the present economic plight of Britain, Elliot Jaques exclaimed in desperation: "Is it not apparent to all that the present wave of disputes has to do with relativities, relativities and nothing but relativities?" The "relativities" of the lower status groups were discussed from a certain point of view earlier in this paper. Those of the higher status groups are, of course, concerned with the preservation of differentials. As I wrote above, we are what we are because "they" are not what we are. But this item of folk wisdom needs to be inserted in a wider context, which is that of the preservation of an individual's satisfactory social identity in a network of social comparisons.

Social identity can be defined as "that part of an individual's self-concept which derives from his knowledge of his membership of a social group (or groups) together with the emotional significance attached to that membership" (Tajfel, 1974a, p. 15). Or, as Berger (1966) wrote: "Society not only defines but creates psychological reality. The individual realizes himself in society—that is, he recognizes his identity in socially defined terms and these definitions become reality as he lives in society" (p. 107).

Several consequences regarding group membership follow upon this "recognition of identity in socially defined terms." They can be described as follows:

(a) It can be assumed that an individual will tend to remain a member of a group and seek membership of new groups if these groups have some contribution to make to the positive aspects of his social identity; i.e. to those aspects of it from which he derives some satisfaction.

(b) If a group does not satisfy this requirement, the individual will tend to leave it *unless*

(i) leaving the group is impossible for some "objective" reasons, or

(ii) it conflicts with important values which are themselves a part of his acceptable social identity.

(c) If leaving the group presents the difficulties just mentioned, then at least two solutions are possible:

(i) to change one's interpretation of the attributes of the group so that its unwelcome features (e.g. low status) are either justified or made acceptable through a reinterpretation;

(ii) to accept the situation for what it is and engage in social action which would lead to desirable changes in the situation. (Of course, there may be various combinations of (i) and (ii) such as, for example, when the negative attributes are justified and social action to remove them is undertaken at the same time).

(d) No group lives alone—all groups in society live in the midst of other groups. In other words, the "positive aspects of social identity" and the reinterpretation of attributes and engagement in social action only acquire meaning in relation to, or in comparisons with, other groups. (Tajfel, 1974a, pp. 15–16)

The inescapable nature of these comparisons is due to the fact that:

The characteristics of one's group as a whole (such as its status, its richness or poverty, its skin colour or its ability to reach its aims) achieve most of their significance in relation to perceived differences from other groups and the value connotation of these differences. For example, economic deprivation acquires its importance in social attitudes, intentions and actions mainly when it becomes relative deprivation; easy or difficult access to means of production and consumption of goods, to benefits and opportunities become psychologically salient mainly in relation to comparisons with other groups; the definition of a group (national, racial or any other) makes no sense unless there are other groups around. A group becomes a group in the sense of being perceived as having common characteristics or a common fate only because other groups are present in the environment.

Thus the psychological aspects and consequences of the membership of a group are capable of any kind of a definition only because of their insertion into a multi-group structure. Consequently, the social identity of an individual conceived as his "knowledge that he belongs to certain social groups together with some emotional and value significance to him of his membership" can only be defined through the effects of social categorizations segmenting an individual's social environment into his own group and others. (Tajfel, 1974a, pp. 17–18)

In situations characterized by the structure of belief in social change "a social group can fulfil its function of protecting the social identity of its members only if it manages to keep its positively valued distinctiveness from other groups" (Tajfel, 1974a, p. 18). The emergence of this structure of beliefs must be understood, in the case of high-status groups, as being dependent on the two conditions just discussed: the high cost of an individual's exit from his group and the very high cost (or impossibility) of the group's exit from the organization. These are also the conditions determining an intense use of the group's voice in the attempts to prevent its comparative decline.

We must now return to the use of voice not as a response to the comparative decline of the in-group but as a response to the decline in the efficiency of functioning of the total organization. Assuming that differentials are perceived by members of a high-status group as being eroded, three possibilities need to be considered:

(1) The comparative decline of the group is not perceived by its members as being associated in one way or another with the decline or the prevention of decline in the functioning of the organization as a whole.

(2) This comparative decline is perceived as being directly associated with the decline in the functioning of the total organization.

(3) This comparative decline is perceived as being directly associated with the *prevention* of decline in the functioning of the total organization.

These are the *psychological* alternatives. The *actual* changes in the functioning of the organization may or may not correspond to the group's perception of what happens. The point is, however, that it is these shared perceptions, tending to become more common and widespread as the group sees itself increasingly beleaguered, which will determine the intensity and the direction of the use of voice. In the first two of the three cases, there is no *perceived* conflict between responding to the threat of comparative decline of the in-group and the wider interests at stake. It can therefore be assumed that the group's "ethnocentric" (or more generally, sociocentric) voice will be given free rein. In turn, it can be assumed that there will be a solid wall of rationalizations (or defensive ideologies) to ward off the uncomfortable thoughts inseparable from the third case.

The emergence and diffusion of these defensive ideologies may at times determine, and at times be determined by, the use of voice. The second alternative would, of course, be predicted from dissonance theory (Festinger, 1957). Independently, however, of the nature of the psychological processes generating these ideologies, we must consider the following relationships between the use of voice by the threatened group and the realities of the decline of the total organization:

(1) As determined by some external criteria (e.g., measures of economic performance) the group is wrong in assuming that its comparative decline is *not* associated either with a decline or with a prevention of decline in the functioning of the total organization.

(2) As determined in the same manner, the group is wrong in assuming that its comparative decline is directly associated with a decline in the total functioning.

(3) The group is right in assuming that its comparative decline is directly associated with a *prevention* of decline in the total organization. But in the ensuing conflict of perceived interests, the former decline turns out to be more important than the latter.

Whenever any of these three relationships comes to materialize, the use of voice by the threatened group may prove catastrophic for the organization as a whole; and the higher is the status of the group threatened by the loss of its superior distinctiveness, the more catastrophic is its use of voice likely to become.

Two notes need to be appended to conclude this discussion of group voice. The first concerns its almost exclusive preoccupation with the "subjective" aspects of the relationships between groups, with the psychological processes of social comparison rather than with the "objective" conflicts of interest. This emphasis was not chosen because of a belief on my part that these social psychological processes are "more important" than, or primary to, the social, economic, and political intergroup processes that form their context. These psychological correlates of the other relationships do, however, exist; and, as I wrote elsewhere (Tajfel, 1974b), the concern is

> with certain points of insertion of social psychological variables into the causal spiral; and [the] argument is that, just as the effects of these variables are determined by the previous social, economic and political processes, so they also acquire in their turn an autonomous function which enables them to deflect in one direction or another the subsequent functioning of these processes. (p. 65)

Finally, I wish to return to the "individual" versus "group" dichotomy discussed earlier in this paper. There is little doubt that many of the points discussed and conclusions presented here apply to interindividual behavior and attitudes as well as to the intergroup scenario. The point of departure (and of arrival) was, however, firmly kept in the area of intergroup relations because of my conviction that it is only when this is explicitly done (at some risk of neglect of other issues) that we have, as social psychologists, a good chance of making a contribution to the understanding of social processes at large.

References

Berger, P. L. Identity as a problem in the sociology of knowledge. *European Journal of Sociology*, 1967, 7, 105–115.

Berkowitz, L. Frustrations, comparisons and other sources of emotion arousal as contributors to social unrest. *Journal of Social Issues*, 1972, 28(1), 77–91.

Billig, M. *Social psychology and intergroup relations*. London: Academic Press (European Monographs in Social Psychology), 1976.

Billig, M., and Tajfel, H. Social categorization and similarity in intergroup behavior. *European Journal of Social Psychology*, 1973, 3, 37–52.

Branthwaite, A., and Jones, J. E. Fairness and discrimination: English vs. Welsh. *European Journal of Social Psychology*, 1975, in press.

Caddick, B. Threat to group distinctiveness and intergroup discrimination. Unpublished manuscript, University of Bristol, 1974.

Coleman, J. Processes of concentration and dispersal of power in social systems. *Social Science Information*, 1974, 13(2), 7–18.

Dann, H. D., and Doise, W. Ein neuer methodologischer Ansatz zur experimentellen Erforschung von Intergruppen–Beziehungen. *Zeitschrift für Sozialpsychologie*, 1973, 5, 2–15.

Danziger, K. The psychological future of an oppressed group. *Social Forces*, 1963, 62, 31–40.

Doise, W., Csepeli, G., Dann, H. D., Gouge, C., and Larsen, W. An experimental investigation into the formation of intergroup representations. *European Journal of Social Psychology*, 1972, 2, 202–204.

Doise, W., and Sinclair, A. The categorization process in intergroup relations. *European Journal of Social Psychology*, 1973, 3, 145–157.

Erikson, E. *Insight and responsibility*. New York: Norton, 1964.

Festinger, L. A theory of social comparison processes. *Human Relations*, 1954, 7, 117–140.

Festinger, L. *A theory of cognitive dissonance*. Evanston, Illinois: Row & Petersen, 1957.

Geber, B. Occupational aspirations and expectations of South African high school children. Unpublished Ph.D. dissertation, University of London, 1972.

Hermann, N., and Kogan, N. Negotiation in leader and delegate groups. *Journal of Conflict Resolution*, 1968, **12**, 332–344.

Hirschman, A. O. *Exit, voice and loyalty: Responses to decline in firms, organizations and states*. Cambridge, Mass.: Harvard Univ. Press, 1970 (2nd ed. 1972).

Hirschman, A. O. The changing tolerance for income inequality in the course of economic development. *Quarterly Journal of Economics*, 1973, **87**, 544–566.

Hirschman, A. O. "Exit, voice and loyalty": Further reflections and a survey of recent contributions. *Social Science Information*, 1974, **13**(1), 7– 26.

Hofstadter, R. *Social Darwinism in American thought*. Philadelphia: Univ. of Pennsylvania Press, 1945.

Lamm, H., and Kogan, N. Risk taking in the context of intergroup negotiation. *Journal of Experimental Social Psychology*, 1970, **6**, 351–363.

Sawyer, J., and Guetzkow, H. Bargaining and negotiation in international relations, in H. C. Kelman (ed.), *International behavior*. New York: Holt, Rinehart & Winston, 1965.

Sherif, M. *Group conflict and cooperation; their social psychology*. London: Routledge & Kegan Paul, 1966.

Tajfel, H. Experiments in intergroup discrimination. *Scientific American*, 1970, **223**(5), 96–102.

Tajfel, H. Experiments in a vacuum, in J. Israel and H. Tajfel (eds.), *The context of social psychology: A critical assessment*. London: Academic Press (European Monographs in Social Psychology), 1972.

Tajfel, H. Intergroup behavior, social comparison and social change. Katz-Newcomb Lectures Univ. of Michigan, Ann Arbor, 1974 (mimeo). (a)

Tajfel, H. Social identity and intergroup behaviour. *Social Science Information*, 1974, **13**(2), 65–93. (b)

Tajfel, H. The exit of social mobility and the voice of social change: Notes on the social psychology of intergroup relations. *Social Science Information*, 1975, in press.

Tajfel, H., and Billig, M. Familiarity and social categorization in intergroup behaviour. *Journal of Experimental Social Psychology*, 1974, **10**, 159–170.

Tajfel, H., Flament, C., Billig, M., and Bundy, R. Social categorization and intergroup behaviour. *European Journal of Social Psychology*, 1971, **1**, 149–175.

Turner, J. Social comparison and social identity: Some prospects for intergroup behaviour. *European Journal of Social Psychology*, 1975, **5**, 1–31. (a)

Turner, J. Social categorization and social comparison in intergroup relations. Unpublished Ph.D. dissertation, University of Bristol, 1975. (b)

SECTION V

ALTERNATIVE FUTURES

THE "POWER STRUCTURE"
IN SOCIAL PSYCHOLOGY*

The discussion reprinted below is from a session of the conference. It followed a stimulating paper by Elaine and William Walster, "The year 2000: The future of small group research," but it might well have occurred at another point in the week's meetings had the Walsters' paper not served as the provocative event it was; the "power" topic was one of real concern for many participants.

The discussion is published here without interpretation to demonstrate this concern to a larger audience, and to show how the sixty-odd social psychologists, representing the full ranges of experience, "visibility," and areas of professional interest, responded when challenged about the distribution of power within their own discipline. The discussion's character is consistent with the rest of the sessions, which featured either by design or by accident a number of sharp exchanges, ranging from intense debates about the scientific and sociocultural value of formal papers to disruption of one meeting by two representatives of a group calling itself a North American Labour Committee.

We have attempted to edit the discussion without losing the essence of its content. Eliminated to save space have been most of the events that involved the chair; this does a disservice to the skillful way in which Tajfel handled a complex and occasionally tense session. Also eliminated have been a few circuitous and redundant statements, along with instances of garbled talking, general laughter, etc. Finally, we have cut several irrelevant, and sometimes personal, digressions. There were few of these; an interaction between the topic's importance, the caliber of the conference participants, and the setting of the session led to a discussion with a degree of focus rarely experienced by the editors. In all, the

* A slightly different version of this discussion has been published in *Representative Research in Social Psychology*. It is reprinted here by permission.

total number of speaking episodes in the present version (43) is 51% of that number of entries in the original manuscript, which was as faithful a version of the taped-recorded events as it was possible to construct, and participants have been allowed to edit their own statements. To an extent, some of the dynamics of the session have been sacrificed for this content-oriented presentation, but an analysis of these by Ian Lubek follows.

Under some circumstances, it would be appropriate for a statement of the discussion's context to precede its presentation. In the present instance, the editors are reluctant to provide this, as it seems problematic as to just whose definition of the context would be most appropriate—the editor's, the initiator's, those of the debate's different participants, or definitions elicited from what proved to be a silent majority. It has been our opinion that the participants' comments are generally articulate and sensitive enough that prior interpretation is unwarranted and possibly risky or unfair. Subsequent interpretation by the reader should be carried out with the understanding that the discussion reflects an interaction among a number of factors: motives, status levels, values, experiences, and quite possibly differences in fatigue and alcohol tolerance. The coherence of the discussion that follows is perhaps as remarkable as the content of the many individual statements of which it is composed. [L. H. Strickland]

Henri Tajfel: I would like to start with the suggestion which seems the most specific, that of Ian Lubek concerning the relationship between the present "power structure" in social psychology and future research. Will you introduce this, Ian?

Ian Lubek: I think Elaine suggested that in the year 2000 just about everyone in this room will be alive and part of the social psychological scene. This has the implication that many of us will be directing theses and controlling social psychology's direction at that time. Therefore, I think we should look at where we are now, at the structure of how we as a discipline produce what we produce. We should look at the whole area of graduate training, at how people higher up in the hierarchy, who have theories, get people lower down in the hierarchy to do the leg work. How does all that contribute to the end products of social psychology, and where will we be in the year 2000 if we continue in this fashion?

Paul Secord: I believe that it's illusory to think that there is any single power structure. As we can see in this room perhaps some of the social psychologists are reasonably powerful, and they don't agree at all on how to proceed. There is great diversity among the people who have influence in terms of directing theses. It may be more relevant that the most important source of power is in the hands of the people who serve on the various research review panels, yet even here I think there is not much agreement in terms of the kind or content of the research to be done. However, I think that there is a tendency toward conservatism in social psychology, in the sense that these panels are put in the position of finding something wrong with each proposal, so this promotes the safer, more traditional research methods. Proposals that involve tightly controlled laboratory experiments tend to receive greater favor in such settings, at least as I have observed them. So although there is some focus of power there, consideration of different universities, and directions, and even people in the same department indicates that there is a lot of diversity in terms of how to proceed, in the methodology, the content, in the whole philosophy of research.

Hilde Himmelweit: I think we (the English) have the wrong system of training. We do not have the apprenticing system as Americans do; this has advantages and disadvantages. For example, we have sometimes to prepare ourselves to work on the students' interests. But this demand that we have, that a man sit there three years doing his own Ph.D. research, is completely wrong.

Allen Turnbull: In terms of rising within the power structure, one needs to publish, and invariably that leads to publishing as many articles as you can and, thus, to little collaborative research with colleagues, either within your department or other fields. It's difficult to undertake a meaningful long-term project or a short-term, cross-cultural project or other projects that involve more than one experimenter and a few subjects in the lab. Within the power structure, we need much more collaborative research.

Henri Tajfel: I think we should consider directly the point that Paul Swingle made, to the effect that in existing systems people who have the power tend to work in a way to maintain the status quo, although this might be irrelevant to lots of things, including the development of social psychology. It is they who determine what is or is not worthwhile, and thus we get into a fairly sterile situation. Are there comments on this particular point?

Bob Zajonc: I think this is an important point, particularly since we do not really have solid criteria of excellence for our products as do other fields. In mathematics, for example, if you see a good piece of work, this is identifiable immediately by almost everybody, and the problem of power is not very critical; however, if the criteria of judgement are ambiguous, then power becomes significant. Perhaps if some of the developments we have been discussing occur, if we develop general theory, if the field becomes more sophisticated, then our criteria for judging a particular individual can become more objective. We will have greater consensus, and the problem of power will not be quite as critical. Power and clarity of criteria are interlocked issues. I have seen reviews of articles, for example, that were so diametrically opposed that one would think they concerned different papers. This should not happen in a field that is sophisticated, which suggests that we are simply babies in our discipline.

Mauk Mulder: I disagree with Bob. We will be at the end of our freedom when we have a general integrative theory without good judgment that it is really the best theory, and when everything new is judged in terms of that theory.

Maybe as a number of small research groups develop, as suggested just now, then the grip of a central system will decrease, and we can forget about a general integrative theory.

Art Shulman: Maybe we should address ourselves not so much to the power structure within social psychology now, but to our power to affect future developments. Who is going to determine whether or not we are involved in studying and resolving future problems, or what effect we will have in terms of power?

Ian Lubek: That is not exactly what I had in mind. If this is a conference concerned with the future of social psychology, we might start by looking at the power structure at this very conference. For example, when a group of social psychologists questioned some of the aims of this conference, they received a reply whose tone seems to suggest that after you had worked hard for a number of years, you too could get invited to a conference to express your views. The conference then proceeds with a number of people who have made strong contributions to the field, who have helped define social psychology's present position. Now we are asking these same people to determine the new directions and to bail us out of the situation in which we now find ourselves. I'm not sure that's appropriate, but I think it's a symptom of the power structure in social psychology. We might look at the structure of this conference right now as a miniature model of the structure of the discipline; other conferences like this will also shape social psychology of the year 2000. Do we want social psychology to continue in the same framework?

John Lanzetta: I think that implicit in the questions and the comments has been the acceptance of the thesis that power is a primary determinant of outcomes—and I think that's a terribly naive theory. I think our own social psychological research indicates that this is a terribly naive theory. I think we do a disservice to the field if we discuss the issue as if we had "origins" and "pawns" and that all outcomes are a function of the relationship between the two. This is the same theory we use with respect to some segments of society. It's a nice, causal, asymmetric model: powerful people control all kinds of outcomes, and the source of their control is something they hold in their heads about what is right and wrong, and if you could just change that, the world would be infinitely improved. There may be some truth in that, but I think there's a hell of a lot of error. I'm not denying that there may be differential control. I deny that one should accept such a model as a theory of how things have come to be and how they will evolve.

Paul Secord: You might reject the view that senior social psychologists are directly and consciously using their power, but it still might be true that the decisions they make or the way they behave do influence the directions in which psychology and social psychology go. This is relevant for the larger question of power in society, as you noted. Many radical Marxists take the view that the capitalists are evil men who are keeping the poor down; but there's another Marxist analysis which argues that the whole problem is structural—businessmen move into government, bureaucrats move into business positions, and this is the way one does things.

John Lanzetta: I was trying to open up the model a little bit—it can't be a simplistic one. Those who are powerful in social psychology are themselves subject to certain forces.

Paul Secord: That's what I mean.

John Carroll: Something occurred to me when Bob Zajonc spoke about two complete difference reviews of one article, and what one does when one is aiming for excellence. Why are we or why is the journal aiming for excellence? I think it is because we are competing for a scarce resource, whether it be support or esteem or whatever. We are co-opting ourselves into an area of scarcity.

Bob Zajonc: This does not happen only with respect to journals—it happens on panels that give money, and you can see a range of ratings from 1 to 5.

Jos Jaspars: There must be a few editors in this room who know the problem. For the *European Journal*, ratings from two reviewers may not correlate, and I was disturbed by that, but what has happened is that some people read it differently. It is rare that one reviewer says "This is good" while the other says that it is bad—they are complementary. I think ratings are not sufficient evidence that we are immature, or that we really conflict with each other on specific points.

Bob Zajonc: I agree in one way, in that good ideas in this field have been identified and have not been lost. I think that *any* good idea in this field has not been buried by a "power structure" or by anything that can be so recognized. But I do think that maybe the A—ideas do not have a good chance, or sometimes have been buried or have waited too long.

Harry Triandis: Bob Scott has been doing intercorrelations of some of the ratings of those papers which he has dealt with for the *Journal of Social Issues,* and these are in the range of .30 to .50. If you look at the comments, it becomes clear that the ratings have been along different dimensions, and that what you have is a multidimensional judgment. One person weights one thing heavily, another weights another, but the final rating doesn't reflect these.

Chuck Kiesler: The lack of correlation between ratings may be a good thing, just as when you're constructing a test. If the thing you are measuring is complex, then you'll want the items to measure different aspects of it, and you'll want them *not* to correlate. To the extent you're seeking advice from reviewers whose orientation is different (and in fairness you're deliberately trying to get different orientations) the correlations must necessarily go down. That can be a good sign. If your correlation is .80, then you've sought out people who, if there is a power structure, are both in it and have exactly the same idea and exactly the same reaction. The idea of being an editor is not necessarily to take a vote, but to try to decide within human limits what sort of fit the paper has in the literature.

Henri Tajfel: This is of course the crucial issue: What sort of fit this has in the literature. This comes right back to the point made by Ian Lubek: does the question, "What sort of fit does this have in the literature?" make it difficult to bring about any innovation?

Chuck Kiesler: Of course, of course, but you are dealing with human beings making judgments. I did my two years, and I'm off now, so whatever bias I had is balanced by whatever bias my replacement has. And I mean these things happen, and I've been on all the panels and all the other junk. I bring my biases, and I try to keep them under control, but then I go off the panel and somebody else comes on with his biases and over the course of the years I'll go back on again, and the biases will balance out. But these are the limitations of human judgment.

Ian Lubek: As initiator of this discussion, I would like to suggest that we now terminate it, as it seems to me rather fruitless. We seem to be arguing on two different levels, if I can use a very simplistic analysis. Those whom I would call high in the hierarchy, whether or not one chooses to call them powerful, seem to be bringing in a number of tangential issues. Those who are low in the hierarchy, like myself, are either scared to engage in a discussion or are keeping silent. It seems that no real dialogue, in the sense of understanding our structures, will come of this, so I would say simply that it was a bad judgment on my part to even suggest the topic.

Henri Tajfel: I disagree that it was a bad judgment, but I agree with your analysis of what has happened. We started with an issue having to do with the future directions of social psychology as they are determined by the power structure in social psychology, and we finish up by discussing procedures of accepting and rejecting papers for journals, along with the general view that there are individual differences between people who have power, these individual differences correcting for the biases which exist. I think you [Ian] are more concerned with the structural problems than with individuals who have power.

Bob Zajonc: He asked whether the same people who have caused the state of social psychology today should be going on making decisions about future social psychology.

Ian Lubek: There's just the fact that some of us in this room are in the status of "student" and have to dance to the tunes of some of those in the room who are in the status of thesis committee members. The same holds true with respect to article writers and journal editors. Here, at this conference, some people are called paper presenters, other people are discussants, and other people are called general audience, and this role differentiation affects what gets said, what gets emphasized, and what gets ignored. The fact that reputations are involved and are invoked in discussions is something which perhaps I'm not polite in bringing up, but we've seen it occur and it will occur again. But it's difficult for me even to bring this power issue up because I have no credentials—I have to work another ten or twelve years before I can deliver a paper bringing these points out. I see that there is a basic structure here; there is a common experience I think that many people have had as graduate students, or are having right now. How they're being supervised will affect the kind of research they do, the kind of problems they look at in the year 2000, and how they in turn will treat the next generation three or four years from now when they get licenses to supervise.

Morton Deutsch: I think that Ian is right, that the discussion has not been productive, but I think for such a discussion to be productive basically alternative paradigms to the ones that exist have to be presented and developed. Otherwise, what we will have will be simply a wandering discussion of what is wrong with the present, and the present is never replaced except by an alternative to the present. I suggest that this is a way of trying to focus the discussion on the really central issues: What are some alternatives to what one thinks are the sources of the present problems?

Nelson Heapy: I think it is always a constructive suggestion to ask for alternative paradigms, but I think when you are talking about an issue of power, as Kuhn pointed out in his discussion of paradigm clash, it's very difficult to bring one paradigm into fair competition with another paradigm at the best of times. When you have one paradigm being supported by extremely powerful kinds of groups as opposed to, let's say, discontent on the part of graduate students, the problem is greater than just dealing with paradigm clash. I think we have to start talking about structures of facilitating paradigm clash. Do I make myself clear? I'm not sure that creating a new paradigm does anything more than indicate the roots of the problem—it may take years and years for the real clash to occur in some kind of productive way. By then we will probably be well socialized into the situation.

Morton Deutsch: I'm not suggesting that this clash will not occur, but I suggest that we won't really have any kind of productive consequences necessary to bring about permanent group change without an alternative paradigm.

Nelson Heapy: I'm just trying to offer an alternative focus of discussion—how, in fact, you break out of paradigms.

Art Shulman: He's given the answer: give us an alternative paradigm.

Warren Thorngate: I'll give an alternative so that it can get stepped on: set a maximum number of publications that everyone can have per year. I mean, there are some people who are flooding the market, and they're taking up valuable space. I don't think that anyone can have more than a couple of profound thoughts per year. Another thing I know that's done among people studying human judgment and decision-making is to pass around newsletters and tech reports. Those of us who do it certainly don't get academic credit for it, but it serves the function of exchanging information. If you can find people who have a common interest, have them do research, send informal papers to one another, and then maybe at the end of five years they can come up with something that's integrative and really significant. Then maybe devote an entire journal issue to it. The only problem with this is really a problem of power. I don't really care whether my name gets in print but the people who are making the decisions about whether or not to keep me in academe care. I really don't think the system can change unless some new method for evaluating the worthiness of psychologists can be invented.

Paul Swingle: In response to what Morton Deutsch was saying, it seems that John Lanzetta has suggested an alternative paradigm: which was that we don't understand power. The idea that there is some sort of hierarchical arrangement in which the boys at the top are playing a tune for the people underneath to dance to is somewhat naive. I'd like to elaborate on that for a few moments. Social psychology is just now coming to terms with the whole concept of "system." The system concept is that the master and slave are equally unfree, because the master must restrain the slave and must have the surveillance system to make sure that the slave is doing what he's supposed to be doing. If you entertain that kind of system, there are some basic questions that you have to ask, like who defines what's problematic, to quote Herb Kelman. Who says that we should be throwing a lot of money into surveys of what goes on in the ghetto? Who submits these proposals, and who or what encourages the submissions? What are the goals? Where are these things coming from? In Canada for a while we had the system of self-replacement on some of our research boards and, of course, it didn't take a very long historical perspective to see what was going on. You simply waited until Charlie got off, and Charlie put you on, and then you put Charlie back on when your tenure on the board had elapsed. Again, the point, as John Lanzetta was suggesting, is that it is not a simply linear structure. Power is a very complicated thing. The question is *what* sets the ball rolling, not who, and to what extent are we as social psychologists obliged to divert it? That is the central question.

Stanley Halpin: Part of the answer to what sets it rolling lies in what was said about the economic question of resource scarcity. We've had one suggestion that we have a more equitable distribution of one available resource, that is, journal credits. An alternative would be to increase the available rewards— triple or quadruple the number of journals. Maybe you should put serious limitations on how many graduate students you are producing, knowing that even one graduate student every year is still "too many," in the sense that we have an exponential expansion of the number of people who are producing bad research. However, a radically different approach would be to limit the number of people who can avail themselves of the rewards.

Harry Triandis: I might mention an experiment that is going to take place with the *Journal of Social Issues*. We are going to try to decentralize and diffuse the process of evaluation, first by having people suggest what topics the society should work on, and what topics the *Journal of Social Issues* should deal with. We will try to pick the topics which are likely to work out and have people self-nominate themselves as consultants to a board of editors and as contributors to the issue. We want very young people to get involved in the preparation of the manuscripts. We will rely on the law of large numbers to get good *mean* judgments. It's going to involve a lot of judgments and paper work; however, I hope it's going to create a situation where the people who are in power will no longer be the ones who are making the judgments—the judges will really be your peers in terms of age and experience. Maybe this will work; we'll just have to keep our fingers crossed.

John Holmes: 1 would like to reply to Ian's question as to who's actually taking part in the discussion here, and why we seem to be getting nowhere. There are two rather obvious reasons for it, Ian. First, if you're going to make accusatory statements, then you must expect the people you are accusing to respond in kind. Second, if you're going to pose the question in such an ambiguous way, then you're going to find the discussion rambling like this. Usually when we discuss power, we talk about power over *what*? You seem to be forgetting the language that we use in our research and general thinking. You seem to forget that when we get into this sort of discussion, you open up the question of power—power over *what*? We've talked about graduate training, publication, one paradigm pitted against another, and so on, but if we continue to pose questions in such general and accusatory ways, we're not going to move in any productive direction. I think the response you're getting is *very* preditable from what we know about social psychology.

Ken Gergen: I think it's very clear what constitutes power. In fact, there's a certain interlocking directorate in social psychology in the United States which controls the journal space, who gets into school, whether you publish or not, whether you get money for research, and you'll find the same people on committees in Washington giving away the money, on the journals, at the heads of social psychology programs. That interlocking directorate is, I think, clearly demonstrable.

John Lanzetta: Would you mind demonstrating that, Ken?

Ken Gergen: Oh, I think it would be so easy to do that. In fact, most of the people who have been invited to this conference from the United States share in, or have shared in, four or five of these capacities, so are senior in the field.

Bob Zajonc: I would support what he says.

Ken Gergen: There are areas of disagreement, but there has been at least a general commitment to the experimental paradigm. There are certain things that are very difficult to do in this field now; individual difference research within social psychology is terribly difficult to do at this point, to get money for, and to publish; that whole paradigm is dying. It's difficult to do correlational research of any kind within that power center; it's difficult to do case studies; it's difficult to do longitudinal studies because it takes time, and so on. It's difficult to do theory building within that power structure because journal space doesn't allow it and we don't give money away for it. Further, any young person is going to undergo probably quadruple jeopardy at least from the people who sit at the head of the structure. If you're working in an area, you're constantly exposed to work of younger people who are trying to make it in social psychology, and if you're in the vanguard of that structure you're exposed to it over and over again. You virtually have control over that person's whole career, whether he gets advancement, whether he even stays in the discipline. I've seen it too many times.

One thing we could do is try to dilute that interlocking directorate in some way. I think that people can't serve in multiple capacities and do a very good job anyway. The same people are constantly asked to sit in one committee after another and to judge one paper after another. After they become visible, they are continuously invited and voted in. But that's a two-way street, in the sense that young people cater to it. They perceive this group as being experimentally oriented, and they send in papers and they write proposals that cater to these people because that's the major avenue to ascend to that position of power and control. Young people are indeed participating in and supporting that system as it stands now. Perhaps one way out is to break up that structure somewhat. To amplify a couple of suggestions a bit, one thing we could do is limit the number of positions within the field that one could hold at any one time. A second one would be to take graduate students—not necessarily on the basis of your selection but on the basis of their selection—and place them on these boards and committees to give them at least some input into that decision-making system.

Art Shulman: Perhaps the system we're working under now *is* best in terms of what the problem is. The "power" problem, as I'm trying to define it, is not one of my concern for the distribution of power so I can become more well known. The problem is, what are we best able to direct our talents at and contribute something to? Perhaps something has evolved—the so-called "power structure" that exists. Those who do it best are at the top, and they should be at the top—we should entertain this possibility. I'm much more concerned about using the talent we have rather than how each one of us can further ourselves. I don't know too many people who have not been able to do the research they wanted to do. They may not be able to do it in a very big way, but they can get started. One of the beautiful things about social psychology, which I think differentiates it from a lot of other fields, is that we can do our studies with very little funding, on a small scale. On a big scale, we do need that larger funding.

Henri Tajfel: I think this is as far as we can go now.

CRITIQUE
Some Tentative Suggestions for Analyzing and
Neutralizing the Power Structure in Social Psychology

IAN LUBEK

The preceding discussion (Strickland *et al.,* 1976) occurred during a session of
the conference, *Research Paradigms and Priorities*, but not as a preplanned
agenda item on the program; rather, it sprang up *autogénéré* from the floor.
While the editors have suggested that the transcript will speak saliently for itself
to readers who were not present, I have taken the position that for the full
meaning and impact to be transmitted, an attempt should be made to describe
both the social context of the original discussion, and the structure of the group
that produced it. Thus it will be argued that the power relationships among the
discussion group members *themselves* had a strong influence on the content and
direction of the discussion, and that it may prove informative to attempt to
analyze the "power structure" of the discussion on the "power structure" of
social psychology.

In raising the topic of the power structure in social psychology, I was hoping
to see whether others, too, assumed the existence of a "pecking order" in

IAN LUBEK · University of Guelph, Guelph, Ontario, Canada. This article was written
while the author was at the Laboratoire de Psychologie Sociale (Centre National de la
Recherche Scientifique), Université Paris VII, Paris, France. The author wishes to thank
Erika Apfelbaum and Lloyd Strickland for extensive comments on earlier drafts. Their
encouragements, as well as those of Ken and Mary Gergen, and colleagues at University of
Guelph and Laboratoire de Psychologie Sociale are appreciated. As well, a joint grant from
the Canada Council and le Ministère des Affaires Etrangères de France aided the writing.

the discipline—a structure of relationships involving unequal power ("power" in the sense of X's ability to control Y's outcomes). Examples of these power relationships are journal editor—article writer, professor—student, Ph.D. committee member—candidate, grantor—grantee, paper presenter (communicator)—audience, and experimenter—subject. While the last two relations involving unequal power have received considerable research attention, those that are more embedded in the structure of the discipline are not "hot" research areas.[1] Social psychologists are perhaps too busy living in their power relations to analyze them. It seems that one could ask how *all* the above power relationships in social psychology affect the final output of the discipline—the findings that get reported in the journals, summarized in the texts, and committed to memory by thousands of undergraduates (some of whom then go on to become the next generation of social psychologists).

For a preliminary attempt to answer that question, the preceding discussion can represent the outputs of a sampling of the discipline. Therefore, it is suggested that the effects of power relationships in social psychology can be demonstrated among *those who attended the conference and participated in the "power structure" discussion.* By analyzing the social structure of this discussion, some insights may be gained, in addition to those derived from the content, as to why such a topic was raised for discussion in the first place.

The Social Context of the Conference

The joint financial backing for this conference from NATO, Canada Council, and Carleton University made possible the assembly of 62 individuals of different backgrounds and persuasions: Europeans, North Americans, graduate students, journal editors, etc. The conference program involved participation in an intellectually stimulating series of ten sessions, during each of which the presentation of an invited paper was followed by comments from two or three discussants, before being opened up for further discussion by members of the

---

[1] Some attempts to unravel the mysteries of the "politics of publishing" have been made by Schaeffer (1970), who found some bias in that editors and their friends were more likely to publish regular-length articles in the *Journal of Peronsality and Social Psychology*, and by Bowen, Perloff, and Jacoby (1972), who reinterpreted the Schaeffer data and found a "modest degree of bias due to shared standards and criteria about what constitutes research of publishable quality" (p. 233). Crane (1967) has looked at certain aspects of editor—article writer relationships for articles in three social science journals, including *Sociometry*.

The professor-student relation is discussed by Seeman (1973; p. 901). The literature on persuasive communications (e.g., Hovland, Janis, Kelley, 1953) and experimenter effects (e.g. Adair, 1973) is generally well known.

audience. There were also certain external elements, not preplanned by the conference organizers, to which all participants became exposed, Each participant received at the conference a packet containing program information as well as copies of a sequence of correspondence between two groups concerned about priorities and paradigms in social psychology: the conference organizers, Strickland and Tajfel, on the one hand, and on the other, a group of social psychologists and students at the State University of New York at Stony Brook. This interchange culminated in the latter group's publication of a newsletter (*Psych Agitator*, 1974) highly critical of the conference, NATO, links between social psychology and the military, etc. This correspondence raised directly, or indirectly, certain questions of a different nature from those normally asked about methodology and theory in social psychology. These questions were somewhat critical, with overtones capable of polarizing opinion along the political spectrum, from far left to far right. Included were the following (some of the responses proffered at the conference are listed as well):

(a) Who might best give suggestions for new directions and priorities in social psychology? Should those who have in the past contributed heavily to the current position of the discipline now define the new directions? Although raised in the "power structure" discussion, this question was left unresolved.

(b) Are there implications, beyond financial, of NATO sponsorship of a social psychology conference? This question, raised in the *Psych Agitator*, was discussed in the correspondence from the coordinators, and at the conference in remarks by Dean Wendt, a member of the Human Factors Panel of NATO.

(c) Would the conference be visited or disrupted by those critical of it? The *Psych Agitator* group did not show up although the conference organizers did maintain a program flexibility that would have allowed them at least one session to debate their views. Instead, however, a group from the "Labour Committee" disrupted one session in order to denounce and present indictments for "war crimes" to several participants, for whom they used titles such as "Nazi doctors" and "CIA agents." However, many of the more established social psychologists did not remain in the room to hear their criticisms, citing as reasons for leaving the undemocratic takeover of the microphone and the fact that they had previously heard these charges before at other conferences, or in their own classrooms.

(d) Should the conference go on strictly as planned, or should some time be devoted to discussing these matters? Here the organizers juggled the schedule to accommodate discussions, such as that on the power structure. As well, small interest groups met informally during meals, free time, etc. At least one participant, Mulder, incorporated an analysis of the event of (c) into his presentation.

Thus, onto the bond paper of the "legitimate" conference program was imprinted a watermark of "critical" questions. By legitimate I mean both "having the sanction of established custom" and "being valued as right and proper"; by critical, I imply both "analytical evaluation" and "pertaining to a decisive transition point." The critical questions did not come only from outside the conference, but given the wide range of participants' backgrounds, were also present within the legitimate program: the intermingling of critical and legitimate elements could be seen clearly on the very first day. In the first session Zajonc's contribution (of the type acceptable for publication in an APA journal) received rather sharp criticism from one discussant, Moffitt, who questioned many of the underlying assumptions of the method and theory from a philosophy of science viewpoint. In the afternoon session that same day, a presentation by Apfelbaum questioned certain political and ideological assumptions of past conflict research (thus probably making it *not* acceptable for an APA journal). One discussant, Deutsch, reacted negatively to the presentation, while the other, Swingle, was positive about the ideas and even extrapolated them to another research area.[2]

Therefore, given the intellectual excitement generated by the very first day's sessions, the clashing and blending of contrasting views within the structure of the sessions, the formation of small spontaneous discussion groups outside the sessions, and the flexibility of the organizers and participants in clearing the time needed, the discussion of the power structure was initiated as a critical challenge of the legitimate conference structure.

Editing the Manuscript

The discussion was tape-recorded (with the written consent of all participants) and a typed transcript (26 pages, approximately 843 lines) was prepared. To avoid losing the essence of the discussion, yet to save space, some deletions have been made in the original transcript (also with the consent and cooperation of the participants). Strickland *et al.* (1976) have described the editing criteria used. Only limited cosmetic surgery was needed to take the rough edges off the discussion. The editing of the typewritten transcript of the taped session has produced a final version that contains 46% of the number of lines in the typewritten original. The editorial work has attempted to spare the reader some of the boredom and confusion ordinarily caused by literal transcription of a live discussion. The essence of the *content* of ideas has been skillfully preserved. In so doing, however, editorial efficiency may not have satisfied other needs of the reader: there is always the risk that too much polishing of historical documents may give them a more polite and cogent demeanor, but do a disservice to the reader and the historian of science, in removing the dynamics that help determine the social context of the discussion.

[2] The papers by Zajonc, Moffitt, Apfelbaum, Deutsch, and Swingle all appear in this volume; see also Zajonc and Markus (1975).

A "Critical" Look at a "Legitimate" Discussion

While the contents of the edited transcript convey clearly all the major ideas expressed, deletion of some of the discussion dynamics, and the lack of information available to the reader about the context in which this discussion has taken place, may create an unrealistic impression of how the participants actually approached this question. As initiator of the discussion topic, I have felt some discrepancy between the impressions I received while participating (and re-reading the original transcript) and those received from studying the edited version. For me, the latter creates the impression of a group of 20 concerned social psychologists sitting around at a session of a conference to discuss the topic of the power structure in social psychology, much as they might discuss "attitudes," "consistency theories," or any of the other scheduled, legitimate conference themes. In what follows, then, I shall attempt to analyze some of the dynamics that I perceived to be present, but which may not be evident in the preceding edited transcript. Behind this attempt is the question: To what extent does the social structure of the group discussing the power structure affect the content of that discussion?

For example, one can, somewhat arbitrarily, divide the 62 conference participants into two groups according to their relative visibility in social psychology. Such a division will create two groups of almost equal size: 27 participants who may be designated "visibles" (i.e., whose names will be recognized by a large number of North America and European social psychologists), and 35 participants who can be labeled "not-so-visibles" (i.e., graduate students and recent Ph.D.s whose contributions to the cumulative literature are not yet so well recognized).[3] Examining the *original* transcript of the discussion, one notes that at first glance the two groups appear equally prominent in the discussion,

---

[3] Using a list of conference participants distributed after its conclusion, the 62 names were rated either visible or not-so-visible by the author (in March 1975) and by two Canadian social psychologist colleagues (in June 1975) using the above definitions. For 79% of the names, the judgments of the author were supported by both colleagues; in 10% of the cases, one colleague disagreed, and in 11%, both colleagues disagreed. For the 13 participants for whom unanimous agreement was not reached, 7 cases involved European names judged visible by the author (who has worked in both North America and Europe), three North Americans listed as visible by the author were not recognized by at least one colleague, and three North Americans rated as not-so-visible by the author were visible to his colleagues (all three were Canadians). For the specific discussion on power, for 17 of the 20 participants, there was unanimity of the author and both colleagues; for one case, one colleague disagreed with the author's not-so-visible rating of a Canadian, and for two cases, neither colleague recognized European social psychologists listed as visible by the author. Overall, no drastic disagreements seem to arise in dividing the participants into the two categories.

i.e., of the 20 speakers, 12 are labeled visibles,[4] and 8, not-so-visibles.[5] However, further analysis reveals that of the 78 separate speeches made, 59 were by visibles. Counting lines in the typed transcript, 69% of the discussion was by visibles.[6] (The edited version, has 63% coming from the visibles, which includes 6% from the chair.) About half-way through the transcript, I made the suggestion that the discussion be terminated as it seemed to be getting carried by those "higher up" in the hierarchy. Examination of the original transcript indicates that prior to this point, 79% of the content (transcript lines) was generated by 9 visibles making 21 speeches, while 4 not-so-visibles made 5 speeches for 21%. After this attempted termination, the discussion continued, but now only 62% of the content came from the visibles.

Was the discussion, initiated as a critical challenge to the legitimate program, "co-opted," "managed," or "taken over" by the visibles?[7] Clearly, the lion's share of the discussion, *quantity*-wise, emanated from this group. The reader may wish to evaluate the *content* both in terms of the *quality* of the ideas, as well as the *source* of the communications. The discussion's contents reflect the dynamics of the group that produced it—at a conference where over 60 people gather to discuss *future* directions for social psychology, and in a session where the formal conference structure is abandoned, 20 people engage in discussion, a disproportionate[8] amount of which emanates from the visible minority of the conference, i.e., *those who have a history of having made past contributions to the current position of social psychology.* What started out as a critical probe appears to end up, neatly edited, as a testimony to the openness and willingness of social psychologists to confront these issues (with the implicit proviso that the confrontation be dominated by the visible group).

Thus, this discussion should perhaps be considered as only one of many possible permutations of collections of ideas on the power structure in social psychology. One can speculate on how the discussion could have taken different turns had the participants been (a) a group of graduate students before (or after) comprehensive exams, (b) participants at a conference called Alternatives to Social Psychology, (c) the executive officers of Division 8 or 9 of APA, (d) discussion participants mutually unaffected by considerations of their own status in the discipline, etc. Social psychologists have long studied the influence processes

---

[4] Visibles: Secord, Zajonc, Mulder, Jaspars, Lanzetta, Triandis, Swingle, Kiesler, Deutsch, Gergen, Himmelweit, and Tajfel (chair).

[5] Not-so-visibles: Lubek, Turnbull, Shulman, Carroll, Heapy, Thorngate, Halpin, and Holmes.

[6] The chair, a visible, contributed 19% both in his capacity as helmsperson and in substantive contributions to the content.

[7] It is probably evident in the transcript that several of the more visible participants are critical; conversely, some of the not-so-visibles manifest clear aspirations to the legitimate order.

[8] With visibles making up 44% of the conference, the Chi-squares are all significant.

in experimentally created discussion groups; turning a reflexive eye inward on the discussion of power structure should not be such an alien task. The preceding transcript should therefore be taken with a grain of salt, or at least a pinch of social context.

Toward a Social Psychology of Social Psychology

If we accept the above demonstration that the power relationships among social psychologists may affect the current (or *mainstream*) output of the discipline, we might speculate about the appearance of output from a discipline devoid of such relations, i.e., an uninfluenced, destructured, or *neutral* discipline. To exhaust a logical possibility, we might also contemplate the outputs of a discipline with *reversed* power relationships, wherein, e.g., graduate students dominate and control program selection for conferences, award funds, evaluate their "supervisors" for promotion, and edit journals (cf. the University of North Carolina's *Representative Research in Social Psychology*, and the State University of New York at Buffalo's philosophy journal *Telos*).

Outputs from authors working on the same problem, but from differing perspectives within mainstream, neutral, and reversed social psychology, could then be compared, thus presenting a wider range of social psychological ideas. In a book such as the present one, the preceding discussion by participants in mainstream social psychology could be juxtaposed with a similar discussion involving a neutral cross section, i.e. a group of social psychologists unaware of (and unaffected by) each other's identity, role, or status in the discipline. (Perhaps, at this point, someone working within mainstream social psychology will suggest using the hood and bulky lab coats of deindividuation experiments!) Finally, the editors could solicit a contribution from a reversed power structure group—these might be an experimental breakaway group, such as the Radical Therapist/Rough Times collective (Agel, 1973); the *Psych Agitator* group at Stony Brook, whose membership is mostly made up of graduate students (*Psych Agitator*, 1974); and certain experimental colleges, where students hire and fire their resource persons.

But given the tenacious structure of the institutions in which most social psychology research is currently conducted, it seems unlikely that much data will be forthcoming from participants in reversed-relationship environments. However, some suggestions have already been put forward in the preceding discussion (Strickland *et al.*, 1975) that may help to reduce the effects of some power relationships in the mainstream strcture and may lead to output of a more neutral nature: (a) limitation of journal page allotment per person, (b) using nonjournal, informal paper exchange networks (Thorngate), (c) limitation of the interlocking directorate's committee assignments, and (d) permitting graduate students access to the decision-making system (Gergen). However, before the fruits of a more neutral social psychology can be observed, unaffected by the current power structure, a number of other steps may be necessary.

The first step would be to develop an intradisciplinary structural awareness—this would involve reflexively examining the relationships of social influence within the discipline—in fact, developing a *social psychology of social psychology*. Steps have been already taken in a number of surrounding areas toward such an analysis, including work in history and philosophy of science (Kuhn, 1970a, 1970b, 1970c), sociology of science (DeGré, 1955; Ashby, 1972), sociology of knowledge (Andreski, 1974; Buss, 1975), sociology of sociology (Albrow *et al.*, 1970), politics of science (Greenberg, 1971; Blissett, 1972), studies of diffusion of innovation (Katz, Hamilton, and Levin, 1966), analyses of communication influence networks (Crane, 1969; Xhignesse and Osgood, 1967; Griffith and Mullins, 1972; APA Project on Scientific Information Exchange in Psychology, 1968), and studies of the social structure of those working in a particular problem area (Cartwright, 1973). Within a social psychology of social psychology one could focus on at least three sources of influence affected by unequal power relationships: (a) pressures to preserve the paradigm, (b) pressures in the publication relation (author—editor), and (c) apprenticeship education. I shall discuss each of these three briefly.

(A) Pressures to Preserve the Paradigm

Consider the following three observations on the scientific enterprise, which, although differing on several dimensions (e.g., country of origin, discipline of author, date of statement, and degree of dispassion), nonetheless provide a common analysis of certain pressures existing within most disciplines:

> Long ago we learned, of course, that if a scientist were content with being a foot soldier, if he would concentrate upon filling in detail, upon increasing the preciseness of reports and tables, upon minor fretwork rather than upon major architecture, his labors would not be likely to shake an institutional applecart and would be appreciated and rewarded ... [for the physical and biological sciences] so many of their devotees become institutional functionaries, that is to say, become housebroken or bureaucratized. Their work may have objectivity, but it has other points resembling that of monastic scholars. Such technicians accept the major intellectual framework of a cult, and they spend their lives polishing and sometimes reworking trivia. (Lee, 1954, p. 518)

> Most scientists are prepared to work most of the time within the framework of ideas developed by their acknowledged leaders. In that sense, within any discipline, science is ruled by oligarchs who hold influence as long as their concepts and systems are accepted as the most successful strategy. (Price, 1965, cited in Blissett, 1972, p. 119)

> All but a very few scientists are confined within the conventional framework of concepts which their colleagues regard as "sound"; the invisible college of other scientists imposes belief in these concepts upon all its members as a condition of belonging to the scientific community. This degree of orthodoxy is essential for the progress of science. (Ashby, 1972, p. ii)

Is science generally (and social psychology in particular) locked into such a constricting social system? Those concerned with analyzing science's structure sociologically, e.g., Mulkay (1972), argue that workers in a particular research network share preconceived notions about their technical and cognitive framework. Therefore, there will be a narrow range both of problems regarded as significant and of solutions accepted as legitimate. As Mulkay (1972) notes, this implies "that the members of research networks are not independent openminded puzzle-solvers. They are rather men concerned to solve a limited range of problems which are rigidly defined in terms of certain cognitive and technical standards or norms. Research which does not conform to these norms tends to be rejected out of hand" (pp. 6–7). He further seeks to demonstrate how this set of social arrangements leads to conformity in science:

> The social structure of basic research consists of a complex web of social networks . . . the central objective of researchers is to supply valued information to their colleagues and the main institutional reward for providing such information is professional recognition. [Despite competition] considerable conformity to current cognitive and technical expectations is maintained. To some extent this is done informally as the individual scientist, in order to gain recognition as having made a valuable contribution to knowledge, comes to adopt his colleagues' definitions of what constitutes knowledge in his field. (p. 10)

Mulkay's conclusions are based largely on the work of others; Blissett (1972), however, has interviewed and surveyed systematically a number of scientists, and his evidence supports conclusions remarkably similar to the above. His major concern is an analysis of "the role of politics in science." He argues "that 'hidden systems' of influence and persuasion" shape the output of science (p. xiii). Moreover, there exist, he argues, certain "institutional elites," who are called upon to decide among conflicting scientific views, but contrary to the "official" image projected by science these scientific judgments do not always transcend politics. But what sort of mechanisms could be at work behind the scenes? Blissett offers evidence for his notion of "circles of influence." Two important factors in describing the "regime conditions" in the "politics of science" will be (a) the maturity of theoretical development, and (b) "the number of decision-makers who are prominent in evaluating the significance of scientific work." He then argues that

> within all disciplines there are expanding circles of influence that define the scope of relevant decisions . . . It may be hypothesized that at the core of each discipline is a group of scientists who, in Polyani's terminology, are the "Chief Influentials"–those men likely to influence the direction of fundamental research by controlling appointments, promotions, publications, and the distribution of special subsidies and awards. (pp. 114–115)

Following these "influentials" come, in descending order of influence, the "scientific statesmen," "student-oriented leaders," "intradepartmentally oriented scientists," and "marginal scientists" (following Hagstrom's system of classification). Depending on the degree of theoretical unity in the discipline, the controlling elites will be either highly interlocked, or, as is probably the case in psychology, competitive. From a director of a prominent research institute and member of the National Academy, Blissett (1972) offers the following interview material:

> In my profession there is a canonizing of views. These are the views that are subscribed to by the most influential members of the profession. That is, those who are the editors of journals and the leading members of professional societies. These people are the defendants and judges of particular points of view. They are able to crush incompatible thoughts. But, of course, they do it under the guise that there is not enough evidence, or that the evidence is incomplete . . . the barrier to the advancement of science lies between the whole of the discipline and the in-group that controls the flow of discoveries. (pp. 116–117)

Whether one prefers discussion about a "web of social networks" in a discipline, "expanding circles of influence," or how a group of visibles dominate a particular discussion, the underlying commonality is that persons of differential status, influence, or power exert pressures (often informal) that have a direct influence on the output of the discipline, such that individual work conforms to the dominant framework.

(B) Pressures in the Publication Relation (Author–Editor)

The informal control system described above "is supplemented by the institutionalized mechanism of the journals which take care to reject submissions deviating from current cognitive and technical norms" (Mulkay, 1972, p. 10). Some efforts have been made to shed some empirical light on the function of the relationship between author and editor (Whitley, 1970; Schaeffer, 1970; Bowen, Perloff, and Jacoby, 1972). Crane (1967) speaks of the gatekeeping function, while Mulkay (1972) describes the conformity-inducing function of the journals: "New recruits to research . . . must build up a sound professional reputation, which can be achieved only by publishing information regarded as valuable by those working within the same research network. The professional journals therefore, constitute the main institutionalized mechanism whereby scientific conformity is maintained" (1972, p. 16).

Our scientific writing in social psychology (as elsewhere in the sciences) is firmly wedded to an authority-based system. In the *introduction* to an article, our new ideas or hypotheses are embedded into the theory, framework, language, and findings of older published work.[9] The *methods* section is often repetitious of a previously successful experimental design, procedure, set of instructions, etc., showing how, with perhaps a little bending of conceptual

---

[9] The average age of the 1754 citations in the *Journal of Abnormal and Social Psychology* (1960) is estimated at just under 12 years, using data from Xhignesse and Osgood (1967).

variables, our ideas of conflict can be accommodated within a Prisoner's Dilemma game, those of aggression within the shock-box-learning method, etc. While the *results* section usually shows new (and often exciting) data, the *discussion* section that follows is not always overburdened with creative speculation about new paradigms and priorities, but rather represents another attempt to fit the new findings into the framework of the old—what one long-time psychology journal editor (Melton, 1962) has called "the relation of necessity between the predicted relationships and other previously or concurrently demonstrated effects . . . but an isolated finding, especially when embodied in a 2 X 2 design, at the .05 level or even the .01 level was frequently judged not sufficiently impressive to warrant archival publication" (p. 554).

Rarely will an article appear with three or fewer citations: reviewers may kindly suggest additional authorities to document points raised (these suggestions often allowing more experienced writers a fair guess at the identity of the anonymous reviewer!). In 1960, articles in the *Journal of Abnormal and Social Psychology* averaged 11.4 citations; indeed, Xhignesse and Osgood (1967) considered this measure, density of citation, to be "perhaps the best single index of a journal's scholarliness—in the sense that its authors depend more or less heavily upon their knowledge of the works of others" (pp. 781–782).

Authors whose papers are rejected, on the other hand, do not get the opportunity to red-pencil the ideas of others (cf. Rodman, 1970, for an enlightening look at how one journal editor views such marginal noncontributors). Generally then, it has been argued that the journal system exemplifies a highly institutionalized power structure in the double sense of (a) the authority-based system for public display of ideas (of which the last five pages of this paper have been exemplary) and (b) the unequal power relationships between contributor and judge. I suspect that many of the above comments would also hold for the relationship between members of granting review boards and grant applicants.

(C) Apprenticeship Education

The authority-based publication system mirrors the educational system that produces new researchers. The apprentice system, described by Festinger *et al.* (1959) resembles closely the authority-centered education system, described less dispassionately by Rossman (1972). The latter argues that "the creation of knowledge, usually conceived of as either 'research' or 'scholarship' becomes an expert's job. The teacher's task is to transmit it; the student's task is to learn it. In this model of education, problems are identified for the student by authorities ('experts') who also define the supply problem-solving approaches" (p. 48).

The English system, as noted by Himmelweit in the power structure discussion, is different in its mode of training. It, too, has its limitations, but at times the supervisor may have to "update" himself on the student's interests!

The reader is invited to compare the graduate education relation in his/her own department, with the following two "hypothetical" meetings between a new graduate student and a supervisor.[10]

> Supervisor A: Here are reprints of all my (important) papers, and the outline of the grant I'm currently working on. Familiarize yourself with them. You'll be running the next three studies on this list, to give you practice with the equipment and procedure. One of my other students, working on his dissertation, is in charge of the lab—he'll show you the ropes. For these three studies, you'll be third author if the results are significant. For your thesis, you can choose any of the studies on this list, and add to it one variable of your own choosing. You'll get senior authorship on the first paper coming out of your thesis data. I'll write up all the others, and you'll be second author.

> Supervisor B: Find a topic that interests you, and we'll sit down frequently to discuss and develop your ideas. We can jointly explore the literature together, develop a new methodology if appropriate, and apply for a grant together if needed. We'll try to expand the existing theory and test out some of the implications from it. We'll critically analyze ideas, brainstorm, and if necessary, cross interdisciplinary lines to develop the intellectual tools to tackle your chosen problem. As we'll be working together on this problem area for a number of years, pick a topic of sufficient importance to you to maintain your curiosity and to allow you sufficient enthusiasm to motivate mine.

It would indeed be tempting to finish this analysis of the authority-centered apprenticeship system by resorting to a classical study purporting to show the superiority of democratic, or laissez faire, over authority-centered leadership, but we have already relied too heavily on authorities up to this point. Suffice it to say that initiation into the power structure of social psychology can be traced back to most graduate learning environments.

What Is to Be Done?

Clearly, these three sources of social influence that affect the output of a discipline such as social psychology are interrelated—researchers "locked into" a particular framework participate in the publication enterprise and transmit the description of their intellectual Plato's cave to the next generation. Once the sources of influence have been described and the intradisciplinary structural awareness achieved, the researcher may very well find it to his liking to continue on within mainstream social psychology. Thus, one expected reaction to the preceding discussion from a number of readers will be: "But of course (old chap), that's the way things are." Other social psychologists may wish to change some, or all, of the influence relations. Kelman (1970), for example, wishes graduate students "to relate themselves to a tradition and a discipline—even if

[10] The author is probably not the only psychologist who can claim to have met supervisors closely resembling the caricatures drawn here.

that relationship is largely one of overturning what has been done in the past. Training in the fundamental concepts and methods of the field is thus essential if social science is to maintain its integrity" (p. 93).

How might the North American training system allow for learning devoid of the superimposed master–apprentice relation? Consider the function of the research assistantship–in return for assisting in a faculty member's research activities, a stipend sufficient to maintain an apprentice social psychologist at, or just above, the poverty level for four years, is offered.[11] The vital link between subsistence and research interest in the projects of one's supervisor is thus economically forged. Contrast this relationship with the notion of awarding a student a four-year, independent research grant (including salary, and modest research funds, which may be used to purchase equipment for the laboratory of a supervisor willing to collaborate on the student's project). This would create independent, rather than career-dependent, apprenticeships. Departments that regularly assign all their graduate students to the pool of professors requiring research assistance, regardless of the source of funds (Canada Council, NIMH, teaching assistantships, research assistantships, block training grants, etc.) on the grounds of providing an equal and valuable research experience for all, may have to redefine their source of "willing" labor. Collaboration on research projects with graduate students, independently financed, would change the output of some supervisors markedly–the generation of novel ideas might emanate from those not necessarily committed, as yet, to a particular framework. The most productive supervisors would then become those most flexible in adapting to new ideas from their graduate collaborators, rather than the technicians adept at grinding out a series of grant-related studies, one after the other.

As for the publication system, this conference (and several sections of this book) offers an interesting format, such that a paper which presents new perspectives is followed by several critiques. Unlike symposia where each speaker addresses the topic from his/her own perspective, or conferences where independent papers are grouped together by apparent title similarity, the interchange of ideas fostered by a critical review of a paper (without the necessity of running an experiment and providing contrary data) may be a useful concept for communications in social psychology. Levine (1974) has proposed an adversary model; Rychlak (1970) argues that perhaps dialectical argument would be again useful (Freud having made earlier use of it). DeGré (1955) had also argued:

If the selection of the subject matter of knowledge as well as the conceptual apparatus of interpretation are bound up with existential factors of social position and cultural norms, then it becomes very important for the scientific enterprise that the broadest confrontation of opposing standpoints be encouraged by the society's institutional arrangements. For it is only by the juxtaposition of conflicting and

---

[11] At one point, graduate students supporting families on these funds were eligible for United States poverty program food stamps.

partial viewpoints that we can expect a more inclusive world view to arise. (pp. 38–39)

An argument for a debate-style journal would be supported by the numerous references in texts to (and reprintings of) the Skinner–Rogers debate; the juxtaposition of Ring's provocative (1967) article with a response from McGuire (1967); the response by Schlenker (1974) to Gergen's (1973) important comments on social psychology as history, etc. Similarly, debates about replicability of findings should be systematically encouraged. To give but one example: Page and Scheidt (1971) failed to replicate the Berkowitz and LePage (1967) "weapons effect." Berkowitz (1971) offered a rejoinder, and the debate was then terminated when Scheidt and Page's (1971) response was not given journal space.

Other attempts to replicate the original experiment, for the most part unsuccessful, have, however, appeared (e.g., Schuck and Pisor, 1974; Turner and Simons, 1974; Buss, Booker, and Buss, 1972; Ellis, Weinir, and Miller, 1971). Another valuable source of "debate" would be the comments of the reviewers, especially when opinion is split. Their publication alongside the article would be very useful in developing critical, analytical skills, instead of the "reliance-on-authority" response often engendered in graduate student readers. Opening up the journals to a debate format would serve to divert some researchers from the trend to tack on one (or two) novel variable(s) to a proven (i.e., published) finding, and more toward activities such as replication, theoretical criticism, discussions of methods, ethics, transhistorical validity, relevance, and applicability. The function of editor, in seeking out and compiling the elements of debate stirred up by a particular article (wtihin a 12–18 month period, for example), would become more one of housekeeper than gatekeeper.

Similarly, a *Journal of Grant Proposals in Social Psychology* would offer space to short versions of all major grant proposals, which could then be publicly debated, rather than the decision being made within an "old-boys network" of grant reviewers. Here too, a cross section of psychologists could have a say in whether a line of work should continue to receive attention and large-scale funding, or if a change were due. The ability to engage in critical thought (and receive publication credit for such debate activities) might reduce the tendencies for researchers to create mini-empires, wherein only they, and a handful of like-minded colleagues (or former students), generate the majority of studies. Similarly, the practice of an in-group forming their own journal to give vent to their particular framework might be lessened if they could participate in debates, thus encouraging a broader scope of opinions within social psychology. And would all this continual debating not be bothersome and confusing to graduate students (who as undergraduates often showed prodigious skill in memorizing the "facts" in their social psychology textbooks)? Perhaps no more so than viewing the debates that occur during the question period at a departmental colloquium, at a dissertation committee meeting to discuss a thesis proposal, or, for those universities that still keep it as a proper moment for finally accepting or rejecting four years of work, the thesis defense itself.

Throughout the above, it has been suggested that paradigms and priorities are maintained within a certain system of power relationships within the discipline, and that for change in direction to occur, it might be instructive first to analyze these influence relations (especially as they relate to paradigm preservation, publishing activities, and graduate training) and then to speculate about ways to neutralize (or possibly reverse) them. Comparisons of outputs from mainstream, neutral, and reverse networks, in both graduate training and journal debates, may produce an awareness not only of how these influence processes work in the discipline (and hence the beginnings of a social psychology of social psychology) but may also permit a vision of, and actions toward producing, the fuller range of theory and research possible in social psychology.

References

Adair, J. G. *The human subject: The social psychology of the psychological experiment.* Boston: Little, Brown, 1973.

Agel, J. (producer) *Rough times.* New York: Ballantine Books, 1973.

Albrow, M., Banks, J. A., Bramson, L., Cherns, A. B., Kelman, H. C., Klausner, S. Z., Mitchell, G. D., Rex, J. A., and Whitley, R. D. The sociology of sociology. *The Sociology Review Monograph*, 1970, **16**.

Andreski, S. *Social science as sorcery.* Harmondsworth, Middlesex, England: Penguin, 1974.

APA Project on Scientific Information Exchange in Psychology. Networks of informal communication among scientifically productive psychologists: An exploratory study. Report no. 21, December 1968.

Ashby, Sir E. (ed.) The sociology of science. *The Sociological Review Monograph*, 1972, **18**.

Berkowitz, L. The "weapons effect," demand characteristics, and the myth of the compliant subject. *Journal of Personality and Social Psychology*, 1971, **20**, 332–338.

Berkowitz, L., and Le Page, A. Weapons as aggression-eliciting stimuli. *Journal of Personality and Social Psychology*, 1967, 7, 202–207.

Blissett, M. *Politics in science.* Boston: Little, Brown, 1972.

Bowen, D. D., Perloff, R., and Jacoby, J. Improving manuscript evaluation procedures. *American Psychologist*, 1972, **27**, 221–225.

Buss, A., Booker, A., and Buss, E. Firing a weapon and aggression. *Journal of Personality and Social Psychology*. 1972, **22**, 296–302.

Buss, A. R. The emerging field of the sociology of psychological knowledge. *American Psychologist,* 1975, **30**, 988–1002.

Cartwright, D. Determinants of scientific progress: The case of the risky shift. *American Psychologist*, 1973, **28**, 222–231.

Crane, D. The gatekeepers of science: Some factors affecting the selection of articles for scientific journals. *American Sociologist*, 1967, **2**, 195–201.

Crane, D. Social structure in a group of scientists: A test of the "invisible college" hypothesis. *American Sociological Review*, 1969, **34**, 335–352.

DeGré, G. *Science as a social institution: An introduction to the sociology of science.* New York: Random House, 1955.

Ellis, D. P. Weinir, P., and Miller, III, L. Does the trigger pull the finger? An experimental test of weapons as aggression-eliciting stimuli. *Sociometry*, 1971, **34**, 453–465.

Festinger, L., Garner, W. R., Hebb, D. O., Hunt, H. F., Lawrence, D. H., Osgood, C. E., Skinner, B. F., Taylor, D. W., and Wertheimer, M. Education for research in psychology. *American Psychologist*, 1959, **14**, 161–179.

Gergen, K. J. Social psychology as history. *Journal of Personality and Social Psychology*, 1973, **26**, 309–320. (Reprinted this volume, pp. 15–32.)

Greenberg, D. S., *The politics of pure science*. New York: New American Library, 1971.

Griffith, B. C., and Mullins, N. C., Coherent social groups in scientific change. *Science*, September 15, 1972, **177**, 959–963.

Hovland, C. I., Janis, I. L., and Kelley, H. H. *Communication and persuasion.* New Haven: Yale Univ. Press, 1953.

Katz, E., Hamilton, H., and Levin, M. L. Traditions of research on the diffusion of innovation, in C. W. Backman and P. F. Secord (eds.), *Problems in social psychology: Selected readings*, pp. 153–166. New York: McGraw-Hill, 1966.

Kelman, H. The relevance of social research to social issues: Promises and pitfalls. *Sociological Review Monograph,* 1970, **16**, 77–99.

Kuhn, T. S. *The structure of scientific revolutions*, 2nd ed. Chicago: Univ. of Chicago Press, 1970. (a)

Kuhn, T. S. Logic of discovery or psychology of research? In I. Lakatos and A. Musgrave (eds.), *Criticism and the growth of knowledge,* pp. 1–23. Cambridge: Cambridge Univ. Press, 1970. (b)

Kuhn, T. S. Reflections on my critics, in I. Lakatos, and A. Musgrave (eds.), *Criticism and the growth of knowledge*, pp. 231–278. Cambridge: Cambridge Univ. Press, 1970. (c)

Lee, A. McC. Social pressure and the values of psychologists. *American Psychologist*, 1954, **9**, 516–522.

Levine, M. Scientific method and the adversary model: Some preliminary thoughts. *American Psychologist*, 1974, **29**, 661–677.

McGuire, W. J. Some impending reorientations in social psychology: Some thoughts provoked by Kenneth Ring. *Journal of Experimental Social Psychology*, 1967, **3**, 124–139.

Melton, A. W. Editorial. *Journal of Experimental Psychology*, 1962, **64**, 553–557.

Mulkay, M. J. Conformity and innovation in science. *Sociological Review Monograph*, 1972, **18**, 5–23.

Page, M. M., and Scheidt, R. J. The elusive weapons effect: Demand awareness, evaluation apprehension and slightly sophisticated subjects. *Journal of Personality and Social Psychology*, 1971, **20**, 304–318.

Price, D. K. *The scientific estate.* Cambridge, Mass: Harvard Univ. Press, 1965. Cited in Blissett, M., *Politics in science.* Boston: Little, Brown, 1972.

Psych Agitator, 1974, **1**(1). Department of Psychology, State Univ. of New York at Stony Brook, Stony Brook, New York.

Ring, K. Experimental social psychology: Some sober questions about some frivolous values. *Journal of Experimental Social Psychology*, 1967, **3**, 113–123.

Rodman, H. Notes to an incoming journal editor. *American Psychologist,* 1970, **25**, 269–273.

Rossman, M. *On learning and social change.* New York: Vintage Books, 1972.

Rychlak, J. F. The human person in modern psychological science. *British Journal of Medical Psychology*, 1970, **43**, 233–240.

Schaeffer, D. L. Do A.P.A. journals play professional favorites? *American Psychologist*, 1970, **25**, 362–365.

Scheidt, R. J., and Page, M. M. Myth versus reality in the social psychological experiment. Unpublished manuscript, Univ. of Nebraska, Lincoln, Nebraska, 1971.

Schlenker, B. R. Social psychology and science. *Journal of Personality and Social Psychology*, 1974, **29**, 1–15.

Schuck, J., and Pisor, K. Evaluating an aggression experiment by the use of simulating subjects. *Journal of Personality and Social Psychology*, 1974, **29**, 181–186.

Seeman, J. On supervising student research. *American Psychologist*, 1973, **28**, 900–906.

Strickland, L. H. (ed.). The "power structure" in social psychology in L. H. Strickland, K. J. Gergen, and F. J. Aboud (eds.), *Social psychology in transition,* pp. 307–316. New York: Plenum Press, 1976.

Turner, C. W., and Simons, L. S. Effect of subject sophistication and evaluation apprehension on aggressive response to weapons. *Journal of Personality and Social Psychology*, 1974, **30**, 341–348.

Whitley, R. D. The formal communication system of science: A study of the organization of British social science journals. *The Sociological Review Monograph*, 1970, **16**, 163–179.

Xhignesse, L. V., and Osgood, C. E. Bibliographical citation characteristics of the psychological network in 1950 and in 1960. *American Psychologist*, 1967, **22**, 778–791.

Zajonc, R. B., and Markus, G. B. Birth order and intellectual development. *Psychological Review*, 1975, **82**, 74–88.

Ziman, J. M. *Public knowledge: An essay concerning the social dimension of science.* Cambridge: Cambridge Univ. Press, 1968. Cited in Blissett, M., *op. cit.*

RESEARCH METHODS AND THE FUTURE

ANDRÉ C. DeCARUFEL

The two major concerns of the participants at the conference might be sum-marized as follows: (1) the lack of, and need for, a general integrative theory, and (2) the relevance of data generated in the traditional laboratory context to "real world" phenomena. On the surface, these might appear to be divergent foci of concern. The former maintains that more attention should be devoted to abstraction and theoretical refinement. A comprehensive theory would sum-marize existing knowledge into a coherent framework and provide direction for research aimed at further reclarification of the theory. The latter holds that research should be directed toward solving important social problems. The goal is not necessarily to advance knowledge in general but rather to provide practical advice on a specific problem. McGuire's recent (1973) article eloquently ex-presses the ambivalence within the field as to which direction might ultimately prove to be more fruitful. At this conference, several of the papers (e.g., Keisler, 1974; Rommetveit, 1974) attempted to integrate the literature within broad areas, while others (e.g., Apfelbaum, 1974) used social events as the main source for research and thinking.

This dichotomy has not always been so marked, however. Ring (1967) noted that early experimental social psychology under the direction of Kurt Lewin was

ANDRÉ C. DECARUFEL · University of North Carolina at Chapel Hill, North Carolina. Preparation of this paper was facilitated by a doctoral fellowship awarded to the author by the Canada Council (W754005). I would like to thank Arie W. Kruglanski for his helpful comments on an earlier draft of this paper.

"a complex interplay of theory, research, and social action" (p. 113). The dictum often attributed to Lewin clearly reflects this integration: no research without action, no action without research. A number of more recent papers reflect modern concern for the relation between psychological theory and method and the problems of society (Campbell, 1969; Skinner, 1971). Unanimity is far from imminent, however, as Gergen (1973) has articulated some deeply rooted concerns about the usefulness of social psychological knowledge. It is the purpose of this paper to argue that both of the aims noted above can be achieved, and to propose that an expansion of our research strategies might be one way to gear this "rapprochement" between theory and social action.

It is the opinion of the present author that research methods as a topic was largely ignored in the discussion of the papers at the conference. This was true despite the fact that a number of the papers (e.g., Triandis, 1974) dealt directly with issues of a methodological nature. On a broader scale, attention to methods has been of importance to social psychologists as a result of the concern about possible artifacts operating in the traditional laboratory study (cf. Rosenthal and Rosnow, 1969; Miller, 1972a). This paper will not evaluate the basis for these concerns but rather will attempt to argue that the theoretical and practical development of social psychology has been somewhat constrained by an over-reliance on laboratory experiments. By expanding our stable of "acceptable" techniques, some concrete gains in these areas might be forthcoming. Note that it is *not* the intent to make the laboratory experiment the "goat" for all the problems encountered by social psychologists. It is my belief that the laboratory experiment has been our greatest tool in discovering what we now know about social behavior, and that it will continue to make a large contribution to the social psychology of the future. Nor is it my intent to suggest alternative methodologies as a panacea for the shortcomings of social psychological methodology as we now know it. It will be argued, however, that supplementary techniques are available which may contribute something over and above that suggested by our present methods. Several different approaches to research will be briefly described which offer unique and different approaches to the study of social behavior, yet retain much of the rigor that has characterized research in the traditional laboratory context. The implications of these methods for the development of theory and the application to social problems will be discussed. The important point to remember in this discussion is that the use of alternative methodologies is only one avenue to aid in achieving an integrated theory as well as concrete social action. The role of methodology in this regard is seen as a catalyst that facilitates the study of processes, such as rate of occurrence of events, which are largely inaccessible using current methods. The payoff is that existing theories could be extended to include these processes or new theories could be developed which incorporate them. The fallacy exists, of course, that we could come to be ruled by our methods, studying only what is conveniently operationalized. Nevertheless, it is true that much of what is considered an acceptable area of investigation is that for which there exists the possibility of operationalization. In addition to opening up new areas of investigation, using different methods to study phenomena of interest would perhaps cause us to look at them somewhat differently. The opportunity for a successful integration of different areas might await new perspectives as much as it does new data. Finally, in terms of social action, one reason that applied work is not attempted as often as it might be is that our methods, which are based on randomization and control of extraneous variables, are often inappropriate in the field. The use of somewhat different techniques might make the prospect of applied work seem less forbidding.

Let us go on to briefly describe several different approaches to methodology and their implications for integrating theory and initiating social action. These techniques again are intended as supplements to traditional methods and not as substitutes for them. The approaches to be discussed are (1) quasi- and non-experimental methods for research on society as a whole, (2) exploratory tactics such as role playing, and (3) experimentation in which the procedures are computer assisted.

(1) Approaches to Experimentation on Society as a Whole

One of the major characteristics of modern industrialized societies is the emphasis on planning. Social reforms are usually aimed at improving the quality of life and satisfaction of the citizens (see Brickman and Campbell, 1971). Despite these good intentions and the desire to be planful, it is often the case that the impact of these reforms on the target population is not to increase their satisfaction but to decrease it, or as is more often the case, the impact is unknown. Consider, for example, the case of members of a minority group who are dissatisfied with the living conditions in their slum neighborhood. Let us say that they make their displeasure known, a reform is instituted, and before they know it they are living in a newly constructed housing project near a middle-class neighborhood. In an "objective" sense they are better off now than they were when they were living in the slums, but are they happier? The assumption is that they are, but usually little effort is made to assess whether or not this is in fact the case, i.e., there is no attempt to evaluate the reform program. An attempt to assess the impact of this innovation might reveal information that would be useful to know before going on to construct other similar projects. As just one example of an unexpected outcome from a reform such as the one noted above, it might be that these slum residents had never been exposed to the "good things in life." Now, with the middle-class neighborhood so close by, they become aware of all the things they did without for so long, perhaps leading to a sense of moral outrage and anger. If such reactions are typical then it calls for future planners of such projects to take this information into account. This information, as was noted above, would only be forthcoming from a properly evaluated program. (The reader interested in the evidence relating to improvement of outcomes and satisfaction should consult Thibaut, 1950; and Folger, 1975.)

The point of the above example is to illustrate the possibilities for the use of social psychological theory and method at the societal level. It is undoubtedly true that social policy would benefit to some degree from an explicit consideration of social psychological theory. To wit, the assumption made by those designing the housing project for the slum dwellers is that they will be using a temporal comparison standard, i.e., comparing their present outcomes with past ones. It is possible though that they could use a social comparison standard and feel deprived relative to their new middle-class neighbors, leading to dissatisfaction. In this case, social psychological theory could be brought to bear in helping decide the site of the housing project. But what of research methods?

Campbell (1969) has noted that one function of psychological methodology in society is to evaluate programs and their effectiveness. He suggests that an explicit shift to experimental approaches should be adopted by administrators, changing the focus from a commitment to the success of a particular policy to a commitment to solve the problem by whatever means are appropriate. A particular program that fails would be replaced by another until an efficient solution has been found rather than sticking with the original because of inadequate information about its success.

The difficulties of experimental control involved in instituting reforms make attractive a number of flexible quasi- and nonexperimental techniques. It is often difficult to have "full control over the scheduling of experimental stimuli" (Campbell and Stanley, 1963, p. 34) and so other approaches aimed at rejecting inadequate hypotheses must be found. While it is beyond the scope of this paper to give detailed consideration to the different quasi-experimental designs, it is clear that in the case of the project tenants, an evaluation program predicated on the random assignment of "subjects to conditions" would have been difficult. In this case a quasi-experimental design such as a nonequivalent control group design would be of some value in evaluating the impact of the program. While it is certainly true that these designs have limitations (see Campbell and Stanley, 1963, pp. 34–61), nevertheless these are preferable to no evaluation at all. Similarly, nonexperimental techniques such as path analysis and cross-lagged correlation may be useful in situations where more orthodox experimental techniques are difficult to implement. Examples of these techniques may be found in a recent article by Kraut and Lewis (1975) on political socialization, as well as in several of the studies in the Surgeon General's report on *Television and Social Behavior*, relating to violence on television. Again the purpose is not to evaluate these particular techniques but to point out that they may have value in the context of evaluating the impact of reforms when the conditions for true experimental designs are not present.

A second use of a scientific approach to social change is what Fairweather (1972) has called "experimental social innovation." The emphasis here is not only on the evaluation of existing programs but also on the experimental *production* of social change. In this case, a social problem would be attacked within the context of a research program with a view to clarifying the operation of the relevant variables. Specific experimental and control groups could be included in order that the reforms be introduced into areas at different rates based on the needs of the community and the requirements of the research design. Fairweather himself has applied these principles to the area of community mental health and one would expect that areas more germane to social psychology such as intergroup behavior and attitude change would benefit from this approach as well.

It should be clear that these procedures promise gains in terms of social action, but do these approaches have any implications for the future of social psychological theory? One is that the simple linear cause and effect models that are so prevalent in our current thinking will have to be replaced with more complex models. Without the strict control procedures that are possible in lab experiments, the investigator would have to consider the workings of larger groups of factors than is currently the practice. In addition, the impact of reform programs would have to be assessed on numerous dimensions to ensure that no noxious "side effects" occur. As an example of a side effect, using our housing project tenants as subjects, it is possible that they might be very happy with their homes but the contrast between this and their "crummy" work surroundings might produce dissatisfaction—a sort of spatial comparison standard. It would seem clear that our theories would benefit from situations in which we are forced to think more complexly about social behavior. Second, it would be the case that demands for "robustness" due again to the difficulty of controlling the environment would help in establishing more clearly what the important variables in a situation are. Some sort of ordering of the most important features of a situation, in conjunction with a sketch of how they relate to the lesser variables, would help clear up some of the muddle as to what occurs under which conditions. Third, our theories would be forced to deal with issues for which we have no immediate answers: Under what conditions will the project dwellers use a temporal, social, or spatial comparison standard, and how will the adoption of one or the other of these standards affect their satisfaction and sense of fairness? We would be forced into dealing with issues of potentially great theoretical impact due to the requirements of clear specification of what should be done, for example, with the slum dwellers. New perspectives gleaned from observation of unexpected reactions, or the intrusion of new factors would help broaden the base of our theories and make them more responsive to social reality. In sum, quasi- and nonexperimental research strategies could be used to evaluate social reform programs and to introduce planned change. In addition to the obvious benefits in terms of social action, social psychological theory would be strengthened by having to come to grips with new problems in the relatively uncontrolled field setting. The resulting new perspectives and new data would help push our theories to include different processes and specify new causal relations. The insights gained from this approach could then be taken back to the lab and studied more closely to establish clearly the cause and effect linkages. The application of new and existing methods to society in general represents one way that the achievement of the dual aims of theory and social action could be facilitated.

(2) Exploratory Techniques in Experimentation: Role Playing

Mixon (1971) has argued for the use of role-playing procedures in research. While it is true that certain reservations have been expressed about the usefulness of role playing (e.g., Freedman, 1969; Miller, 1972b), it would seem that much of this uneasiness is prompted by a misdirected view of the nature and uses of role-playing methodology. Role playing, in Mixon's (1971) view "proceeds in a manner that is the reverse of the usual experimental approach" (p. 28). Experiments examine unique situations in order to determine the direction, intensity, etc., of an as yet unknown outcome. Role playing by contrast "aims at abstracting the determining features of a social situation whose outcome is known" (Mixon, 1971, p. 28). As such it becomes clear that role playing and experimental methods are complementary rather than antagonistic as was (and still is in some quarters) believed formerly. It would seem inappropriate then to ask whether role playing should replace laboratory experiments. Clearly it cannot, and was not intended to in the first place. One might ask, however, if role playing can contribute to the research enterprise over and above that to be derived from the lab experiment.

Role playing involves the construction of social situations from their component parts. Subjects take a role, specified by the experimenter, which can either be themselves or some other person. The experimenter then arranges a social setting that includes all of the relevant factors that would be required to elicit the desired (as defined in dvance) response. The experimenter might then alter certain features of the situation so as to produce variations in behavior. Because the desired outcome is already known, the researcher has immediate feedback as to whether his construction of the situation is adequate. This procedure would fit into the context of research as it is now practiced in at least two ways. One way would be as part of an exploratory research program as a prelude to the more exacting experimental procedures. For example, an interesting response to a social situation might be noted. Accordingly, subjects could be brought to the lab, and placed into a social setting and encouraged to play a specific role in responding to the stimuli. The researcher would be present, asking the subject to expand on his performance or to reflect on his behavior.

Certain elements of the situation could be altered and changes in subjects' behavior observed. In this way, the researcher's experimental setting would be purified of nonessential or misleading elements, such as unintended cues in the instructions or distractions in the lab. In addition, sessions such as these could provide a source of hypotheses to be explored using an experiment. All of this, plus an enthusiastic and meaningful interaction with the subject, would seem to argue for the virtue of an extended exploratory session, especially when entering a new area. There is always the danger of "piddling" but it seems clear that in the hands of a competent researcher this technique would help provide a more complete knowledge of the circumstances surrounding a research project. It is possible too that researchers would be inclined to follow up on these leads gained in interaction with subjects, leading to more research programs instead of the one-shot study. More time and more care taken in the setting up of research projects would perhaps discourage a lot of "flitting" about from one topic to another without really understanding either. A second use of role playing might be in the form of a "retest" in which a "general" situation is set up that embodies the features of a number of the experiments conducted as part of a research program. Elements could be added or substracted from this situation and the expected variations in the subjects' behavior noted. This would provide some "summary" evidence that one understands the crucial features of the situation. Further, the necessity of additional control groups might be suggested by deviations in the subjects' behavior. All in all, such an approach would seem to aid our understanding of the situations to which our research efforts are directed. What advantages (if any) does this technique have for advancing theory or social action though?

One advantage possessed by this method is in a new perspective on the analysis of social situations. The current practice involves the study of processes that are important in a situation but do not fully explain it. For example, a social greeting might be analyzed as an instance of sociolinguistic convention, a data point that sheds light on sociolinguistic theory. It appears that more than this is involved; for example, the status and mood of the person doing the greeting, his attitude toward the target, and his attributions about the other's moods and expectations would all affect the choice of greeting. Role-playing techniques shift the emphasis from an attempt to define processes that are central to many behaviors but fail to explain any of them fully, to the construction of intact social situations. Thus, in our example of a social greeting, the intent would be to define all the necessary elements, sociolinguistic conventions, attributions, attitudes, etc., that go into eliciting that particular response. Variations could also be attempted to alter the behavior in question in specific ways. What is to be gained or lost from this new perspective? Certainly it would help break down some of the barriers between areas of research. It is the case in many of our textbooks that equity theory, for example, is discussed as a topic totally separate from social comparison, when it is clear the two are intimately intertwined. This attention to specific situations and their expanation using constructs from different research traditions would perhaps lead theorists to see connections among these traditions that were not seen before. This might lead to more integration, paving the way for more general theory. One limitation of this approach is that many of the formulations would then have to be studied by more rigorous experimental techniques in order to disentangle the cause and effect web. This would be necessary, but by this stage perhaps some of the advantages noted above will have already taken effect. Further, one would have to be careful not to lose sight of the more general processes that we currently study. This latter point emphasizes again the complementarity of the role-playing and experimental methods.

The gain in terms of concrete social action is less impressive. It lies mainly in the fact that since one is trying to produce a specific effect that has already occurred, one may choose his topics carefully. A specific response that is of interest to a societal group could be singled out for detailed attention. The role-playing perspective could be of some use here, with its focus on detailed recreation of a specific situation. This would then pave the way for more concrete experimentation to deal with the underlying dynamics that the situation holds in common with others. Perhaps this would give a more balanced view of the problem at hand.

There is one final way in which role playing would prove complementary to more traditional experimentation. When we speak of an experimental design, we commonly refer to a set of independent variables derived from theory. Less attention is usually given to the dependent variable; in fact, the measure is often chosen so as to follow from the cover story rather than reflecting on the issue at hand. What effect does this have? Kruglanski and Kroy (1976) have argued that the fundamental issue in experimental research is that of "representation" or class membership. This applies on two levels, how we actually operationalize or measure our variables, and how we derive our variables from theory. If we do not represent the theoretical construct or do not measure what we intend to measure, invalidity results. Kruglanski contends that the issue of representation applies not only to the independent variable but also to other aspects of the research proposition, including the dependent variable. It would seem advisable to consider our measurements more carefully because failure to do so invites invalidity as surely as does sloppy operationalization of the independent variable. This is especially true with multivariate analysis of variance, which is becoming more popular. It is often the case tha the overall multivariate F is significant for a particular effect but this effect does not show up on all of the relevant dependent variables. In these cases, we should be very careful about drawing general conclusions because the effect may in fact hold only for a particular subset of variables. These variables may be measuring something quite different despite passing the usual "face validity comparability test." Perhaps the role-playing technique, with its emphasis on the construction of the response (dependent variable), provides one avenue by which to correct the overbalance of attention to the independent variable. In sum, role playing as a technique for exploratory experimentation seems to possess a number of advantages. These advantages appear to complement those of the experimental method and thus offer an interesting supplement to them.

(3) Use of Computers in Experiments

Thus far this paper has addressed itself to methods which might be said to increase the mundane realism (Aronson and Carlsmith, 1968) of research, that is, relating the design to events that are likely to occur in the real world. A second aim has been to encourage thinking about social behavior in slightly different and somewhat more complex fashion. While retaining this latter theme, let us go on to see if increasing the experimental realism through the use of computers relates to theory and social action. This paper will not be concerned with computer simulation but rather with using the computer to aid in running a more traditional laboratory experiment.

Using a computer to assist an experiment allows one to examine areas of social behavior that would be relatively inaccessible using standard research tactics. Before going further with this, however, it should be noted that results obtained in computed-assisted experiments are not always directly comparable to those employing human experimenters. For example, Johnson and Baker (1973) have demonstrated that on difficult tasks with low time pressure and wide response latitude, subjects' performance was more highly related to intellectual ability in the computer-conducted sessions. Factors such as these should be kept in mind during the following discussion.

Two types of advantages seem to stem from the use of computers in experiments. One involves the ability to manipulate independent variables that possess special properties, such as timing or sequence. In such cases, the computer can ensure that all of the testing sessions are identical and do not reflect human factors such as boredom, fatigue, or nervousness on the part of the experimenter. The ability to include manipulations such as these in designs would make the time spent theorizing about them more goal oriented. The inclusion of these variables might suggest qualifications on existing theories as well. With respect to the dependent variable, more "behavioral" measures might be encouraged. It is often the case that computers allow for a broader range of response options than exist with seven-point scales. These measures could be assessed using an involving display screen in order to capture more closely the theoretical constructs.

A second advantage is that computer-assisted experiments can often increase experimental realism directly. It has been the observation of the author that many subjects who report to the lab in a bored, sleepy fashion perk up considerably when they learn they will be interacting with a computer. This is especially true if the situation is a compelling representation of a real world event. Many real-life problems lose their force in the lab when they are presented as pencil and paper tasks or as conceptual analogs. Through the use of attractive visual displays and considerable response latitude the participant becomes an enthusiastic partner rather than just another sleepy subject.

To illustrate these points, I shall briefly describe a recently completed computed-assisted experiment designed by deCarufel and Schopler (unpublished). These investigators were interested in how groups of subjects would respond to a rapidly changing social environment. Three subjects were each assigned to a role in a community known as Carfax. The roles were that of town manager, home owner, or housing project tenant, and each carried with it a salary of a particular amount (this was a perceived control manipulation). Subjects were told that it was their task to maintain the living standard of the community as a whole and to be financially successful as private citizens as well. They were told that a number of events (e.g., a fire or a federal development grant) would occur in Carfax which would threaten or bolster its financial stability. By investing a part or all of their salaries in one of a variety of response options they could counteract or enhance the effects of these events. Subjects were seated before an attractive display scope, which presented the events. These occurred at either a very rapid rate or at a much more leisurely pace. The scope also provided them with performance feedback either after every event or only periodically throughout the session. Subjects indicated their choice of response option by punching keys, which thus kept an accurate record of their behavior. These response categories were then combined to yield measures of tendencies to hoard, to take risks, and so on. One of the major advantages of this approach was that many of the subjects spontaneously reported how exciting and enjoyable their participation had been and that the "mood" of the community had been effectively conveyed. Very few suspected the deceptions and there was complete constancy of sessions despite the complexity of the experiment. An added bonus was the fact that several terminals were run at once, yielding a highly efficient system.

While these advantages were the icing on the cake, the real bonus lies in the fact that such complex social behavior became amenable to rigorous experimentation. A general theory of behavior will undoubtedly include more complex behaviors, which are often the product of real world concerns. While computers are not being presented as a cure-all for the ills of present-day laboratory experimentation, nevertheless it is felt that their continued use should be encouraged. Any method that allows for tightly controlled experiments on complex social issues will benefit social psychological theory by extending it to cover these issues. In addition, bringing social problems into the lab for study with much of their original force and meaning would surely make the resulting data more applicable to those situations. This would seem to be an instance where increasing the experimental realism of the experiment has implications for the study of real world events as well as for theory building.

Concluding Remarks

The purpose of this paper has been to comment on what the author felt was a slighted issue in the conference discussion, that of research methods. An attempt was made to show that one possible way of making progress toward the dual goal of an integrative theory and social relevance is to expand our list of acceptable research methods to include some different approaches. The use of quasi- and nonexperimental research designs on society as a whole, exploratory tactics such as role playing, and the use of computers in experiments might provide some impetus toward thinking about social behavior in new and different ways. The altered perspective of examining entire situations, attention to measurement, and more accessibility to processes such as sequence or rate were some of the advantages mentioned. In addition, application of these methods to social problems is sometimes more direct than in the case of the traditional lab experiment, especially in the case of research on society as a whole. Again the caution should be noted that these methods were *not* being presented as the only way to achieve the dual goals noted above. It may be that their application will make no difference, but it seems that they possess some value toward these ends. It is simply felt that these methods would function as something of a catalyst, facilitating new perspectives, attention to new processes, etc. By making the study of these processes more practical, it frees the creative mind to wander in these directions. It is felt that theory and social action are directly linked and that one of the ways to gear a "rapprochement" between them is to begin to use new research strategies that affect how we deal with these issues. After all, as Lewin has said, "There is nothing as practical as a good theory."

References

Apfelbaum, E. Conflicts: Resolution or revolution? In quest of the implicit and the invisible. Paper presented at the conference Research Paradigms and Priorities in Social Psychology, Ottawa, July 1974.

Aronson, E., and Carlsmith, J. M. Experimentation in social psychology, in G. Lindzey and E. Aronson (eds.), *The handbook of social psychology*, Vol. 2, pp. 1–79. Reading, Mass.: Addison-Wesley, 1968.

Brickman, P., and Campbell, D. C. Hedonic relativism and planning the good society, in M. H. Appely (ed.), *Adaptation-level theory: A symposium*, pp. 287–304. New York: Academic Press, 1971.

Campbell, D. C. Reforms as experiments. *American Psychologist*, 1969, **24**, 409–429.

Campbell, D. C., and Stanley, J. C. *Experimental and quasi-experimental designs for research*. New York: Rand-McNally, 1963.

deCarufel, A., and Schopler, J. An exploratory study of coping with social change. Unpublished data.

Fairweather, G. W. Social change: The challenge to survival. New York: General Learning Press, 1972.

Folger, R. G. Effects of "voice" and improvement on the experience of inequity. Unpublished doctoral dissertation, University of North Carolina, Chapel Hill, 1975.

Freedman, J. Role-playing: Psychology by consensus. *Journal of Personality and Social Psychology*, 1969, **13**, 107–114.

Gergen, K. J. Social psychology as history. *Journal of Personality and Social Psychology*, 1973, **26**, 309–320.

Johnson, E. S., and Baker, R. F. The computer as experimenter: New results. *Behavioral Science*, 1973, **18**, 377–385.

Keisler, C. A. A motivational theory of stimulus incongruity with application for such phenomena as dissonance and self-attribution. Paper presented at the conference Research Paradigms and Priorities in Social Psychology, Ottawa, July 1974.

Kraut, R. E., and Lewis, S. H. Alternate models of family influence on political ideology. *Journal of Personality and Social Psychology*, 1975, **31**, 791–800.

Kruglanski, A. W., and Kroy, M. Outcome validity in experimental research: A reconceptualization. *Representative Research in Social Psychology,* 1976, in press.

McGuire, W. The yin and yang of progress in social psychology. *Journal of Personality and Social Psychology*, 1973, **26**, 446–456.

Miller, A. G. *The social psychology of psychological research.* New York: The Free Press, 1972. (a)

Miller, A. G. Role-playing: An alternative to deception? A review of the evidence. *American Psychologist*, 1972, **27**, 623–636. (b)

Mixon, D. Behavior analysis treating subjects as actors rather than organisms. *Journal for the Theory of Social Behavior*, 1971, **1**, 19–32.

Ring, K. Experimental social psychology: Some sober questions about some frivolous values. *Journal of Experimental Social Psychology*, 1967, **3**, 113–123.

Rommetveit, R. On the architecture of intersubjectivity. Paper presented at the conference Research Paradigms and Priorities in Social Psychology, Ottawa, July 1974.

Rosenthal, R., and Rosnow, R. (eds.) *Artifact in Behavioral Research.* New York: Academic Press, 1969.

Skinner, B. F. *Beyond freedom and dignity.* New York: Knopf, 1971.

Thibaut, J. W. An experimental study of the cohesiveness of underprivileged groups. *Human Relations,* 1950, **3**, 251–278.

Triandis, H. C. Social psychology and cultural analysis. Paper presented at the conference Research Paradigms and Priorities in Social Psychology, Ottawa, July 1974.

PARTICIPANTS IN THE CONFERENCE
"Priorities and Paradigms in Social Psychology"

Virginia Andreoli
University of North Carolina

Erika Apfelbaum
University of Paris

John Barefoot
Carleton University

David Bernhardt
Carleton University

John W. Berry
Queens University

Richard Bourhis
University of Cardiff

John Carroll
Carnegie-Mellon University

André deCarufel
University of North Carolina

Richard deCharms
Washington University

Morton Deutsch
Columbia University

Marjorie N. Donald
Carleton University

Ronald Dyck
University of Alberta

J. Richard Eiser
University of Bristol

Robert Ellis
University of Waterloo

Mary Gergen
Swarthmore College

Howard Giles
University of Cardiff

Michael Girodo
University of Ottawa

Paul D. Guild
Carleton University

Stanley Halpin
*U.S. Army Research Unit
Arlington, Virginia*

Nelson Heapy
University of Western Ontario

Hilde Himmelweit
*London School of Economics
and Political Science*

John Holmes
University of Waterloo

Shirley Housch
Carleton University

Jak Jabes
University of Ottawa

Gustav Jahoda
University of Strathclyde

Jos Jaspars
Catholic University

Charles Kiesler
University of Kansas

Robert Knox
University of British Columbia

W.E. Lambert
McGill University

John Lanzetta
Dartmouth College

Ian Lubek
University of Guelph

Sally Luce
Carleton University

Monique Lussier
University of Ottawa

Dale Miller
University of Waterloo

Alan Moffitt
Carleton University

Mauk Mulder
University of Rotterdam

Terry Nosanchuk
Carleton University

John T. Partington
Carleton University

Daniel Perlman
University of Manitoba

Ragnar Rommetveit
University of Oslo

Brendan Rule
University of Alberta

Peter Schönbach
University of Bochum

Paul Secord
Queens College, CUNY

Dennis Shea
Washington University

Arthur Shulman
Washington University

David Stang
Queens College, CUNY

Caryll Steffens
Carleton University

Thomas Stephens
Health and Welfare Canada

Wolfgang Stroebe
University of Marburg

Paul Swingle
University of Ottawa

Henri Tajfel
University of Bristol

Warren Thorngate
University of Alberta

Harry Triandis
University of Illinois

Allen Turnbull
Carleton University

Elaine Walster
University of Wisconsin

David Wilson
Cornell University

Stephen Worchel
University of Virginia

Lawrence Wrightsman
George Peabody College for Teachers

Robert B. Zajonc
University of Michigan

AUTHOR INDEX

351

SUBJECT INDEX